ETHICS
IN THE WORKPLACE

To my colleagues.

ETHICS IN THE WORKPLACE

Tools and Tactics for Organizational Transformation

CRAIG E. JOHNSON

George Fox University

SAGE Publications
Thousand Oaks ▪ London ▪ New Delhi

For information:

Sage Publications, Inc.
2455 Teller Road
Thousand Oaks, California 91320
E-mail: order@sagepub.com

Sage Publications Ltd.
1 Oliver's Yard
55 City Road
London EC1Y 1SP
United Kingdom

Sage Publications India Pvt. Ltd.
B-42, Panchsheel Enclave
Post Box 4109
New Delhi 110 017 India

Printed in the United States of America

Library of Congress Cataloging-in-Publication Data

Johnson, Craig E. (Craig Edward), 1952-
Ethics in the workplace : tools and tactics for organizational transformation / Craig E. Johnson.
p. cm.
Includes bibliographical references and index.
ISBN 1-4129-0538-9 or 978-1-4129-0538-1 (cloth)—
ISBN 1-4129-0539-7 or 978-1-4129-0539-8 (pbk.)
1. Business ethics. I. Title.
HF5387.J64 2007
174′.4—dc22 2006011640

This book is printed on acid-free paper.

06 07 08 09 10 10 9 8 7 6 5 4 3 2 1

Acquisitions Editor: Al Bruckner
Editorial Assistant: MaryAnn Vail
Production Editor: Laureen A. Shea
Copy Editor: J. G. Robinson
Typesetter: C&M Digitals (P) Ltd.
Proofreader: Kevin Gleason
Indexer: Michael Ferreira
Cover Designer: Candice Harman

Contents

Acknowledgments

Writing this text would have been impossible without assistance at every stage of the project. Editor Al Bruckner encouraged me to submit the proposal to Sage. A grant from the George Fox University faculty development committee then enabled me to devote more time to the book. During the writing process, student employees, under the direction of Kelly Borror, gathered books and photocopied materials. Reference librarians Janis Tyhurst, Louise Newswanger, and Alex Rolfe helped me navigate a variety of databases. Sandee Robinson checked references. Faculty in the School of Management provided ideas for case studies, and students enrolled in my classes provided feedback on chapter material. My colleagues around the university have given me a greater appreciation of what it means to live in an ethical community.

Three reviewers offered helpful critiques on the completed manuscript, and the editorial staff at Sage made it possible to release the text in a timely fashion.

I am grateful to all the individuals and groups named above. Thanks, too, to my wife, Mary, who is all too aware of the demands that writing makes on my time but supports my efforts nonetheless.

Finally, I want to acknowledge the ethics scholars whose research and analysis provide the foundation of this book. Their continuing efforts make me optimistic that a great many more organizations will experience ethical transformation in the years to come.

Introduction

"We've got to draw a line on unethical behavior and then get as close to that line as possible."

Making the Case for Transformation

Scarcely a day goes by without revelations of a new organizational scandal. We read and hear about ethical failures in every sector of society—business, education, social service, environmental, entertainment, military, religious, government. Here is just a small sample of the prominent organizations accused of immoral behavior:

- Enron, WorldCom, Zerox, Rite-Aid, Waste Management, HealthSouth, AIG Insurance, Fannie Mae Mortgage Corporation, Quest, Parmalat (Italy), Ahold (the Netherlands): accounting fraud

- Arthur Andersen: certifying fraudulent accounting statements, shredding documents wanted in a criminal investigation
- Bridgestone-Firestone: delaying the recall of defective tires
- Boeing: stealing secrets from a competitor; colluding with a federal procurement officer to secure contracts
- Salomon Smith Barney, Merrill Lynch: lying to investors
- Putnam Investments, Charles Schwab, Alliance Capital, Janus Capital, Strong Funds, Canary Capital Partners, Morgan Stanley, PBHG Fund: illegal trading practices, high management fees, steering clients to funds in return for commissions
- Halliburton: overcharging for wartime products and services
- Adelphia, Tyco: insider loans to corporate executives and families; corruption; theft of corporate funds
- Major League Baseball: player steroid use; lax drug testing policies and punishments
- The Nature Conservancy: making favorable real estate deals with board members
- The United Nations: diversion of funds from the Iraqi Food for Oil program, widespread waste and corruption
- The Catholic Church: clergy sexual abuse and subsequent cover up
- The Air Force Academy: sexual assault, religious proselytizing by faculty
- Army Intelligence, the National Guard: prisoner abuse in Iraq and Afghanistan
- The City of Chicago: forcing companies to pay for city contracts through bribes, donating to campaigns of or doing free work for government officials
- U.S. Congress: accepting campaign donations, meals, and trips from lobbyists in return for political favors

Negative publicity generated by this wave of organizational scandals has spotlighted the importance of ethical behavior. Workplaces that previously ignored or downplayed ethical considerations now recognize that their health is tied to their moral performance. Fallen organizations pay a high price for their moral shortcomings in the form of damaged reputations; declining revenues, earnings, donations, and stock prices; downsizing and bankruptcy; increased regulation; and civil lawsuits and criminal charges. Managers and employees are looking for better, more effective ways to integrate ethical values into their work structures and processes. They realize that promoting ethical behavior should be their top priority. Unfortunately, many don't know how to translate their good intentions into reality.

Too often organizations settle for superficial ethical measures that have little influence on day-to-day operations. Surveys of large North American companies drive home this point. Nearly all major firms have ethical strategies in place to ensure compliance with legal requirements, including formal codes and policies, ethics officers, and systems for registering and dealing with ethical concerns and complaints.[1] However, most of these efforts are disconnected or "decoupled" from corporate decisions and policies. Many ethics officials only devote a small portion of their time to their ethical duties, and complaint hotlines are rarely used. CEOs typically discuss ethical topics with their ethics officers only once or twice a year, attend no meetings focusing primarily on ethics, and rarely communicate to employees about ethics. Followers generally don't receive more than one ethical message annually, and one fifth to one third of lower level workers receive no ethics training at all over a 12-month period. Employees quickly skim written ethics statements and file them away.

The poor track record of contemporary work organizations is proof that the decoupled approach to ethics doesn't work. A new perspective is in order, one that (a) recognizes the moral dimension of every aspect of organizational life, and (b) leads to significant improvement in ethical performance. Investigators use a variety of terms to describe such an ethics-based approach, including *integrated, integrity focused, purpose driven,* and *values centered.*[2] However, *transformational* is a more inclusive descriptor. This broader label incorporates integration, integrity, purpose, and values. To transform something means to alter its very nature or essence for the better, producing fundamental, long-lasting positive change.[3] When applied to ethics, transformation goes beyond lip service to moral values or grudging compliance to legal requirements. Transformation places ethics at the center of the workplace, significantly altering attitudes, thinking, communication, behavior, culture, and systems. Key values drive individual decisions, interpersonal relationships, group interaction, and organizational goals.

There is no one widely accepted list of the characteristics of ethically transformed organizations. However, I offer Box 0.1 (which introduces concepts from upcoming chapters) as an initial step in building such a catalog. In Box 0.1 the qualities of ethically decoupled and ethically transformed organizations are contrasted with one another. Moving organizations from the disconnected column to the transformed column takes change agents. And that's where this book comes in. I believe that when we join organizations as employees we assume the burden of making them better places. *Ethics in the Workplace: Tools and Tactics for Organizational Transformation* is a resource for those who want to join me in carrying out this task.

Box 0.1 Characteristics of Ethically Decoupled and Ethically Transformed Organizations

Ethically Decoupled Organizations	*Ethically Transformed Organizations*
See ethics as a means to an end (profit, better public image)	See ethics as an end in and of itself
Comply with legal requirements	Exceed legal requirements
Exhibit organizational behavior inconsistent with stated values	Take actions that reflect collective values; the transformed organization "walks its Talk"

(Continued)

(Continued)

Are insensitive to potential moral issues	Are highly sensitive to moral dilemmas
Control behavior through rules and penalties	Control behavior through adherence to shared values
Have a low awareness of ethical duties	Have a high awareness of individual and collective ethical responsibilities
Rarely discuss ethics; rarely use moral vocabulary	Routinely discuss ethics using moral vocabulary
Omit ethics from daily decisions and operations	Make ethics part of every decision and operation
Are driven by practical or pragmatic considerations (the bottom line)	Are driven by mission and values
React to destructive behaviors	Prevent destructive behaviors
Have ethically inconsistent reward structures	Have reward systems that promote moral behavior
Show a high concern for self	Show a high concern for others
Sacrifice individual rights for organizational good	Honor and protect individual rights
Engage in self-centered communication (monologue)	Engage in other-centered communication (dialogue)
Have low to moderate trust and commitment levels	Have high trust and commitment levels
Have teams that routinely fall victim to unethical group processes	Have teams that are rarely victimized by unethical group processes
Show high concern for the organization	Show high concern for stakeholders, society, and the global environment
Hold and build power bases	Give power away
Exhibit low-level moral reasoning	Base reasoning on universal ethical principles
Prevent members from making moral choices	Equip members to make moral choices
Respond to changes in the ethical environment	Anticipate changes in the ethical environment

Invest little in building a positive ethical climate	Invest significantly in creating and maintaining an ethical workplace (i.e., training, socialization, leader involvement)
Are at significant risk of ethical misbehavior and scandal	Are at low risk of ethical misbehavior and scandal

Acting as a transformational change agent requires knowledge and skills—the basic tools of transformation. We also need strategies or tactics for putting these tools to work in the transformational process. Tools and tactics will be blended throughout this text. I'll describe theories and concepts, present research findings, identify key skills, and offer implementation tips and guidelines. Self-assessments and chapter end exercises are designed to help you apply these principles, practices, and plans.

Assuming the role of ethical change agent also means identifying and dispelling misunderstandings or myths that serve as barriers to ethical transformation. I call the first of these myths "There's nothing to it." Those who fall victim to this misconception believe that changing ethical performance is easy. They are seriously mistaken. Acting morally can be a tough task, as you've probably discovered when you tried to do the right thing in the face of peer pressure or were punished for telling the truth. At times you will be called upon to put aside your self-interest to meet the needs of others, to stand alone, and to endure criticism. You could risk losing your job because you "aren't a team player" or because you have to bring organizational wrongdoing to the attention of outside authorities (see Chapter 7). Further, ethical decisions are complex, without any clear answers. They may require choosing between what appear to be two "rights" or two "wrongs."

The second myth is "It won't do any good." This myth comes out of widespread cynicism about organizations and stands at the opposite end of the spectrum from the first misconception. According to this perspective, change is too hard, not too easy. The individual can have little impact on the ethical climate of an organization. Organizations are too complicated and have a life of their own. Even people with high personal moral standards leave their scruples at the door when they go to work. They end up following company dictates, no matter how immoral.

This misconception contains an element of truth. Situational pressures are important determinants of ethical or unethical behavior. In recognition of that fact, a great deal of this text is devoted to how we can reshape the ethical climates of our groups and organizations. There is little doubt that many of us do act contrary to our personal convictions due to outside pressures. However, this myth overlooks the fact that organizations are the products of choices.

Organizations become embroiled in scandals because individuals and groups decided to lie, steal, abuse their positions and power, and cover up crimes. The same members that create and sustain unhealthy practices, values, and structures can develop more productive alternatives. Granted, your ability to make significant systemwide changes will be limited if you are a college graduate entering your first job. Nevertheless, you do have the power to manage your own behavior, and your coworkers will note how you react to ethical issues. Your influence will likely grow over time, as those with undergraduate and graduate degrees generally end up in management positions. (If you question the ability of one person to make a difference, turn to the profile of former Supreme Court Justice Sandra Day O'Connor in Box 0.2.)

Box 0.2 From Cowgirl to Supreme Court Justice

Newsweek magazine called the story of Sandra Day O'Connor "a uniquely American tale."[1] The retired Supreme Court justice started her life on a cattle ranch on the Arizona-New Mexico border, 35 miles from the nearest town. There she learned to deal with the challenges of living without electricity, running water, doctors, and neighbors. At the same time, Sandra's parents promoted a love of knowledge. The Day family traveled widely, subscribed to the *New Yorker* magazine, and sent their daughter to a private girls' school and then to Stanford University.

O'Connor graduated third in her class from Stanford law school, but major West Coast law firms refused to hire her or only offered her secretarial positions. She finally landed a job at a county attorney's office by offering to work for free. Later, after taking time to give birth to three sons, she went to work as an assistant attorney general and was elected majority leader of the Arizona state senate. She then served nearly 6 years on state and federal appellate courts before she was appointed by Ronald Reagan to the Supreme Court in 1981 and became the first female Supreme Court justice.

O'Connor's vote became a key swing vote on the Court. Over her last 10 years on the bench she voted with the majority in more than three quarters of court rulings that were decided by a 5–4 margin. For example, she cast the deciding vote in reaffirming *Roe v. Wade* (which permits abortions), stopping the Florida recount in the 2000 presidential elections, and supporting affirmative action in the University of Michigan's law school admissions. Based on her pivotal role in these decisions, one observer noted: "We are all living now in Sandra Day O'Connor's America."[2]

Regardless of whether or not you agree with her politics and judicial opinions, the fact remains: Justice O'Connor is living proof that one person can make a difference. From her humble origins O'Connor went on to influence state government, the state and federal appellate court systems, the Supreme Court, and the entire nation. Her opinions shaped the debate over some of the most controversial moral and legal issues of our time.

Notes

1. Thomas, Taylor, Murr, Wingert, Clift, & Meadows (2005), p. 25.
2. Lemonick & Novak (2005), p. 31.

Sources:

Lemonick, M. D., & Novak, V. (2005, July 11). The power broker. *Time,* pp. 30–33.

Romano, A., & Guide, K. (2005, July 11). The O'Connor verdicts. *Newsweek,* pp. 28–29.

Thomas, E., Taylor, S., Jr., Murr, A., Wingert, P., Clift, E., & Meadows, S. (2005, July 11). Queen of the center. *Newsweek,* pp. 24–31.

The third myth is "Too little, too late." Proponents of this view (including some university faculty) argue that our ethical values and standards are set in childhood. Studying ethics in college or on the job is a waste of time if that's the case. If we don't have strong values by the time we are adults, coursework will do little good.

Research does not support this argument, as we'll see in Chapter 3. Psychologists have established that moral development, like physical and psychological development, continues beyond childhood.[4] Discussing ethical issues in the classroom does increase moral reasoning abilities all the way through graduate school. Most of us, whatever our stage in life, can point to ways that our views on moral issues like the death penalty, cloning, gay marriage, stem cell research, and recycling have changed over a period of years.

The fourth myth is labeled "Been there, done that." Proponents of this view argue that current excitement about organizational ethics is just a fad. They note that right now organizational ethics is a "hot" topic; interest in the subject will dissipate as our memory of recent scandals fades. These critics have a point. Discussion of organizational ethics did peak during earlier scandals like Watergate, the My Lai Massacre, the Iran Contra affair, the Sears auto repair scandal, and the failure of the savings and loan industry. Ethical talk subsided as time passed. Yet ethics is not a fad. Popular attention may shift to other concerns but, as the recent spate of scandals demonstrates, moral decision making is more important than ever.

The fifth and final myth I've entitled "We can't afford it." The argument here is that adopting high ethical standards is too costly. Adherents believe that ethically transformed organizations can't compete in the modern marketplace. Groups that do the right thing, like refusing to bribe foreign officials to gain contracts, lose out to less scrupulous competitors. Proponents of this view also point out that unethical behavior often goes undetected and that good intentions, by themselves, are no guarantee of organizational success.

There is no doubt that ethical behavior can be costly. Unethical behavior often does go unpunished and careful planning and execution must back lofty goals. However, there is evidence that ignoring ethics is more costly than pursuing ethics. Business ethicists report that, more often than not, it pays to be ethical. High moral standards and outstanding performance often go hand in hand. For example, large firms rated as socially responsible corporate citizens typically outperform other companies that make up the S & P 500.[5] Being perceived as ethically responsible, as we will discover in Chapter 10, is an asset rather than a liability in today's business environment.

At the very least, transformed organizations reduce the risk that they will be damaged, sometimes fatally, by scandal. Yet reducing exposure to risk is only part of the story. Many of the transformational characteristics to be described in the chapters to come—shared purpose and mission, a trusting atmosphere, core values, empowerment, and concern for others—create a high performance climate. In such environments members are more committed, work harder, share information, and act responsibly; maintain positive relationships with customers and suppliers; take more initiative and generate more creative ideas; and persist in the face of obstacles.[6]

Defining Ethics in the Workplace

With the exception of those who work entirely on their own, paid labor takes place in the organizational context. Organizations consist of three or more people engaged in coordinated action in pursuit of a common purpose or goal. They function as socially constructed, structured, interconnected systems.[7] Let's look at the elements of this definition in more detail.

Three or more people. The presence of three or more persons sets the stage for the formation of organizations, allowing for the development of structure, coalitions, shared meanings, and so forth.

Coordination of activities. Completion of any complex task, whether it be making a film, repairing a highway, or starting a health club, requires the coordination of people and units. Coordination, in turn, produces synergy. Synergy describes the way in which organizations are greater than the sum of their parts. The achievements of an organization as a whole are much greater than could be reached by a collection of individuals working on their own.

Goal directed. Organizations don't form by chance. Instead, they are intentionally formed to meet specific needs and to serve specific purposes like educating elementary school children, developing and selling automobiles, passing legislation, and combating crime. These objectives focus the collective energies of members.

Socially constructed. Organizations are human creations shaped through the collective decisions and actions of their members. The socially constructed nature of organizations is particularly apparent in their cultures. No two organizations are exactly alike. Every group has its unique way of seeing the world and culture developed through shared meaning and experiences. New employees often undergo a form of culture shock as they move into an organization with a different language, customs, and attitudes about work and people.

Structured interaction. The word *organization* frequently conjures up images of organizational charts, policy manuals, discipline policies, articles of incorporation, and other official documents. Bureaucratic organizations in particular do their best to leave nothing to chance, spelling out everything from how to apply for sick leave and retirement benefits to the size of office cubicles. They also carefully detail how tasks like processing auto insurance payments and registering students are to be managed. However, some of the most important elements of structure aren't formalized. Communication scholars, for instance, study communication networks, which are patterns of messages sent between individuals and organizational units. These networks may have little resemblance to the flow of information outlined in the official organizational chart.

Roles and hierarchy are two particularly important aspects of structure. Roles are sets of expectations, responsibilities, and duties associated with organizational positions. Failure to meet role expectations generates sanctions in the form of criticism, reprimands, lower wages, and termination. Hierarchy grants certain individuals and groups more power, status, and privileges. These differences in status and power are part of every interaction between organizational members.

Interconnectedness (systems). Organizations function as interconnected systems, Consider all the departments involved in the introduction of a new product, for instance: research and development, design, purchasing, production, marketing, finance, human resources. The success of the product introduction depends on each division doing its part. Marketing can do an effective job of promoting the new item, but first purchasing must secure the necessary components at the right cost and production must meet manufacturing deadlines. Because organizations function as systems, a change in any one component will influence all the others. A new accounting system, for example, will change the way that every department records expenses, books revenue, and determines profits.

Ethics involves judgments about the rightness or wrongness of human behavior. To illustrate this point, I've collected definitions of the term from a variety of sources. Notice how each highlights the evaluative nature of ethical study and practice.

> "Ethics is concerned with how we should live our lives. It focuses on questions about what is right or wrong, fair or unfair, caring or uncaring, good or bad, responsible or irresponsible, and the like."[8]
>
> "[Ethics includes] the principles, norms, and standards of conduct governing an individual or group."[9]
>
> "Ethical judgments focus . . . on degrees of rightness and wrongness, virtue and vice, and obligation in human behavior."[10]
>
> "Ethics refers to the rules or principles that define right and wrong conduct."[11]
>
> "[An ethical act or decision] is something judged as proper or acceptable based on some standard of right and wrong."[12]

There are some scholars who make a distinction between ethics and morals, drawing in part on the origins of each word.[13] Ethics comes from the Greek term *ethos,* which refers to "custom" or "usage" or "character." Moral is derived from the Latin *mos* or *moris,* which refer to "conduct" or "way of life." From this perspective, ethics has to do with the systematic study of general principles of right and wrong behavior. Morality and morals, on the other hand, describe specific, culturally transmitted standards of right and wrong ("Thou shall not steal"; "Treat your elders with respect"). Maintaining this distinction is becoming more difficult, however. Both ethics and morality involve decisions about right and wrong. When we make such evaluations we draw upon universal principles as well as upon our cultural standards. Further, scholars from a number of fields appear to use the terms *ethics* and *morals* interchangeably. Philosophers interested in ethics study moral philosophy, for example, while psychologists examine moral reasoning and educators promote moral education. For these reasons, I will use the terms synonymously in the remainder of this text. You, of course, are free to disagree. You may want to engage in a class discussion about whether these two concepts should be integrated or treated separately.

Workplace ethics applies moral standards and principles to evaluate the behavior of employees in work organizations. Organizations are well suited for ethical analysis because, as we've seen, they are the products of conscious, goal-directed behavior. Whatever form they take (small family owned restaurants, community-based nonprofits, large multinational corporations, international relief agencies), all employers share the common features described above. These shared elements mean that members in every type of organization face some common ethical temptations and dilemmas. Further, a common body of theory, principles, strategies, and skills can be used to address these moral challenges.

I am convinced there is much to be gained in looking at ethical problems and solutions across organizational boundaries. No matter what particular type of organization we work in, we can learn from the experiences of others in different settings (see Box 0.3). Knowing how corporate managers communicate important values, for instance, can be useful to those of us working in the federal government. If we work in business, we can gain important insights into how to empower employees from watching how nonprofit executives recruit and motivate volunteers.

CASE STUDY

Box 0.3 Blurring the Line Between Profits and Nonprofits

Telling the difference between for-profit and nonprofit organizations is getting harder. In recent years nonprofit groups have adopted many strategies traditionally associated with businesses, like hiring MBAs, conducting market research, advertising, and jettisoning unproductive programs.

Goodwill Industries in the Portland, Oregon area is a prime example of how the line between the business and charitable sectors is blurring. Goodwill Industries employs thousands of disabled and disadvantaged workers at thrift stores in 172 cities around the country. When Michael Miller became president of Portland Goodwill in the mid-1980s, he adopted a corporate approach to running the charity. He laid off executives, closed a money-losing location while opening and remodeling other outlets, made donating items for sale more convenient, hired research consultants to develop a growth strategy, and formed a marketing department to produce commercials for Goodwills nationwide. His efforts paid off. Per-store sales tripled and total sales increased tenfold (from $5.3 million to $51.6 million). Revenues of the Portland branch are the highest in the nation. The local Goodwill workforce increased threefold at the same time the charity reduced its reliance on government funding.

Miller and his team have been handsomely rewarded for their superior performance. The CEO receives the highest compensation package of any Goodwill president. He earns over a half million a year in pay and such additional perks as a Lincoln Navigator and a $400,000 severance package. Four other executives receive more than $100,000 in salary and benefits. These compensation packages, while considerably higher than those at other nonprofits in the area, are similar to those given to business executives running companies with comparable sales.

Many are troubled by Miller's salary package. According to Pat Libby, director of the Nonprofit Leadership and Management program at the University of San Diego: "A half-million dollars sounds like too much to me. There is a moral obligation for nonprofits to compensate their top staff in a way that is respectful of their mission. When you're running an organization that's about social justice, there should be some reflection of that."[1]

A former client has filed suit, claiming that Goodwill has lost sight of its mission and should pay rank-and-file workers better (a small percentage of workers make subminimum wages, for example). Some donors are troubled that Goodwill executives are being richly rewarded for selling items that they contribute. Clothing retailers complain that the charity's tax-exempt status gives it an unfair advantage.

The Portland Goodwill board defends Miller's pay package by pointing out that a large business or another nonprofit could easily hire him away. Board members believe that his "incredible results" justify his high compensation. Miller argues that high pay enables him to retain and motivate the best possible management team in order to help the greatest number of disadvantaged workers. "It would be unrealistic for me to expect any segment of those people [the executive team] to work here at a discount," he contends.[2] However, the board was forced to reduce Miller's pay package 24 percent when the Oregon attorney general ruled that his salary was "unreasonable."

Controversy over Miller's generous salary package is part of a larger, nationwide debate about how much nonprofit executives should earn. In one well-publicized case, New York Attorney General Eliot Spitzer sued former New York Stock Exchange president Richard Grasso to force him to return most of the $140 million he received when ousted from his position. Charities that adopt a corporate model pit themselves against businesses when recruiting talented executives, pushing nonprofit salaries up. As a result, the IRS is beginning to investigate more cases of excessive compensation for nonprofit administrators.

In coming years society will have to determine if a nonprofit that operates like a business should pay taxes like a business. If the answer to this question is yes, then distinguishing between the for-profit and nonprofit sectors will become even more difficult.

DISCUSSION PROBES

1. Should nonprofit groups operate like businesses? What are some of the potential benefits of doing so? The potential dangers?
2. Should businesses operate more like nonprofits? What are some of the potential benefits of doing so? The potential dangers?
3. Should charities that compete against businesses be forced to pay taxes?
4. Should managers at charities be expected to work for less than their colleagues in corporations? Why or why not?
5. Is Miller's compensation package immoral? Why or why not?
6. What standards should be used to determine if a nonprofit administrator is receiving excessive compensation?
7. Would you donate your used items to Portland, Oregon, Goodwill?

NOTES

1. Kosseff (2004), p. A11.
2. Kosseff (2004), p. A1.

SOURCES

Denson, B., & Kosseff, J. (2005, December 20). Goodwill chief agrees to pay cut. *Oregonian,* p. A1. Retrieved January 25, 2006, from NewsBank database.

Fonda, D., & Kadlec, D. (2004, May 31). The rumble over executive pay. *Time,* pp. 62–63.

Kosseff, J. (2004, March 14.). Charity Inc. *Oregonian,* pp. A1, A11.

Kosseff, J. (2004, March 14). Goodwill gives, gets hand from disabled. *Oregonian,* p. A10.

Looking Ahead

You'll note several unique features of this text. First, this is a book about transforming ethics in all sorts of workplaces (not just businesses) for the reasons cited above. Second, *Ethics in the Workplace: Tools and Tactics for Organizational Transformation* has an interdisciplinary focus. In recent years, a significant number of social scientists have begun to examine ethics in the organizational setting. I cite findings from the fields of management, moral psychology, communication, and social psychology in addition to philosophy. This research is cited in the chapter endnotes as well as in the comprehensive References section at the end of the book. Third, expect to confront the dark side of individuals, leaders, and organizations. Acknowledging dysfunctional attitudes and behaviors is the first step in curbing them. Fourth, my goal is to write in a reader-friendly style in order to make the discussion of ethics less intimidating. Fifth, I don't hesitate to reveal my biases. You are likely to take issue with some of my conclusions. I hope you do. Discussion and dialogue are essential to the learning process.

Every chapter begins with a preview and includes a feature called "Implications" which reviews important concepts and their ramifications for you as an ethical change agent. There are two cases in each chapter as well as a self-assessment that measures your (or your organization's) performance on an important behavior, skill, or concept. The Application Projects ask you to engage further reflection, analysis, and implementation. Some of these activities can be completed on your own; others require group participation.

Ethics in the Workplace is organized around levels or layers of organizational behavior to provide a framework for ethical transformation. Part I lays the groundwork. Chapter 1 concludes this introductory section by introducing ethical theories and principles frequently used in ethical problem solving. Part II, Transforming Individual Ethics in the Organization, examines individual motivations and decisions. Chapter 2 surveys personal moral development. Chapter 3 describes ethical action, decision-making processes, and formats. Part III, Transforming Interpersonal Ethics in the Organization, looks at the moral issues raised by our connections to other organizational members. Chapter 4 outlines an ethical framework for interpersonal communication. Chapter 5 addresses questions of power and influence. Part IV, Transforming Group and Leadership Ethics, focuses on the ethical dilemmas that are part and parcel of organizational groups and teams (Chapter 6) as well as the leadership and followership roles (Chapter 7). Part V, Transforming the Ethics of Organizational Systems, examines organizations as integrated units. Chapter 8 provides strategies for combating destructive behavior. Chapter 9 looks at the components of ethical culture and cultural change efforts. Chapter 10 discusses tactics for promoting global citizenship.

Endnotes

1. Weaver, G. R., Trevino, L. K., & Cochran, P. L. (1999). Corporate ethics practices in the mid-1990s: An empirical study of the *Fortune 1000. Journal of Business Ethics, 18,* 283–294; Weaver, G. R., Trevino, K. L., & Cochran, P. L. (1999). Integrated and decoupled corporate social performance: Management commitments, external pressures, and corporate ethics practices. *Academy of Management Journal, 42,* 539–552; Lindsay, R. M., & Irvine, V. B. (1996). Instilling ethical behavior in organizations: A survey of Canadian companies. *Journal of Business Ethics, 15,* 393–407.

2. See, for example: Pearson, G. (1995). *Integrity in organizations: An alternative business ethic.* London: McGraw-Hill; Schminke, M. (Ed.). (1998). *Managerial ethics: Moral management of people and processes.* Mahwah, NJ: Lawrence Erlbaum; Paine, L. S. (1996, March-April). Managing for organizational integrity. *Harvard Business Review,* pp. 106–117; Paine, L. S. (2003). *Values shift: Why companies must merge social and financial imperatives to achieve superior performance.* New York: McGraw-Hill.

3. Burns, J. M. (2003). *Transforming leadership: A new pursuit of happiness.* New York: Atlantic Monthly Press, p. 24.

4. Kohlberg, L. A. (1984). *Essays on moral development: Vol. 2: The psychology of moral development: The nature and validity of moral stages.* New York: Harper & Row; Rest, J. R. (1993). Research on moral judgment in college students. In A. Garrod (Ed.), *Approaches to moral development* (pp. 201–211). New York: Teachers College Press.

5. Paine, L. S. (2000). Does ethics pay? *Business Ethics Quarterly, 10,* 319–330; Paine, L. S. (2003). *Value shift: Why companies must merge social and financial imperatives to achieve superior performance.* New York: McGraw-Hill; Trevino, L. K., & Nelson, K. A. (2004). *Managing business ethics: Straight talk about how to do it right* (3rd ed.). Hoboken, NJ: John Wiley; Waddock, S. A., & Graves, S. B. (1997). The corporate social performance-financial performance link. *Strategic Management Journal, 18,* 303–319.

6. Kalwies, H. H. (1989). Ethical leadership: The foundation for organizational growth. *Howard Journal of Communication, 1,* 113–130; Bass, B. M., & Avolio, B. J. (1994). Transformational leadership and organizational culture. *International Journal of Public Administration, 17,* 541–554

7. Newstrom, J. W., & Davis, K. (1993). *Organizational behavior: Human behavior at work* (9th ed.). New York: McGraw Hill; Sims, R. R. (2002). *Managing organizational behavior.* Westport, CT: Quorum Books.

8. Jaska, J. A., & Pritchard, M. S. (1994). *Communication ethics: Methods of analysis.* Belmont, CA: Wadsworth, p. 3.

9. Trevino & Nelson (2004).

10. Johannesen, R. L. (2002). *Ethics in human communication* (5th ed.). Prospect Heights, IL: Waveland Press, p. 1.

11. Sims, R. R. (1994). *Ethics and organizational decision making: A call for renewal.* Westport, CT: Quorum Books, p. 5.

12. Ferrell, O. C., & Gardiner, G. (1991). *In pursuit of ethics: Tough choices in a world of work.* Springfield, IL: Smith Collins, p. 2.

13. Day, L. A. (2003). *Ethics in media communications: Cases and controversies* (4th ed.). Belmont CA: Thomson/Wadsworth; Jarrett, J. L. (1991). *The teaching of values: Caring and appreciation.* London: Routledge; Johannesen (2002).

Part I

Laying an Ethical Foundation

1

Ethical Perspectives

Chapter Preview

Ethical theories are critical to organizational transformation. We will employ them repeatedly throughout the remainder of this text. Ethical perspectives help us identify and define problems, force us to think systematically, encourage us to view issues from many different vantage points, and provide us with decision-making guidelines. In this chapter I'll introduce five widely used ethical approaches. I'll briefly summarize each perspective and then offer an evaluation based on the theory's advantages and disadvantages.

Resist the temptation to choose your favorite approach and ignore the rest. Use a variety of theories when possible. Applying all five approaches to the same problem (practicing ethical pluralism) is a good way to generate new insights about the issue. You can discover the value of ethical pluralism by using each theory to analyze the Chapter End Case (see Application Project 7 on page 24). You may find that some perspectives are more suited to this problem than others. Combining insights from more than one theory might help you come up with a better solution. At the very least, drawing from several perspectives should give you more confidence in your choice and make you better prepared to defend your conclusion.

Utilitarianism: Do the Greatest Good for the Greatest Number

Many people weigh the advantages and disadvantages of alternatives when making significant decisions. They create mental balance sheets listing the pluses and minuses of each course of action. When it's a particularly important choice, such as deciding which job offer to take or where to earn a graduate degree, they may commit their lists to paper to make it easier to identify the relative merits of their options.

Utilitarianism is based on the premise that our ethical choices, like other types of decisions, should be based on their consequences.[1] English philosophers Jeremy Bentham (1748–1832) and John Stuart Mill (1806–1873) argued that the best decisions (1) generate the most benefits as compared to their disadvantages, and (2) benefit the largest number of people. In other words, Utilitarianism is attempting to do the greatest good for the greatest number of people. *Utility* can be defined as what is best in a specific case (Act Utilitarianism) or as what is generally preferred in most contexts (Rule Utilitarianism). We can decide, for example, that telling a specific lie is justified in one situation (to protect a trade secret) but, as a general rule, believe that lying is wrong because it causes more harm than good.

Utilitarians consider both short- and long-term consequences when making ethical determinations. If the immediate benefits of a decision don't outweigh its possible future costs, this alternative is rejected. However, if the immediate good is sure and the future good uncertain, decision makers generally select the option that produces the short-term benefit. Utilitarians are also more concerned about the ratio of harm to evil than the absolute amount of happiness or unhappiness produced by a choice. In other words, a decision that produces a great amount of good but an equal amount of harm would be rejected in favor of an alternative that produces a moderate amount of good at very little cost. Further, the Utilitarian decision maker keeps her or his own interests in mind but gives them no more weight than anyone else's.

Making a choice according to Utilitarian principles is a three-step process. First, identify all the possible courses of action. Second, estimate the direct as well as indirect costs and benefits for each option. Finally, select the alternative that produces the greatest amount of good based on the cost-benefit ratios generated in step two. Government officials frequently follow this process when deciding whether or not to impose or loosen regulations. Take decisions about raising rural highway speed limits, for instance. States have the option of maintaining the 55 mile per hour limit or selecting from a range of higher speeds. Raising speed limits produces immediate benefits—reduced travel and delivery times. Fewer motorists are tempted to break the law. These benefits, however, must be weighed against the short-term cost of greater fuel consumption and the long-term risk of higher fatalities. After balancing the costs and benefits, a great many states have opted to loosen speed restrictions.

EVALUATION

Utilitarianism is a popular approach to moral reasoning. We're used to weighing the outcomes of all types of decisions, and the Utilitarian decision-making rule covers every conceivable type of choice. Few could argue with the ultimate goal of evaluating consequences, which is to promote human welfare by maximizing benefits to as many people as possible. Utilitarianism is probably the most defensible approach in emergency situations, such as in the wake of the massive earthquake that hit Pakistan in 2005. In the midst of such widespread devastation, medical personnel ought to give top priority to those who are most likely to survive. It does little good to spend time with a terminal patient while a person who would benefit from treatment dies.

Despite its popularity, Utilitarianism suffers from serious deficiencies.[2] Sometimes identifying possible consequences can be difficult or impossible. Many different groups may be affected, unforeseen consequences may develop, and so on. Even when consequences are clear, evaluating their relative merits can be challenging. Being objective is difficult because we humans tend to downplay long-term risks in favor of immediate rewards (see Box 1.1) and to favor ourselves when making decisions. Due to the difficulty of identifying and evaluating potential costs and benefits, Utilitarian decision makers sometimes reach different conclusions when faced with the same dilemma. States have opted to raise highway speeds but they don't agree as to what the new limits should be. Some state legislatures determined that traveling at 65 miles per hour produces the greatest good; others decided that 70 or 75 miles per hour generates the most benefits.

CASE STUDY

Box 1.1 Stronger, Faster, Bigger: Sacrificing the Future for High Performance

Athletes demonstrate how easy it is to ignore long-term consequences when making choices. They are all too willing to sacrifice their futures for immediate results. Baseball stars Ken Caminiti and Jose Canseco have admitted to taking steroids. Competitors in a variety of other sports, including track, cricket, soccer, rugby, cycling, tennis, ice hockey, and orienteering, have been suspended for taking illegal performance drugs. In professional football, linemen are bulking up to land jobs. The number of players listed at over 300 pounds soared from 130 to 350 between 1996 and 2004, and 70 percent of this group is made up of offensive linemen.

The dangers of performance-enhancing drugs are well documented. Users of anabolic steroids, which imitate the effects of testosterone, can experience mood swings; become hyperaggressive; suffer a higher likelihood of injury and liver damage; and risk high blood pressure, heart disease, strokes, and blood clots. Males may also experience impotence, early onset of baldness, and breast development. Females may grow more body and facial hair and develop a deeper voice. Their breasts may shrink and menstrual problems may develop. Quitting can also be dangerous. Those who stop taking the drugs face a drastic drop in testosterone levels, which can lead to severe depression and suicide among men. Ken Caminiti, the 1996 National League MVP, believed that his drug addiction problem started with his use of steroids (he later died of an overdose).

The dangers of drastic weight gain are just as real as those linked to steroids, though not as well publicized. All professional football players face a 90 percent chance of permanent physical injury if they compete for 3 years. However, the risk to massive linemen is even greater. A study conducted by *The New England Journal of Medicine* found that the rate of sleep apnea among NFL players is five times higher than among other males in the same age groups. Apnea victims suffer from repeated interruptions of breathing during sleep that can sometimes result in an irregular heartbeat. Over time, sufferers are more likely to experience high blood pressure and congestive heart failure. Apnea is believed to have contributed to the death of former pro-bowl defensive lineman Reggie White, who died in his sleep at age 43. In addition to developing apnea, heavy players, like other heavy Americans, are much more likely to develop diabetes and suffer from strokes.

Why do athletes risk their reputations and lives to further their careers? Because the rewards for doing so are so great. Enhanced performance can literally mean millions of dollars in higher salaries and endorsement contracts, not to mention celebrity status. Steroid-enhanced performance can make baseball players into highly sought after free agents. Bulking up allows football players to earn fortunes while playing the sport they love in front of adoring fans. Then, too, it's easy to discount future risks by rationalizing that "it won't happen to me" or to argue that the dangers don't outweigh the immediate payoffs. After all, earning a substantially higher salary now can guarantee a comfortable (if not luxurious) lifestyle for an athlete and his or her family after retirement. The trade-offs—a shorter life span, serious health problems, and chronic pain—appear to be worth the risk.

Professional athletes may seem shortsighted. Nevertheless, millions of average citizens also mortgage their futures in order to reach their career goals. They work 80-hour weeks, eat unhealthy food, deprive themselves of sleep, ignore their families, and endure high stress levels in order to earn more money and to get promoted. The sacrifices may be worth it, but few conduct the rational cost-benefit analysis required to determine what will generate the greatest good in the long run.

DISCUSSION PROBES

1. Imagine that you are a professional athlete in your favorite sport. How far would you go to improve your performance?
2. Athletes use a variety of tactics to boost their performance (training at high altitudes or in oxygen deprivation chambers, going on special diets and training regimens). Where do you draw the line between ethical and unethical tactics? What criteria do you use to make this determination?
3. Do you hold fans partly responsible for the poor health choices of athletes? Why or why not?
4. What steps can you take to better balance long-term consequences against short-term rewards when making ethical choices?

SOURCES

Adler, A., Underwood, A., Scelfo, J., Juarez, V., Johnson, D., Shenfeld, H., Reno, J., Murr, A., Breslau, K., & Raymond, J. (2004, December 20). Toxic strength. *Newsweek,* pp. 44–52.

Ever farther, ever faster, ever higher? (2004, August 7). *Economist,* pp. 20–22.

Hiestand, M., & Mihoces, G. (2004, December 29). Apnea common for NFL linemen. *USA Today,* p. 1C.

Saraceno, J. (2004, December 29). White's death sends message to super-sized NFL. *USA Today,* p. 12C.

Starr, M. (2004, August 16). A long jump. *Newsweek,* pp. 52–53.

Ironically, one of the greatest strengths of Utilitarian theory—its concern for collective human welfare—is also one of its greatest weaknesses. In focusing on what's best for the group as a whole, Utilitarianism discounts the worth of the individual. The needs of the person are subjugated to the needs of the group or organization. This type of reasoning can justify all kinds of abuse. For example, a number of lawsuits accuse Wal-Mart of cheating individual employees out of overtime pay to cut labor costs for the greater good of the company.[3]

Kant's Categorical Imperative: Do What's Right No Matter What the Consequences Are

Like the Utilitarians, German philosopher Immanual Kant (1724–1804) developed a simple set of rules that could be applied to every type of ethical decision. However, he reached a very different conclusion about what those principles should be. Kant argued that moral duties or imperatives are *categorical*—they should be obeyed without exception. Individuals should do what is morally right no matter what the consequences are.[4] His approach to moral reasoning falls under the category of deontological ethics. Deontological ethicists argue that we ought to make choices based on our duty to follow universal truths, which we sense intuitively or identify through reason (*deon* is the Greek word for duty). Moral acts arise out of our will or intention to follow our duty, not in response to circumstances. Based on this criterion, an electric utility that is forced into reducing its rates is not acting morally; a utility that that lowers its rates to help its customers is.

According to Kant, "what is right for one is right for all." We need to ask ourselves one question: Would I want everyone else to make the decision I did? If the answer is yes, the choice is justified. If the answer is no, the decision is wrong.

Based on this reasoning, certain behaviors, like honoring our commitments and being kind, are always right. Other acts, like cheating and murder, are always wrong. Kant cited borrowing money that we never intend to repay as one behavior that violates the Categorical Imperative. If enough people made such false promises, the banking industry would break down because lenders would refuse to provide funds.[5] Deliberate idleness also violates the principle, because no one would exercise his or her talents in a culture where everyone sought to rest and enjoy himself or herself.

Kant also argued for the importance of "treating humanity as an end." Others can help us reach our objectives, but they should never be considered solely as a means to an end. We should, instead, respect and encourage the capacity of others to choose for themselves. It is wrong under this standard for companies to expose manufacturing workers to hazardous chemicals without their consent or knowledge. Managers shouldn't coerce or threaten employees, because such tactics violate freedom of choice. Coworkers who refuse to help one another are behaving unethically because ignoring the needs of others limits their options.

EVALUATION

Kant's imperative is a simple yet powerful ethical tool. Not only is the principle easy to remember, but asking if we would want our behavior to be made into a universal standard should also prevent a number of ethical miscues.

Emphasis on duty builds moral courage. Those driven by the conviction that certain behaviors are either right or wrong no matter what the situation are more likely to blow the whistle on unethical behavior (see Chapter 8), resist group pressure to compromise personal ethical standards, follow through on their choices, and so on. Kant's emphasis on respecting the right of others to choose is an important guideline to keep in mind when making ethical choices in organizations. This standard promotes the sharing of information and concern for others while condemning deceptive and coercive tactics.

Critiques of Kant's system of reasoning often center on his assertion that there are universal principles that should be followed in every situation. In almost every case, we can think of exceptions. For instance, many of us agree that killing is wrong yet support capital punishment for serial murderers. We value privacy rights but have given many up in the name of national security. Then, too, how do we account for those who honestly believe they are doing the right thing even when they are engaged in evil? "Consistent Nazis" were convinced that killing Jews was morally right. They wanted their fellow Germans to engage in this behavior; they did what they perceived to be their duty.

Conflicting duties also pose a challenge to deontological thinking. Complex ethical dilemmas often involve competing obligations. For example, we should be loyal to both our bosses and coworkers. Yet being loyal to a supervisor may mean breaking loyalty with peers, such as when a supervisor asks us to reveal the source of a complaint when we've promised to keep the identity of that coworker secret. How do we determine which duty has priority? Kant's imperative offers little guidance in such situations.

There is one final weakness in Kant's theory that is worth noting. By focusing on intention, Kant downplayed the importance of ethical action. Worthy intent does little good unless it is acted out. We typically judge individuals based on what they do, not on their motives.

Rawls's Justice as Fairness: Balancing Freedom and Equality

Limited organizational resources make conflicts inevitable. There are never enough jobs, raises, corner offices, travel funds, laptop computers, and other benefits to go around. As a result, disputes arise over how to distribute these goods. Departments battle over the relative size of their budgets, for example, and employees compete for performance bonuses, promotions, and job titles. Participants in these conflicts often complain that they have been the victims of discrimination or favoritism.

Over the last third of the twentieth century, Harvard philosopher John Rawls developed a set of guidelines for justly resolving disputes like these that involve the distribution of resources.[6] His principles are designed to foster cooperation in democracies. In democratic societies, all citizens are free and equal before the law. However, at the same time, citizens are unequal. They vary in status, economic standing, talents, and abilities. Rawls's standards honor individual freedom—the foundation of democratic cultures—but also encourage more equitable distribution of societal benefits. The theorist primarily focused on the underlying political structure of society as a whole. Nevertheless, his principles also apply to organizations and institutions that function within this societal framework.

Rawls rejected the use of Utilitarian principles to allocate resources. He believed that individuals have rights that should never be violated no matter what the outcome. In addition, he asserted that seeking the greatest good for the greatest number can seriously disadvantage particular groups and individuals. This can be seen in modern Israel. In an attempt to build a lasting peace, the Israeli government has removed Jewish settlements from Palestinian land. The whole region will benefit if this strategy succeeds. However, the displaced settlers are understandably angry at the loss of their homes.

As an alternative to basing decisions on cost-benefit ratios, Rawls argued that we should follow these principles of justice:[7]

> *Principle 1:* Each person has an equal right to the same basic liberties that are compatible with similar liberties for all.
>
> *Principle 2:* Social and economic inequalities are to satisfy two conditions. A) They are to be attached to offices and positions open to all under conditions of fair equality of opportunity. B) They are to be to the greatest benefit of the least advantaged members of society.

The first principle, the "principle of equal liberty," has priority. It states that certain rights are protected and must be equally applied to all. These liberties include the right to vote, freedom of speech and thought, freedom to own personal property, and freedom from arbitrary arrest. Invading employee privacy and pressuring managers into contributing to particular political candidates would be unethical according to this standard. So would failing to honor contracts, since such behavior would reduce our freedom to enter into agreements for fear of being defrauded.

Principle 2A, "the equal opportunity principle," asserts that everyone should have the same chance to qualify for offices and jobs. Job discrimination based on race, gender, or ethnic origin is forbidden. Further, all citizens ought to have access to the training and education needed to prepare for these positions. Principle 2B, "the difference principle," recognizes that inequalities exist but that priority should be given to meeting the needs of the disadvantaged.

Rawls introduced the "veil of ignorance" to support his claim that his principles should guide decision making in democratic societies like Great Britain, the United States, and Canada. Imagine, he said, a group of people who are asked to come up with a set of guidelines that will govern their interactions. Group members are ignorant of their characteristics or societal position. Faced with such uncertainty, these individuals will likely base their choices on the "maximin rule." This rule states that the best option is the one whose worst outcome is better than the worst outcomes of all the other options. Or, to put it another way, the best choice is the alternative that guarantees everyone a minimum level of benefits.

Rawls argued that individuals standing behind the veil of ignorance would adopt his moral guidelines because they would ensure the best outcomes even in the worst of circumstances. Citizens would select (1) equal liberty, because they would be guaranteed freedom even if they occupy the lowest rungs of society; (2) equal opportunity, because if they turned out to be the most talented societal members, they would not be held back by low social standing or lack of opportunity; and (3) the difference principle, because they would want to be sure they were cared for if they ended up disadvantaged.

EVALUATION

Rawls became one of the most influential philosophers of his time because he offered a way to reconcile the long-standing tension between individual freedom and social justice. His system for distributing resources and benefits encompasses personal liberty as well as the common good. Individual rights are protected. Moreover, talented, skilled, or fortunate people are free to pursue their goals, but the fruits of their labor must also benefit their less fortunate neighbors. Applying Rawls's principles would have a significant positive impact on the moral behavior of organizations. High achievers would continue to be rewarded for their efforts, but not, as is too often the case, at the expense of their coworkers. All of an organization's members would be guaranteed a minimum level of benefits, such as a living wage and health insurance. Everyone would have equal opportunity for training, promotion, and advancement. The growing gap in compensation between the top and bottom layers of the organization would shrink.

Rawls's theory addresses some of the weaknesses of Utilitarianism outlined earlier. In his system, individuals have intrinsic value and are not to be treated as means to some greater end. There are certain rights that should always be protected. The interests of the organization as a whole do not justify extreme harm to particular groups and individuals.

Stepping behind a veil of ignorance does more than provide a justification for Rawls's model; it can also serve as a useful technique to use when making moral choices. Status and power differences are an integral part of organizational life. Nonetheless, if we can set these inequities aside temporarily, we are likely to make more just decisions. The least advantaged usually benefit when status differences are excluded from the decision-making process. We need to ask ourselves if we are treating everyone fairly or if we are being unduly influenced by someone's position or her or his relationship to us. Classical orchestras provide one example of how factoring out differences can improve the lot of marginalized groups. Orchestras began to hire a much higher percentage of female musicians after they erected screens that prevented judges from seeing the gender of players during auditions.[8]

Rawls's influence has not spared his theory from intense criticism. Skeptics note that the theory's abstractness limits its usefulness. Rawls offered only broad guidelines, which can be interpreted in a number of different ways. Definitions of justice and fairness vary widely, a fact that undermines the usefulness of his principles. What seems fair to one group or individual often appears grossly unjust to others. Take programs that reserve a certain percentage of federal contracts for minority contractors, for example. Giving preferential treatment to minorities can be defended based on the equal opportunity and difference principles. Members of these groups claim that they should be favored in the bidding process to redress past discrimination and to achieve equal footing with whites. On the other hand, such policies can be seen as impinging upon the equal liberty principle because they limit the freedom of Caucasians to pursue their goals. White contractors feel that these requirements unfairly restrict their options. They are denied work when they believe they can provide better quality at lower cost than those given the work.

By trying to reconcile the tension between liberty and equality, Rawls left himself open to attack from advocates of both values. Some complain that he would distribute too much to the have-nots; others believe that his concern for liberty means that he wouldn't give enough. Further, philosophers point out that there is no guarantee that parties who step behind the veil of ignorance would come up with the same set of principles as Rawls. They might not use the maximin rule to guide their decisions. Rather than emphasize fairness, these individuals might decide to emphasize certain rights. Libertarians, for instance, hold that freedom from coercion is the most important human right. Every individual should be able to produce and sell as he or she chooses, regardless of the impact of his or her business on the poor. Capitalist theorists believe that benefits should be distributed based on the contributions each person makes to the group. They argue that helping out the less advantaged rewards laziness while discouraging productive people from doing their best. Because decision makers may reach different conclusions behind the veil, skeptics contend that Rawls's guidelines lack moral force, that other approaches to distributing resources are just as valid as the notion of fairness.

Communitarianism: Promoting Shared Moral Values

Communitarianism is the newest of the five perspectives presented in this chapter. While communitarian ideas can be traced back as far as ancient Israel and Greece, the modern (responsive) Communitarian movement began in the Unites States in 1990. That year, sociologist Amatai Etzioni gathered a group of fifteen ethicists, social scientists, and philosophers together to address their concerns about the health of American society. Members of this gathering took the name "Communitarian" to highlight their desire to shift the focus of citizens from individual rights to communal responsibilities.[9] The next year, the group started a journal (*The Responsive Communitarian*) and organized a teach-in that produced the Communitarian platform. Communitarian thinkers like Philip Selznick, William Galston, and Robert Bellah have produced a steady stream of journal articles, books, and position papers outlining Communitarian principles and stands on a variety of modern social issues, like children's television, sobriety checkpoints, airport security screening, and privacy rights. At the same time, Communitarian philosophy has taken hold in Great Britain.

Many of the major tenets of Communitarianism are outlined in the movement's platform.[10] Important platform planks include: (1) Human dignity is intertwined with the health of the community. Liberty flourishes in a healthy society, but no community can exist for long unless members contribute their time, attention, resources, and energy to shared projects. (2) The success of a democratic society depends not on force or government intervention but upon building shared values, practices, and habits. (3) Communal values in responsive communities are developed by the group but are subject to universal standards. (4) The institutions of civil society are charged with reinforcing moral values. (5) Citizens should reject selfishness and care for the material and social well-being of others. (6) Community members have a responsibility to stay active in political and civil matters by staying informed, voting, paying their taxes, serving on juries, and so forth.

Communitarians argue that organizations are essential to character formation. Together, societal institutions speak with a moral voice, articulating and reinforcing communal values. The family plays the greatest role in shaping character. For that reason, Communitarian theorists urge women to leave the workforce to serve as full-time parents and encourage men to become equal partners in child rearing. School is the most important source of moral education and character formation after the family. Government has a duty to encourage civil participation and to be responsive to the needs of citizens. Voluntary associations (such as soccer leagues, churches, and Rotary clubs) reinforce social connections and informally sanction those who violate important values and standards. Businesses encourage concern for others by responding to community needs.

Etzioni describes Communitarianism as the second environmental movement. Protecting nature was the concern of the first environmental movement; creating a "good society" is the focus of the second. As social environmentalists, Communitarians hope to restore the social fabric of society, which shows plenty of evidence of decay—high divorce and crime rates, child neglect, declining schools, excessive materialism, illiteracy, drug use, and teen pregnancy. The United States needs renewal that can only come through the creation of healthy communities. Communities (including organizations) form when individuals develop a web of relationships and are committed to a shared history and identity.

Organizational consultants Juanita Brown and David Isaacs identified seven core processes ("the Seven Cs") that are essential to building and maintaining organizational communities.[11] As you read the list, consider how you would rate your organization (turn to Application Project 4 on page 23).

1. Commitment

Communities emerge around shared commitment. Commitment develops when employees work together toward something they find important. They invest their resources, pool their efforts, overcome obstacles, learn together, and so on. Using a common language, stories, metaphors, and other symbols to help members develop common understandings supports commitment. According to Brown and Isaacs, budget cuts and workforce reductions pose a very real danger to commitment levels. Business and nonprofit leaders must be honest about economic realities, seek input about how to respond, and endure their fair share of the cuts. Employees should be tangibly rewarded if the company is saved from bankruptcy through their efforts.

2. Competence

Successful communities are populated with people who have the knowledge, skills, and qualities needed by the group as a whole. Leaders in these organizations encourage followers to keep on learning by providing training, tuition remission for college courses, and funding for conferences. They also foster the capacity of the organization as a whole to learn. Learning organizations reflect (a) the capacity of *aspiration* (the ability to create the desired future rather than leaving the future to chance), (b) the capacity for *reflective conversation* in which members dialogue about their work and reflect on completed projects, and (c) the capacity for *conceptualization*—the ability to think about how the organizational parts work together as a system.

3. Contribution

Organizational communities help employees recognize how their work contributes to the group's success. They recognize and draw upon the diverse talents of each person. Doing so encourages the extra effort that contributes to high performance.

4. Collaboration

Collaboration is nurtured by "reliable interdependence." Members need to know that they can count on others as they pursue their tasks. True communities foster collaboration by involving a variety of stakeholder groups in pursuit of a common goal (see Chapter 10). They encourage the free flow of information through e-mail, newsletters, bulletin boards, and other means. At the same time, communities recognize the importance of fostering personal relationships that produce trust.

5. Continuity

Lack of continuity (acquisitions, mergers, reorganization, retirements, turnover) threatens the continued existence of community. Wise leaders encourage experienced employees to stay put rather than moving on. They reward organizational veterans for learning new skills and encourage them to share their knowledge. Community-minded managers insure institutional memory by recording learning (the best practices for introducing a new product, for example) and by developing processes for passing on the culture to new members.

6. Conscience

Conscience mechanisms reinforce shared values, purpose, and ethical standards. They include, for instance, codes of ethics, mission statements, official corporate values, and ethics hotlines. (We'll examine these elements and socialization processes in Chapter 9.)

7. Conversation

Verbal interaction creates shared purpose and worldviews, fosters relationships, and solves problems. Organizational communities are marked by ongoing electronic and face-to-face discussions about strategy and issues. They create a climate where individuals can have honest conversations with one another, drawing upon their diverse perspectives to generate solutions that benefit the common organizational good. (Turn to Chapter 4 for a closer look at interpersonal dialogue.)

Concern for the common good is an underlying theme of the Communitarian movement. Citizens work towards shared purposes, shoulder their responsibilities, reinforce common values, and express concern for others. Focus on the common good discourages selfish, unethical behavior. Although practices like false advertising and withholding taxes may serve the needs of an organization, such actions are unethical because they rarely benefit society as a whole. Further, if each group looks out only for its own welfare, the community as a whole suffers. Competing special interests have made it extremely difficult to tackle major societal problems like Social Security and Medicaid reform.

EVALUATION

There are several reasons why Communitarianism is a promising approach to moral reasoning. First, Communitarians recognize the social basis of morality. Our views of what is right or wrong, acceptable or unacceptable are largely the product of the cultures we live in. Second, Communitarianism highlights the dangers posed by the individualistic focus of Western culture. We have paid a high price for trying to maintain our freedom and autonomy at all costs. Selfishness needs to be supplanted by a commitment to communal responsibilities and a focus on the common good.

Third, Communitarianism promotes the benefits of participation and dialogue. Citizens need to be involved in molding values, debating ethical issues, and evaluating policies. Fourth, the rise of Communitarianism coincides with renewed interest in virtue ethics, which will be our focus in Chapter 2. Both Communitarian theorists and virtue ethicists are concerned with the development of moral character. Virtuous citizens build moral communities that, in turn, encourage further character formation. Fifth, Communitarianism addresses the role of organizational communities. Schools, churches, governments, businesses, and voluntary associations are to communicate important values.

The Communitarian movement has more than its share of detractors. Some critics fear that individual rights will be eroded in the pursuit of the common good. (Turn to the Chapter End Case to see how privacy concerns can clash with the need for public safety.) Other critics worry about promoting one set of values in a pluralistic society. Who decides, for example, which values are taught in the public schools? Still other critics take issue with the portrait of community painted by the Communitarians. Many collectives fall well short of the Communitarian ideal. They are homogeneous, repressive and exclusive, not responsive and inclusive. Gated communities springing up all across the nation are symptomatic of this tendency to segregate into different economic and social groups and to shut others out. Feminists accuse Communitarians of trying to recreate the patriarchal patterns of the past by encouraging women to stay at home to raise children.

The "toughest question" responsive Communitarians face is determining how to judge community values, according to Etzioni.[12] Local values should be respected because they reflect the unique history of the group. Community standards can be oppressive, however, as in the case of American cities that tolerate police brutality. As a consequence, local preferences need to be accountable to the larger society. Etzioni argued that broad deontological ethical principles should be used to evaluate community standards when groups can't reconcile their values differences. Yet, invoking these principles may not resolve such disputes, because parties may prioritize principles differently. Proponents of abortion put a much higher value on privacy rights and personal freedom than do foes of abortion, for example.

Altruism: Concern for Others

Altruism is based on the principle that we should help others regardless of whether or not we profit from doing so.[13] Assisting those in need may be rewarding (we may feel good about ourselves or receive public recognition, for example). Nevertheless, altruistic behavior seeks to benefit the other person, not the self. The most notable cases of altruism are those that involve significant self-sacrifice, as when a soldier jumps on a grenade to save the rest of his platoon or when an employee donates a kidney to another worker in need of a transplant. The word *altruism* comes from the Latin root *alter,* which means "other." Advocates of altruism argue that love of one's neighbor is the ultimate ethical standard. People are never a means to an end; they *are* the ends.

Not everybody agrees that prosocial behavior is possible. One group of evolutionary biologists believes that humans are conduits of "selfish genes." For instance, they believe that anything we do on behalf of family members is motivated by the desire to transmit our genetic code. Some skeptical philosophers argue that people are egoists. Every act, no matter how altruistic on the surface, always serves our needs, like when we help others because we expect to get paid back at some later time. However, a growing of body of research in sociology, political science, economics, social psychology—and other fields—establishes that true altruism does exist and is an integral part of the human experience.[14] In fact, altruistic behavior is common in everyday life:

> We humans spend much of out time and energy helping others. We stay up all night to comfort a friend who has suffered a broken relationship. We send money to rescue famine victims halfway round the world, or to save whales, or to support public television. We spend millions of hours per week helping as volunteers in hospitals, nursing homes, AIDS hospices, fire departments, rescue squads, shelters, halfway houses, peer-counseling programs and the like. We stop on a busy highway to help a stranded motorist change a flat tire,

or spend an hour in the cold to push a friend's—even a stranger's—car out of a snowdrift.[15]

Care for others appears to be a universal value, one promoted by religions the world over. Representatives from a variety of religious groups agree that every person deserves humane treatment, no matter what his or her ethnic background, language, skin color, political beliefs, or social standing (see Chapter 10).[16] Western thought has been greatly influenced by the altruistic emphasis of Judaism and Christianity. The command to love God and to love others as we love ourselves is the most important obligation in Judeo-Christian ethics. Since humans are made in the image of God and God is love, we have an obligation to love others no matter who they are and no matter what their relationship to us. Jesus drove home this point in the parable of the Good Samaritan. In this tale a generous businessman stops (at great risk to himself and his reputation) to befriend a wounded Jewish traveler—a person he could have considered his enemy. (See Box 1.2 for another story that highlights the importance of loving one's neighbor.)

Box 1.2 The Rabbi Goes to Heaven

In Nemirov, a small town in eastern Europe not unlike the town where the now famous Tevye of *Fiddler on the Roof* fame lived, a story is told of a Chassidic rabbi, his devoted flock, and a skeptic. The people, of course, were very, very poor, the rabbi very, very holy, and the skeptic very, very unbelieving. The story is as follows: The people believed that each year, just prior to the Penitential Season marking the Days of Awe which began the Jewish New Year, their rabbi went to heaven. After all, the Jews, however poor, still needed to eke out some kind of a livelihood, even as they needed good health and good matches for their sons and daughters and they believed that their rabbi went to heaven to intercede on their behalf. One day, a skeptic, a Jewish shoemaker from Lithuania, arrived in town, and on that day the Jews of the town were very happy because some time within the next twenty-four hours their rabbi was going to heaven, they said, to plead for them before the Throne of the Most High.

The skeptic called them foolish Jews for believing this. Not even Moses ascended to heaven, let alone a poor rabbi. Nevertheless, the skeptic was intrigued, so he decided to follow the rabbi, even to hide in the rabbi's house so that he would be able to see everything the rabbi did that day and thereby discredit the notions of the rabbi's foolish flock.

That evening, when the Jews of Nemirov journeyed to the river to symbolically rid themselves of their sins, their rabbi was not among them, nor was he in the house of prayer. "He must be in heaven," a congregant announced, and all of the others agreed.

Meanwhile the skeptic, hiding under the rabbi's bed, saw the rabbi dress himself in the clothing of a Polish peasant. On his feet he placed high boots, and on his head a woodsman's cap, and on his body a greatcoat. The rabbi then placed a sack in the inner pocket of the coat and tied a large leather belt about his waist. The skeptic could not imagine what was going on until the rabbi took hold of an axe. "For sure," thought the skeptic, "the rabbi knows I'm here and he is going to kill me."

Instead the rabbi put the axe in his belt, exited his small house, and walked deep into the woods. The skeptic followed and watched the rabbi fell a tree, chop it into logs, and then chop some of the logs more finely into sticks. The rabbi then bundled the wood and placed it into the large sack, which he took from his greatcoat. He then dragged the sack of wood even more deeply into the forest to a small hut where a poor widow lived.

The rabbi knocked on the door. "Who is there?" cried the widow. "It is Ivan," said the rabbi, "Ivan the woodcutter. I have heard that you are ill, and it is very cold, so I have brought you some wood." The woman opened the door and, from behind the tree where he was hiding, the skeptic heard the woman say, "I have no money to pay for wood." She coughed. "My son is looking for work in the next town, but he has found none," she said. The rabbi, alias Ivan, said, "He will find work soon; then you will pay. Plenty of time." The rabbi then entered the widow's hut. Through the window, the skeptic saw him light a fire, give the woman a crust of bread from his pocket, and then exit the house.

At daybreak, when the Jews were going to synagogue for morning prayers, they once again encountered the skeptic. "Well," one said to him, "our beloved rabbi went to heaven last night. Next year will surely be a little better for us. But you don't believe us, do you?" he asked.

Quietly the skeptic said, "Yes, I do. He went to heaven, if not higher. In fact, I saw him do it."

Source: Modified and reproduced by special permission of the Publisher, Davies-Black Publishing, an imprint of CPP, Inc., Mountain View, CA 94043 from *Connections Between Spirit & Work in Career Development* by Deborah P. Bloch, Lee J. Richmond, Eds.

Concern for others promotes healthy relationships. Society functions more effectively when individuals help one another in their daily interactions. This is particularly apparent in organizations. Many productive management practices, like empowerment, mentoring, and teambuilding, have an altruistic component. Researchers use the term *organizational citizenship behavior* to describe routine altruistic acts that increase productivity and build trusting relationships.[17] Examples of organizational citizenship behavior include an experienced machine operator helping a newcomer master the equipment, a professor teaching a class for a colleague on jury duty, and an administrative assistant working over break to help a coworker meet a deadline. Such acts play an important if underrecognized role in organizational success. Much less work would get done if members refused to help out. Take the case of the new machine operator. Without guidance, he or she may flounder for weeks, producing a number of defective parts and slowing the production process. Caring behaviors also break down barriers of antagonism between individuals and departments. Communication and coordination increase, leading to better overall results. You can determine your likelihood to engage in organizational citizenship behavior by completing the instrument in Box 1.3.

Self-Assessment

Box 1.3 Organizational Citizenship Behavior Scale

Instructions

Take the following test to determine your willingness to engage in altruistic behavior in the work setting. Respond to each item on a 5-point scale ranging from 1 (*never engage in this behavior*) to 5 (*nearly always engage in this behavior*). Reverse the scale where indicated, so that it ranges from 5 (*never engage in this behavior*) to 1 (*nearly always engage in this behavior*). Generate a total by adding up your scores. Maximum possible score: 80.

1. Help other employees with their work when they have been absent.
2. Exhibit punctuality in arriving at work on time in the morning and after lunch and breaks.
3. Volunteer to do things not formally required by the job.
4. Take undeserved work breaks. (Reverse)
5. Take the initiative to orient new employees to the department even though it is not part of the job description.
6. Exhibit attendance at work beyond the norm; for example, take fewer days off than most individuals or fewer than allowed.
7. Help others when their work load increases (assist others until they get over the hurdles).

8. Coast toward the end of the day. (Reverse)
9. Give advance notice if unable to come to work.
10. Spend a great deal of time in personal telephone conversations. (Reverse)
11. Do not take unnecessary time off work.
12. Assist others with their duties.
13. Make innovative suggestions to improve the overall quality of the department.
14. Do not take extra breaks.
15. Willingly attend functions not required by the organization but that help its overall image.
16. Do not spend a great deal of time in idle conversation.

Source: From *Organizational Citizenship Behavior: The Good Soldier Syndrome* by Organ, D. W. Copyright © 1988 by Lexington Books. Reproduced with permission of Lexington Books via Copyright Clearance Center.

EVALUATION

Altruism has much to offer. First, concern for others is a powerful force for good. It drives people to volunteer to care for the dying, teach prisoners, act as Big Brothers and Sisters, provide medical relief, and answer crisis calls. Clinical psychologist Kathleen Brehony found hundreds of cases of what she calls "ordinary grace"—average men and women doing extraordinary good on a daily basis.[18] She describes, for example, one 72-year-old woman who rises at 4:30 every morning to deliver food and clothing donations to poverty-stricken Native Americans in the Phoenix area. A retired Air Force physician reduces the isolation of chronically ill children around the country by providing them with computers.

Second, following the principle of caring helps prevent ethical abuses. We're much less likely to take advantage of others through accounting fraud, stealing, cheating, and other means if we put their needs first. (We'll return to this theme in our discussion of servant leadership in Chapter 7.) Third, altruistic behavior, as we've seen, promotes healthy relationships and organizations. There are practical benefits to acting in a caring manner. Fourth, altruism lays the foundation for high moral character. Many personal virtues, like compassion, hospitality, generosity, and empathy, reflect concern for other people. Finally, altruism is inspiring. When we hear of the selfless acts of Gandhi,

Desmond Tutu, and the Rwandans who risked their lives to save their neighbors from genocide, we are moved to follow their example.

While compelling, altruism suffers from serious deficiencies. All too often our concern for others only extends to our immediate family, neighbors, or communities.[19] Sadly, well-intentioned attempts to help others can backfire. They fail to meet the need, have unintended negative consequences, or make the problem worse. For example:

- Panhandlers use the money they collect from compassionate passers-by to feed their drug habits.
- A large proportion of the money donated to some charities pays for fund-raising costs rather than client services.
- Wealthy nations fail to follow through on their pledges to provide money for disaster relief, sparking bitterness and resentment in victims.
- Medicines donated for rural health care in a developing nation are stolen and sold on the black market.
- Recipients of welfare assistance become dependent on it.
- Buying children out of slavery increases the slave trade by making it more profitable for the slavers.

Altruism is not an easy principle to put into practice. For every time we stop to help a stranded motorist, we probably pass by several others that need assistance. Our urge to help out a coworker is often suppressed by our need to get our own work done or to meet a pressing deadline. Common excuses for ignoring needs include: (1) Somebody else will do it so I don't need to help; (2) I didn't know there was a problem (deliberately ignoring evidence of poverty, domestic violence and other problems); (3) I don't have the time or energy; (4) I don't know enough to help; (5) People deserve what they get (disdain for those who need help); (6) It won't matter anyway because one person can't make much of a difference; and (7) What's in it for me? (looking for personal benefit in every act). [20] There's also disagreement about what constitutes loving behavior. For example, firing someone can be seen as cruel or as caring. This act may appear punitive to outsiders. However, terminating an employee may be in that person's best interests. For someone who is not a good fit for an organization, being fired can open the door to a more productive career.

Implications

- Mastering widely used ethical theories greatly enhances your chances of success as an ethical change agent.
- Each ethical perspective has its weaknesses, but each makes a valuable contribution to moral problem solving.
- Whenever possible, apply a variety of ethical approaches when faced with a moral dilemma. Doing so will help you generate new insights into the issue.

- Utilitarian decisions are based on their consequences. The goal is to select the alternative that achieves the greatest good for the greatest number of people. To apply Utilitarian principles, identify all the possible courses of actions, estimate the direct and indirect costs and benefits of each option, and select the alternative that produces the greatest amount of good based on the cost-benefit analysis.
- Kant's Categorical Imperative is based on the premise that decision makers should do what's morally right no matter what the consequences. Moral choices flow out of a sense of duty and are those that we would want everyone to make. Always respect the worth of others when making ethical decisions.
- Justice as Fairness Theory provides a set of guidelines for resolving disputes over the distribution of resources. Assure that everyone in your organization has certain rights like freedom of speech and thought, the same chance at positions and promotions, and receives adequate training to qualify for these roles. Excess benefits should go to the least advantaged organizational members.
- Communitarianism encourages the creation and transmission of shared moral values. Focus on your responsibilities, not your rights. Make choices that promote the common good. Create an organizational community marked by commitment, competence, contribution, collaboration, continuity, conscience, and conversation.
- Altruism seeks to benefit the other person, not the self. By making caring for others the ethical standard, you can encourage practices (empowering, mentoring, teambuilding, organizational citizenship behavior) that build trust and increase productivity.

Application Projects

1. Reflect on one of your ethical decisions. Which approach(es) did you use when making your determination? Evaluate the effectiveness of the approach(es) as well as the quality of your choice. What did you learn from this experience?

2. Form a group and develop a list of behaviors that are always right and behaviors that are always wrong. Keep a record of those behaviors that were nominated but rejected by the team and why. Report your final list, as well as your rejected items, to the rest of the class. What do you conclude from this exercise?

3. Join with classmates and imagine that you are behind a veil of ignorance. What principles would you use to govern society and organizations?

4. Rate your organization on the seven core processes of organizational communities. Which characteristics does it possess? Which does it need to develop? How can your organization become more like the ideal? What steps should it take?

5. During a week, make note of all the altruistic behavior you witness in your organization. How would you classify these behaviors? What impact do they have on your organization? How would your organization be different if people didn't engage in organizational citizenship behavior? Write up your findings.

6. Write a case study based on an individual or group you admire for its altruistic motivation. Provide background and outline the lessons we can learn from this person or persons.

7. Apply all five ethical perspectives presented in the chapter to the Chapter End Case. Keep a record of your deliberations and conclusions using each one. Did you reach different solutions based on the theory you used? Were some of the perspectives more useful in this situation? Are you more confident after looking at the problem from a variety of perspectives? Write up your findings.

CHAPTER END CASE

Truro's DNA Dragnet

In January 2002, former fashion writer Christa Worthington was stabbed to death in the small coastal town of Truro, Massachusetts. One important clue to the killer's identity was the presence of semen on her body. After searching in vain for her murderer for 3 years, state and local police decided to gather DNA samples from all 790 of the village's full-time male residents. They hoped to identify the person who had sex with Worthington shortly before her death, even if he wasn't the killer. Police fanned out to local businesses, the town dump, and other locations to gather cheek swabs.

The decision to conduct a DNA dragnet divided the town's male population. Some were outraged. They contacted the police and the American Civil Liberties Union to protest and threatened litigation. Resisters viewed the DNA sweep as an invasion of privacy and worried that their samples wouldn't be destroyed as promised if they didn't match the evidence. Other men considered it their civic duty to be tested and came to the police station voluntarily.

Town residents faced significant pressure to cooperate. Police recorded the license plate numbers of those men who refused to provide DNA. Social sanctions were also applied to resisters. "I wish I could be bold enough to refuse," reported a Truro Little League coach. "[But] it's a difficult situation. It's a small town. . . . The word gets out. You already hear who has refused."[1]

Truro's DNA dragnet is part of a larger trend. More such collections are being held as testing becomes cheaper and faster. In Baton Rouge, police swabbed 1,200 men and some of the samples entered the state of Louisiana's crime database. In the largest sweep, conducted to identify a serial killer in Miami, authorities tested 2,300 men.

DNA dragnets in the United States have a low success rate. Of 19 publicized sweeps, only one (limited to 25 workers at a nursing home) resulted in a conviction. The rate of success in Britain, where the procedure is more common and the public less resistant, has been higher. Twenty percent of British DNA sweeps have produced matches leading to suspects and often convictions.

Even proponents of DNA dragnets acknowledge that such tactics pose significant ethical dilemmas. According to a spokesperson of the Baton Rouge police: "Let's face it. If we took a DNA sample from every male child at birth, we could solve a lot of crimes. But is that a price we're willing to pay?"[2]

In April 2005 a suspect was charged with Worthington's murder after his DNA matched the sample collected from the crime scene. The accused lived in a nearby town and had been the victim's trash collector. His DNA had been collected, not as a result of the sweep, but after he had attracted the attention of the police when he was charged with threatening a girlfriend.

DISCUSSION PROBES

1. Would you voluntarily submit to the DNA test if you were a male resident of Truro? Why or why not?
2. What rights and values are in conflict here?
3. How could each ethical perspective discussed in the chapter be applied to the case? Do you reach different conclusions about the ethics of DNA dragnets based on the ethical approach you take?
4. Should organizations (business, civic associations, schools) encourage their members to participate in DNA sweeps like the one in Truro?
5. What guidelines should be created to guide local police and other law enforcement agencies conducting DNA searches?
6. Why do you think Americans are more resistant than the British to this procedure?
7. Do you think the United States will ever develop a national DNA database that includes all citizens? Would you support such a system? Why or why not?

NOTES

1. Ripley (2005), p. 40.
2. Ripley (2005), p. 40.

SOURCES

Belluck, P. (2005, April 15). DNA test leads, at last, to arrest in Cape Cod case. *New York Times,* p. A6. Retrieved October 8, 2005, from LexisNexis.

Ripley, A. (2005, January 24). The DNA dragnet. *Time,* pp. 39–40.

Endnotes

1. Material for this summary of utilitarian theory is drawn from the following sources: Barry, V. (1978). *Personal and social ethics: Moral problems with integrated theory.* Belmont, CA: Wadsworth; Bentham, J. (1948). *An introduction to the principles of morals and legislation.* New York: Hafner; De George, R. T. (1995). *Business ethics*

(4th ed.). Englewood Cliffs, NJ: Prentice Hall, chap. 3; Troyer, J. (Ed.). (2003). *The classical Utilitarians: Bentham and Mill.* Indianapolis, IN: Hackett; Velasquez, M. G. (1992). *Business ethics: Concepts and cases* (3rd ed.). Englewood Cliffs, NJ: Prentice Hall, chap. 2; West, H. R. (2004). *An introduction to Mill's Utilitarian ethics.* Cambridge, UK: Cambridge University Press.

2. Hartman, E. (1996). *Organizational ethics and the good life.* New York: Oxford University Press, chap. 2; Barry (1978); Valesquez (1992).

3. Takeuchi, C. L. (2004, July 5). Wal-Mart's gender gap. *Time Canada,* p. 25. Retrieved January 21, 2006, from Academic Source Premier database.

4. Kant, I. (1964). *Groundwork of the metaphysics of morals* (H. J. Ryan, Trans.), New York: Harper & Row.; Christians, C. G., Rotzell, K. B., & Fackler, M. (1990). *Media ethics* (3rd ed.). New York: Longman.; Leslie, L. Z. (2000). *Mass communication ethics: Decision-making in postmodern culture.* Boston: Houghton Mifflin;Velasquez (1992).

5. Graham, G. (2004). *Eight theories of ethics.* London: Routledge, chap. 6.

6. Material on Rawls's Theory of Justice and its critics is taken from the following sources: Rawls, J. (1971). *A theory of justice.* Cambridge, MA: Belknap Press; Rawls, J. (1993). Distributive justice. In T. Donaldson & P. H. Werhane (Eds.), *Ethical issues in business: A philosophical approach* (4th ed., pp. 274–285). Englewood Cliffs, NJ: Prentice Hall; Rawls, J. (1993). *Political liberalism.* New York: Columbia University Press; Rawls, J. (2001). *Justice as fairness: A restatement* (E. Kelly, Ed.). Cambridge, MA: Belknap Press; Barry (1978); Blocker, H. G., & Smith, E. H. (Eds.). (1980). *John Rawls' theory of justice: An introduction.* Athens: Ohio University; Velasquez (1992); Mulhall, S., & Swift, A. (1992). *Liberals and Communitarians.* Oxford, UK: Blackwell.

7. Rawls (2001), p. 42.

8. Gladwell, M. (2005). *Blink: The power of thinking without thinking.* New York: Little, Brown.

9. Etzioni, A. (1993). *The spirit of community: The reinvention of American society.* New York: Simon & Schuster. See also: Etzioni, A. (Ed.). (1995). *New Communitarian thinking: Persons, virtues, institutions, and communities.* Charlottesville: University Press of Virginia; Etzioni, A. (Ed.). (1995). *Rights and the common good: A Communitarian perspective* (pp. 271–276). New York: St. Martin's Press; Johnson, C. E. (2000). Emerging perspectives in leadership ethics. *Proceedings of the International Leadership Association,* pp. 48–54. College Park, MD: International Leadership Association; Eberly, D. E. (1998). *America's promise: Civil society and the renewal of American culture.* Lanham, MD: Rowman & Littlefield; Tam, H. (1998) (1978). *Communitarianism: A new agenda for politics and citizenship.* New York: New York University Press.

10. Etzioni, A., Volmart, A., & Rothschild, E. (2004). *The Communitarian reader: Beyond the essentials.* Lanham, MD: Rowman & Littlefield, pp. 13–23.

11. Brown, J., & Isaacs, D. (1995). Building corporations as communities: The best of both worlds. In K. Gozdz (Ed.), *Community building: Renewing spirit and learning in business* (pp. 69–83). San Francisco: Sterling & Stone.

12. Etzioni, A. (2000). Epilogue. In E. W. Lehman (Ed.), *Autonomy and order: A Communitarian anthology* (pp. 219–236). Lanham, MD: Rowman & Littlefield, p. 221. See also: Etzioni, A. (1996). *The new golden rule: Community and morality in a democratic society.* New York: Basic Books.

13. Batson, C. D., Van Lange, P. A. M., Ahmad, N., & Lishner, D. A. (2003). Altruism and helping behavior. In M. A. Hogg & J. Cooper (Eds.), *The Sage handbook of social psychology* (pp. 279–295). London: Sage; Post, S. G. (2002). The tradition of agape.

In S. G. Post, L. G. Underwood, J. P. Schloss & W. B. Hurlbut (Eds.), *Altruism and altruistic love: Science, philosophy, & religion in dialogue* (pp. 51–64). Oxford, UK: Oxford University Press.

14. Piliavin, J. A., & Charng, H. W. (1990). Altruism: A review of recent theory and research. *American Sociological Review, 16*, 27–65.

15. Batson, Van Lange, Ahman, & Lishner (2003), p. 279.

16. Kung, H. (1998). *A global ethic for global politics and economics.* New York: Oxford University Press.

17. Kanungo, R. N., & Conger, J. A. (1993). Promoting altruism as a corporate goal. *Academy of Management Executive, 7*, 37–49; Organ, D. W. (1988). *Organizational citizenship behavior: The good soldier syndrome.* Lexington, MA: Lexington Books.

18. Brehony, K. A. (1999). *Ordinary grace: Lessons from those who help others in extraordinary ways.* New York: Riverhead Books.

19. Sorokin, P. A. (1954). *The ways and power of love: Types, factors, and techniques of moral transformation.* Boston: Beacon Press.

20. Kottler, J. A. (2000). *Doing good: Passion and commitment for helping others.* Philadelphia: Brunner-Routledge.

Part II

Transforming Individual Ethics in the Organization

2

Personal Ethical Development

Chapter Preview

"Is it bad apples or bad barrels?" Observers sometimes ask this question when trying to account for organizational misbehavior or "rottenness." Do work groups engage in immoral behavior because unethical individuals (the "bad apples") spoil those around them or do unethical organizations (the "bad barrels") corrupt their employees? Truth is, *both* individual and contextual factors contribute to ethical failure.[1] That means we'll have to address both the person and the situation when attempting to transform organizations. While we could begin by examining the organizational barrel, I believe that we are better off starting with the apples. Before addressing the organizational context, we need to prepare for our role as change agents by examining and then developing our motivations, personal mission, values, character, and moral reasoning. In this chapter we'll identify the elements that should be part of any personal ethical development plan. In the next chapter we will zero in on the process of moral reasoning and moral action.

Components of Personal Ethical Development

COMPONENT 1: FACING THE SHADOW SIDE OF THE PERSONALITY

Any personal change effort should be based on a realistic self-assessment. In particular, we need to acknowledge our potential to do harm as well as good. Many of the causes of aggression, discrimination, and other destructive behaviors (competitiveness, hostility, prejudice) lie within the individual, as we'll see in Chapter 8.

Psychotherapist Carl Jung introduced the shadow metaphor to account for those parts of ourselves that fall short of what we want to be and that we don't want to share with others.[2] These elements could be embarrassing ("I'm afraid of the dark."), socially unacceptable ("I'm bigoted."), or dangerous ("I'm filled with hostility."). In most cases the shadow is considered a negative force, but it can fuel creativity and spontaneity.

Jung and others interested in the dark side of the personality have argued that ignoring this side of ourselves puts us at great risk. Repressing these impulses (anger, jealousy, rage, insecurity, pride) doesn't make them go away. According to Jung, "mere suppression of the shadow is as little of a remedy as beheading would be for headache."[3] The shadow is likely to surface under stressful conditions. If you think of yourself as a caring person, for example, you may be surprised when you lash out at your family or roommates as homework begins to pile up. Under this stressful situation the anger hiding in the shadow side of your personality might suddenly emerge. The same dynamic occurs in organizations when supervisors cope with their own fear of failure by making unreasonable demands on employees or when coworkers respond to their own insecurities by belittling members of other work teams.

Leaving the shadow side unattended also leaves us vulnerable to projection. In projection we unconsciously transfer or project undesirable characteristics onto others. Jung believed that racial hatred is a projection of the shadow side of the personality, as when the Nazis cast their shadows on the Jews. Another sign of projection is reacting negatively when others reflect the very characteristics (selfishness, dogmatism, a critical attitude) we dislike in ourselves.

Confronting the shadow side of the personality brings many benefits. First, acknowledging that we have undesirable characteristics begins to break their hold over us. We can't master them until we admit that they exist. Second, facing the shadow side provides us with a clearer sense of who we really are. Third, knowing that we harbor destructive tendencies humbles us, making us more understanding and forgiving of others. Fourth, we are less likely to project our shadow on others in the workplace, thus reducing the frequency of destructive behaviors and improving the ethical climate. Fifth, acknowledging our weaknesses can encourage others to do the same, building healthier work relationships.

There is no blueprint for controlling the shadow side of the personality. However, these tips can help you better manage the unpleasant aspects of the self.[4]

- Take personal responsibility for your actions. You are ultimately accountable for how you act. You have a choice as to how to respond to shadow forces.
- Determine if the negative images you have of others are the result of projecting your undesirable qualities on them. If so, address these negative characteristics in yourself.
- Learn from your mistakes. When your behavior contradicts your self-image, probe for the underlying reasons for your misbehavior. Determine how you can respond more appropriately in the future.
- Find a supportive partner. Create a trusting relationship where you can explore your weaknesses with one another through listening and feedback.
- Accept criticism. Your critics (supervisors, coworkers, customers) can provide you with valuable insights into your weaknesses.
- Keep yourself out of harm's way. You may need to adjust your behavior or environment to keep from unleashing shadow forces. For example: If high stress levels at work are harming your relationships with your family and coworkers, you may need to reduce your hours or find another job.

COMPONENT 2: DISCOVERING VOCATION

Any strategy for personal ethical development should address two questions: (1) "Who am I?" and (2) "Where am I headed?" A number of authors suggest that we can best determine our identity and life direction through understanding our vocation or calling. In popular usage, the word *vocation* refers to a job or occupation. However, the original meaning of the term was much broader. The English word is drawn from the Latin *vocare,* which means "to call" or "calling."[5] Discovering our vocation means determining our purpose in life. That purpose is based on a clear understanding of our unique skills, abilities, and desires. Or, to put it another way, our vocation (the answer to "Where am I headed?") flows out of our individual identity (the answer to "Who am I?").

For many of us, the work we do is essential to fulfilling our vocation. At times, however, the pursuit of vocation has little to do with paid employment. Some use the money they earn from their jobs to pursue their vocations (working with homeless youth, performing music, inventing, researching) in their spare time. Others, such as stay-at-home parents, retirees, and the voluntarily unemployed, follow their callings without earning a salary.

Whether or not we hold a full time job, we need to recognize that vocational calling encompasses every aspect of life, including our relationships to others, our roles in public (as citizens and volunteers), our attempts to recreate ourselves through leisure, and our participation in spiritual communities.[6] A social worker, for instance, may exercise her calling by assisting clients at a state agency, by befriending her elderly neighbors, and by volunteering her time to lobby for greater health care coverage for the poor.

Finding our calling produces important ethical benefits. One, when we are using our abilities and interests, we enjoy a feeling of personal satisfaction or self-actualization. This sense of satisfaction increases our level of commitment and reduces the likelihood that we will poison the ethical climate of the organization. Two, having a clear direction makes us better stewards. Instead of wasting time and energy on tasks that aren't central to our purpose, we can focus on more meaningful projects that make effective use of our abilities. Three, vocation equips us for service to others. This outward focus is captured in writer Frederick Buechner's description of vocation as "the place where your deep gladness and the world's deep hunger meet."[7] Because we are more productive when pursuing our vocation, we are better able to serve others, whether as engineers, architects, graduate students, software developers, nursing home administrators, or scientists.

Philosophy professor Lee Hardy offers some practical advice for discovering how you can use your gifts to serve others in the workplace.[8] The first step is to determine your unique gifts. Pay particular attention to past experiences. Ask yourself,

- What have I done and done well?
- What kinds of skills did I make use of?
- What kind of knowledge did I acquire?
- What kind of objects did I work with?
- In what capacity was I relating to others?
- Was I working in a position with a lot of freedom and responsibility, or was I working in a highly structured situation, where my activity was thoroughly and carefully structured?

Hardy suggests that you try out a variety of jobs. Even if you don't like a particular position, you will learn from the experience. Identify your personality type (see Box 2.1) and get feedback about your strengths and weaknesses from those who know you well.

Box 2.1 Holland's Personality and Career Types

John Holland, a professor emeritus at Johns Hopkins University, offers the following personality types on which career choices can be based.[1] These types are the product of both genetic background and experience. A child who has musically gifted parents may inherit the ability to recognize pitch and melody, for example. However, to become a professional musician, she will need plenty of practice and encouragement (lessons, attendance at concerts, special schools).

Holland identifies six patterns that impact career choices:

The Realistic Type

The Realistic person likes carefully structured, ordered activities that involve the use of objects, tools, machines, and animals. He or she acquires mechanical, electrical, agricultural, and other competencies in order to achieve goals. Sample professions: surveyor, mechanic.

The Investigative Type

An Investigative person seeks to observe and understand the physical and cultural world. Such an individual strives to acquire scientific and mathematical skills. Sample professions: medical technician, chemist, physicist.

The Artistic Type

An individual with the Artistic preference prefers unstructured activities that allow for the creation of art forms and new products. This type masters artistic skills that draw from music, art, drama, and language. Sample professions: artist, musician, writer.

The Social Type

Heredity and experience encourage the Social person to inform, train, and enlighten others. This requires the acquisition of interpersonal skills and knowledge along with a strong educational background. Sample professions: teacher, counselor.

The Enterprising Type

The Enterprising individual wants to reach goals and make money through others. As a result, he or she works on acquiring persuasive, interpersonal, and leadership competencies. Sample professions: salesperson, executive.

(Continued)

(Continued)

The Conventional Type

A Conventional individual gravitates to tasks that involve the systematic manipulation of data through keeping records, filing, analyzing numbers, and use of databases. This type focuses on developing clerical, computational, and computer skills. Sample professions: accountant, clerk.

Note

1. For a complete copy of Holland's career inventory, see Holland (1997).

Source: Holland, J. L. (1997). *Making vocational choices* (3rd ed.). Odessa, FL: Psychological Assessment Resources.

Professor Hardy's second and third steps to finding vocation consist of identifying your specific concern for others and your interests. You may be concerned about the housing needs of immigrant populations, for instance, or environmental and educational problems. Your interests—like the love of art, music or literature, bird watching, hiking, photography, film production, current events—can motivate you to develop skills and knowledge which later can be employed in service. For example, one of my colleagues was prompted by his boyhood hobby of collecting baseball statistics into pursuing a career as a professor of mathematics.

The final step is to find the right job fit. Locate a place where your gifts, concerns, and interests can be put to best use. According to Hardy, finding the right fit goes beyond matching your talents to the job description. It should also include an evaluation of the values and goals of the work setting. You may be well suited for a position (for example, a position writing copy for tobacco ads), yet refuse it on moral grounds.

Sadly, the call of vocation often falls upon deaf ears. Ambition is one significant barrier to obeying our callings. Following our heart's desires may put us in direct conflict with what the world defines as success. We may want to study art, protect wildlife, or teach, but our culture encourages us to pursue other objectives, like making money, getting promoted, and achieving status. (See the Case Study in Box 2.2 for one example of the clash between worldly values and personal calling.) Emory University professor Brian Mahan argues that to follow our vocation we must "forget ourselves on purpose."[9] After determining what is most satisfying and meaningful to us, we then need to discover what is preventing us from hearing its call. We can uncover our preoccupations by asking, "What is keeping me from living fully for the thing I want to live for?" Setting aside distractions enables us to acknowledge that pride and the trappings of success are constant temptations. By understanding their power, we can begin to break their hold over us. Then we are ready to respond to our life purpose.

Avoidance is another obstacle to vocation. Like the biblical figure Jonah, who headed in the opposite direction when God sent him to the city of Nineveh, many of us resist our call. We may do so out of a sense of caution, doubts about our own abilities, self-imposed limitations, or compliance with orders from authority figures. Resistance can take the form of

- waiting for just the right moment
- analyzing the call to death
- lying to ourselves
- replacing one call with another, more socially acceptable one
- sabotaging our own efforts
- filling our lives with other activities[10]

In order to overcome resistance, we need to break free of our low self-esteem. Fortunately, our chances of success are much greater when we respond to a genuine call. That realization should make it easier to leave our self-doubts behind and move forward.

CASE STUDY

Box 2.2 Pam's Choice

Many college seniors aren't sure what they're going to do once they finish school. Not so with Pam. Pam had a clear direction before the end of the first semester of her senior year. At a Christmas party, she told ethics professor Brian Mahan that she had been accepted into Yale Law School but turned down this offer to enter the Peace Corps instead.

Mahan uses Pam's story to illustrate the tension between worldly values and answering our call. When Mahan told his ethics classes about his conversation with Pam, students' responses went through a series of phases. At first, class members were content to let Pam do anything she wanted. "Well, I'd probably have gone to Yale," said one. "I'd like that. But it's fine that Pam chose the Peace Corps. More power to her."[1] This initial consensus soon gave way to questions like "Do you think her parents were upset?" and "Didn't she know that she could have done more for the poor if she went to Yale Law School first?"[2]

In the final phase of the discussion, students became more critical, arguing that Pam might have been afraid of the competition at Yale or out to prove how "sensitive" she was. One went so far to as to suggest that Pam was lying: "I don't mean to be insensitive, but did it occur to you that, well, she might have lied to you—that maybe she didn't really get into Yale Law School? If she got in—let's face it—I really think she would've gone."[3]

DISCUSSION PROBES

1. Do you believe Pam's story? Why or why not?
2. Did Pam make the right decision, assuming her story is true?
3. What might have motivated Pam to choose the Peace Corps over Yale Law School?
4. Would you make the same choice if you were in her position?
5. What does Pam's story tell us about answering our vocational call?

NOTES

1. Mahan (2002), p. 3.
2. Mahan (2002), p. 4.
3. Mahan (2002), p. 5.

SOURCE

Mahan, B. J. (2002). *Forgetting ourselves on purpose: Vocation and the ethics of ambition.* San Francisco: Jossey-Bass.

COMPONENT 3: IDENTIFYING PERSONAL VALUES

Personal moral values are "desirable goals, varying in importance, that serve as guiding principles in people's lives."[11] Values drive a good deal of our decision making and behavior on the job, including how hard we work, how we treat coworkers and subordinates, how we evaluate performance, and so on. For example, those who put a high value on responsibility are rarely late to work and may show up even when they are sick. Those who place more value on enjoying life may skip work to go skiing or to the beach. We also use our values as standards to determine right from and wrong and to set our priorities. I value justice, for example, so I become incensed when I read about the growing gap between the wages of top executives and average workers. I value relationships with students, so an advising appointment is likely to take precedence over my administrative duties.

One way to identify or clarify your values is by sitting down and generating a list. Chances are, you'll have no trouble coming up with at least a few of your core values. However, there may be some potentially important values that you overlook. For that reason, you may want to consider rating a list of values supplied by values experts. Hebrew University professor Shalom Schwartz developed one widely used value system. Schwartz argues that, due to the human condition, people around the world organize themselves around the same set of universal values.[12] While the values remain constant, their priority changes based on personal experiences and cultural differences. You are more likely to respect authority, for instance, if you grew up in a strongly religious family. Tradition and conformity often motivate behavior in collectivist cultures that seek to subordinate the individual to the group. Self-direction, hedonism, and stimulation are more likely to drive behavior in individualistic societies that encourage personal autonomy. Further, the pursuit of one type of value (personal achievement and success) may conflict with pursuit of another (benevolent concern for others).

To determine your value priorities and those of your organization, complete the Self-Assessment in Box 2.3. If your rankings agree with those of the larger group, your organizational commitment and job satisfaction are likely to be high. You might have others in your work group complete the same inventory and then compare rankings. (See Application Project 5 on page 54.)

Self-Assessment

Box 2.3 Schwartz's Value System

Take a few moments and rank the items below. Each value is described along with sample behaviors produced by that value. These will serve as your anchor points. Next, rate each value according to its importance as a guiding principle in your life. Use a 9-point scale ranging from –1 (*opposed to my principles*) to 0 (*not important*) to 7 (*of supreme importance*). When you finish you'll have a sense of how important each value is to you as well as how it rates in comparison to the other values on the list. Then rank and rate the values for your workgroup or organization as a whole. Compare the two sets of scores. What do they reveal?

Power: Social status and prestige, control, or dominance over people and resources (social power, authority, wealth)

Behaviors: pressure others to go along with my preferences and opinions; choose friends and relationships based on how much money they have

Personal rank _____ rating ______Organizational rank _____ rating _____

Achievement: Personal success through demonstrating competence according to social standards (successful, capable, ambitious, influential)

(Continued)

(Continued)

Behaviors: study late before exams even though I studied well in the semester; take on many commitments

Personal rank _____ rating ______Organizational rank _____ rating _____

Hedonism: Pleasure and sensuous gratification for oneself (pleasure, enjoying life)

Behaviors: take it easy and relax; consume food or drinks even when I'm not hungry or thirsty

Personal rank _____ rating ______Organizational rank _____ rating _____

Stimulation: Excitement, novelty, and challenge in life (daring, a varied life, an exciting life)

Behaviors: watch thrillers; do unconventional things

Personal rank _____ rating ______Organizational rank _____ rating _____

Self-direction: Independent thought and action—choosing, creating, exploring (creativity, freedom, independent, curious, choosing my own goals)

Behaviors: examine the ideas behind rules and regulations before obeying them; come up with novel set-ups for my living space

Personal rank _____ rating ______Organizational rank _____ rating _____

Universalism: Understanding, appreciation, tolerance, and protection for the welfare of all people and for nature (broad-minded, wisdom, social justice, equality, a world at peace, a world of beauty, unity with nature, protecting the environment)

Behaviors: use environmentally friendly products; make sure everyone receives equal treatment

Personal rank _____ rating ______Organizational rank _____ rating _____

Benevolence: Preservation and enhancement of the welfare of people with whom one is in frequent personal contact (helpful, honest, forgiving, loyal, responsible)

Behaviors: agree easily to lend things to neighbors; keep promises I have made

Personal rank _____ rating ______Organizational rank _____ rating _____

Tradition: Respect, commitment, and acceptance of the customs and ideas that traditional culture or religion provide the self (humble, accepting my portion in life, devout, respect for tradition, moderate)

Behaviors: observe traditional customs on holidays; show modesty with regard to my achievements and talents

Personal rank _____ rating ______Organizational rank _____ rating _____

Conformity: Restraint of actions, inclinations, and impulses likely to upset or harm others and violate social expectations or norms (politeness, obedient, self-discipline, honoring parents and elders)

Behaviors: obey my parents; avoid confrontation with people I don't like

Personal rank _____ rating ______Organizational rank _____ rating _____

Security: Safety, harmony, and stability of society, of relationships, and of self (family security, national security, social order, clean, reciprocation of favors)

Behaviors: refrain from opening my door to strangers; buy products that were made in my country

Personal rank _____ rating ______Organizational rank _____ rating _____

Source: Bardi, A., & Schwartz, S. (2003). Values and behavior: Strength and structure of relations. *Journal of Personality and Social Psychology, 29,* 1207–1220, p. 1211. Used by permission of the publisher.

COMPONENT 4: DEVELOPING CHARACTER

Character plays an important role in ethical decision making and behavior. Your chances of making wise decisions and following through on your choices will be higher if you demonstrate the positive moral traits or qualities referred to as *virtues.* The notion that good people make good choices is the premise of virtue ethics. Virtue ethics is one of the oldest ethical traditions, dating back to the times of Plato, Aristotle, Confucius, and before.[13] In contrast to the rules-based theories presented in the last chapter, virtue theory highlights the person or actor instead of general ethical principles. Virtue ethicists note that ethical decisions are typically made under time pressures in uncertain conditions.[14] Individuals in these situations don't have time to weigh possible consequences or to select an abstract guideline to apply. Instead, they respond based on their character. Those with high (virtuous) character will immediately react in ways that benefit themselves, others, and the greater good. They will quickly turn down bribes, reach out to help others, and so on. (Read the Chapter End Case to see character demonstrated under horrific conditions.)

Virtues are "deep-rooted dispositions, habits, skills, or traits of character that incline persons to perceive, feel, and act in ethically right and sensitive ways."[15] It takes a long time for such qualities to develop and become part of our core identities. Being virtuous increases sensitivity to ethical issues and encourages moral behavior. Further, virtues aren't bound by context. A virtue may be expressed differently depending on the situation (courage takes different forms in the boardroom and on the battlefield, for example). Nonetheless, a virtuous person doesn't abandon his or her principles to please others or act civilly to some people but not to others.

Aristotle and Plato identified primary or cardinal virtues appropriate for the Greek city-state: prudence (discernment, discretion), justice (righteousness, integrity), courage (strength in the face of adversity), and self-restraint (temperance). Christians added faith, hope, and love.[16] Later a number of other virtues, such as compassion, generosity, empathy, hospitality, modesty, and civility, were derived from the original seven. Contemporary lists expand the number of virtues still further. For example, ethicist Robert Solomon suggests that the following virtues are relevant to business:[17]

honesty	tactfulness	trustworthiness
helpfulness	cool-headedness	openness
tolerance	courage	liveliness
prudence	decency	benevolence
loyalty	wittiness	cheerfulness
cooperativeness	warmth	magnanimity
reasonableness	reliability	sensitivity
resourcefulness	modesty	amiability
sincerity	gracefulness	persistence
civility	hospitality	

Agreeing on one comprehensive list of virtues is not as important as developing desirable character traits that will promote moral behavior. Deliberately moralizing (telling people how to behave) may spark resistance. That means we have look for other, less direct, ways to encourage character development. These include:

Habits

According to Aristotle, we cannot separate character from action. We acquire virtues through exercising them: "Men [and women] become builders by building, and lyre-payers by playing the lyre, so too we become just be doing just acts, temperate by doing temperate acts, brave by doing brave acts."[18] Good habits are voluntary routines or practices designed to foster virtuous behavior. Every time we engage in a habit (telling the truth, giving credit to others, giving to the less fortunate), it leaves a trace. Over time, these residual effects become part of our personality and the habit becomes "second nature." In other words, by doing better we become better. We also become more skilled in demonstrating the virtue. Practicing self-restraint, for example, improves the ability to demonstrate self-restraint under pressure. Conversely, practicing bad habits encourages the development of vices that stunt character development. This was the case at Microsoft, according to some critics who claimed that chair Bill Gates and president Steve Ballmer did not appear to have ever admitted mistakes. When they faced an antitrust suit, this pattern repeated itself, damaging the reputation and standing of the company. The Microsoft executives were unrepentant and saw no reason to change their business practices even though the judge in the case ruled that they were monopolistic.[19]

Character-building habits include being honest in every transaction, no matter how small; never hiding the bad news from the boss; and treating every person with respect. Stephen Covey has described seven habits that characterize highly effective, ethical individuals.[20] You can use his list of habits as you strive to develop your character on the job. One, be proactive—choose how to respond to events. Two, begin with the end in mind. Identify desired results and follow through. Base goals on inner principles rather than external factors like money, friends, or work. Three, put first things first. Organize time around priorities, not emergencies. Four, think win/win by cooperating to generate a solution that benefits both parties. Five, seek first to understand, then to be understood. Listen to comprehend, not evaluate, and build trusting relationships. Six, synergize by generating solutions that exceed the ability of either party to create on their own. Seven, sharpen the saw by continually renewing the physical, mental, social/emotional, and spiritual dimensions of the self.

Role Models

Virtues are more "caught than taught" in that they are often acquired through observation and imitation. We learn what it means to be courageous, just, compassionate, and honest by seeing these qualities modeled in the lives of others. Role models can be drawn from the people we know (managers, friends, teachers); historical figures; or contemporary political, business and military leaders. For example, those interested in careers in government can turn to a set of exemplars provided by the American Society for Public Administration.[21] These examples of virtue include Harvard W. Wiley, the chief chemist of the U.S. Department of Agriculture who engineered passage of the Food and Drug Act in 1906; former U.S. Comptroller General Elmer Stats

Source: © Scott Adams/Dist. By United Features Syndicate, Inc.

(1966–1981), who used the General Accounting Office to root out corruption and inefficiency; William Ruckelshaus, the attorney general who refused to follow President Nixon's orders to fire the independent prosecutor investigating the Watergate scandal; former Surgeon General C. Everett Koop, who fought against smoking and for treatment of AIDS as a medical, not moral problem in the 1980s; and Marie Ragghianti, a Kentucky official who, in 1977, uncovered a scheme by the governor of Kentucky to sell paroles.

Stories

Stories help us understand the world and promote desired behaviors.[22] The narratives told by our families, schools, and religious bodies are designed to impart values and to encourage caring, self-discipline, and other virtues. When we learn of the bravery of a distant relative, for instance, we get a better grasp of our family's heritage. At the same time we are encouraged to follow his or her example in order to maintain the family name. A similar process unfolds in the organizational setting. The story of a coworker who went to extraordinary lengths to serve a customer inspires us to do likewise. (See Chapter 9 for more information on organizational stories.)

Character growth not only comes from hearing narratives but also comes from "living up" to our roles in the stories we share with others.[23] When we align ourselves with an organization, we become actors in its ongoing narrative. We should seek out transformed organizations that will bring out the best in us or work to change the collective story of which we are a part.[24]

Fictional stories can also enhance character development. Literature, theatre productions, films, and television shows all play a role in our moral education. Fiction forces us to confront unpleasant realities like aging, death, and the fact that the vast majority of events are beyond our control. We are introduced to new ethical dilemmas and improve our moral judgment by evaluating the actions of important characters.[25]

Passages

Intense experiences—those that push us out of our comfort zones—play a critical role in character development. These crossroads events, called *passages,* fall into four categories: (1) diversity of work experiences (joining a company, accepting a major new assignment); (2) work adversity (significant failure, losing a job, coping with a bad boss); (3) diversity of life experiences (living abroad, blending work and family into a meaningful whole); (4) life adversity (death or divorce, illness).[26]

All four types of passages offer significant potential for character growth. Through them we can gain more empathy for others, develop resiliency, let go of our ambitions, become more vulnerable and authentic, and so forth. However, we'll only benefit from these experiences if we view them as learning opportunities. We must accept responsibility for our actions and failures, admit our need to grow, and engage in reflection to draw out important lessons.

COMPONENT 5: DRAWING UPON SPIRITUAL RESOURCES

A growing number of organizational members are discovering that spiritual resources are essential to inner transformation. Spiritual insights can provide the strength to face our shadow sides, direct us to our vocations, and shape our values and character.

By all indications, interest in spirituality in the workplace is booming.[27] Hundreds of books have been written on the topic. Thousands of Bible study and prayer groups meet in corporate settings. Spiritual seekers can find business and spirituality courses at a number of colleges and universities or attend conferences and seminars devoted to the subject. Tom's of Maine, Herman Miller, TD Industries, Medtronic, Bank of Montreal, and Toro are just a few of the companies that base their organizational culture on spiritual values.

A number of factors account for the surge of interest in workplace spirituality.[28] Among the most important are (1) aging baby boomers (many of whom have no connection to religious congregations) seeking greater meaning in the workplace; (2) greater societal emphasis on self-discovery and self-knowledge; (3) heightened employee insecurity brought about by widespread layoffs and downsizing; (4) recognition in organizations that workers are whole persons with personal values, emotions, and spiritual commitments; (5) companies hoping to enhance employee commitment and productivity through fostering purpose, collaboration, and community.

Organizational spirituality encompasses a number of themes or threads (see Box 2.4). Ian Mitroff and Elizabeth Denton provide one popular definition of spirituality based on the theme of interconnectedness. Drawing upon their interviews with managers and executives, they define workplace spirituality as "the basic feeling of being connected with one's complete self, others, and the entire universe."[29] Connection with self involves getting in touch with our deepest longings and emotions. Connection with others takes form in concern for coworkers, respect, teamwork, and community involvement. Connection with "the entire universe" refers to developing relationships with larger forces like nature and God. It should be noted that most scholars distinguish between religion and spirituality. The two overlap but are not identical. Religious institutions encourage and structure spiritual experiences, but spiritual encounters routinely occur outside formal religious channels.

Box 2.4 Workplace Spirituality: Definitional Threads

Self-actualization; self-fulfillment; self-awareness; self-consciousness; self-discovery

Wholeness, holism; integration; integrity; authenticity; balance; harmony

Meaning; purpose

Emotion; passion; feeling

Life force; energy; vitality; life; intrinsic motivation

Wisdom; discernment; courage; creativity

Morality; values; peace; truth; freedom; justice

Interconnectedness; interdependence; interrelationship; cooperation; community; teamwork

Source: From Hicks, D. A., *Religion and the Workplace: Pluralism, Spirituality and Leadership,* copyright © 2003. Reprinted with the permission of Cambridge University Press.

Spiritual resources need to be nurtured. Psychotherapist and best-selling author Thomas Moore uses the phrase "caring for the soul" to describe the ongoing process of cultivating the inner emotional and spiritual self.[30] In an organizational setting, Moore says you can feed your soul through the following.

Intimacy (Closeness and Connection)

Organizations foster intimacy through encouraging friendship, repeating the history of a business to foster employee attachment, opening up contact between departments, storytelling, creating a sense of family, and sensitivity to the community.

Creative Work

Creativity is a drive or impulse that needs to be supported by allowing people to work in their own ways and by accepting their failures. Even routine tasks are creative because they produce products and profits, further careers, and generate new organizational structures.

Nature and Beauty

Refreshment comes through encounters with nature, whether in the form of landscaping, interior design, a park, or the countryside. Nature is a provider of what every soul must have—beauty. Unfortunately, by focusing on success, the modern organization sacrifices beauty for efficiency. Colors, textures, and sounds are essential to the soul but are often forgotten in the rush to build drab, inexpensive, and efficient buildings. Stopping to contemplate beauty is seen as a barrier to progress instead of as a vital way to nourish the soul.

Spirituality

The term *sacred* need not be reserved solely for personal beliefs. Work can be dedicated to higher purposes, as we've seen. In addition, business activity is sacred because it has a dramatic impact on the lives of individual workers, the community, and the economy as a whole. Corporations attuned to the soul recognize that making a profit can work in harmony with other important values like concern for the poor and the environment. These groups establish a strong business identity and earn the trust of outsiders. (We'll take an in-depth look at organizational citizenship in Chapter 10.)

So far we've focused on ways to better care for the soul. However, one important question remains—how do we know if we are making any spiritual progress? Management educator Peter Vaill provides one list of milestones. These markers or avenues of spiritual growth emphasize its ongoing development. We'll never "arrive" as spiritual seekers. Instead, we need to be progressing toward the following mileposts.[31]

1. Toward Embracing New Values and the Possibilities They Imply, and the Relativity of Values to Each Other

The first measure of spiritual development is the ability to see the world in shades or gray instead of as black and white, right or wrong. Spiritually developed leaders reflect a "largeness of spirit." They are willing to hear all sides of issues, try to discover how organizational members come to the understanding of truths, and recognize that people can be simultaneously right and wrong.

2. Toward a Passionate Reason

Spiritual growth embraces the whole person, mental and emotional, calm and passionate. Courage, for example, blends both reason and emotion. Acting courageously requires a clear understanding of the situation along with an emotional commitment to press on despite significant obstacles. Faith, too, is a blend of passion and reason. Faith based solely on emotion is likely to be discredited. On the other hand, faith based solely on logic may not withstand outside pressures and challenges.

3. Toward the Development of an Open Value System

The relationship between a person's values is key to spiritual growth. Values don't operate in isolation but function as a system. For instance, an employee may value independence but, because of a greater need for security, submit to closer supervision in order to keep his or her job. Those with open values systems can step out of their own moral frameworks and understand the belief structures of people of other professions and cultures. They also develop a deeper understanding of their organizations' values systems.

4. Toward Spiritual Development That Is Shared With Others

Spiritual growth is reflected in a willingness to enter into fellowship with others. In addition, taking a collaborative approach to spirituality pays significant dividends. Those who join with others experience a greater sense of interdependence and are better able to deal with loneliness and failure.

5. Toward a New Vocabulary and Grammar of Spirituality

Willingness to use such words as *faith, soul, redemption,* and *spirit* is an important marker of spiritual development. Those making spiritual progress also try to understand the deeper meaning behind these terms. Further, they consciously seek contact with the spiritual side of life through prayer and other means.

6. Toward Appreciation of the Spirit in Larger and Large Wholes

Spiritually sensitive leaders see how they and their units contribute to the organization as a whole. Managers who understand the underlying essence or spirits of their organizations are better able to attend to the many details required to keep them running smoothly. In addition, they realize that the spirits of their organizations are connected with those of other groups, society, and the global community.

7. Toward Centering in the Present

Vaill believes that this last element of spiritual growth is most important because it integrates the first six. Personal effectiveness depends on balance, which he defines as paying attention simultaneously to what is going on both inside and outside the self. When members of an organization lose their balance by ignoring either their thoughts or feelings, or by ignoring other people and events, they are more likely to fail. Spiritual energy can be found in the events of the moment. New organizational visions and other breakthroughs rarely come when an organization is exhausted. They arise instead when group members have sufficient energy because they are successfully managing the anxieties of the present.

Transformation in Action: Advanced Change Theory

University of Michigan management professor Robert Quinn offers an organizational change model that integrates many of the components of personal development.[32] For that reason, his Advanced Change Theory is a fitting conclusion to this chapter. Quinn argues that systemwide change starts from inside the individual and then moves outward. He contrasts his from the inside out approach to more traditional change strategies that rely on telling (rational persuasion) or on forcing others to comply. Trying to change others from the outside in is both unproductive and unethical. Those targeted for change frequently resist and become locked into their current behavior patterns. Change agents then assume that the problem lies with the change targets. Instead of examining their own motivations and behaviors, they blame their audiences and treat them as objects standing in the way of progress.

Instead of imposing their will, change agents must model the change process. For instance, parents faced with rebellious teenagers often try to bring their children into line with additional rules and sanctions. A better approach would be for parents to examine their own attitudes, making sure that their love is unconditional, not based on their children's performance.

Individuals in the organizational setting can start social change movements through their actions. When even one member of an organization changes, the whole system is affected. To demonstrate this principle, begin to treat an enemy at work as a friend. He or she must take notice and decide how to respond. More often than not, this individual's behavior will become less hostile and the atmosphere of the group as a whole will improve.

Quinn offers these principles or "seed thoughts" that can help you succeed in producing organizational transformation:

ENVISION THE PRODUCTIVE COMMUNITY

We all carry mental images of human relationships. Often these images reinforce the traditional, top-down organizational hierarchy. Visions of productive communities, in contrast, include the notion that members are inner directed, focused on the needs of others, and look beyond their self-interests. Transformational change agents practice higher-level moral reasoning by asking, "What is the right thing to do?" and "What result do I want?" (see Chapter 3).

FIRST LOOK WITHIN

Transformational change agents look inward. They make a "fundamental choice" to be true to their own values and calling. This choice provides a touchstone to return to when facing challenges and decisions. Because authentic change agents understand themselves, they avoid knee-jerk reactions to events. They realize that they can choose their responses to organizational conditions.

EMBRACE THE HYPOCRITICAL SELF

The presence of the shadow side of the personality means that few of us live up to our personal standards on every occasion. We keep silent when we should speak up, lie when we advocate the truth, impose our will when we proclaim the importance of empowering others. When challenged about our integrity gap, we become defensive. We either deny that anything is wrong or blame others for our failures. Recognizing personal hypocrisy can be a source of transformational power because we can make a conscious choice to rewrite our scripts or narratives. If we align the ideal and actual self, we model authenticity. Authenticity, in turn, attracts colleagues to the change movement.

TRANSCEND FEAR

Many personal behaviors and organizational systems are driven by fear. We fear failure, meeting with disapproval from our friends and colleagues, and not living up to expectations. Organizations built on these fears encourage conformity through top-down authority systems, rules and regulations, and punishing dissent and deviance. Transcending our fears requires separating ourselves from how others define us. This is easier when we have identified our vocation. Understanding our purpose makes us more internally driven and provides us with a greater sense of power. We then become change leaders who take risks to speak out, challenging traditions and widely accepted "truths."

EMBODY A VISION OF THE COMMON GOOD

The most effective change agents act as living symbols, personifying the values of productive communities. Gandhi, for example, backed up his call for sacrifice by simple living. He made his own clothes and had little money. Martin Luther King dreamed of a country in which his children would be judged by their character, not their racial background. He lived out this value by courageously facing beatings, jailings, and, ultimately, death. We, as ordinary change agents at any level of the organization, can follow their example. We can decide to choose the collective interest over personal interest, bring uncomfortable topics out into the open, and listen to others in order to create a shared organizational vision.

DISTURB THE SYSTEM

Organizations and other living systems are maintained by negative feedback. Any action too far outside the norm is treated as a problem and then controlled through punishment or other means. Successful change agents disrupt the system to overcome negative feedback. They know when and how to introduce new ideas and procedures that break members out of their old mind-sets and behavioral patterns.

SURRENDER TO THE EMERGENT PROCESS

Those in a transformational state try to live out their message and focus on being in the right state of mind or being in order to promote change. The most effective transformational change agents have "bold-stroke capacity." They understand the system so well that they can alter it with just a single statement, question, or action. Former Coca Cola CEO Roberto Goizueta performed such a bold stroke in the 1980s. At that time, Coke was locked in a market share battle with Pepsi and losing. Goizueta found that the average per-capita daily consumption of fluids around the world was 64 ounces; the daily per-capita consumption of Coke was less than 2 ounces. He then asked: "What's our market share of the stomach?" This question greatly enlarged Coca Cola's market, shifting the focus from beating Pepsi to winning a larger share of the total global consumption of fluids. Goizueta's bold stroke helped transform Coke from a stagnant company into one of the stock market's top performers.[33]

ENTICE THROUGH MORAL POWER

Powerful change agents put a high value on both tasks and persons. They pursue excellence and at the same time build strong relationships with others. Such individuals "do things for their own sake." They set their own goals, find satisfaction in the task, and evaluate their performance according to their own standards. Those who find their rewards in their work exert more control over the quality of their lives. They aren't trapped by circumstances but control their attitudes, seeing even a lousy job as an opportunity for personal growth and learning. Effective change agents also offer emotional and practical support to others who join the transformational movement.

Implications

- You need to acknowledge your potential to do harm as well as good. The shadow side of your personality contains the parts of yourself that are embarrassing, socially unacceptable, or dangerous. To confront your shadow side: (1) take personal responsibility for your actions; (2) determine if your negative images of others are the result of projecting undesirable qualities on them; (3) learn from those times when your behavior contradicts your self-image; (4) find a supportive partner to help you explore your urges and failings; (5) accept criticism that reveals your weaknesses; and (6) adjust your behavior and your environment to keep from unleashing shadow forces.
- Discovering your vocation means determining your purpose in life, which is based on a clear understanding of your unique skills, abilities, and desires. Following your vocation produces greater self-fulfillment, makes you a better steward, and equips you for more productive service to others. To hear your call you'll need to set aside ambition, distractions, and resistance based on fears and low self-esteem.
- Moral values serve as guiding principles that drive behavior and help us determine right from wrong. You can clarify your values by generating a list or rating a list of values. If your values agree with those of your organization, you are more likely to be committed to the group and satisfied with your job.
- High moral character will better enable you to make wise ethical choices. You can foster the virtues that make up character by (a) developing moral habits, (b) observing and imitating ethical role models, (c) telling and living collective stories, and (d) learning from passage experiences.
- Spiritual resources can play an essential role in inner transformation. Nourish your soul through intimacy (closeness and connection), exposure to nature and beauty, and recognition of the sacred nature of work.
- Advanced Change Theory argues that the direction of organizational change is from the inside out, starting with the individual and spreading outward. Begin the transformation process by modeling the desired behaviors instead of imposing them on others. Remember that, even as one person, you can bring about systemwide change.

Application Projects

1. Analyze the life of a fallen leader. Which elements of the shadow side of the personality contributed to this individual's downfall? What do you learn from this person's failure that you can apply in your own life? Write up your findings.
2. Use the steps outlined in the chapter to identify a job that fits your vocation.
3. Identify distractions that might be keeping you from hearing your call. Determine how you might put these pressures and preoccupations aside.

4. With classmates, create a list of six to eight virtues that you think are most important in the workplace. Present your list and defend your choices to the rest of the class.
5. Complete the Self-Assessment in Box 2.3 and reflect upon the findings. What does this instrument reveal about your values and those of your organization? How do your values impact your behavior at work? What values conflicts do you have with coworkers? How good is the match between your values and those of your employer?
6. What habits do you want to develop? How will you go about developing them?
7. Analyze a popular television show from an ethical perspective. Identify the issues raised by the program, the values it promotes, and the virtues and vices demonstrated by the important characters.
8. Identify some key passages in your life. What have you learned from these experiences?
9. Choose two strategies for nurturing your soul and implement them on a daily basis for 2 weeks. Note any changes in your attitudes and behavior.
10. Assess your spiritual development using Vaill's guidelines presented in the chapter.
11. Test the Advanced Change Theory by engaging in more positive behavior toward a friend, family member, coworker, or fellow student. How does this person respond? How does your relationship change or improve? Record the results of your experiment.

CHAPTER END CASE

Heroism in the Twin Towers

In the terrorist attacks of September 11, 2001, 1 hour and 42 minutes elapsed between the crash of the first plane into the North Tower of the World Trade Center and its subsequent collapse. During that period, from 8:46 to 10:28, the South Tower was also destroyed. What went on inside the towers during those 102 minutes? To find out, *New York Times* reporters Jim Dwyer and Kevin Flynn interviewed hundreds of survivors and rescue workers and examined masses of phone, radio, and e-mail transcripts. They report that 12,000 people were able to evacuate in large part because office workers behaved calmly and civilly, guided by volunteer fire wardens who helped them file out.

Dwyer and Flynn also uncovered many cases where individuals banded together to help others. For example, fire commander Orio Palmer and his colleagues ran up to the 78th floor of the South Tower (the impact zone) to organize survivors and rescue an elevator car filled with people who had been trapped for 45 minutes. The building collapsed shortly after they arrived. In the North Tower, a "committee of the willing—self-selected civilians and self-assigned uniformed rescuers" stationed themselves at the mezzanine level to direct people away from the plaza where pieces of the building were raining down.[1] A group of firefighters and New York Port Authority police were able to drag an overweight man to safety moments before the tower disintegrated.

One particularly heroic group, led by manager Frank De Martini and coworker Pablo Ortiz, was made up of members of the Port Authority's construction team. Housed on the 88th floor of the North Tower, these individuals first scouted for unblocked stairways on their level, removed debris, and organized the evacuation of other Port Authority workers. Then they headed to other floors, using crowbars to break through drywall and open stairway doors to help victims escape. At the 102nd minute they were rescuing workers on the 78th floor. The construction team is credited with saving the lives of 70 people.

Reporters Dwyer and Flynn point out that De Martini's team was charged with overseeing remodeling projects, not emergency operations. However, group members wasted no time in reaching out to others, sacrificing their lives so that others could live.

> It was hardly the job of Frank De Martini and Pablo Ortiz and the others from 88 to go around prying open doors. Their responsibilities at the trade center during an emergency were to get themselves out of the building. The sprinklers, the fireproofing, the smoke venting systems were all supposed to kick in automatically. This network of emergency systems succumbed, one by one, on September 11, replaced by a lethal web of obstacles. Only when people like De Martini and his crew took it upon themselves to attack those barriers—broken rubble, stuck doors, disorientation—could people go free. . . .
>
> And below 92, across all or parts of ten floors, dozens of people had been unable to open doors, or walk through burning corridors to the stairs and find their way past the rubble. Then help appeared. With crowbar, flashlight, hardhat, and big mouths, De Martini and Ortiz and their colleagues had pushed back the boundary line between life and death.[2]

DISCUSSION PROBES

1. Why do some people act heroically in emergencies while others do not?
2. What character traits did the rescuers demonstrate?
3. How can we prepare ourselves to respond effectively and ethically to crises?
4. Have you ever faced an emergency situation? How did you react?
5. What ethical insights do you draw from the stories of the heroes of 9/11?

NOTES

1. Dwyer & Flynn (2005), p. 240.
2. Dwyer & Flynn (2005), p. 88.

SOURCE

Dwyer, J., & Flynn, K. (2005). *102 Minutes: The untold story of the fight to survive inside the Twin Towers.* New York: Times Books.

Endnotes

1. Trevino, L. K., & Youngblood, S. A. (1990). Bad apples in bad barrels: A causal analysis of ethical decision-making behavior. *Journal of Applied Psychology, 75,* 378–385; Trevino, L. K. (1986). Ethical decision making in organizations: A person-situation interactionist model. *Academy of Management Review, 11,* 601–607.

2. Mattoon, M. A. (1981). *Jungian psychology in perspective.* New York: Free Press; Hall, C. S., & Nordby, V. J. (1973). *A primer of Jungian psychology.* New York: New American Library.

3. Storr, A. (1983). *The essential Jung.* Princeton, NJ: Princeton University Press, p. 89.

4. Miller, W. A. (1981). *Make friends with your shadow.* Minneapolis, MN: Augsburg; Johnson, R. A. (1993). *Owning your own shadow: Understanding the dark side of the psyche.* San Francisco: HarperSanFransisco.

5. Rayburn, C. A. (1997). Vocation as calling. In D. P. Bloch & L. J. Richmond (Eds.), *Connections between spirit and work in career development* (pp. 162–183). Palo Alto, CA: Davies-Black.

6. Fowler, J. W. (1984). *Becoming adult, becoming Christian: Adult development and the Christian faith.* San Francisco: Harper & Row; Fowler, J. W. (1991). *Weaving the new creation: Stages of faith and the public church.* San Francisco: HarperSanFrancisco.

7. Buechner, F. (1973). *Wishful thinking: A theological ABC.* New York: Harper & Row, p. 95.

8. Hardy, L. (1990). *The fabric of this world: Inquiries into calling, career choice, and the design of human work.* Grand Rapids, MI: Eerdmans.

9. Mahan, B. J. (2002). *Forgetting ourselves on purpose: Vocation and the ethics of ambition.* San Francisco: Jossey-Bass.

10. Levoy, G. (1997). *Callings: Finding and following an authentic life.* New York: Three Rivers Press.

11. Schwartz, S. H., & Sagiv, L. (1995). Identifying culture-specifics in the content and structure of values. *Journal of Cross-Cultural Psychology, 26,* 92–116.

12. Schwartz, S. H. (1994). Are there universal aspects in the structure and contents of human values? *Journal of Social Issues, 50,* 19–45; Schwartz, S. H. (1994). Beyond individualism/collectivism: New cultural dimensions of values. In U. Kim, H. C. Triandis, C. Kagitcibasi, S, Choi, & G. Yoon (Eds), *Individualism and collectivism: Theory, method and applications* (pp. 85–119). Thousand Oaks, CA: Sage; Bardi, A., & Schwartz, S. H.

(2003). Values and behavior: Strength and structure of relations. *Journal of Personality and Social Psychology, 29,* 1207–1220.

13. See, for example: Cooper, T. L. (1992). Prologue: On virtue. In T. L. Cooper & N. D. Wright (Eds.), *Exemplary public administrators: Character and leadership in government* (pp. 1–8). San Francisco: Jossey-Bass; Deverettere, R. J. (2002). *Introduction to virtue ethics: Insights of the ancient Greeks.* Washington, DC: Georgetown University Press; McKinnon, C. (1999). *Character, virtue theories, and the vices.* Ontario: Broadview Press; Statman, D. (1997). Introduction to virtue ethics. In D. Statman (Ed.), *Virtue ethics* (pp. 1–41). Washington, DC: Georgetown University Press.

14. Johannesen, R. L. (2002). *Ethics in human communication* (5th ed.). Prospect Heights, IL: Waveland Press.

15. Johannesen (2002), p. 11.

16. Hart, D. K. (1994). Administration and the ethics of virtue. In T. C. Cooper (Ed.). (1994). *The handbook of administrative ethics* (pp. 107–123). New York: Marcel Dekker.

17. Solomon, R. C. (1997). Corporate roles, personal virtues: An Aristotelian approach to business ethics. In D. Statman (Ed.), *Virtue ethics* (pp. 206–225). Washington, DC: Georgetown University Press.

18. Aristotle. (350 B.C.E./1962). *Nichomachean ethics* (Martin Ostwald, Trans.). Indianapolis, IN: Bobbs-Merrill, Book II, p. 1.

19. Sison, A. J. G. (2003). *The moral capital of leaders: Why virtue matters.* Northampton, MA: Edward Elgar.

20. Covey, S. R. (1989). *The seven habits of highly effective people.* New York: Simon & Schuster.

21. Cooper, T. L., & Wright, N. D. (1992). *Exemplary public administrators: Character and leadership in government.* San Francisco: Jossey-Bass.

22. Kirkpatrick W. K. (1992). Moral character: Story-telling and virtue. In R. T. Knowles & G. F. McLean (Eds.), *Psychological foundations of moral education and character development: An integrated theory of moral development* (pp. 169–184). Washington, DC: Council for Research in Values and Philosophy.

23. MacIntyre, A. (1984). *After virtue: A study in moral theory* (2nd ed.). Notre Dame, IN: University of Notre Dame Press, p. 216. See also: Hauerwas, S. (1981). *A community of character.* Notre Dame, IN: University of Notre Dame Press.

24. O'Connor, E. S. (1997). Compelling stories: Narrative and the production of the organizational self. In O. F. Williams (Ed.), *The moral imagination: How literature and films can stimulate ethical reflection in the business world* (pp. 185–202). Notre Dame, IN: University of Notre Dame Press.

25. Lisman, C. D. (1996). *The curricular integration of ethics: Theory and practice.* Westport, CT: Praeger.

26. Dotlich, D. L., Noel, J. L., & Walker, N. (2004) *Leadership passages: The personal and professional transitions that make or break a leader.* San Francisco: Jossey-Bass. See also: Moxley, R. S. (2004). Hardships. In C. D. McCauley, R. S. Moxley, & E. Van Velsor (Eds.), *Handbook of leadership development* (2nd ed., pp. 183–204). San Francisco: Jossey-Bass; Bennis, W. G., & Thomas, R. J. (2002). *Geeks and geezers: How era, values and defining moments shape leaders.* Boston: Harvard Business School Press.

27. Pauchant, T. C. (2002). Introduction: Ethical and spiritual management addresses the need for meaning in the workplace. In T. C. Pauchant (Ed.), *Ethics and*

spirituality at work (pp. 1–27). Westport, CT: Quorum Books; Wagner-Marsh, F., & Conley, J. (1999). The fourth wave: The spiritually based firm. *Journal of Organizational Change Management 12,* 292–301; Mitroff, I. I., & Denton, E. A. (1999). *A spiritual audit of corporate America.* San Francisco: Jossey-Bass.

28. Hicks, D. A. (2003). *Religion and the workplace: Pluralism, spirituality and leadership.* Cambridge UK: Cambridge University Press.

29. Mitroff I. I., & Denton, E. A. (1999, Summer). A study of spirituality in the workplace. *Sloan Management Review,* p. 83.

30. Moore, T. (1995). Caring for the soul in business. In B. Defoore & J. Renesch (Eds.), *Rediscovering the soul of business: A renaissance of values* (pp. 341–356). San Francisco: Sterling & Stone. See also: Moore, T. (1992). *Care of the soul: A guide to cultivating depth and sacredness in everyday life.* New York: HarperCollins.

31. Vaill, P. B. (1998). *Spirited leading and learning: Process wisdom for a new age.* San Francisco: Jossey-Bass.

32. Quinn, R. E. (2000). *Change the world: How ordinary people can achieve extraordinary results.* San Francisco: Jossey-Bass. See also: Quinn, R. E. (1996). *Deep change.* San Francisco: Jossey-Bass.

33. Charan, R., & Tichy, N. (1988). *Every business is a growth business: How your company can prosper year after year.* New York: Random House.

3

Ethical Decision Making and Action

In making and implementing decisions, we put widely accepted ethical principles, as well our vocation, values, character and spiritual resources, into practice. This chapter focuses both on the how (processes) and the how to (formats) of moral thinking and action. Our chances of coming up with a sound, well-reasoned conclusion and executing our plan are greater if we understand how ethical decisions are made and take a systematic approach to problem solving.

Components of Ethical Behavior

Breaking the process down into its component parts enhances understanding of ethical decision-making and behavior. Moral psychologist James Rest identifies four elements of ethical action. Rest developed his Four-Component Model by asking: "What must happen psychologically in order for moral behavior to take place?" He concluded that ethical action is the product of these psychological subprocesses: (1) moral sensitivity (recognition); (2) moral judgment or reasoning; (3) moral motivation; and (4) moral character.[1] The first half of the chapter is organized around Rest's framework. I'll describe each factor and then offer some tips for improving your performance on that element of Rest's model.

COMPONENT 1: MORAL SENSITIVITY (RECOGNITION)

Moral sensitivity is the recognition that an ethical problem exists. Such recognition requires being aware of how our behavior impacts others, identifying possible courses of action, and determining the consequences of each potential strategy. Moral sensitivity is key to transformational ethics. We can't solve a moral dilemma unless we know that one is present.

Empathy and perspective skills are essential to identifying and exploring moral issues. Understanding how others might feel or react can alert us to the potential negative effects of our choices and makes it easier to predict the likely outcomes of various options. For example, the central figure in the "Is It Better to Ask for Permission or to Ask for Forgiveness?" Chapter End Case empathizes with neighborhood residents and understands their point of view. As a result, he realizes that he faces an ethical problem.

According to University of Virginia ethics professor Patricia Werhane, many smart, well-meaning managers stumble because they are victims of tunnel vision.[2] Their ways of thinking or mental models don't include important ethical considerations. In other words, they lack moral imagination. Take the case of the Nestlé Company. The European food producer makes a very high quality infant formula, which the firm successfully marketed in North America, Europe, and Asia. It seemed to make sense for the company to market formula in East Africa using the same communication strategies that had worked elsewhere. However, Nestlé officials failed to take into account important cultural differences. Many East African mothers could not read label directions, were so poor that to make the product last longer they overdiluted it, and used polluted water to mix it. In a society that honors medicine men, parents felt pressured to use formula because it was advertised with pictures of men in white coats. As a result, many poor African mothers wasted money on formula when they could have breast-fed their children for free. Thousands of their babies died after drinking formula mixed with polluted water. Nestlé refused to stop its marketing campaign despite pressure from the World Health Organization and only quit after being faced with a major boycott. Company leaders didn't consider the possible dangers of marketing to third world mothers and failed to recognize that they were engaged in unethical activities.

To exercise moral imagination, managers and employees step outside their current frame of reference (disengage themselves) to assess a situation and evaluate options. They then generate creative solutions. Werhane uses Chicago's South Shore Bank as an example of moral imagination at work. In the early 1970s, a group of investors bought a failing bank in the impoverished South Shore neighborhood and began loaning money for residential restoration. Few people in the area qualified for traditional bank loans, so South Shore managers developed a new set of criteria. Loan officers gave credit to individuals of limited means who had good reputations. The bank prospered and, at the same time, the neighborhood became a desirable place to live. South Shore's morally imaginative owners and managers envisioned a profitable financial institution in a depressed, poverty stricken area. They disproved traditional "bank logic" by demonstrating that they could make money in a responsible manner under tough conditions.

Moral muteness, like lack of moral imagination, interferes with the recognition of moral issues. Managers can be reluctant to talk about their actions in ethical terms. They may want to avoid controversy or believe that keeping silent will help them appear practical, efficient, powerful, and capable of handling their own problems.[3] Describing a situation in moral terms breaks this ethical code of silence. Such terms as *values, justice, immoral, character, right,* and *wrong* encourage listeners to frame an event as an ethical problem and to engage in moral reasoning.[4]

Tips for Enhancing Your Ethical Sensitivity

Engage in active listening and role-playing. The best way to learn about the potential ethical consequences of choices, as well as the likely response of others, is through listening closely to what others have to say. (See Chapter 4 for a closer look at the process of active listening.) Role-play can also foster understanding. Taking the part of another individual or group can provide you with important insight into how the other party is likely to react.

Challenge mental models or schemas. Recognize the dangers of your current mental models and try to visualize other perspectives. Distance yourself from a situation to determine if it does indeed have moral implications. Remember that you have ethical duties that extend beyond your group or organization.

Be creative. Look for innovative ways to define and to respond to ethical dilemmas; visualize creative opportunities and solutions.

Speak up. Don't hesitate to discuss problems and your decisions using ethical terms. Doing so will help frame an argument as an ethical one for you and your colleagues.

COMPONENT 2: MORAL JUDGMENT

After determining there is an ethical problem, decision makers then choose among the courses of action identified in Component 1. They make judgments about what is the right or wrong thing to do in this specific context.

Moral judgment has been studied more than any other element of the Rest model. There is far too much information to summarize it here. Instead, I'll focus on two topics that are particularly important to understanding how problem solvers determine whether a solution is right or wrong—cognitive moral development and defective reasoning.

Cognitive Moral Development

Before his death, Harvard psychologist Lawrence Kohlberg was the leading champion of the idea that individuals progress through a series of moral stages just as they do physical ones.[5] Each stage is more advanced than the one before. As individuals develop, their reasoning becomes more sophisticated. They become less self-centered and develop broader definitions of morality (see Box 3.1).

Box 3.1 Stages of Moral Development

	Content of Stage	
Level and Stage	*What Is Right*	*Reasons for Doing Right*
LEVEL I—PRE-CONVENTIONAL		
Stage 1—Heteronomous Morality	To avoid breaking rules backed by punishment, obedience for its own sake, and to avoid physical damage to persons and property.	Avoidance of punishment; the superior power of authorities.

Stage 2—Individualism, Instrumental Purpose, and Exchange	Following rules only when it is in your immediate interest; acting for your own interests and needs and letting others do the same. Right is also what's fair, what's an equal exchange, a deal, an agreement.	To serve your own needs or interests in a world where you have to recognize that other people have their interests, too.
LEVEL II—CONVENTIONAL		
Stage 3—Mutual Interpersonal Expectations, Relationships, and Interpersonal Conformity	Living up to what is expected by people close to you or what people generally expect of people in your role as son, brother, friend, etc. "Being good" is important and means having good motives, showing concern about others. It also means keeping mutual relationships with trust, loyalty, respect, and gratitude.	The need to be a good person in your own eyes and those of others. Your caring for others. Belief in the Golden Rule. A desire to maintain rules and authority which support stereotypical good behavior.
Stage 4—Social System and Conscience	Fulfilling the actual duties to which you have agreed. Laws are to be upheld except in extreme cases where they conflict with other fixed social duties. Right is also contributing to society, the group, or institution.	To keep the institution going as a whole, to avoid a breakdown in the system or to fulfill a sense of personal obligation
LEVEL III—POST-CONVENTIONAL, PRINCIPLED		
Stage 5—Social Contract or Utility and Individual Rights	Being aware that people hold a variety of values and opinions, that most values and rules are relative to your group.	A sense of obligation to law because of one's social contract to make and abide by laws for the welfare of all and for the

(Continued)

(Continued)

	These relative rules should usually be upheld, in the interest of impartiality and because they are the social contract. Some nonrelative values and rights like *life* and *liberty* must be upheld in any society and regardless of majority opinion.	protection of all people's rights. A feeling of contractual commitment, freely entered upon, to family, friendship, trust, and work obligations. Concern that laws and duties be based on rational calculation of overall utility, "the greatest good for the greatest number."
Stage 6—Universal Ethical Principles	Following self-chosen ethical principles. Particular laws or social agreements are usually valid because they rest on such principles. When laws violate these principles, one acts in accordance with the principle. Principles are universal principles of justice: the equality of human rights and respect for the dignity of human beings as individual persons.	The belief as a rational person in the validity of universal moral principles, and a sense of personal commitment to them.

Source: Kohlberg, L. A. (1986). A current statement on some theoretical issues. In S. Modgil & C. Modgil (Eds.), *Lawrence Kohlberg: Consensus and controversy* (pp. 485–546). Philadelphia: Falmer Press, pp. 488–489.

Pre-conventional thinking is the most primitive and is common among children. Individuals at Level I decide on the basis of direct consequences. In the first stage they obey to avoid punishment. In the second they follow the rules in order to meet their own interests. Stage 2 thinkers believe that justice is giving a fair deal to others—you help me and I'll help you.

Conventional (Level II) thinkers look to other people for guidance in how to act. They strive to live up to the expectations of family members and significant others (Stage 3) or recognize the importance of going along with the laws of society (Stage 4). Kohlberg found that most adults fall in stages 3 and 4, which suggests that the typical organizational member looks to work rules, leaders, and the situation to determine right from wrong.

Post-conventional or principled (Level III) thinking is the most advanced type of thinking and relies on universal values and principles. Stage 5 individuals are guided by Utilitarian principles, seeking to do the greatest good for the greatest number. They recognize that there are a number of value systems within a democratic society and that regulations may have to be broken to serve higher moral purposes. Stage 6 thinkers operate according to internalized, universal ethical principles like the Categorical Imperative or Justice as Fairness. These principles apply in every situation and take precedence over the laws of any particular society. According to Kohlberg, only about 20 percent of Americans can be classified as Stage 5 post-conventional moral thinkers. Very few individuals ever reach Stage 6.

Kohlberg's model has drawn heavy criticism from philosophers and psychologists alike.[6] Some philosophers complain that it draws too heavily from Rawls's Theory of Justice and makes deontological ethics superior to other ethical perspectives. They note that the theory applies more to societal issues than to individual ethical decisions. A number of psychologists have challenged the notion that people go through a rigid or "hard" series of moral stages. They argue instead that individuals can engage in many ways of thinking about a problem, regardless of their age.

Rest (who was a student of Kohlberg's) responded to these criticisms by replacing the hard stages with a staircase of developmental schemas. *Schemas* refer to a general structures or patterns in our memories. We use these patterns or structures when we encounter new situations or information. When you enrolled in college, for example, you probably relied on high school experiences to determine how to act in the university classroom. Rest and his colleagues contend that decision makers shift upward, adopting more sophisticated moral schemas as they develop. Rest's group redefined the post-conventional stage to make it less dependent on one ethical perspective. In their "neo-Kohlbergian" approach, the most advanced thinkers reason like moral philosophers.[7] Post-conventional individuals look behind societal rules to determine if they serve moral purposes. These thinkers appeal to a shared vision of an ideal society. Such a society seeks the greatest good for the entire community and assures rights and protections for everyone.

Rest developed the Defining Issues Test (DIT) to measure moral development. Subjects taking the DIT respond to six scenarios and then choose statements that best reflect how they went about making their choices. The statements (which correspond to the levels of moral development) are then scored. In the best-known dilemma, Heinz's wife is dying of cancer and needs a drug he cannot afford to buy. He must decide whether or not to steal the drug to save her life.

Over 800 studies have been conducted using the DIT.[8] Among the findings:

- Moral reasoning ability generally increases with age.
- The total college experience, both inside and outside the classroom, increases moral judgment.[9]
- Those who love learning, taking risks, and meeting challenges generally experience the greatest moral growth while in college.
- Ethics coursework boosts the positive effects of the college experience, increasing moral judgment still further.
- Older students (those in graduate and professional school) gain a great deal from moral education programs.
- When education stops, moral development plateaus.
- Moral development is a universal concept, crossing cultural boundaries.
- There are no consistent differences between the moral reasoning of men and women.
- Principled leaders can improve the moral judgment of the group as a whole, encouraging members to adopt more sophisticated ethical schemas.

Defective Reasoning

No discussion of moral judgment would be complete without consideration of why this process so often breaks down. Time after time very bright people make very stupid decisions. Former President Bill Clinton illustrates this sad fact. By all accounts Clinton was one of the country's brightest leaders. Not only was he a Rhodes scholar with a nearly photographic memory, but his former advisor David Gergen reports that Clinton could hold conversations with aides and visitors while completing the *New York Times* crossword puzzle.[10] Somehow the former chief executive thought he could have sex with an intern and keep the affair quiet despite being under constant media scrutiny. Further, he didn't think he would suffer any serious consequences if word got out. He was wrong on both counts.[11]

The moral stupidity of otherwise intelligent people can be explained in part by the power of their internal enemies. Employees and managers must always be alert to the presence of the "dark side" of the personality introduced in Chapter 2. Unless acknowledged and confronted, internal forces can seriously disrupt moral reasoning. Three such factors are particularly damaging: insecurities, greed, and ego.

1. *Insecurities.* As we saw in the last chapter, low self-esteem and inner doubts can drive individuals to use others to meet their own needs, and insecure people fall into the trap of tying their identities to their roles. Those plagued by self-doubt are blind to larger ethical considerations and, at the same time, they are tempted to succeed at any cost.

2. *Greed.* Greed is more likely than ever to undermine ethical thinking because we live in a "winner take all" society.[12] The market economy benefits the few at

the expense of the many. Professional sports are a case in point. Superstars like Kobe Bryant and Shaquille O'Neal account for the vast majority of the payroll while others sit on the bench making league minimums. Or consider the inequity of the salary structure at the Banana Republic clothing chain. The average employee at a Banana Republic store makes near minimum wage with no health benefits. Store managers do better, receiving an adequate salary and benefits. Professionals working at the headquarters of the Gap (the parent of Banana Republic) make several times the wages of local managers. Those at the top earn a fortune. Former CEO Millard Drexler engineered a $25 million pay raise in one year and left the company with $500 million.

A winner-take-all culture encourages widespread cheating because the payoff is so high. In addition, losers justify their dishonesty by pointing to the injustice of the system and to the fact that they deserve a larger share of the benefits. When greed takes over, altruism disappears along with any consideration of serving the greater good.

3. Ego. Even the most humble of us tend to (a) think we are above average, (b) believe we are more ethical than most of the people we know, (c) give ourselves the benefit of the doubt, (d) overestimate our control over events, (e) assume that we are immune from harm, (f) have all the information we need, and (g) overstate our value to the organization.[13] Such self-serving biases put us in danger. We can become overconfident, ignore the risks and consequences of our choices, take too much credit when things go well and too little blame when they don't, and demand more than our fair share of organizational resources.

Inflated egos become more of a problem at higher levels of the organizational hierarchy. Top managers are often cut off from customers and employees. Unlike the rest of us, they don't have to wait in line for products or services or for a ride to work. Subordinates tell them what they want to hear and stroke their egos. All these factors make it easier for executives to excuse their unethical behavior (outrageous pay packages, diverting company funds to private use) on the grounds that they are vital to the organization's success.

Harvard psychologist Robert Sternberg believes that people in positions of great power, like Bill Clinton, former WorldCom CEO Bernie Ebbers, and former House majority leader Tom Delay, develop three dispositions that lead to foolish decisions.[14] Their access to so many sources of information tricks them into thinking that they are all-knowing (the sense of omniscience). Because they possess great power, top government and business figures mistakenly believe that they can do anything they want in or outside their organizations (the sense of omnipotence). Entourages of subservient staff members seduce these leaders into believing that they will be protected from the consequences of their actions (the sense of invulnerability).

The formidable forces of insecurity, greed, and ego become even more powerful when managers and subordinates adopt a short-term orientation. Modern workers are under constant time pressures as organizations cut staffing levels while demanding higher performance in the form of shorter product development cycles, better customer service, and greater returns on investment. Employees are sorely tempted to do what is expedient instead of what is ethical. As ethics expert Laura Nash puts it: "Short-term pressures can silence moral reasoning by simply giving it no space. The tighter a manager's agenda is, the less time for contemplating complex, time-consuming, unpragmatic issues like ethics."[15]

Time pressed managers lose sight of the overall purpose of the organization and fail to analyze past conduct. They don't stop to reflect on their choices when things are going well. Overconfident, rushed decision makers are only too willing to move on to the next problem. Eventually they begin to make mistakes that catch up with them. In addition, short-term thinkers begin to look for immediate gratification, which feeds their greedy impulses.

The damage caused by rushing to judgment can be seen in the results of a study by Ohio State professor Paul Nutt.[16] Professor Nutt examined 400 poor organizational decisions over a period of 20 years, including construction of Euro Disney, Ford's failure to recall the Pinto, and NASA's decision to launch the Challenger space shuttle. Adopting a short-term perspective helps to account for many of the decision-making blunders he uncovered. Nearsighted decision makers (a) overlooked important ethical questions, (b) came to premature conclusions, (c) failed to consult with important stakeholders, (d) lacked a clear direction, (e) limited their search for information, (f) demonstrated little creativity, and (g) learned little from either their successes or their failures.

Tips for Improving Your Moral Judgment

Stay in school. The general college experience (including extracurricular activities) contributes greatly to moral development. However, you'll gain more if you have the right attitude. Focus on learning, not grades; be ready to take on new challenges.

Be intentional. While the general college experience contributes to moral development, focused attention on ethics also helps. Take ethics courses and units, discuss ethical issues in a group, reflect on the ethical challenges you experience in internships.

Reject ethical pessimism. Ethical values and thought patterns are not set in childhood as pessimists claim, but continue to grow and develop through college and graduate school and beyond.

Take a broader view. Try to consider the needs and positions of others outside your immediate group; determine what is good for the community as a whole.

Look to underlying moral principles. Since the best ethical thinkers base their choices on widely accepted ethical guidelines, do the same. Draw upon important ethical approaches like Utilitarianism, the Categorical Imperative, and Justice as Fairness for guidance.

Acknowledge your dark side. Before coming to a conclusion, try to determine if your decision is shaped by feelings of self-doubt and self-interest as well as your need to feed your ego. If so, then reconsider.

Step outside yourself. We can't help but see the world through our own selfish biases. However, we have a responsibility to check our perceptions against reality. Consult with others before making a choice, consider the likely perspective of other parties (refer back to our earlier discussion of role-taking), and double-check your assumptions and information.

Keep your ego in check. Stay close to those who will tell you the truth and hold you accountable. At the same time, don't punish those who point out your deficiencies. Use the questions in the Self-Assessment in Box 3.2 as tools for breaking the ego barrier.

Self-Assessment

Box 3.2 Ego-Busting Questions

Apply the following questions to an important ethical decision you face. After you have answered these queries, summarize what this exercise tells you about the soundness of your moral reasoning.

- What is my intention?
- Have I invited and tolerated dissent?
- Have I rubbed elbows with subordinates? (peers?)
- What have I omitted from my analysis?
- What if I get caught?
- Have I listened to other opinions? Can I tolerate hearing them directly, or only filtered through company communication channels?
- Did I address the facts? Precisely what value am I creating?
- At whose expense am I creating value?
- Have I articulated factual information in as objective and impartial a way as possible?

(Continued)

(Continued)

- Are my decisions or behavior having a negative impact on the relationships involved?
- Am I rewarding ego-dominant, relationship-destroying attitudes in others?
- Have I laughed at myself recently?

Source: Nash, L. 1990, *Good intentions aside: A manager's guide to resolving ethical problems.* Boston: Harvard Business School Press, p. 212. Used by permission.

Take a long-term perspective. In an emergency (when lives are immediately at stake, for example), you may be forced to make a quick decision. In all other situations, provide space for ethical reflection and deliberation. Resist the temptation to grab on to the first solution. Take time to consult with others, gather the necessary data, probe for underlying causes, and set a clear direction. Adopting a long-term perspective also means putting future benefits above immediate needs. In most cases, the organization and its clients and consumers are better served by emphasizing enduring relationships. You may make an immediate profit by selling low quality products, but customers will be hurt and refuse to buy again, lowering corporate performance.

COMPONENT 3: MORAL MOTIVATION

After reaching a conclusion about the best course of action, decision makers must be motivated to follow through on their choices. Moral values often conflict with other important values like job security, career advancement, social acceptance, and wealth. Ethical behavior will only result if moral considerations take precedence over competing priorities.

Two factors—rewards and emotions—play an important role in ethical follow through. It is easier to give priority to ethical values when rewarded for doing so. Conversely, moral motivation drops when the reward system honors inappropriate behavior.[17] Individuals are much more likely to act ethically when they are evaluated on how well they adhere to important values and when they receive raises, bonuses, promotions, and public recognition for doing so. On the other hand, they are motivated to lie, steal, act abusively, take bribes, and cheat when offenders prosper. At Merrill Lynch, for instance, brokers generated large commissions by lying to investors. Lynch employees encouraged clients to buy stocks that they referred to in private as "crap," "junk," and "horrible."[18] (Reward and performance evaluation systems will be discussed in more detail in Chapter 9.)

Emotional states also influence moral motivation. Research continues, but so far investigators have found the following:[19]

- Positive affect (joy, happiness) makes individuals more optimistic and therefore more likely to live out their moral choices.
- Jealousy, rage, envy, and feelings of aggression have been linked to a wide variety of antisocial behaviors in organizations, including stealing, sabotage, revenge, lying, and unwarranted lawsuits.
- People in positive moods are more likely to help coworkers and others. In other words, feeling good leads to doing good.
- Helping others maintains positive feelings.
- Depression lowers motivation by lowering self-confidence and energy levels. In contrast, sadness may motivate individuals to repair their moods by doing what they believe is right.
- Guilty people are more likely than shamed people to try to rectify what they've done wrong through asking for forgiveness and making restitution.
- Feeling sympathy leads to more prosocial (altruistic) behavior toward both individuals and groups.
- Experiencing high personal stress reduces prosocial behavior.
- Anger and frustration often lead to aggressive behavior.
- Regulating moods can improve moral motivation. Those who recognize and modify their feelings increase the likelihood that they will carry through on their choices. For example, they put themselves in a better frame of mind by replacing angry thoughts with calmer ones and by engaging in behaviors (listening to music, reading, walking) that cheer them up.

Tips for Increasing Your Moral Motivation

Seek out ethically rewarding environments. When selecting a job or volunteer position, consider the reward system before joining the group. Does the organization evaluate, monitor, and reward ethical behavior? Are rewards misplaced? Are organizational leaders concerned about how goals are achieved?

Reward yourself. Sometimes ethical behavior is its own best reward. Helping others can be extremely fulfilling, for example, as is living up to the image we have of ourselves as individuals of integrity. Congratulate yourself on following through even if others do not.

Monitor your emotions. Some emotions (happiness, optimism, joy, guilt) can have a positive effect on ethical implementation. Determine if your feelings (depression, anger, personal distress) are inhibiting your ability to carry out your ethical choice.

Regulate your emotions. Master your moods to bring them in line with your goals. Put a brake on destructive feelings; try to shift into a more positive frame of mind.

COMPONENT 4: MORAL CHARACTER

Carrying out the fourth and final stage of moral action—executing the plan—requires character. Moral agents must overcome active opposition, cope with fatigue, resist distractions, and develop sophisticated strategies for reaching their goals. In sum, they must persist in a moral task or action despite obstacles.

Persistence can be nurtured like other positive character traits (see Chapter 2), but it is also related to individual differences. Those with a strong will, as well as confidence in themselves and their abilities, are more likely to persist. So are individuals with an internal locus of control.[20] Internally oriented people (internals) believe that they have control over their lives and can determine what happens to them. Externally oriented people (externals) believe that life events are beyond their control and are the product of luck or fate. Because internals take personal responsibility for their actions, they are motivated to do what is right. Externals are more susceptible to situational pressures. As a consequence, they are less likely to persist in ethical tasks.

Successful implementation demands that persistence be complemented with competence. A great number of skills can be required to take action, including, for instance, relationship building, organizing, coalition building, and public speaking. Pulitzer Prize–winning author and psychiatrist Robert Coles discovered the importance of ethical competence during the 1960s.[21] Coles traveled with a group of physicians who identified widespread malnutrition among children of the Mississippi Delta. They brought their report to Washington, D.C., convinced that they could persuade federal officials to provide more food. Their hopes were soon dashed. The secretaries of agriculture and education largely ignored their pleas and Southern senators resisted attempts to expand the food surplus program. The physicians were skilled in medicine, but they didn't understand the political process. They only got a hearing when New York Senator Robert Kennedy took up their cause. A highly skilled politician, Senator Kennedy coached them on how to present their message to the press and public, arranged special committee meetings to hear their testimony, and traveled with them to the South to draw attention to the plight of poor children.

Tips for Fostering Your Moral Character

Take a look at your track record. How well do you persist in doing the right thing? How well do you manage obstacles? Consider what steps you might take to foster the virtue of persistence.

Believe that you can have an impact. Unless you are convinced that you can shape your own life and surroundings, you are not likely to carry through in the midst of trials.

Master the context. Know your organization, its policies, and important players so you can better respond when needed.

Be good at what you do. Competence will better enable you to put your moral choice into action. You will also earn the right to be heard.

Decision-Making Formats

Decision-making guidelines can help us make better moral choices. Formats incorporate elements that enhance ethical performance while helping us avoid blunders. Step-by-step procedures ensure that we identify and carefully define ethical issues, resist time pressures, investigate options, think about the implications of choices, and apply key ethical principles. I'll introduce three decision-making formats in this the second half of the chapter. You can test these guidelines by applying them to the scenarios described in the Chapter End Case. You'll probably find one format more interesting and useful than the others. Which format you prefer is not as important as approaching moral problems systematically.

KIDDER'S ETHICAL CHECKPOINTS

Ethicist Rushworth Kidder acknowledges that ethical issues can be "disorderly and sometimes downright confusing."[22] They can quickly arise when least expected, are complex, may lack a clear cause, and generally have unexpected consequences. However, Kidder argues that there is an underlying structure to the ethical decision-making process. Following his nine steps or checkpoints can help you cut through the confusion and generate a well-grounded solution.

Checkpoint 1: Recognize that there is a moral issue.

In this step determine if there are ethical considerations in the situation that demand attention. Sort out genuine ethical issues from those involving etiquette, personal taste, or custom. I may be irritated at someone who burps at the next table at my favorite restaurant. However, such behavior is not morally wrong but is a breach of etiquette or a reflection of cultural differences. (See Box 3.3 to consider an issue that has been defined as both a violation of etiquette and a moral dilemma.)

CASE STUDY

Box 3.3 A Violation of Etiquette or Ethics?[1]

Sorting out the difference between ethical violations and breaches of etiquette is not always easy. Take the case of cell phones. Worldwide, cell phones have become more common than fixed telephones. As their popularity has soared, so have concerns about their use in public spaces. Common complaints include:

High volume conversations referred to as "cell yell." Many users yell into their phones because (a) they don't receive the type of aural feedback they get with traditional phones, (b) coverage is spotty and filled with static, or (c) they don't trust tiny cell microphones to pick up the sound of their voices.

Irritating rings. Rings are programmed with tunes ranging from the "Star Spangled Banner" to "Jesu Joy of Man's Desiring."

Inappropriate timing. Not only do cell phones ring at inopportune moments (during films, plays, weddings, funerals, church services, classes), but some cell users compound the problem by carrying on discussions after they answer.

Inane conversations. Many cell conversations consist of the kind of talk that keeps the social wheels turning—reports, brief orders, announcements. While this type of conversation is vital to everyday life, sharers of public space are forced to listen to these banal messages.

Forced intimacy. Not all cell conversations are innocuous. Private conversations in public expose listeners to unwanted details of money problems, rebellious children, and sexual encounters. The problem is greatest when strangers are stuck in the same enclosed space (train, bus) for a long period of time.

Disregard for immediate others. Cell phone users often seem oblivious to those sharing the same territory. In their quest to connect with intimates and business colleagues, they ignore the people around them. Cell abusers may take offense when confronted with their transgressions.

The public outcry over boorish cell phone behavior apparently has wireless providers worried. They have begun to publish guidelines for cell phone etiquette on their Web sites in hopes that users will change their ways before further restrictions (like the ban on talking and driving in New York State) are put into place. Etiquette experts like Emily Post and Miss Manners now offer advice on wireless behavior in their books and columns. Advocates of the etiquette approach believe that societal norms will soon catch up with wireless technology. Users will modify their behaviors once they learn the rules. In fact, treating conflicts over public cell phone behavior as violations of manners may be working. One survey found that the percentage of cell phone owners using their devices in public places had decreased.[2]

Adopting the etiquette approach may not do justice to the issues triggered by public mobile phone use. Cell phone abuse sparks intense emotional reactions.[3] Those victimized by thoughtless callers can feel violated, embarrassed, and angry. Such strong emotional responses suggest that there are moral issues raised by cell phone use in public spaces and that these issues ought to be taken seriously.

A number of ethical principles could be applied to the controversy surrounding cell use. For instance, in deciding whether or not to carry on a conversation in public, callers might ask themselves if they would want everyone to do the same (the Categorical Imperative). Or they might also ask themselves if such conversations promote the common good (Communitarianism) or concern for others (altruism). Those pondering how to respond to cell violations could take a Utilitarian approach, considering what would bring the greatest benefits (to keep silent? confront the offender quietly? be more assertive?).

DISCUSSION PROBES

1. Is public cell phone abuse a matter of etiquette or ethics or both? Why?
2. How does etiquette differ from ethics?
3. Do you think that cell phone abuse is becoming less or more of a problem? What evidence can you offer for your conclusion?
4. How do you respond to someone misusing a cell phone in public? Is your response ethical?
5. What ethical principle would you choose to best explain and prevent cell phone misuse?

NOTES

1. This case is adapted from Johnson (2003).

2. Research updates America's view on cell phone etiquette. (2002, September 3). *Business Wire*. Retrieved September 8, 2003, from LexisNexis Academic database.

3. Terrell, K., & Hammel, S. (1999, June 14). Call of the riled. *U.S. News & World Report*. Retrieved August 12, 2003, from Academic Search Premier database.

SOURCE

Johnson, C. E. (2003, November). *Aural space violations and unwanted intimacy: The ethics of cell phone use*. Paper presented at the National Communication Association convention, Miami Beach, FL.

Checkpoint 2: Determine the actor.

Kidder makes a distinction between involvement and responsibility. Because we're members of larger communities, we're involved in any ethical issue that arises in the group. Yet we are only responsible for dealing with problems that we can do something about. I may think that police use excessive force in a neighboring town, but there is little I can do as a nonresident to address this issue.

Checkpoint 3: Gather the relevant facts.

Become a reporter and gather important information. For example: the history of the problem, key actors, motives, what was said and who said it, patterns of behavior. Consider the future as well. What will be the likely consequences if the problem continues? The likely outcome of one course of action or another? The likely future behavior of those involved in the issue?

Checkpoint 4: Test for right-versus-wrong issues.

Determine if there is any wrongdoing in the case. Four tests can be applied to make this determination. The *legal test* asks if lawbreaking is involved. If so, then the problem becomes a legal matter, not a moral one. Resolution will come through legal proceedings. The *stench test* relies on intuition. If you have a vague sense of unease about the decision or course of action, chances are it involves right-versus-wrong issues. The *front-page test* asks how you would feel if your private decision became public by appearing on the front page of tomorrow's newspaper. If that thought makes you uncomfortable, then you had better choose another alternative. The *Mom test* asks how you would feel if your mother or some other important role model got wind of your choice. Once again, if such a thought makes you queasy, you had better revisit your choice.

Checkpoint 5: Test for right-versus-right paradigms.

If an issue doesn't involve wrong behavior, then it likely pits two important positive values against each other. These right-versus-right dilemmas generally fall into four categories or paradigms.

Justice versus mercy. Norms of fairness and equality often clash with the desire to extend mercy and forgiveness. Consider the dilemma of the professor who catches an honors student cheating on an exam. According to university regulations, the student should automatically receive a zero on the test that would cost him his scholarship. The student then appeals to the instructor for partial credit. The professor wants to be fair to other class members who didn't cheat and to mete out the necessary punishment. Nonetheless, she feels sympathy for the student who appears to be a first-time offender with a great deal to lose.

Short term versus long term. Short-term advantages often come at the expense of long-term benefits. For instance, shifting money from research and development into marketing may generate more immediate sales but undermine a company's future by cutting off the flow of new products and ideas. Ethical decision makers balance immediate needs against long-range consequences. The economic benefits of cutting timber in national forests, for example, must be weighed against the long-term costs to the environment.

Truth versus loyalty. This ethical tension pits our loyalty to friends, family, groups, and organizations against our desire to tell the truth. It arises when we have to determine whether or not to lie to the boss to protect a coworker, to keep quiet about safety violations at the plant or to go public with our allegations, or to award a contract to a friend or to another supplier with a better bid.

Checkpoint 6: Apply resolution principles.

Once the options or sides are clear based on Checkpoints 4 and 5, apply the ethical perspectives described in Chapter 2.

Checkpoint 7: Look for a third way (investigate the "trilemma" option).

Compromise is one way to reveal a new alternative that will resolve the problem. Both the state and federal governments have used compromise to deal with the manufacture and marketing of cigarettes and alcohol. Many religious and public health groups want to ban these products. Yet, they are widely used by Americans. Government officials have tried to strike a balance, which recognizes the dangers of smoking and drinking while allowing citizens to engage in these activities. Tobacco and alcoholic beverages can't be sold to minors and there are limits to where they can be consumed.

The third way can also be the product of moral imagination. Setting up "pay for play" online music libraries is one such innovative concept. The music industry and millions of consumers have been locked in a legal and ethical battle over downloading copyrighted tunes for free. Now listeners can get just the songs they want without violating copyright laws. Record producers, who have seen a steady decline in CD sales, are enjoying a new source of revenue.

Checkpoint 8: Make the decision.

Exhausted by wrestling with the problem, we may overlook this step. Yet no decision, no matter how well grounded, is useful unless it is put into action.

Kidder argues that this step requires moral courage. Such courage, along with our ability to reason, sets us apart from the animal kingdom.

Checkpoint 9: Revisit and reflect on the decision.

Return to the decision later, after the issue has been resolved, to debrief. Reflect on the lessons to be learned. In some instances, the problem can be shaped into a case or example that can be used in ethics teaching and training.

THE MORAL COMPASS

Harvard ethics professor Lynn Paine offers a four-part "moral compass" for guiding managerial decision making.[23] The goal of the compass is to ensure that ethical considerations are factored into every organizational decision. Paine believes that we can focus our attention (and that of the rest of the group) on the moral dimension of even routine decisions by engaging in the following four frames of analysis. Each frame or lens highlights certain elements of the situation so that they can be carefully examined and addressed. Taken together, the lenses increase moral sensitivity, making it easier for organizational members to recognize and discuss moral issues.

Lens 1: Purpose—Will this action serve a worthwhile purpose?

The first frame examines end results. Proposed courses of action need to serve worthy goals. To come up with the answer to the question of purpose, we need to gather data as well as make judgments. Important subsidiary questions include:

- What are we trying to accomplish? What are our short- and long-term goals?
- Are these goals worthwhile? How do they contribute to people's lives?
- Will the course of action we are examining contribute to achieving these goals?
- Compared to the possible alternatives, how effectively and efficiently will it do so?
- If this is not the most effective and efficient course, do we have a sound basis for pursuing the proposed path?

Lens 2: Principle—Is this action consistent with relevant principles?

This mode of analysis applies ethical standards to the problem at hand. These guidelines can be general ethical principles, norms of good business practice, codes of conduct, legal requirements, and personal ideals and aspirations. We need to determine:

- What norms of conduct are relevant to this situation?
- What are our duties under these standards?
- What are the best practices under these standards?
- Does the proposed action honor the applicable standards?
- If not, do we have a sound basis for departing from these standards?
- Is the proposed action consistent with our own espoused standards and ideals?

Lens 3: People—Does this action respect the legitimate claims of the people likely to be affected?

The third frame highlights the likely impacts of decisions. Identifying possible harm to stakeholder groups can help us take steps to prevent damage. Such analysis requires understanding the perspectives of others as well as careful reasoning.

- Who is likely to be affected, both directly and indirectly, by the proposed action?
- How will these parties be affected?
- What are these parties' rights, interests, expectations, and concerns?
- Does our plan respect the legitimate claims of the affected parties?
- If not, what are we doing to compensate for this infringement?
- Have we mitigated unnecessary harms?
- Are there alternatives that would be less harmful or more beneficial on balance?
- Have we taken full advantage of opportunities for mutual benefit?

Lens 4: Power—Do we have the power to take this action?

The final lens directs attention to the exercise of power and influence. Answers to the first three sets of questions mean little unless we have the legitimate authority to act and the ability to do so. Subsidiary questions of power include:

- What is the scope of our legitimate authority in view of relevant laws, agreements, understandings, and stakeholder expectations?
- Are we within our rights to pursue the proposed course of action?
- If not, have we secured the necessary approvals?
- Do we have the resources, including the knowledge and skills as well as tangible resources, required to carry out the proposed action?
- If not, do we have the ability to marshal the needed resources?

Paine uses the example of a failed product introduction to illustrate what can happen when organizational decision makers fail to take moral issues into account. In the early 1990s, Lotus Development and Equifax teamed up to create a product called Lotus Marketplace: Households. This compact disc and software package was designed to help small businesses create targeted mailing lists from their desktop computers. For $695, purchasers could draw from a database of 80 million households (created from credit information collected by Equifax) instead of buying one-time mailing lists from list brokers. Businesses could then tailor their mailings based on income, gender, age, marital status, and lifestyle.

Criticism began as soon as the product was announced to the public. Many consumers didn't want to be included in the database due to privacy concerns and asked if they could opt out. Others worried that criminals might misuse the information by, for instance, identifying and then targeting upper income single women. The system didn't take into account that information would soon be outdated and that data could be stolen. The two firms tried to address these issues by allowing individuals to remove their names from the list, strengthening privacy controls, and improving security. Lotus and Equifax failed to sway the public and the project was scuttled. Equifax subsequently stopped selling credit information to marketers.

THE FIVE "I" FORMAT

Remembering all of Kidder's checkpoints or Paine's subsidiary questions would be difficult without referring to a book or a handout. Sometimes we need to make decisions without access to our notes. For that reason, I offer the easily memorized Five "I" Format as a guide. This approach incorporates elements of the first two models into the following sequence.

Identify the problem. Identification involves recognizing there is an ethical problem to be solved and setting goals. Describe what you seek as the outcome of your deliberations. Will you be taking action yourself or on behalf of the group or organization? Developing recommendations for others? Dealing with an immediate issue or setting a long-term policy?

Investigate the problem. Investigation involves two subprocesses: problem analysis and data collection. "Drill down" to develop a better understanding of the problem. Determine important stakeholders as well as conflicting loyalties, values, and duties. Develop a set of criteria or standards for evaluating solutions. This is the time to introduce important ethical perspectives. You may decide that your decision should put a high value on justice or altruism, for instance. In addition to analyzing the issue, gather more information. Knowing why an employee has been verbally abusive, for example, can make it easier to determine how much mercy to extend to that individual. You will likely be more forgiving if the outburst appears to be the product of family stress (divorce, illness, rebellious children). There may be times when you can't gather more data or when good information is not available. In those cases, you'll need to make reasonable assumptions based on your current knowledge.

Innovate by generating a variety of solutions. Resist the temptation to reach quick decisions. Instead, continue to look for a third way by generating possible options or alternative courses of action that could reach your goals and meet your criteria.

Isolate a solution. Settle on a solution using what you uncovered during the investigation stage. Evaluate your data, weigh loyalties and duties, consider the likely impact on stakeholders, and match the solution to your ethical criteria. The choice may be obvious or you may have to choose between equally attractive or equally unattractive alternatives. When it comes to decisions involving truth and loyalty, for instance, there is no easy way out. Lying for a friend preserves the relationship at the expense of personal integrity; refusing to lie for a friend preserves the truth but endangers the relationship. Remember that you are not looking for the perfect solution, but a well reasoned, carefully considered one.

Implement the solution. Determine how you will follow through on your choice. If you are deciding alone, develop an action plan. If you are deciding in a group, make sure that every team member knows her or his future responsibilities.

Implications

- Moral behavior is the product of moral sensitivity, moral judgment, moral motivation, and moral character. You'll need to master each of these components in order to make and then implement wise ethical decisions.
- You can enhance your ethical sensitivity through active listening, challenging your current ways of thinking, looking for innovative ways to solve problems, and discussing decisions in moral terms.
- Your moral judgment can be impaired if you only look to others for guidance or blindly follow the rules of your organization. Try to incorporate universal ethical principles into your decision-making process.
- Beware of major contributors to defective decision making: insecurities, greed, ego, and a short-term orientation.
- You will be more likely to put ethical values first if you are rewarded for doing so and monitor and regulate your emotions to create a positive frame of mind.
- To succeed at implementing your moral choice, you'll need to be both persistent and competent. Believe in your own ability to influence events, master the organizational context, and develop the necessary implementation skills.

- Decision-making formats can help you make better moral choices. Which format you use is not as important as approaching moral problems systematically. Kidder's Ethical Checkpoints can help you cut through the disorder and confusion surrounding ethical issues, the Moral Compass factors ethical considerations into every organizational decision, and the Five "I" Format offers a shorthand approach which incorporates elements of the first two sets of guidelines.

Application Projects

1. Use the suggestions in the chapter to develop an action plan for improving your moral sensitivity, judgment, motivation, and character.
2. Describe how your college experience has influenced your moral development. What experiences have had the greatest impact?
3. Apply one of the decision-making formats to an ethical dilemma found at the end of the chapter or to another one that you select. Keep a record of your deliberations and your final choice. Then evaluate the format and the decision. Did following a system help you come to a better conclusion? Why or why not? What are the strengths and weaknesses of the format you selected? Would it be a useful tool for solving the ethical problems you face at school and work? Write up your findings.
4. Using the material presented in the chapter, analyze what you consider to be a poor ethical decision. What went wrong? Why? Present your conclusions in a paper or in a presentation to the rest of the class.
5. Develop your own set of guidelines for ethical decision making. Describe and explain your model.

CHAPTER END CASE

Scenarios for Analysis

IS IT BETTER TO ASK FOR PERMISSION OR TO ASK FOR FORGIVENESS?*

Anselmo Escobar is the owner of Stately Homes, a small residential contractor. Stately Vistas is the company's biggest project yet. Escobar is anxious to begin building this new subdivision after a series of costly delays caused by a backlog in the city zoning office. He plans to remove nearly all the mature trees in the area so that he can build more homes and recoup his losses. However, the contractor knows this move will be unpopular with current residents who believe that the trees enhance the neighborhood and improve property values.

Escobar is under no legal obligation to consult with the neighborhood association about his plans. Further, he fears that notifying neighbors might lead to additional delays. A successful protest could force Anselmo to retain some of the trees scheduled for removal. Yet, the builder feels uneasy about moving ahead without talking to neighborhood representatives. Taking unilateral action could generate negative publicity and increase opposition to future Stately Homes developments. More importantly, Escobar wonders about his responsibility to current residents. He knows that he would be upset if another contractor removed trees in his neighborhood without notifying anyone.

As he ponders what to do, Anselmo is reminded of the old saying, "It is easier to ask for forgiveness than to ask for permission." He is torn between consulting with the neighbors before removing the trees (asking for permission) and removing the trees and then dealing with the fall out (asking for forgiveness).

What should Escobar do?

Note

*Not based on actual people or events.

GAMING THE SYSTEM

Alice Hamilton is a primary care physician at a large health maintenance organization (HMO). She enjoys the practice of medicine but feels caught between the needs of her patients and loyalty to her employer. Determined to keep medical costs down, Dr. Hamilton's managed care group routinely denies needed treatments to subscribers. Many of Alice's colleagues lie to ensure that patients get the care they deserve, a practice the doctors at her facility and elsewhere refer to as "gaming the system." Exaggerating symptoms makes it easier for subscribers to see specialists, receive further testing, and stay in the hospital longer. Physicians who game the system claim that doing so is the only way to properly do their jobs under current rules and regulations. At times, however, their cheating is a way to pacify patients who demand unneeded tests and treatments.

Should Dr. Hamilton game the system like many of her fellow professionals? Why or why not?

Source

Callahan, D. (2004). *The cheating culture.* Orlando, FL: Harcourt.

WHEN THE GOOD NEWS IS BAD NEWS*

Employees and administrators at Kentucky College were excited to hear that the incoming freshman class was the largest in the small private school's history. Years of slumping enrollment had left the college, which depended heavily upon tuition dollars, strapped for cash. Now the school's leadership could add new staff, increase faculty salaries, and improve facilities.

Unfortunately, what was good news for the Kentucky College as a whole was bad news for some freshmen. There weren't enough rooms available to house everyone. New students were placed in study rooms and in double rooms that were converted to "triples" by adding an extra bunk bed. All students paid the same price for room and board regardless of their housing arrangements. A few freshmen complained, arguing that they should pay less because their living arrangements weren't equal to those of other students. The housing director refused their request. Less revenue would mean fewer repairs to dorms and apartments. In addition, he believed that conceding to such demands could set a bad precedent. Some dorms are older and more run down than others. Residents living in these facilities might also claim that they should pay less.

Was Kentucky College wrong to admit more students than it could house comfortably?

Was the housing director justified in refusing to reduce fees for those students forced to live in substandard conditions?

Note

*Not based on actual people or events.

MERCY FOR MARGARET?*

Receptionist Margaret Simpson was one of the first employees hired at T Rex Manufacturing when the company opened 20 years ago. The first 2 years of operations were difficult ones and Simpson accepted late paychecks on more than one occasion to help keep the company afloat. For two decades she has been the face of the company to visitors and a friendly voice on the phone for suppliers and employees alike. Company president Gregg Smith often praises Margaret at employee meetings, citing her as an example of what the "T Rex family" is all about.

Sadly, Margaret's job performance has begun to slip. Over the past few months she has often been late to work and has become cold and distant. Outsiders and coworkers alike complain about how difficult the new Margaret is to deal with. They resent her rude comments and brusque manner. Earlier this month president Smith took the receptionist aside to confront her about her poor performance but to no avail. If anything, she is more unpleasant than ever. Smith did discover, however, that Simpson plans to retire in 3 years but that the value of her retirement savings plan has declined dramatically.

Smith knows that he must come to a decision about Margaret soon. In fact, she would have been fired earlier if she had been most any other employee.

However, the T Rex executive knows that the choice is a difficult one given Margaret's loyal service, her age and lack of retirement savings, and his desire to foster a family-like atmosphere at the plant.

What action should Smith take?

Note

*Not based on actual people or events.

Endnotes

1. Rest, J. R. (1994). Background: Theory and research. In J. R. Rest & D. Narvaez (Eds.), *Moral development in the professions: Psychology and applied ethics,* (pp. 1–25). Hillsdale, NJ: Lawrence Erlbaum; Rest, J. R. (1986). *Moral development: Advances in research and theory.* New York: Praeger.

2. Werhane, P. H. (1999). *Moral imagination and management decision-making.* New York: Oxford University Press.

3. Bird, F. B. (1996). *The muted conscience: Moral silence and the practice of ethics in business.* Westport, CT: Quorum Books.

4. Trevino, L. K., & Nelson, K. A. (2004). *Managing business ethics: Straight talk about how to do it right* (3rd ed.). Hoboken, NJ: John Wiley.

5. Kohlberg, L. A. (1984). *The psychology of moral development: The nature and validity of moral stages* (Vol. 2). San Francisco: Harper & Row; Kohlberg, L. A. (1986). *A current statement on some theoretical issues.* In S. Modgil & C. Modgil (Eds.), *Lawrence Kohlberg: Consensus and controversy* (pp. 485–546). Philadephia: Falmer Press.

6. Rest, J. R., Narvaez, D., Bebeau, M. J., & Thoma, S. J. (1999). *Postconventional moral thinking: A neo-Kohlbergian approach.* Mahwah, NJ: Lawrence Erlbaum; Trevino, L. K., & Weaver, G. R. (2003). *Managing ethics in business organizations: Social scientific perspectives.* Stanford, CA: Stanford University Press, chap. 7.

7. Rest, Narvaez, Bebeau, & Thoma (1999).

8. See, for example: Rest, J. R., & Narvaez, D. (1991). The college experience and moral development. In W. M. Kurtines & J. L. Gewirtz (Eds.), *Handbook of moral behavior and development. Vol. 2: Research* (pp. 229–245). Hillsdale, NJ: Lawrence Erlbaum; Rest, J. R. (1979). *Development in judging moral issues.* Minneapolis: University of Minnesota Press; Trevino & Weaver (2003).

9. Not all studies reveal a relationship between education and moral reasoning. See: Loe, T. W., Ferrell, L., & Mansfield, P. (2000). A review of empirical studies assessing ethical decision making in business. *Journal of Business Ethics, 25,* 185–204.

10. Gergen, D. (2000). *Eyewitness to power: The essence of leadership.* New York: Simon & Schuster.

11. Sternberg, R. J. (2002). Smart people are not stupid, but they sure can be foolish. In R. J. Sternberg (Ed.), *Why smart people can be so stupid* (pp. 232–242). New Haven, CT: Yale University Press.

12. Examples of the "winner take all" society come from: Callahan, D. (2004). *The cheating culture.* Orlando, FL: Harcourt.

13. Messick, D. M., & Bazerman, M. H. (1996, Winter). Ethical leadership and the psychology of decision making. *Sloan Management Review,* pp. 9–23.

14. Sternberg (2002).

15. Nash, L. (1990). *Good intentions aside: A manager's guide to resolving ethical problems.* Boston, MA: Harvard Business School Press, p. 166.

16. Nutt, P. (2002). *Why decisions fail.* San Francisco: Berritt-Koehler.

17. James, H. S. (2000). Reinforcing ethical decision making through organizational structure. *Journal of Business Ethics, 28,* 43–58.

18. Benjamin, M. (2002, April 22). Honest opinions. *U.S. News & World Report,* p. 47.

19. Eisenberg, N. (2000). Emotion, regulation, and moral development. *Annual Review of Psychology, 51,* 665–697; Gaudine, A., & Thorne, L. (2001). Emotion and ethical decision-making in organizations. *Journal of Business Ethics, 31,* 175–187; Salovey, P., Hsee, C. K., & Mayer, J. D. (1993). Emotional intelligence and the self-regulation of affect. In D. M. Wegner & J. W. Pennebaker (Eds.), *Handbook of mental control* (pp. 258–277). Englewood Cliffs, NJ: Prentice Hall; Giacalone, R. A., & Greenbergh, J. (Eds.), (1997). *Antisocial behavior in organizations.* Thousand Oaks, CA: Sage.

20. Trevino & Weaver (2003), chap. 7.

21. Coles, R. (2001). *Lives of moral leadership.* New York: Random House.

22. Kidder, R. M. (1995). *How good people make tough choices.* New York: Simon & Schuster. For an example of how Kidder's model can be applied to ethical problems in one industry, see: Baker, S. (1997). Applying Kidder's ethical decision-making checklist to media ethics. *Journal of Mass Media Ethics, 12*(4), 197–210.

23. Paine, L. S. (2003). *Values shift: Why companies must merge social and financial imperatives to achieve superior performance.* New York: McGraw-Hill.

Part III

Transforming Interpersonal Ethics in the Organization

4

Ethical Interpersonal Communication

Chapter Preview

Communication is a logical starting point for any consideration of ethical relationships because organizational partnerships are created through verbal and nonverbal messages. If we want to establish and maintain transformed relationships, we must adopt a moral stance toward our communication with others and master communication skills that foster ethical interactions and decisions.

Dialogue: An Ethical Framework for Interpersonal Communication

The outcome of any conversation is largely dependent upon the attitude we bring to the encounter. Consider how you respond to a request from a coworker you respect as compared to one you distrust, for instance. You're likely to be more friendly and helpful to the former than the latter. Twentieth-century German philosopher Martin Buber argued that our attitudes also set the moral tone for our conversations. He identified two primary human attitudes or relationships: I-It and I-Thou.[1] Communicators in I-It relationships treat others as objects. Centered on their own needs, they are not really interested in the ideas of their conversational partners. Participants in I-Thou (I-You) relationships, in contrast, treat others as unique human beings. They are genuinely committed to understanding the perspectives of their fellow communicators.

Buber identifies three types of communication that reflect varying degrees of interest in the self or the other. *Monologue* is self-centered, I-It communication, which, at its worst, is characterized by deception, exploitation, coercion, and manipulation. *Technical dialogue* reflects a more neutral stance toward the self and other. In this type of interaction the focus is on gathering and processing information. *Dialogue* is the product of an I-Thou relationship. Dialogue occurs between equal partners who focus on understanding rather than on being understood.

All three forms of communication have their place in the organization. There are times when we legitimately engage in monologue to meet our needs, such as when we need emotional support. Technical dialogue enables us to get our work done, and we spend most of our time sending and receiving information-centered messages. However, dialogue has the most potential to build productive relationships and organizational communities. Entering into I-Thou relationships heightens self-esteem by reaffirming the worth of both parties, strengthens interpersonal bonds, and promotes understanding and learning. Yet, before we can pursue dialogue, we need to clear up some common misconceptions about this form of communication, clarify its unique characteristics, and identify the ethical demands dialogue makes of us.

Dialogue is frequently misunderstood. It is *not* merely venting one's feelings (that is a form of monologue). Successful dialogue focuses on what happens between communicators based on the meanings and understandings they jointly develop. For that reason, dialogue can't be forced, only encouraged. Nor is dialogue limited to friendly interactions between friends or intimates. Instead, dialogue is most powerful when acquaintances profoundly disagree but remain in an I-Thou relationship. Buber urged discussants to walk "a narrow ridge" between extreme positions, avoiding the temptation to take up residence in one opposing camp or another.[2] They should stand by their convictions while remaining open to the positions of others. Buber had this type of relationship with Mahatma Gandhi. The two disagreed about whether violence should be used against the Third Reich in World War II. Gandhi urged nonviolent tactics while Buber (who suffered persecution as a Jew) was convinced that such strategies would not sway the Nazis. Had he lived in our era, Buber would likely be distressed by today's highly polarized political environment filled with pitched battles between conservatives and liberals.

Communication experts Kenneth Cissna and Robert Anderson outline the following as characteristics of interpersonal dialogue:[3]

- *Presence.* Partners in dialogue are less interested in a specific outcome than in working with others to come up with a solution. Their interactions are unscripted and unrehearsed.
- *Emergent unanticipated consequences.* Dialogue produces unpredictable results that are not controlled by any one party.
- *Recognition of "strange otherness."* If dialogue is to flourish, discussants must refuse to believe that they already understand the thoughts, feelings, or intentions of others, even people they know well. They are tentative instead, continually testing their understanding of the perspectives of other group members and revising their conclusions when needed.
- *Collaborative orientation.* Dialogue demands a dual focus on self and others. Participants concentrate on coming up with a shared, joint solution that preserves the relationship, not on winning or losing.
- *Vulnerability.* Dialogue is risky because discussants open their thoughts to others and may be influenced by the encounter. They must be willing to change their minds and to be changed as persons. (Turn to the Chapter End Case for an example of someone who signaled her vulnerability in a most unusual way.)
- *Mutual implication.* Speakers engaged in dialogue always keep listeners in mind when speaking. In so doing they may discover more about themselves as well.
- *Temporal flow.* Dialogue unfolds over time—drawing from the past, filling the present and leading to the future. It is a process that can't be cut into segments and analyzed.
- *Genuineness and authenticity.* Participants in dialogue give each other the benefit of the doubt, assuming that the other person is being honest and sharing from personal experience. While speakers don't share all their thoughts, they don't deliberately hide ideas and feelings that are relevant to the topic and to the relationship.

We have to make several ethical commitments if we hope to engage in the kind of conversation described by Cissna and Anderson.[4] First, we must be committed to the good of others in order to treat them as unique beings. Second, we need to value relationships and the common good, recognizing that organizations are made up, not of autonomous individuals, but of people living in relation to one another. Third, we have to be open to influence and be willing to take criticism. Fourth, we ought to allow others to hold and express opinions different from ours. Fifth, we have to commit ourselves to honesty, not just during dialogue, but also when we engage in monologue and technical dialogue. There are times when we need to get others to follow our directions or to change their opinions. However, let's not disguise our motives by pretending to dialogue when we really only want to get our way. Sixth, we need to invest ourselves in the hard work of dialogue. Focusing on the needs and positions of others takes a good deal of time and energy, as does mastering the necessary communication competencies to make dialogue successful. These dialogic skills will be introduced in the next section.

Ethical Communication Competencies

While dialogue can't be forced, it is much more likely to take place when we have the necessary competencies. Productive communication behaviors that foster I-Thou relationships include mindfulness, effective listening, confirmation, emotional sensitivity, trust building, and productive conflict management. These strategies can also help us make better choices. When used in conjunction with the principles and practices of sound moral reasoning introduced in the last chapter, they further increase our likelihood of coming up with a well-reasoned ethical conclusion.

MINDFULNESS

Dialogue demands our complete attention. Not only is it unscripted, unrehearsed, and unpredictable, but this type of interaction also requires that we simultaneously focus on our own thoughts as well as on the positions of our conversational partners. Psychologist Ellen Langer uses the term *mindfulness* to describe the process of devoting full attention to the task at hand.[5] She contrasts mindfulness to *mindlessness*, which is the state of mind in which we find ourselves in most routine encounters. In the mindless condition we operate on "auto pilot" and perform our roles mechanically, without much reflection. Mindlessness can be costly. We get stuck in our current roles and self-perceptions; stop developing intellectually; engage in unintended cruelty by rationalizing our immoral behaviors; lose control of our choices to advertisers and other outsiders; give into helplessness when we can control the situation; and limit our potential.

Langer identifies three psychological processes of a mindful state of being which help us sidestep the dangers of mindless behavior. These characteristics are contrasted to mindlessness in the narrative found in Box 4.1.

Box 4.1 Mindlessness Meets Mindfulness: Napoleon Versus the Russian Bear

When Napoleon invaded Russia, he appeared to the world as a brilliant conquering hero, yet again proving his military genius by daring to march against a giant. But behind the proud banners and eagles, he carried a dangerous mindset, a determination to have Russia no matter what the cost in human life. As Tolstoy describes him in *War and Peace*, Napoleon had no use for alternatives; his determination was absolute.

Opposite Napoleon stood the old Russian bear of a general, Kutuzov, a mellowed veteran who liked his vodka and had a habit of falling asleep at state occasions. An uneven match, or so it would appear.

As Napoleon's army advanced, Kutuzov let his army fall back, and then fall back some more. Napoleon kept coming, deeper into Russia, farther from his supply lines. Finally, as Kutuzov knew would happen, a powerful ally intervened: the Russian winter. The French army found itself fighting the cold, the wind, the snow, and the ice.

When Napoleon at last achieved his single, obsessive goal—Moscow—there was no one there for him to conquer. The Russians had set their holy city on fire to greet the invader. Once more Kutuzov played the seeming loser.

At that moment, when Napoleon had no choice but to retreat—from the burned city, from the winter—the mindful old general attacked. He appealed to Mother Russia, an appeal that Stalin was to use with similar success years later. He appealed to the people to save their land, and that appeal revived all of Russia. The French had everything against them, including the Cossacks, who rode down off the winter steppes. Mother Russia prevailed, just as she would when Hitler was to repeat Napoleon's mistake.

In each case, Napoleon's blind obsession provides a vivid mirror image, a portrait of mindlessness. First of all, Kutuzov was flexible: Evacuating a city would usually fall under the category of defeat, but for him it became the act of setting a trap. Second, his strategy was responsive to the news of Napoleon's advance, while Napoleon did not seem to be taking in information about Kutuzov's moves. Finally, while Napoleon saw his rapid advance and march on Moscow only from the point of view of conquering enemy terrain, Kutuzov could also see that an "invasion" in the context of winter and distance from supplies could be turned into a bitter rout.

Source: From Langer, E., *Mindfulness,* copyright © 1989 by Ellen J. Langer. Reprinted by permission of Da Capo Press, a member of Perseus Books, L.L.C.

The first psychological process is the *creation of new categories.* Being mindful breaks us out of our old rigid categories and makes us more sensitive to differences. These distinctions enhance our thinking and relationships. We become better problem solvers when we realize that moral reasoning can be broken down into smaller stages, as we saw in Chapter 3. We're much less likely to stereotype individuals and act in a prejudiced manner if we refuse to lump people into broad categories based on age, race, gender, or role.

The second psychological process involves *welcoming new information.* In mindful communication we seek new information as we closely monitor our behavior along with the behavior of others. This data allows us to revise our conclusions and adjust our responses. Mindless communication, on the other hand, closes us off to new information. As a result, we make costly mistakes and fail to adjust to changes in our environments. We assume that others hold our ethical values when they don't, settle on the first solution when a better one might be available, fail to meet the changing expectations of our audiences, and so on.

The third psychological process is *openness to different points of view.* Any event or behavior can be viewed from more than one perspective. What seems like thoughtless, hurtful behavior on the part of a coworker may have been intended as playful or harmless. Exploring multiple perspectives gives us more options, reduces the probability that we will get locked into an extreme position, and equips us to change our behavior. For instance, we are more likely to change the way we act when we realize that others take offence at what we're currently doing.

Mindfulness is a mode of thinking, not a personality trait. As a consequence, we can consciously shift to this frame of mind when needed. It's easy to identify situations that clearly demand a mindful state of mind: dealing with strangers and people of other cultural backgrounds, public presentations, brainstorming sessions, interviews, strategy meetings, change efforts. However, even routine interactions like casual conversations with coworkers can be enhanced with a mindful awareness. You can practice shifting your thinking modes by deliberately paying more attention during common communication events. For example, approach a classroom lecture with a mindful attitude, noting elements of delivery, audience response, and other factors you usually overlook. Or you might analyze a film from more than one point of view (see Application Project 2 on page 109).

EFFECTIVE LISTENING

Listening is key to coming to mutual understanding through dialogue. We can't come up with a joint, shared solution or speak to the needs of the other party unless we comprehend the other party's perspective. Skillful listening is also essential to processing the informational messages that make up technical dialogue. According to Judi Brownell of Cornell University, communication is best understood as listening, not speaking, centered.[6] She offers the multistage HURIER model to describe her listener-focused approach to communication.

Component 1: Hearing

The environment is filled with all kinds of stimuli. Listening begins when we focus in on one or more of these elements—music, a radio announcer, the voice of a friend, a supervisor's phone call. What we choose to hear is dependent on our perceptual filters, which are made up of our cultural background, beliefs and values, past experiences, interests, family history, and other factors. Consider how you and a friend respond to the same stimuli, for example. If you are an avid ski boarder, you'll listen carefully to the morning radio report on mountain snow conditions. Your conversational partner (who is not interested in heading for the slopes) may change stations when this segment comes on.

Component 2: Understanding

Once the message is received, it must be processed. Like reading comprehension, listening comprehension is based on the literal meanings of the words and signals received. Shared language and vocabulary greatly increase the likelihood of understanding.

Component 3: Remembering

Memory allows an individual to retrieve information in order to come up with an appropriate response. Memory, like hearing, is especially influenced by our perceptual filters. Information we're interested in is retained; other messages are quickly forgotten.

Component 4: Interpreting

During this stage meaning is assigned to the message based on the words and nonverbal cues like context (location, previous events, participants), vocal qualities, and body language.

Component 5: Evaluating

At this stage the receiver makes a judgment about the accuracy and truthfulness of the message by evaluating evidence and reasoning, source credibility, the situation, emotional appeals, and other factors.

Component 6: Responding

We can only respond appropriately if we've successfully completed the first five steps of the model. Since listening is continuous, we must also adjust our messages even as we're speaking. If a coworker gives us a puzzled look while we're explaining a new technical process, for instance, we need to pause to ask if he or she understands our directions.

Listening can fail at any stage of the HURIER model. We might tune out important messages or fail to comprehend their meanings, forget essential data, come up with an inaccurate interpretation, misjudge the message, or formulate the wrong response. However, listening effectiveness increases when we approach conversations with a mindful attitude and incorporate the skills outlined in Box 4.2.

Box 4.2 Listening Skills

Hear Messages: Focus Attention and Concentrate

- Take a sincere interest in other people and ideas.
- Listen to new and difficult information.
- Stay active by taking notes, paraphrasing, etc.
- Manipulate the physical environment to make listening easier.
- Use the thought-speech differential (extra time generated by the ability to process speech faster than it is delivered) wisely.

Understand What You Hear

- Listen to the entire message.
- Distinguish main ideas from details
- Recognize your personal assumptions and meanings.
- Increase your vocabulary.
- Check your perceptions.

Remember Messages

- Improve your short-term memory.
- Learn long-term memory techniques and use them regularly.
    - Create associations.
    - Use visual imagery.

Interpret Messages

- Develop empathy.
- Increase awareness of and sensitivity to nonverbal cues.

- Take into account the speaker's background attitudes and other variables.
- Take into account the communication context.
- Strive to be a high self-monitor (monitor the impact your behavior has on the other person).

Evaluate What You Hear

- Consider the speaker's credibility.
- Recognize personal bias.
- Understand persuasive strategies.
- Analyze logic and reasoning to identify logical fallacies.
- Recognize emotional appeals.

Source: Brownell, J. (2003, November 22). *The skills of listening-centered communication*. Paper presented at the National Communication Association Convention, Miami, FL. Reprinted with permission of Dr. Judi Brownell.

Understanding how we prefer to listen can also improve our performance as listeners. Listening consultants Larry Barker and Kittie Watson identify four listening preferences.[7] Each has its own unique combination of strengths and weaknesses. Knowing the downside of our listening profiles can help us avoid listening errors.

People-oriented listeners are most concerned with maintaining relationships. They are concerned, caring, and nonjudgmental and provide clear feedback. However, these communicators can get overly involved with others and may overlook their faults. *Action-oriented listeners* concentrate on the task and are good at keeping meetings on topic while encouraging speakers to organize their thoughts. Unfortunately, they often come across as impatient, quick to jump to conclusions, and disinterested in relationships. *Content-oriented listeners* (often those in technical fields) evaluate messages carefully, even highly complex ones, and explore all sides of an issue. Their weaknesses include getting bogged down in details and taking forever to come to a decision. *Time-oriented listeners* value effectiveness and efficiency. They are good at saving time (theirs and others') but tend to interrupt, look at their clocks and watches, and limit creativity by setting time limits.

While most people have one or two preferred styles, effective listeners know how to match their preferences or habits to the communication context. The action-oriented style works well in processing business proposals, for example, but is not so effective in the break room where messages are not likely to be clearly structured. Time-oriented executives often get in trouble when they take this style home to conversations with their spouses and children. In these cases, effective listeners would adopt a people-centered approach.

Conversely, a content-oriented style works better than a people-focused preference when engaged in technical processes like debugging software and creating engineering designs.

CONFIRMATION

Treating the other person as a unique human being is at the heart of dialogue. Buber used the term *confirmation* to describe the process of recognizing and acknowledging the presence and value of others. He made this recognition of personhood the defining characteristic of human society:

> The basis of man's life with man is twofold, and it is one—the wish of every man to be confirmed as what he is, even as what he can become by men; and the innate capacity in man to confirm his fellow men in this way. . . . Actual humanity exists only where this capacity unfolds.[8]

Confirmation occurs when we value ourselves more after interacting with another person; disconfirmation takes place if we value ourselves less. Confirming behaviors (1) express recognition of the other person's existence, (2) acknowledge a relationship or affiliation, (3) express awareness of the significance or value of the other, and (4) accept or "endorse" the other person's experience or way of seeing the world. Disconfirming behaviors send the opposite message.[9]

Expressing confirmation improves interpersonal relationships. Those who feel confirmed or endorsed report greater marital satisfaction, an increased sense of intimacy, and higher self-esteem. Confirmation has also been linked to improved classroom performance. Students report that they are less anxious and learn more from teachers who make an effort to build relationships through such confirming messages as expressing interest in student learning and comments, answering questions fully, and listening attentively.[10]

Examples of disconfirming and confirming responses are outlined below. Ethical communicators try to avoid the first category of remarks and engage in the second set of behaviors.

Disconfirming Responses

Impervious—failing to acknowledge the messages of the other person; ignoring; shunning

Interrupting—cutting the other speaker short; beginning before he or she is finished

Irrelevant—responding in a way that seems unrelated to what the other person has just said

Tangential—acknowledging the previous message but immediately taking the conversation in a new direction

Impersonal—conducting a monologue, speaking in an overly intellectual or impersonal way

Ambiguous—responding with messages containing multiple or unclear meanings

Incongruous—engaging in nonverbal behavior that is inconsistent with the verbal content of the message, like a speaker who denies being angry even as his voice rises and his face turns red

Confirming Responses

Recognition—responding to the presence of the other person; treating the other person with respect

Acknowledgment—providing a direct, relevant response to the message of the other person; asking questions, disagreeing, paraphrasing

Endorsement—accepting the feelings of the other party as legitimate; letting the other person "be" without trying to analyze, blame, or change him or her

EMOTIONAL INTELLIGENCE

Understanding and responding to emotions plays a critical role in building relationships. Emotionally sensitive individuals get along better with people in general, experience few negative interactions with friends, and are more supportive team members. In addition, they make better choices because they recognize how their moods influence their thinking and manage their feelings instead of falling victim to them. Researchers use the term *emotional intelligence* to describe a cluster of competencies that determine our ability to identify and influence emotions in ourselves and others. According to psychologists David Caruso, Peter Salovey, and John Mayer, emotional intelligence is made up of the following four skill sets.[11] Each is increasingly difficult and builds on the levels that come before.

1. Identifying Emotions

Emotions provide important data about what's happening to us, to others, and in the environment. Effective communication depends on accurately reading these signals and on accurately conveying how we feel. Unfortunately, research suggests that, when it comes to interpreting emotional expressions, we are not as skilled as we think.[12] Most people can pick out intense emotional expressions but are less adept at identifying slight or partial displays of the same feelings. Accurate decoding is further complicated by the fact that facial displays of emotion during conversation last only a short time (generally from ½ second to 2½ seconds). Skillful communicators have mastered these challenges and can

- recognize their internal emotional states
- talk about their feelings
- communicate internal emotional states so that their feelings are understood as intended
- accurately read people even when they try to disguise or repress their emotions
- pick up on the emotional meaning of messages sent through body language, vocal cues, and facial expressions

2. Using Emotions

Emotions play an important role in reasoning and can enhance our thinking. Positive moods promote new ideas and risk taking; negative moods focus attention on details and possible errors.[13] Our chances of coming up with a good solution are greatest when we employ both modes of reasoning. For that reason, we might put ourselves in a positive frame of mind for a brainstorming session but wait until the next day to evaluate our ideas when we're not so optimistic and can do a better job of catching potential problems. (Turn to Chapter 3 for more information on the link between emotions and ethical decision making.) Those with high emotional intelligence

- demonstrate creative thinking and imagination
- inspire and motivate others
- closely monitor events that generate strong emotions
- match their emotions to the task and select tasks based on the mood they are in

3. Understanding Emotions

Emotions aren't chaotic but have underlying causes and follow progressions. Annoyance leads to anger and then to rage, for example, but not the other way around. If we understand these patterns, we can better forecast how others will respond to events and plan accordingly. Emotionally sensitive individuals

- make correct assumptions about how others will behave
- have an extensive emotional vocabulary that enables them to accurately communicate what they are experiencing
- appreciate emotional complexity—the fact that communicators can experience contradictory emotions at the same time
- accurately predict how others will respond and choose the right message

4. Managing Emotions

Emotions (even the unwelcome ones) need to be factored into reasoning, evaluation, and behavior. However, we need to manage our feelings instead of being controlled by them. Emotions can generate more productive outcomes if they are integrated into our thinking. Emotionally intelligent people

- resist unhealthy impulses
- know when to follow their feelings and when to set them aside temporarily
- are open to their own feelings and the emotions of those around them
- let emotions activate productive behavior, like fighting against injustice when angry and avoiding risks when afraid
- regulate their moods to achieve their goals; for example, getting "pumped up" before a class presentation; consciously shifting attention from a source of irritation to preparing for an upcoming meeting
- establish genuine interpersonal connections
- manage the feelings of coworkers in appropriate ways (cheer them up, calm them down)

These four skill sets, taken together, provide an "emotional blueprint" for dealing with organizational relationships of all kinds. This blueprint can be used to analyze past encounters or to prepare for important or difficult situations (client presentations, performance evaluations, termination interviews). Caruso and Salovey suggest that one way to raise your emotional intelligence quotient is by evaluating a past conversation from the vantage point of emotion using the set of questions found in the self assessment Box 4.3. You can also use these same queries to analyze an upcoming event.

Self-Assessment

Box 4.3 Emotional Analysis Questions

Think of a recent communication encounter and apply the following questions both to you and the other person involved. Respond to each query. Then apply the same questions to an upcoming conversation. Summarize your conclusions.

1. Questions to Help You Identify Emotions

- How aware are you (was the other party) of your (his or her) emotions?
- Were you aware of how you felt during this situation?

(Continued)

(Continued)

- How do you feel right now?
- How did you feel during this interaction?
- How emotional were you?
- Did you express your feelings to others? Appropriately so?
- Were you expressing your true feelings or trying to cover them up?
- Were you focused only on your feelings, or were you aware of the other person's feelings?

2. Questions to Help You Use Emotions

- Did it help (will it help) you (the other party) to feel this way?
- Did your mood focus you on the issue or away from it?
- Did you find yourself feeling negative or positive about things?
- Did your mood help you see the other person's point of view?
- Were you able to feel what the other person was feeling?
- How much did you pay attention to the problem?
- Did you try to feel the emotions or block them out?

3. Questions to Help You Understand Emotions

- Why did (do) you (does the other party) feel this way?
- What caused you to feel the way you feel?
- Describe the intensity of your feelings.
- How will you feel next?

4. Questions to Help You Manage Emotions

- What did (do) you (does the other party) want to happen?
- What did happen?
- What did you do?
- How did it work out?
- Was there a better way to have handled it?
- Why didn't you handle it better?
- How satisfied were you with the outcome?
- How satisfied do you think the other person was with the outcome?
- What could you have done differently?
- What did you learn from this situation?

Source: From Caruso, D. R., & Salovey, P., *The emotionally intelligent manager: How to develop and use the four key emotional skills of leadership.* Copyright © 2004. Reprinted with permission of Jossey-Bass, an imprint of John Wiley & Sons, Inc.

TRUST BUILDING

Interpersonal trust is often the "glue" that binds organizational members together. Those in trusting relationships feel a greater sense of interdependence, help one another, and are more willing to learn and to take risks, including the risk of engaging in dialogue. A group with members who trust each other makes higher quality decisions, is more productive, and operates more efficiently.[14]

A cluster of attitudes and behaviors defines trusting relationships. First, trust involves optimistic expectations. Trusting individuals believe that the other party will carry through on promises and commitments. Second, those who trust put themselves in a vulnerable position. They depend on the behavior of others and have much to lose if these individuals break their commitments. Third, trust is willingly offered. Participants entering into trust relationships hope to increase cooperation and generate benefits, not only for themselves, but also for the group as a whole. All organizational stakeholders gain from such partnerships. Fourth, trust is hard to enforce. Organizations try to ensure cooperation through contracts, legal requirements, and other means. However, formal enforcement mechanisms don't have much impact on informal relationships between group members and can't, by themselves, create a trusting climate. Fifth, trust imposes an obligation or duty to protect the rights and interests of others. The target of trust is expected to (a) not harm the other party, and (b) act in a way that benefits both individuals.

Interpersonal trust, because it involves obligation or duty, has a moral dimension.[15] More than just a strategy for ensuring cooperation and better results, trust also imposes ethical demands. We have a moral responsibility to protect and promote the interests of those who rely on us (put themselves in a vulnerable position). Breaking trust can be considered unethical because interpersonal trust serves the greater organizational good.

Many definitions of trustworthiness include virtues or values. When it comes to building trust, we need to demonstrate the character virtues described in Chapter 2. In addition to demonstrating knowledge and expertise, we need to express concern, act in a consistent manner, and be honest, open, and loyal. Conversely, when trust is broken by ourselves or by the other party, we need to engage in relational repair. (See Box 4.4 for an example of a situation needing relational repair.)

CASE STUDY

Box 4.4 Taking Credit When Credit's Not Due*

Monique Myerson works for the human resources department of a regional bank in the Southeastern United States. This is her first job after college. Monique's performance reviews are outstanding. After handling the paperwork for benefits packages her first 2 years, she is now in charge of the department's minority hiring initiative. In just twelve months she developed an internship program called Minority Advance in conjunction with her alma mater and other area universities. Students of color receive a stipend for interning with the bank their senior year and, if their performance is satisfactory, are offered permanent positions after graduation. Initial results are very encouraging. The percentage of minority hires is steadily increasing.

The success of Minority Advance attracted the attention of the local newspaper, which was doing a feature on diversity initiatives in business. That's when the trouble began. A reporter came to the bank and interviewed Monique's manager (the Human Resources director) when Monique was on vacation. The director described Minority Advance as her brainchild and took credit for the program's success. When the article came out, it spoke in glowing terms of the program, citing it as a model workplace diversity effort. Monique Myerson was not mentioned once in the article.

Furious at seeing her ideas and hard work "stolen" by the director, Monique has arranged an appointment to meet with her tomorrow morning.

DISCUSSION PROBES

1. Why do you think the Human Relations director claimed credit for this program?
2. What should Monique say during her appointment to address this breach of trust?
3. How should the Human Relations director respond?
4. How can Monique and her manager restore their relationship based on the five steps of relational repair outlined in the chapter? Or can they?
5. Can you think of times when your trust was betrayed on the job? How did you respond? What would you do differently the next time a similar event occurs?

NOTE

*Not based on actual people or events.

According to organizational behavior scholars Roy Lewicki and Barbara Bunker, restoring trust requires the involvement of both parties—the violator and the violated.[16] Violators must take ownership of destroying trust and the violated must commit themselves to the restoration process. The investigators outline five steps to restoring work relationships.

Step 1: Recognize and acknowledge that a violation has occurred.

The violation has to be acknowledged if restoration is to take place. A violator may come to the realization that trust is broken or the victim may have to bring the offending acts to the offender's attention.

Step 2: Determine the nature of the violation—its causes and the offender's responsibility.

Violators must recognize that they have caused harm (broken promises, failed to carry through, shared confidences) and assume responsibility for their actions. They may resist, however, by denying that they caused the problem or that the problem is important enough to warrant correction.

Step 3: Admit that the event damaged trust.

Rebuilding trust requires discussion of what happened and the ensuing consequences. The violator needs to understand the victim's reactions and how the relationship has been undermined.

Step 4: Be willing to accept responsibility for the violation.

Offenders need to take accountability for the relational damage even if their actions were well intentioned and they were unaware of the consequences of what they had done. What's important is the perception of the trustor. If he or she perceives that trust has been broken, then it has been. Failing to acknowledge that fact will intensify the victim's anger and cause further relational deterioration.

Step 5: Trust repair.

In this stage balance is restored to the relationship. The violator tries to atone for the transgression, following the direction of the victim, who sets the conditions for the repair effort. Trust reconstruction can follow four paths. In the first sequence, the victim initially refuses any attempts to reestablish the relationship. He or she may feel too angry or injured or believe that the relationship is not worth saving and/or can't be repaired. The violator then unilaterally takes action to change the victim's perspective by apologizing, asking forgiveness, sending letters, and demonstrating kindness. Both parties move on to trust repair if the offender changes the perspective of the victim.

In the second path, the victim sets unreasonable expectations for the violator out of the desire for revenge. When the violator resists these demands, the relationship is once again put at risk. The parties must come to a common agreement about the conditions for restoration if repair is to continue.

In the third path, the victim offers forgiveness without requiring any further acts of reparation. Both parties try to put the breach of trust behind them and move on. Nonetheless, there will probably be lingering relational tension as the offender feels embarrassed and the offended party remains suspicious.

In the fourth sequence the victim offers forgiveness and spells out reasonable acts of reparation and restoration. These acts are designed to test the violator's sincerity and investment in the relationship to the victim's satisfaction. At the same time, the offender works through any guilt or remorse.

Lewicki and Bunker argue that forgiveness with reparations is more effective at repairing relationships than forgiveness alone. The fourth alternative actively involves both parties, reduces the level of negative feelings, demonstrates commitment to the partnership, and lays the groundwork for slowly rebuilding trust. Yet those who study forgiveness suggest that there is significant benefit to victims who extend mercy even when the offender refuses to acknowledge guilt. Forgivers are less depressed and anxious. They lower their risk of heart attack and blood pressure while they're increasing resistance to disease. Offering forgiveness in serious breaches of trust can help the victim develop a deeper sense of meaning and purpose.[17]

CONFLICT MANAGEMENT SKILLS

Conflict puts dialogue to the ultimate test. Buber encouraged disputants to walk the narrow ridge between opposing points of view. However, the nature of conflict encourages us to set up camp on one side of the ridge or the other. Conflict experts William Wilmot and Joyce Hocker define conflict as "an expressed struggle between at least two interdependent parties who perceive incompatible goals, scarce resources, and interference from others in achieving their goals."[18] Each element of this definition highlights the difficulty of maintaining an I-Thou relationship during disputes. Conflict begins when the parties express their thoughts and feelings to each other through their behaviors. They engage in conflict because they depend to some degree on one another. The choices of one party affect the options of others, as when one employee's choice of vacation time interferes with the vacation plans of a fellow worker. Conflict can be over perceived incompatible goals (if I get promoted, then you don't) or scarce resources in office space, staffing, and budgets. Interference sets the stage for conflict. Goals may be incompatible and resources scarce, but conflict only develops if we perceive that the other party is interfering with our efforts to achieve our goals and to get the resources we want.

While remaining in dialogue during conflict is never easy, we are more likely to succeed if (1) we differentiate between functional and dysfunctional conflicts, and (2) we adopt conflict management guidelines and tactics.

Many of us fear and avoid conflict because of our past experiences. Earlier struggles cost us relationships and left us feeling bruised and battered. Aversion to conflict is counterproductive, however. To begin, organizational conflict is inevitable. Trying to avoid conflict means that we are not equipped to deal with it when it arises. Further, conflicts can promote personal and relational growth.

Resolving a conflict successfully builds our skills and generates a sense of accomplishment. Often conflict over an idea or proposal produces a higher quality solution.

Several factors distinguish between productive and unproductive conflicts.[19] Functional conflicts focus on the content of messages—ideas, values, beliefs, proposals, procedures, budgets, and so on. Participants in these kinds of conflicts are out to solve the problem, not to damage the other party. They make supportive comments, engage in effective listening, signal that they want to collaborate to come up with a solution, and avoid verbal abuse. Dysfunctional conflicts often center on the personalities of those involved, both of whom are out to hurt the other. Strong negative emotions and threats, personal attacks, and other forms of verbal aggression characterize these encounters. Discussants locked in unproductive conflicts engage in fight-or-flight responses. They either escalate the conflict or try to avoid it. Conflict spirals when each party retaliates at a higher and higher level. An employee who feels unjustly treated may retaliate by trying to undermine the authority of her supervisor who, in turn, may retaliate against the subordinate by reducing her work hours. Avoidance, which we noted earlier, is the other common destructive pattern. Participants may reduce their dependence on one another, refuse to cooperate, withdraw, harbor resentment, and complain to third parties. In doing so, they leave conflicts unresolved and poison the relationship.

Setting the right guidelines and using collaborative tactics can help prevent conflicts from deteriorating into dysfunctional exchanges. Organizational communication expert Pamela Shockley-Zalabak offers these principles for managing conflicts.[20]

Monitor your personal behavior and the behavior of the other party for signs of destructive conflict.

Be alert to those behaviors that indicate that you or the other party is contributing to escalation or avoidance cycles.

Identify common goals and interests.

Think about what both parties have in common and want to achieve. Consider overlapping needs, concerns, goals, and fears.

Develop norms to work on problems.

Rules of behavior can be developed for both individual- and group-level conflicts. Relational partners may want to agree to take "time-outs" when discussions get too heated, meet in a neutral location, and avoid personal attacks.

Groups may want to encourage dissent, seek consensus rather than voting on a solution, and resist speedy outcomes that fail to take advantage of productive conflict over ideas.

Focus on mutual gain.

Identify and state what everyone can gain from working through the conflict. Think win-win rather than win-lose. One party does not have to win at the expense of another. Try to expand the pie instead so that both parties can get what they want.

Collaborative conflict management tactics are designed to foster the win-win approach to conflict described above. They reflect a high level of concern for the interests of both parties as well as for the health of the relationship. The focus is on reaching a mutually agreeable solution that benefits everyone. Research findings establish that the collaborative approach is most effective, generating better choices and higher satisfaction with partners.[21] Collaborative tactics are both analytic and conciliatory in nature. Analytic remarks include:[22]

- *Descriptive statements.* Nonevaluative comments which report on observable events surrounding the conflict. ("I was short with you yesterday when you turned in that report.")
- *Disclosing statements.* Nonevaluative statements about conflict events that the partner can't observe—thoughts, feelings, intentions, past history, motivations. ("I didn't intend to criticize you in front of the rest of the staff.")
- *Qualifying statements.* Remarks that qualify the nature and the boundaries of the conflict. ("Tensions between our departments are greatest near the end of the fiscal year when both groups are swamped with work.")
- *Solicitation of disclosure.* Nonhostile queries that seek information from the other party that can't be observed, like thoughts, feelings, intentions, past history, and motivation. ("What was your goal in raising this issue at this time?")
- *Solicitation of criticism.* Nonhostile questions aimed at soliciting criticism of the self. ("Does it frustrate you that I don't get the sales figures in every Monday?")

Conciliatory verbal messages include:

- *Supportive remarks.* Statements that reflect positive affect, understanding, and acceptance for the partner along with shared interest and goals. ("I appreciate the stress you must be under in your new job.")
- *Concessions.* Comments that signal flexibility, a willingness to change, a conciliatory attitude, and concern for reaching mutually acceptable solutions. ("I would be willing to extend the due date for the project an additional month.")
- *Acceptance of responsibility.* Remarks that attribute responsibility to one or both partners. ("I'll admit that I overreacted at first.")

Implications

- Our attitudes set the moral tone for organizational conversations. Treat others as unique human beings (I-Thou) rather than as objects (I-It).
- Monologue (self-centered communication) and technical dialogue (information-centered speech) have their place, but strive for dialogue (I-Thou interaction) whenever possible.
- To engage in dialogue, you will need to commit yourself to (1) seeking the good of others, (2) valuing relationships and the common good, (3) openness to influence, (4) allowing others to hold differing opinions, (5) honesty, and (6) willingness to invest time and energy in the process.
- Learn to be mindful, giving your full attention to an encounter. Create additional categories, welcome novel information, and be open to new points of view.
- Understand communication as listening, not speaking, centered. Keep in mind that listening is a multistage process made up of hearing, understanding, remembering, interpreting, evaluating, and responding (HURIER). This process can break down at any step along the way. Master listening skills and avoid listening errors by understanding the weaknesses of your listening profile.
- Seek to confirm other communicators by recognizing and acknowledging their presence and value.
- Master the four skill sets of emotional intelligence in order to get along better with others and to make wiser choices. These skills include: (1) accurately identifying emotions; (2) using emotions to enhance reasoning; (3) understanding the causes and progressions of emotions to predict events; (4) managing emotions to generate productive outcomes.
- Employees have a moral obligation to protect others who have put themselves in a vulnerable position. If you violate trust, you will need to accept responsibility for what has occurred and engage in trust repair.
- Try to remain in dialogue during conflict by focusing on the content of messages and viewing the dispute as a problem to be solved. Use collaborative tactics to analyze the problem and to signal a willingness to cooperate.

Application Projects

1. Describe a time when you engaged in dialogue. When did it occur and with whom? What did each party say and do? What was the outcome of your encounter? How did both parties feel when it ended? What did you learn from the experience?

2. As a group, select a film and assign each member to view the movie from a different point of view. Then discuss the film based on each perspective. What insights do you gain from this perspective? What does this project reveal about the value of being open to many different points of view?

3. Based on the HURIER listening model, what are your strengths and weaknesses as a listener? What skills do you need to develop to become more effective?

4. As a small or large group, discuss Buber's assertion that confirmation (recognizing one another's personhood) is the defining characteristic of humankind.
5. Write up your responses from the self-assessment exercise in Box 4.3. Compare your current perspective to your thinking before you completed this exercise. How has your understanding of the past conversation changed? How might you prepare differently for the upcoming encounter?
6. Describe a time when trust was broken and then restored in one of your work relationships. Outline the effects of the breach of trust and how trust was restored.
7. Try to employ collaborative guidelines and skills in an ongoing conflict. Report on the success (or lack of success) of your efforts.

CHAPTER END CASE

Opening Conversational Doors With a Chair

Most of us try to hide our vulnerabilities, at least from strangers. Not so with graphic designer Lindsey Hammond. For 5 weeks, the 28-year-old Portland, Oregon, resident carried around a battered 10-pound folding chair covered with such words as "angry" and "mad." Hammond started carrying her "anger chair" at the advice of her counselor, who didn't think that Lindsey knew just how much anger she still held as a result of childhood trauma. This anger was holding her back. She felt "stuck," unable to fix up her house, to do personal artwork, or to enter into romantic relationships.

Lindsey carried her chair everywhere—to business meetings, on hikes, to the bathroom. While she slept, the chair stood at the end of her bed. At first Hammond was "absolutely terrified" at how others would respond to her companion, but she soon discovered that the chair opened up opportunities for dialogue. An important client shared the story of a lost love. A number of strangers complimented her for her bravery, and some admitted that they had so much anger they would have to cart around a couch instead of just a chair. One man reported that he should be waving a white flag of surrender because he had trouble giving things up. A woman said she should carry a mirror with the word "ego" written all over it. Reflecting on these encounters, Hammond noted:

> Right then I realized through the chair I am connected to humanity. The human race is really pretty neat, and to think about how separate we are is sad. It took carrying around all that anger to let people into my world a little bit. And it happened wherever I went. People opened their hearts.[1]

As the weeks passed, Lindsey's anger diminished and her life improved. She reestablished relationships with people who had hurt her, began work on redecorating her house, and started creating art for fun. However, she decided to hold onto her chair until she was absolutely sure the time was right to put it down for good. That time came when Hammond was speaking to a group of church youth at the invitation of their pastor who had heard of her story. At the end of the presentation, the seventh and eight graders wrote down things that angered them, ripped them up, and put them in a basket on Lindsey's chair. Lindsey decided to leave her chair and walk away from her anger. "I put down my anger," she says. "It's just gone. I carried it everywhere I went, subconsciously, for my whole life, and I carried it consciously for a month and a half everywhere I went, and it took the power away from it."[2]

DISCUSSION PROBES

1. Are you surprised at the response Lindsey got from carrying her chair? What might account for these reactions?
2. Where you do you think Lindsey got the courage to carry the anger chair?
3. Why are we so reluctant to be vulnerable to others?
4. What "chair" do you need to carry to reduce its power over your life?
5. What strategies can we use to open the door to dialogue, to better connect with others at work and in other organizational settings?

NOTES

1. Boule, M. (2005, February 27), p. L3.
2. Boule, M. (2005, February 27), p. L3.

SOURCES

Boule, M. (2005, January 9). She doesn't want to sit in her chair of anger any longer. *Oregonian*, p. L1.

Boule, M. (2005, February 27). Woman's "anger chair" got lighter each day, until it was time to let go. *Oregonian*, pp. L1, L3.

Endnotes

1. Buber, M. (1970). *I and thou.* (R. G. Smith, Trans.). New York: Scribner's; Arnett, R. C., & Arneson, P. (1999). *Dialogic civility in a cynical age: Community, hope, and interpersonal relationships.* Albany: State University of New York Press; Johannesen, R. L. (2002). *Ethics in human communication* (5th ed.). Prospect Heights, IL: Waveland Press, chap. 4; Biemann, A. D. (2002). (Ed.). *The Martin Buber reader: Essential writings.* New York: Palgrave Macmillan; Mayhall, C. W., & Mayhall, T. B. (2004). *On Buber.* Belmont, CA: Wadsworth-Thomson Learning.

2. Arnett, R. C. (1986). *Communication and community: Implications of Martin Buber's dialogue.* Carbondale: Southern Illinois University Press; Czubaroff, J. (2000). Dialogic rhetoric: An application of Martin Buber's philosophy of dialogue. *Quarterly Journal of Speech, 2,* 168–189.

3. Cissna, K. N., & Anderson, R. (1994). Communication and the ground of dialogue. In R. Anderson, K. N. Cissna, & R. C. Arnett (Eds.), *The reach of dialogue: Confirmation, voice, and community* (pp. 9–30). Cresskill, NJ: Hampton Press.

4. Brown, C. T., & Keller, P. W. (1994). Ethics. In R. Anderson, K. N. Cissna, & R. C. Arnett (Eds.), *The reach of dialogue: Confirmation, voice, and community* (pp. 284–290). Cresskill, NJ: Hampton Press.

5. Langer, E. J. (1989). *Mindfulness.* Reading, MA: Addison-Wesley; Langer, E. J. (1997). *The power of mindful learning.* Reading, MA: Addison-Wesley; Trenholm, S., & Jensen, A. (2004). *Interpersonal communication* (5th ed.). New York: Oxford University Press, chap. 7; Langer, E. J., (1989) Minding matters: The consequences of mindlessness-mindfulness. *Advances in Experimental Social Psychology, 22,* 137–173.

6. Brownell, J. (2003, November 22). *The skills of listening-centered communication.* Paper presented at the National Communication Association convention, Miami, FL.; Brownell, J. (2002). *Listening: Attitudes, principles, and skills* (2nd ed.). Boston: Allyn & Bacon.

7. Barker, L., & Watson, K. (2000). *Listen up: How to improve relationships, reduce stress, and be more productive by using the power of listening.* New York: St. Martin's Press.

8. Buber, M. (1965). *The knowledge of man: Selected essays* (M. Friedman, Ed.). New York: Harper & Row, pp. 67–68.

9. Cissna, K. N., & Sieburg, E. (1990). Patterns of interactional confirmation and disconfirmation. In J. Stewart (Ed.), *Bridges not walls: A book about interpersonal communication* (5th ed., pp. 237–246). New York: McGraw-Hill; Laing, R. D. (1994). Confirmation and disconfirmation. In R. Anderson, K. N. Cissna, & R. C. Arnett (Eds.), *The reach of dialogue: Confirmation, voice, and community* (pp. 73–78). Cresskill, NJ: Hampton Press.

10. Ellis, K. (2004). The impact of perceived teacher confirmation on receiver apprehension, motivation, and learning. *Communication Education, 53,* 1–20; Ellis, K. (2000). Perceived teacher confirmation: The development of validation of an instrument and two studies of the relationship to cognitive and affective learning. *Human Communication Research, 26,* 264–291.

11. Caruso, D. R., & Salovey, P. (2004). *The emotionally intelligent manager: How to develop and use the four key emotional skills of leadership.* San Francisco: Jossey-Bass. See also: Mayer, J. D., & Salovey, P. (1993). The intelligence of emotional intelligence. *Intelligence, 17,* 433–442; Mayer, J. D., & Salovey, P. (1995). Emotional intelligence and the construction and regulation of feelings. *Applied and Preventive Psychology, 4,* 197–208; Mayer, J. D., & Salovey, P. (1997). What is emotional intelligence? In P. Salovey & D. J. Sluyter (Eds.), *Emotional development and emotional intelligence: Educational implications* (pp. 3–31). New York: Basic Books; Mayer, J. D., Caruso, D. R., & Salovey, P. (2000). Emotional intelligence meets traditional standards for an intelligence. *Intelligence, 27,* 267–298.

12. Ekman, P. (2003). *Emotions revealed: Recognizing faces and feelings to improve communication and emotional life.* New York: Times Books.

13. Gaudine, A., & Thorne, L. (2001). Emotion and ethical decision-making in organizations. *Journal of Business Ethics, 31,* 175–187.

14. Examples of the effects of trust and its qualities are drawn from the following sources: Brockner, J., Siegel, P. A., Daly, J. P., Tyler, T., & Martin, C. (1997). When trust matters: The moderating effect of outcome favorability. *Administrative Science Quarterly, 42,* 558–583; Dirks, K. T. (1999). The effects of interpersonal trust on work group performance. *Journal of Applied Psychology, 84,* 445–455; Dirks, K. T., & Ferrin, D. L. (2002). Trust in leadership: Meta-analytic findings and implications for research and practice. *Journal of Applied Psychology, 87,* 611–628; Mayer, R. C., & Davis, J. H. (1995). An integrative model of organizational trust. *Academy of Management Review, 29,* 709–734; McAllister, D. J. (1995). Affect- and cognition-based trust as foundations for interpersonal cooperation in organizations. *Academy of Management Journal, 38,* 24–61; Mishra, A. K. (1996). Organizational responses to crisis: The centrality of trust. In R. M. Kramer & T. R. Tyler (Eds.), *Trust in organizations: Frontiers of theory and research* (pp. 261–287). Thousand Oaks, CA: Sage; Shaw, R. B. (1997). *Trust in the balance: Building successful organizations on results, integrity and concern.* San Francisco: Jossey-Bass; Zand, D. E. (1972). Trust and managerial problem solving. *Administrative Science Quarterly, 17,* 229–239.

15. Hosmer, L. T. (1995). Trust: The connecting link between organizational theory and philosophical ethics. *Academy of Management Review, 20,* 279–403. See also: Michalos, A. C. (1995). *A pragmatic approach to business ethics.* Thousand Oaks, CA: Sage, chap. 6.

16. Lewicki, R. J., & Bunker, B. B. (1996). Developing and maintaining trust in work relationships. In R. M. Kramer & T. R. Tyler (Eds.), *Trust in organizations: Frontiers of theory and research* (pp. 114–139). Thousand Oaks, CA: Sage.

17. Enright, R. D., Freedman, S., & Rique, J. (1998). The psychology of interpersonal forgiveness. In R. D. Enright & J. North (Eds.), *Exploring forgiveness* (pp. 46–62). Madision: University of Wisconsin Press; Thoresen, C. E., Harris, H. S., & Luskin, F. (2000). Forgiveness and health: An unanswered question. In M. E. McCullough, K. I. Pargament, & C. E. Thoresen (Eds.), *Forgiveness: Theory, research and practice* (pp. 254–280). New York: Guilford Press.

18. Wilmot, W. W., & Hocker, J. L. (2001). *Interpersonal conflict* (6th ed.). New York: McGraw-Hill, p. 41.

19. Scileppi, P. A. (2005). *Values for interpersonal communication: How then shall we live?* Belmont, CA: Star, chap. 10; Folger, J., Poole, M., & Stutman, R. (1993). *Working through conflict.* New York: HarperCollins; Wilmot & Hocker (2001).

20. Shockley-Zalabak, P. (2003). *Fundamentals of organizational communication: Knowledge, sensitivity, skills, values* (5th ed.). Boston: Allyn & Bacon.

21. Isenhart, M. W., & Spangler, M. (2000). *Collaborative approaches to resolving conflict.* Thousand Oaks, CA: Sage

22. Wilmot & Hocker (2001), p. 164.

5

Exercising Ethical Influence

Chapter Preview

On the job, you can expect to devote much of your time to influencing others. Over the course of a day you may find yourself urging the mailroom to ship your package first, asking a subordinate to complete a project on time, negotiating for the best price with a supplier, convincing a customer to place another order, and persuading your boss to increase the budget for your department. The exercise of influence is not an option in the workplace. We must influence others if we are to fulfill our roles. If we don't, our work groups and organizations (not to mention our careers) will suffer.

While we don't have much choice as to whether or not we exert influence, we do have control over *how* we go about modifying the behaviors of others. These choices will go a long way toward determining the ethical health of our organizations. In this chapter we'll conclude our discussion of transforming interpersonal relationships by addressing ethical questions that arise when influencing others. We'll begin with a look at power and then address moral issues related to impression management, emotional labor, and the communication of expectations.

Questions of Power

The exercise of ethical influence is founded on an understanding of power, the capacity to control the behavior of others. Power is the foundation for influence. The greater the power we have, the more likely that others will comply with our wishes no matter what particular strategy we employ. However, to wield power ethically, we need to answer some important questions.

"But how do you know for sure you've got power unless you abuse it?"

Source: © The New Yorker Collection, 1992, Robert Mankoff from cartoonbank.com.

QUESTION 1: ARE SOME FORMS OF POWER MORE ETHICAL THAN OTHERS?

Power comes from a variety of sources. The most popular power classification system identifies five power bases.[1] *Coercive power* is based on penalties or punishments like verbal warnings, wage cuts, staffing reductions, and student suspensions. *Reward power* depends on being able to deliver something of value to others, whether tangible (bonuses, health insurance, grades) or intangible (praise, recognition, cooperation). *Legitimate power* resides in the position. Supervisors, judges, police officers, and instructors have the right to control our behavior within certain limits. A professor sets the requirements in her course, for example, but has no influence over what we do in our other classes. In contrast to legitimate power, *expert power* is based on the characteristics of the individual regardless of his or her official position. Knowledge, skills, education, and certification all build expert power. As a result, those without positions of authority can be very influential because they possess valued information. *Referent (role model) power* rests on the admiration one individual has for another. We're more likely to do favors for a peer we admire or to agree to work over the weekend for a supervisor we respect.

No form of power is inherently immoral. In fact, we need to draw from a variety of power sources. The manager who is appointed to lead a task force is granted legitimate power that enables her to reward or punish. In order to succeed, she'll also have to demonstrate her knowledge of the topic, skillfully direct the group process, and earn the respect of task force members through hard work and commitment to the group. The effective use of one form of power can increase other power bases.[2] A widely admired employee who demonstrates expertise is more likely to be promoted. Conversely, the boss who has more access to information is better equipped to solve problems and thus will appear more expert. (Complete the Personal Power Profile in Box 5.1 to determine how you prefer to influence others.)

Self-Assessment

Box 5.1 Personal Power Profile

Instructions

Below is a list of statements describing possible behaviors of leaders in work organizations toward their followers. Carefully read each statement, thinking about *how you prefer to influence others*. Mark the number that most closely represents how you feel.

(Continued)

(Continued)

	Strongly Disagree	*Disagree*	*Neither Agree nor Disagree*	*Agree*	*Strongly Agree*
I prefer to influence others by					
1. increasing their pay level	1	2	3	4	5
2. making them feel valued	1	2	3	4	5
3. giving undesirable job assignments	1	2	3	4	5
4. making them feel like I approve of them	1	2	3	4	5
5. making them feel that they have commitments to meet	1	2	3	4	5
6. making them feel personally accepted	1	2	3	4	5
7. making them feel important	1	2	3	4	5
8. giving them good technical suggestions	1	2	3	4	5
9. making the work difficult for them	1	2	3	4	5
10. sharing my experience and/or training	1	2	3	4	5
11. making things unpleasant here	1	2	3	4	5
12. making work distasteful	1	2	3	4	5
13. helping them get a pay increase	1	2	3	4	5
14. making them feel they should satisfy job requirements	1	2	3	4	5
15. providing them with sound job-related advice	1	2	3	4	5
16. providing them with special benefits	1	2	3	4	5
17. helping them get a promotion	1	2	3	4	5
18. giving them the feeling that they have responsibilities to fulfill	1	2	3	4	5
19. providing them with needed technical knowledge	1	2	3	4	5
20. making them recognize that they have tasks to accomplish	1	2	3	4	5

Scoring

Record your responses to the 20 questions in the corresponding numbered blanks below. Total each column, then divide the result by 4 for each of the five types of influence.

	Reward	Coercive	Legitimate	Referent	Expert
	1 _____	3 _____	5 _____	2 _____	8 _____
	13 _____	9 _____	14 _____	4 _____	10 _____
	16 _____	11 _____	18 _____	6 _____	15 _____
	17 _____	12 _____	20 _____	7 _____	19 _____
Total	_____	_____	_____	_____	_____
Divide by 4	_____	_____	_____	_____	_____

Interpretation

A score of 4 or 5 on any of the five dimensions of power indicates that you prefer to influence others by using that particular form of power. A score of 2 or less indicates that you prefer not to employ this particular type of power to influence others. Your power profile is not a simple addition of each of the five sources. Some combinations are more synergistic than the simple sum of their parts. For example, referent power magnifies the impact of other power sources because these other influence attempts are coming from a "respected" person. Reward power often increases the impact of referent power, because people generally tend to like those who can give them things. Some power combinations tend to produce the opposite of synergistic effects. Coercive power, for example, often negates the effects of other types of influence.

Source: Modified version of Hinken, T. R., & Schreisheim, C. A. (1989). Development and application of new scales to measure the French and Raven (1959) Bases of Social Power. *Journal of Applied Psychology, 74,* 561-567. Reprinted with permission.

Ultimately, the morality of a particular power source depends on the ends or goals that it serves. We need to ask if our exercise of power serves worthy objectives. However, arguing that no form of power is unethical in and of itself should not obscure the fact that some types of power are more likely to be abused. Power linked to organizational position (coercive, reward, and legitimate) is more dangerous than that linked to the person (expert, referent). Positional power gets immediate results, securing compliance and boosting short-term performance. But at a high cost. The use of legitimate, reward, and coercive power reduces trust and lowers task satisfaction and performance over the long term.[3] Of the three forms of positional power, coercive tactics pose the greatest risk. Extreme coercion can be devastating to individuals, attacking their dignity and value while threatening their mental and physical health.

QUESTION 2: IS IT POSSIBLE TO HAVE TOO MUCH POWER?

Concentration of power produces a wide range of unethical behavior, as Britain's Lord Acton noted in the 1800s. "Power corrupts," asserted Acton, "and absolute power corrupts absolutely." Lord Acton could have been commenting on the organizational scandals of our day. In case after case, powerful individuals abused their positions and put their organizations at risk. Enron CEOs Kenneth Lay and Jeffrey Skilling intimidated employees, making it harder for them to object to the unethical schemes that drove the company into bankruptcy.[4] John Rigas of the Adelphia Cable Company stole from his firm and gave the money to family members.[5]

Positional power is most susceptible to abuse. Lord Acton probably had this type of control in mind when he noted power's corrosive effects. The world's most infamous leaders—Nero, Stalin, Hitler, Pol Pot, Milosovic, Idi Amin—used their lofty positions to darken the lives of followers through purges, torture, murder, and other means. However, many of these same leaders also misused their personal power. Followers believed that they were endowed with special gifts and looked to them as role models. (In Chapter 9 we'll examine the relationship between leadership and power in more depth.)

There are a number of possible explanations for why unfettered power is so susceptible to misuse. The first ties in with our discussion of the shadow side of the personality in Chapter 2. Powerful individuals who fail to master their inner monsters are free to project their inner darkness on others. Without checks and balances, they cast deeper and deeper shadows on larger and larger audiences. Second, powerful people are more susceptible to judgment biases.[6] They typically devote little attention to finding out how others think and feel. As a consequence, they are more likely to hold and act on harmful stereotypes, which justify their lofty positions. In addition, they believe they deserve their high status because those who are powerless aren't as capable as they are. Third, powerful people protect their positions by attacking those they perceive as threats. Fourth, those in power often ignore the needs of others. They see subordinates as a means to achieving their ends. (Turn to the Chapter End Case for an example of someone who frequently ran roughshod over his followers.) Fifth, powerful individuals are tempted to rely upon positional power. Rather than building personal power bases, they employ coercion. Power holders are more likely to order subordinates to complete a task when a softer tactic (making a request, offering a reason) would achieve the same result at less emotional and relational cost.[7]

Having too little power also poses ethical dilemmas.[8] Powerless members can't achieve worthy objectives and feel like they have no control over their environments. They focus on maintaining the little power they have instead of achieving collective goals. Along with taking out their frustrations on other employees, they harm the organization through work slowdowns, breaking equipment, calling in sick, and other aggressive behaviors.

QUESTION 3: HOW DO I USE POWER WISELY?

Ethical power use begins with proper motivation. You need to ask yourself why you want to influence others, making sure your objectives are ethically justified. Recognize that your positional power is entrusted to you; you act on behalf of the group. If you seek to serve others, you'll be much less likely to take advantage of your position of authority.[9]

Next, select power bases carefully. Positional power should be used with caution. Reduce your reliance on authority, reward, and coercion by developing your skills and knowledge while modeling the behaviors you want to see in others. Coercion should only be employed as a last resort. It is best used for preventing and punishing incivility, dishonesty, aggression, discrimination, criminal activities, sexual harassment, and other destructive behaviors described in Chapter 8.

Third, be open to influence. Influence needs to be reciprocal, with leaders exerting power but, at the same time, responding to the influence attempts of followers. Enact formal mechanisms like appeals procedures, subordinate feedback, recalls, and elections to encourage yourself to be responsive to your less powerful colleagues.[10]

Finally, give power away. Paradoxically, you gain more power by distributing it to others.[11] People like their jobs more and work harder when they feel like they have a significant voice in shaping decisions. They're more likely to cooperate as well. Performance and perceptions of your power increase as a result. Empowerment also fosters the personal growth of followers. Sharing power can help them learn new skills, tackle new challenges, and find greater fulfillment.

QUESTION 4: WHAT FACTORS CONTRIBUTE TO EMPOWERMENT?

Psychological empowerment refers to increased motivation to carry out tasks associated with work roles. According to organizational scholars Kenneth Thomas and Betty Velthouse, this heightened motivation is the product of four factors:[12]

Meaning

Meaning is the value placed on a task, goal, or purpose based on personal standards. The better the fit between the purpose of the task and our standards, the greater our motivation to do the job.

Competence

Competence is the belief that we can do the job required. It is part of a broader sense of personal power or self-efficacy. Self-efficacy is the conviction that we can deal with the events, people, and situations at work and in other environments.[13]

Self-Determination

Self-determination is the sense that we have a choice in how we carry out our jobs—when to start, how fast to work, how to prioritize tasks.

Impact

Impact is the extent to which we can influence the larger organizational environment. Those with a high sense of impact believe that they make a difference in the work group's operating procedures, plans, and goals.

All four of the cognitive components of empowerment are shaped by elements of the work group environment. As a consequence, we can boost perceptions of empowerment as managers by modifying the setting where work occurs, including reward systems, job duties, organizational structure and workflow, rules, and physical layout. Elimination of situational factors that create feelings of powerlessness is an excellent place to start. Get rid of petty regulations, authoritarian supervision, and strict routines. Next, shift more decision-making authority to followers. Allow those assigned to do the task a great deal of leeway in how the task gets done. Invite employees into organizational decision-making processes. At the same time, supply resources. Completing a task depends on having adequate funds and supplies, sufficient time to devote to the job, and a place to work. Political support is essential for major projects. The introduction of new products, accounting systems, and software programs requires the endorsement of important individuals who also encourage other leaders to buy-in to initiatives.[14]

Information may be the most important resource for empowerment. Data about the competition, consumers, and strategy help members see the "big picture." They gain a better understanding of their roles in the organization and how their efforts help achieve collective goals. Access to information builds self-efficacy and enables individuals to make better decisions while exerting influence over the direction of their work units. Newly empowered followers, in particular, need information in order to carry out more demanding assignments. At one pet supply manufacturer, managers gave employee teams the power to shut down the production line and set production schedules. To prepare workers for this added responsibility, they provided employees with production schedules and information on customer requirements. The company developed a set of criteria for shut downs, gave teams training on how to diagnose line malfunctions, and told them how much it cost to shut down and restart production. Workers discussed case studies involving line-shutdown decisions. They then exercised their new powers for 3 months with review by managers. At the end of that period they controlled the production process entirely on their own.[15]

QUESTION 5: HOW DO I OVERCOME BARRIERS TO EMPOWERMENT?

Empowerment efforts face significant obstacles. Keeping, not sharing, authority is rewarded in traditional top-down organizations. Managers in these systems are afraid to let go of their power for fear of failure. Adopting any new approach is risky, particularly when it comes to empowerment. Managers lose control and have to rely on the efforts of team members. They may be punished if their subordinates fail to produce. Success in a more equalitarian system also requires a different skill set. Empowering managers must provide resources instead of direction, share information, and facilitate the group process. Newly empowered followers are anxious too. They're used to having one person make the final decision and must take on greater responsibilities. Some are not eager to learn new skills and are afraid of making mistakes.

Management professor and consultant Alan Randolph admits that empowerment is hard to put into practice but notes it has been successfully implemented at such companies as the Marriott Corporation, General Electric, AES, Springfield Remanufacturing, and Pacific Gas and Electric. Companies who want to take "the long journey to empowerment" must pass through three stages.[16]

Stage 1: Starting and Orienting the Process of Change

Any major empowerment initiative must begin, not with a grand vision, but with practical answers to personal concerns. People want to know why the change is needed and what's wrong with the ways things operate now. Further, they want to understand how the change will impact them and how they stand to gain (or lose). Providing information—financial statements and projections, data on market changes—motivates members to do a better job. At the same time, managers need to set boundaries so members don't feel overwhelmed. Boundaries can be set through setting goals and by providing training that equips employees to reach those objectives. Most successful empowerment efforts replace hierarchy with self-directed work teams.

Stage 2: Making Changes and Dealing With Discouragement

In this stage the focus shifts to concerns about implementation and impact. Workers wonder what they need to do to be empowered, where to go for help, and why the process is so difficult. They also question whether the effort is worth it and doubt that any progress is being made. Once again, members desire data, this time about how to proceed. They need to know where to get help, what to do if things go wrong, and whether the initiative is producing results. Instead of backing off empowerment efforts, leaders need to expand boundaries further. Work teams ought to be given even more responsibility for work flow, not less. The good news is that once results begin to appear, members will promote the advantages of empowerment to their colleagues. One key during this step is changing performance appraisal systems to reward collaboration instead of individual efforts.

Stage 3: Adopting and Refining Empowerment to Fit the Organization

At this stage a culture of empowerment emerges. Concerns turn to collaboration and refinement. Individuals in this final step want help getting everyone involved in the process because they know empowerment works. They also want to learn how to perform even better. Managers and teams share data with each other about how to make improvements. Employees internalize commitment to the values and goals of the organization.

Organizational empowerment has its share of critics.[17] Some complain that empowerment is just a management fad and that far too many organizations give it lip service only, resisting any meaningful change efforts. Employees then become disillusioned and resentful as trust breaks down. Others complain that managers and employees understand the term *empowerment* differently. Empowered employees may expect to be treated equally, while managers view empowerment as a means for better getting the work done. The most cynical observers believe that empowerment is a form of exploitation. In participative systems, workers contribute more ideas and energy but don't get rewarded for their additional efforts.

These criticisms are valid. Empowerment can be faddish and exploitive. Yet it doesn't have to be. Truly empowering organizations back up their talk with their walk, following through on their commitment to change. These groups recognize that genuine empowerment benefits both workers and management. They boost compensation for those who accept more responsibility.

Ethical Issues in Influence

Selecting the appropriate tactic is one of the most important choices we make when exerting influence. Ethical considerations should always play a central role in this determination. In the remainder of this chapter we'll look at the ethical issues raised by three widely used organizational influence strategies: impression management, emotional labor, and the communication of expectations.

IMPRESSION MANAGEMENT

In the organizational setting, you'll have little chance of getting what you want unless you create the desired image. Want a raise? Then you must convince your supervisor that you are hard working and productive. Want to be assigned to be a project leader? Then you must be seen as competent and able to manage others. Want to make a sale? Then customers must perceive that you are honest and trustworthy. Want more staff for your work group? Then you'll have to convince the management team that your group is critical to the organization's success.

Scholars use the term *impression management* to describe how people try to control the images others have of them through their behaviors.[18] Impression management is a part of all human interaction, but it is particularly evident in the organizational setting. In a very real sense, organizations act as stages. On the organizational stage, members perform a variety of roles for different audiences. Consider the average professor, for example. Faculty members are typically evaluated on their teaching, scholarship (research), and service. To succeed, our instructor will have to perform well in the classroom, write for scholarly publications and present papers to academic peers, and take leadership at the university and in the local community. Each of these audiences requires a different performance. The highly technical jargon of the academic journal or presentation won't work well, for instance, with community audiences. The ability to accurately evaluate student work is essential to a successful teaching performance but has little relevance to research and service.

There are a variety of ways to manage the image that others have of us in the organizational setting, ranging from what we say and wear to the layout of our dorm rooms and offices. These tactics can be divided into two major categories: *acquisitive impression management* and *protective impression management.* [19] Acquisitive tactics are attempts to be seen in a positive light; protective tactics are attempts to avoid looking bad. Both sets of tactics, in turn, can be directly or indirectly applied. Parties use direct tactics during interactions, while indirect tactics involve the process of association. If Dan wants to convince Mary that he deserves a raise, he might point out how hard he works. Or he might take a more indirect approach, counting on her to remember that he was part of the team that launched the company's hottest new product. A catalog of organizational impression management tactics is found in Box 5.2.

Box 5.2 Impression Management Tactics

Acquisitive/Direct Tactics

1. *Ingratiation*

   Goal: To appear more likeable and attractive.
   Examples: expressing similar attitudes, doing favors, flattering, complimenting, publicizing one's desirable qualities

2. *Self-Promotion*

   Goal: To appear competent.
   Examples: claiming relevant work experience on a resume, mentioning a high grade point average in a job interview

3. *Intimidation*

   Goal: To gain social power and influence by appearing dangerous.
   Examples: using coercive power to ensure follower compliance, using counterpower (law suits, a tough image) to intimidate superiors

4. *Exemplification*

   Goal: To generate impressions of integrity and morality.
   Examples: publicizing self-sacrifice (working over the weekend or while sick), going beyond the call of duty

5. *Supplication*

   Goal: To secure help by appearing incompetent.
   Examples: asking for help with a new computer program, claiming poor speaking skills to get someone else to make the class presentation

Acquisitive/Indirect Tactics

1. *Acclaiming*

   Goal: To highlight a relationship or association with a successful occurrence.
   Examples: claiming to be responsible for success (softball team victory, higher sales), maximizing the value of a positive event (noting that not only did you graduate from college, but that you graduated from one of the country's top rated universities)

2. *Nonverbal Impression Management*

   Goal: To encourage liking through nonverbal behaviors.
   Examples: smiling and leaning forward during a job interview, renting expensive office furniture to create an image of financial stability

Protective/Direct Tactics

1. *Accounts*

   Goal: To lessen or repair the damage after a failure has occurred.
   Examples: making excuses—admitting that an action is wrong but denying responsibility for it ("it wasn't my fault"), offering justifications—accepting responsibility but claiming that the event wasn't as bad as it seemed or that the behavior was justified

2. *Disclaimers*

   Goal: To lessen the potential damage that might be caused by an upcoming failure event.
   Examples: claiming credentials to make racist comments ("some of my best friends are . . ."), claiming an exception to the rules, asking for a suspension of judgment

3. *Self-Handicapping*

   Goal: To put self-imposed barriers in place when outcomes are uncertain, in order to maximize the value of success and to minimize the penalties for failure.
   Examples: claiming to be coming back from an injury prior to a racquetball game with a coworker, mentioning an illness that prevented you from doing as much research as you wanted

4. *Apologies*

   Goal: To obtain pardon by admitting responsibility and blame.
   Examples: expressions of remorse, offers of restitution, requests for forgiveness

Protective/Indirect Tactics

1. *Blaring*

   Goal: To dissassociate from a negative event or person.
   Examples: publicizing a lack of connection with the occurrence or individual ("I had nothing to do with that project"; "I was always suspicious of him.")

2. *Blasting*

   Goal: To exaggerate the bad qualities of a person to whom we are connected but don't want to be.
   Examples: pointing out the poor work habits of another team member, claiming that a supervisor is abusive

---

Source: Rosenfeld, P., Giacalone, R. A., & Riordan, C. A. (1995). *Impression management in organizations: Theory, measurement, practice.* London: Routledge. Reprinted with permission.

Some observers equate impression management with manipulation. To them, impression managers are phonies who try to deceive others by projecting a false image when they should strive to reflect their "true" selves instead. They note that competent performers get passed over in favor of employees who ingratiate themselves with the boss.

It is easy to see why impression management would be viewed with suspicion. We probably have all encountered individuals who are "all style and no substance." These coworkers are all too ready to change their behaviors and standards to conform to the wishes of others. They get ahead by playing politics instead of through hard work. Our academic and work careers may have languished because professors and supervisors played favorites.

Research confirms that we are right to be concerned about the ethics of impression management. Skilled impression managers are more likely to be hired and promoted regardless of ability. This puts women, who are more likely to rely on their performance to get ahead, at a disadvantage. Careerists who care little about coworkers and organizational goals use self-promotion to advance themselves at the expense of others.[20] Deceit can quickly turn impression management into manipulation, as in the case of job applicants who overstate their skills and background (see the Case Study in Box 5.3). One study reported that 95 percent of college students were willing to make at least one false statement in order to get a job. More than 40 percent of the respondents in the same study had already done so. This happens despite the fact that falsifying credentials and past accomplishments can serve as grounds for dismissal. Padded resumes cost George O'Leary the opportunity to coach at Notre Dame and Kenneth Lonchar his job as Veritas Software's Chief Financial Officer.[21]

CASE STUDY

Box 5.3 To Pad or Not to Pad*

When Johann Schultz decided to earn a computer science degree several years ago, the market for computer savvy graduates was red hot. Promising students from well-established programs were often hired before they could finish their coursework. Market demand drove salaries well above the norm for college graduates. Unfortunately, the high tech bubble burst before Johann (who is a part-time student) could finish his program. Jobs in everything from Web design and programming to software engineering and development dried up. Now employers have their pick of applicants to choose from. Johann knows that he will have to stand out in order to be noticed.

Recently a local consulting firm announced it would open a division to provide computer security advice and systems to large corporations. Some of the positions in the division will require extensive work experience but others will be open to college graduates. In addition to a degree in computer science, requirements for the entry-level openings include oral and written communication skills, a working knowledge of the SpyEye X security program, a 3.5 grade point average, and the ability to lead project teams.

Meeting the communication criteria is no problem for Schultz, who always found writing papers and making presentations easier than taking tests. Fulfilling the other requirements will be more of a problem, however. Johann is familiar with the other leading security programs but not SpyEye X. He knows someone who works with the program, though, and could practice with it before being interviewed and hired. His cumulative GPA is 3.3, not 3.5. Further, while he was a member of several successful project groups in school, Johann's work schedule prevented him from taking a leadership role in any of these teams.

Johann believes that some of the criteria (like the GPA) were arbitrarily selected to weed out applicants and aren't a true reflection of ability. He is convinced that, if he can land this job, he can succeed and help this employer.

DISCUSSION PROBES

1. Should Johann alter any details on his resume in order to land this job? Why or why not? If you answered yes, which information should he change?
2. Are slight exaggerations more justified than outright lies on resumes?
3. Why is lying on resumes and in job interviews so widespread?
4. What are the potential long-term consequences to an applicant for lying or withholding part of the truth on a resume to the applicant? To the employer?
5. What responsibility do organizations have to check up on the claims that applicants make on their resumes? What actions should they take when they discover deceit?

NOTE

*Not based on actual people or events.

Recognition that impression management is prone to abuse does not mean we should abandon this form of influence. In fact, it would be impossible to do so. Impression management is found in every culture. Whatever the particular setting, humans want to achieve their goals and to be seen in a favorable light. Impression management is also hard to eliminate because it can occur at the unconscious or semiconscious level. For example, you may not have given much thought to why you brushed your teeth this morning or chose a particular shirt or top to wear. Yet both of these activities help shape the impressions you make on others throughout the rest of the day.

Other organizational members are forming impressions of us, whether we are intentional about our behaviors or not. Even our attempts to avoid impression management tactics influence the impressions of others. Take the example of the job applicant who thinks that dressing up for an interview is "fake." His sloppy appearance manages the impressions of the employer, only in a negative manner. The interviewer may think that the applicant doesn't understand what the business world is like, that he didn't care enough about this job to make an effort to look good, or that his work habits may match his appearance.

Impression management serves many useful purposes. More often than not, individuals use IM to project an image that is congruent with who they think they are. Rather than deceiving or manipulating others, they want to accurately reflect their identities. Impression management is also essential to accomplishing moral objectives. Convincing management that a department legitimately needs more resources benefits both the work unit and the total organization. Department members will feel fairly treated and produce more. Organizational performance will likely increase because budget and personnel will be strategically allocated.

Organizational impression management experts Paul Rosenfeld, Robert Giacalone, and Catherine Riordan offer the following standards for determining if impression management is beneficial or detrimental to an organization.[22] Beneficial impression management (1) facilitates positive interpersonal relationships both inside and outside the organization; (2) accurately portrays positive people, products, and events to insiders and outsiders; (3) facilitates effective decisions. Dysfunctional impression management (1) inhibits or obstructs internal and external relationships; (2) inaccurately casts persons, events, and products in a bad light; (3) distorts information, which leads to erroneous conclusions and decisions.

These standards place ethical demands on impression managers as well as on their audiences. We have a responsibility to generate accurate images. In particular, we need to resist the temptation to exaggerate, for example, by claiming more than our fair share of the credit for a class group project or overstating how much we like the bosses' ideas. Self-interest should always take a back seat to the interests of others, which means that impression management ought to be a tool for carrying out our roles in a way that benefits both the organization and its constituencies. One way to ensure that our performances are honest and effective is through pursuing our vocations (see Chapter 2). Finding the right job fit will put us in roles that we are passionate about and are well suited to fill.

Targets of impression management tactics have an ethical responsibility to ensure that agents aren't unduly or unfairly shaping decisions and outcomes.

Job interviewers and human resource personnel need to use objective criteria in hiring decisions. Managers need to be aware that they are susceptible to ingratiation and beware of playing favorites. They too need to base personnel decisions on objective criteria, knowing that women in particular may not trumpet their accomplishments as much as men. Careerists should be confronted. Their success should be tied to how well they cooperate in a group, not on how well they promote themselves.

EMOTIONAL LABOR

Emotional labor is a special form of impression management that is increasingly common in the modern service economy.[23] In emotional labor, frontline workers (baristas, sales clerks, servers, counter staff, receptionists, retail clerks) manage their feelings so that they can present the desired bodily and facial displays to the public. Their ability to portray friendliness and to give personal attention is often just as important to consumers as the price and quality of the product or service itself. Profits depend on how well company representatives manage both their emotions and behaviors when dealing with customers. Service personnel may have to hold back their anger at obnoxious clients, project enthusiasm to everyone entering the store, or answer the same question with a "smile in their voices" time after time after time. Emotional labor is different from other forms of impression management because (a) control of feelings is done for pay; (b) emotional laborers interact with outsiders, not with other organizational members; and (c) this form of influence raises its own special set of ethical issues.

Sociologist Arlene Hochschild, who coined the term *emotional labor,* studied the emotional performances of Delta flight attendants who had to project a warm, helpful persona to passengers, even rude ones. Subsequent researchers examined the emotional labor of frontline service workers in a wide variety of settings, including, for example, convenience stores, fast food restaurants, a cruise ship, Disneyland, door-to-door insurance sales, and a 911 call center.[24] Investigators discovered that emotions can be managed for neutral or negative displays as well as for "nice" ones. For example, psychiatric workers try to remain calm in the face of abuse, and police officers and bill collectors express irritation and anger to intimidate suspects and to collect delinquent accounts.[25]

Organizations go to great lengths to control the emotional behavior of their frontline workers. Managers ("emotional supervisors") may only hire individuals deemed to have "friendly, outgoing" personalities. Once hired, new employees go through orientation and training sessions that introduce them to the corporation's guidelines and formulas for customer service. Emotional routines or scripts tell workers both what to say and how to act. They are given lines like "Welcome to Blockbuster!" "How are you today?" and "Have a great day!" These lines are packaged with uniforms (smocks, aprons, name tags, blazers), smiles, eye contact, attentive posture, and vocal enthusiasm.

All these programmed emotional displays can be costly to employees. (To reflect upon your experiences as an emotional laborer, turn to Application Project 4 on page 137.) Emotions, traditionally considered the worker's private concern, are now "owned" by the organization.[26] As service providers, we feel the tension between wanting to maintain our ideal or authentic selves and following organizational rules. Being forced to display emotions that aren't felt (or that contradict feelings) can produce dissonance. This dissonance may lead to stress, cynicism, burnout, low self-esteem, illness, job turnover, and difficulties in work relationships. Intrusive emotional scripts threaten the dignity of the individual and can reinforce gender stereotypes. Women programmed to be flirtatious, outgoing, and friendly (such as waitresses at Hooters restaurants) run a higher risk of becoming the targets of sexual harassment.

Emotional labor can also take a toll on us as customers.[27] Consider the tensions inherent in the pleasant service encounter, for instance. All displays of positive emotion in this setting, no matter how authentic they appear, are suspect because they are designed to sell products and services. These emotional routines are logically and ethically inconsistent because they attempt to standardize "personal" service.

Service recipients offered pleasant performances must determine how to react. Most of us play along, acting the role of the "good customer," even when we're in a foul mood. A few consumers resist. When dining out, for instance, they complain to management when the wait staff is too attentive and friendly. They may use put-down lines like "What's the worst thing on the menu?" or "Hi, my name's Dave, and I'll be your customer tonight."[28] Those who play along run the risk of lying about how they really feel (unhappy, tense, angry). Those who resist may maintain their integrity but little else. They come across as mean-spirited and have little impact on organizational policy. Instead, resisters make the job of the emotional laborer (generally underpaid and overworked) all the harder.

Not everyone is convinced that emotional labor is harmful.[29] Some researchers defend these performances. They point out that service providers aren't robots. Frontline employees sometimes fight the organization's attempts to control their feelings and can adjust their performances when needed. Convenience store clerks are friendlier during slow periods, for instance. When lines develop, they adopt a more efficient manner. Emotional labor can also be enjoyable. One group of 911 dispatchers reported that emotional work was the highlight of their jobs, providing comic relief and excitement. Further, there is some evidence that acting cheerful, even when we are not feeling particularly cheerful, reduces levels of stress hormones and increases resistance to disease.

Neither side of the emotional labor debate—critics or defenders—seems to adequately address the ethical questions raised by this form of impression management. On the one hand, there is evidence that emotional labor can generate dissonance, become intrusive, reinforce stereotypes, and put customers in a moral bind. Such encounters may seem routine, but need to be treated as potential moral dilemmas. On the other hand, emotional labor can be a boon to some employees, helping them to reach their goals and to have fun. Those who embrace their roles experience little dissonance and often find their moods shifting to fit their performances. For their part, customers generally prefer pleasant service personnel and want their shopping experiences to be fast and efficient.

The most ethical approach to the dilemma of emotional labor lies between outright rejection and unthinking acceptance. *Bounded emotionality* is one attempt to identify this middle ground.[30] Bounded emotionality is a feminist approach to organizational behavior that emphasizes caring and connection. In this model, organizations accomplish tasks and put a high value on emotion. Members are encouraged to express a wide range of emotions but to constrain their feelings so that they don't damage interpersonal relationships. Managers exert less control over the expression of feelings, allowing employees to express empathy for clients, frustration about the demands of the job, and so on. Service personnel try to avoid the dissonance that comes from expressing inauthentic emotions while they build an organizational community.

The Body Shop is one large organization that tries to operate under the principles of bounded emotionality. Employees routinely talk about their fears, sadness, joy, and other emotional topics. Managers are evaluated on their emotional competency, including how well they encourage the expression of emotions among their subordinates.[31]

Taking a bounded emotionality approach to emotional labor would mean less reliance on scripts and more opportunity for us as service providers to express our feelings and to develop our own performance styles. As customers we would respect the autonomy of agents to express a variety of emotions. We might encourage supervisors and organizations to give their workers more freedom of expression. We could strive for personal consistency and authenticity in the consumer role by responding tactfully but honestly to emotional displays. For instance: "I'm not doing too well today, but thanks for asking"; "I appreciate your friendliness, but it is a little overwhelming this early in the morning."

COMMUNICATION OF EXPECTATIONS

The communication of expectations is a powerful organizational influence tool. That's because we have a tendency to live up to the expectancies others place on us. Researchers refer to this phenomenon as self-fulfilling prophecy, or the Pygmalion Effect after the prince of Greek mythology. Prince Pygmalion created a statue of a beautiful woman whom he named Galatea. After the figure was complete, he fell in love with his creation. The goddess Venus took pity on the dejected prince and brought Galatea to life.

Evidence of the Pygmalion Effect has been discovered in a variety of organizational settings. For example:[32]

- Nursing home residents are less depressed and less likely to be admitted to hospitals when staff believe that these clients will respond more favorably to rehabilitation.
- Industrial trainees designated as "high aptitude personnel" learn more quickly and are less likely to drop out.
- Patients in medical experiments improve when they receive placebos because they believe they will get better.
- The high expectations of teachers lead to higher student test and IQ scores.
- Military personnel labeled as having high potential perform up to the expectations of their superiors. Those told that they can succeed are more likely to volunteer for dangerous special duty.

The Pygmalion Effect has more effect on some individuals than others. Disadvantaged groups (those stereotyped as low achievers) tend to benefit most from positive expectations, as do those who lack a clear sense of their abilities or find themselves in a novel situation. Men seem to be more influenced by the expectancies of their managers than are women.[33] Negative expectations also have an impact on performance. This is sometimes referred to as the Golem Effect (*golem* means dumbbell in Yiddish). Unless counteracted, these reduced expectancies lower performance.[34]

Verbal persuasion is the straightforward way to communicate expectations. For example: offering compliments, assuring others that they have the necessary ability, and stating you expect great things from them. However, self-fulfilling prophecies are most often communicated indirectly through these four channels:[35]

1. Climate

Climate describes the social and emotional atmosphere individuals create for others. Communicators act in a friendly, supportive, accepting, and encouraging manner with people they like. This is done through using nonverbal behaviors that portray respect and warmth while avoiding behaviors that communicate disrespect, coolness, and superiority. Supervisors, for example, signal positive expectations by giving adequate time to employees, holding appointments in pleasant surroundings, sitting or standing close to workers, nodding and smiling, making frequent eye contact, and using a warm tone of voice.

2. Input

Positive expectations are also communicated through the number and type of assignments and projects given workers. High expectations create a positive performance spiral. As employees receive and successfully complete more tasks, they gain self-confidence and the confidence of superiors. These outstanding performers are then given further duties, which they are more likely to complete as well.

3. Output

Those tagged as high performers are given more opportunities to speak, to offer their opinions, and to disagree. Superiors pay more attention to these employees when they speak and offer more assistance to them when they're problem solving. In the classroom, teachers call on "high achievers" more than "low achievers," wait less time for low achievers to answer questions, and provide fewer clues and follow-up questions to low achievers.[36]

4. Feedback

Supervisors give more frequent positive feedback when they have high expectations of employees, both praising them more often for success and criticizing them less often for failure. In addition, managers provide more detailed performance feedback to high expectation employees. Just the opposite occurs with those labeled as poor performers. Supervisors praise their minimal performance more, reinforcing the impression that they expect less from these employees.

Pygmalion investigators wrestle with the ethical implications of this influence strategy, beginning with the use of deception. Experimenters typically deceive leaders by informing them that groups differ in abilities even though they have been randomly assigned. Such tactics could be used in the organizational setting by telling managers that selected subordinates have more potential when, in reality, there are no data to support that assertion. Some researchers argue that this deceit would be justified because the organization would benefit from the superior performance of those described as high performers. However, to carry off this deception, managers would have to be misled by their supervisors or staff personnel, undermining trust. Deliberately privileging one group of people is unjust and might result in lawsuits.

Even when deception isn't involved, the separation of groups into different ability groupings is problematical. Organizations routinely label some individuals as exceptional employees according to some set of criteria. These members are then given extra training, assigned to mentors, placed into more challenging assignments, and so on. These measures generate the Pygmalion

Effect for the chosen few and the Golem Effect for everyone else. Those labeled as average or low performers receive fewer benefits and may live down to reduced expectations.

Communicating high expectations to everyone in the organization is an ethical alternative to deception and ability grouping.[37] Such an approach not only maintains integrity, it encourages everyone to function at his or her best. Strategies for improving organizationwide performance include (a) building follower self-efficacy (a sense of personal power) through breaking down tasks into manageable segments, role modeling, and verbal persuasion; (b) encouraging a learning orientation that emphasizes improvement over perfection; (c) creating a friendly atmosphere; (d) raising consciousness of the impact of negative expectations; (e) creating opportunities for employees to start anew in different departments and assignments; (f) fostering a culture that demands high productivity.

Even if our organization doesn't adopt a high expectations orientation, we can do so as individuals. The power of self-fulfilling prophecy places a moral burden upon us. If others are to reach their full potential, we need to communicate positive expectations to them, not negative ones. We should carefully monitor our behavior to reduce inequities in how we treat others, particularly in subtle ways. The strategies for communicating high expectations outlined above can be employed in our peer relationships and organizational units. Also, we can use the Galatea Effect to insulate ourselves from the negative expectations of our leaders. The Galatea Effect (named after the statue in the Greek myth) refers to expectations of the self. High self-expectancies can keep us from lowering our standards when others expect little. We can encourage others to raise their expectations of us by meeting and exceeding standards.

Implications

- While the exercise of influence is not an option in the workplace, you do have control over how you go about modifying the behaviors of others.
- Understand that no form of power is inherently immoral, but positional power (legitimate, coercive, reward) is more likely to be abused than person-centered power (expert, referent).
- Use a variety of power sources when pursuing worthy objectives.
- Recognize that concentration of positional power (in yourself or others) is dangerous, producing a wide range of unethical behavior.
- Use power wisely. Seek to serve others, use positional power with caution, be open to influence, and empower others.
- Increase the motivation of others to carry out tasks by modifying the work setting and supplying adequate resources.
- Overcome barriers to empowerment by managing the journey though the three stages of the empowerment process: (1) starting and orienting the process of

change, (2) making changes and dealing with discouragement, (3) adopting and refining empowerment to fit the organization.

- You'll have little chance of getting what you want unless you project the desired image. However, you have a moral responsibility to ensure that you use impression management tactics to build positive relationships, to accurately portray your personal image and that of your organization, and to facilitate effective decisions. You also have a duty to ensure that others don't manipulate you through their use of impression management strategies.
- Emotional labor, the management of feelings by frontline workers that leads to facial and bodily displays, can pose significant dilemmas for employees and customers. These dilemmas can be solved in part by allowing workers to express a wide range of emotions while constraining feelings that might damage interpersonal relationships.
- Communication of expectations can be one of your most powerful influence tools. Your individual moral responsibility is to encourage those around you to live up to their full potential. Generate positive self-fulfilling prophecies (the Pygmalion Effect) through creating a warm emotional climate, providing valuable assignments, giving opportunities for others to express their opinions, and offering frequent positive feedback.

Application Projects

1. Analyze a leader's use of power. Determine if this leader acted ethically or unethically. Explain why. Write up your findings.

2. Debate the following propositions:

   Empowerment takes advantage of workers.

   Empowerment should not be practiced in some organizations.

   Impression management is unethical.

   The costs of emotional labor are overstated.

   Communicating positive expectations to everyone in a work group is impossible.

   Communicating high expectations to people you don't like is unethical.

3. Create a case study based on an organization's attempts to empower its employees. What went right? What went wrong? What conclusions can you draw from this organization's experience?

4. In a small group, discuss your experiences as emotional laborers. What characteristics did you have to demonstrate to land your jobs? What training did you receive and what scripts did you have to follow? What did it take to be successful? What were the costs of your performances? The benefits of engaging in emotional labor? What do you conclude about the ethics of emotional labor? Report to the rest of the class.

5. Have you ever been the victim of low expectations (the Golem Effect)? How did you respond? What happened as a result? Share your story orally or in writing.

CHAPTER END CASE

An Intimidator at the U.N.

President George W. Bush's nomination of State Department official John Bolton to be the country's U.N. ambassador in 2005 was controversial. Not only was Bolton highly critical of the international body, but also he was anything but diplomatic when dealing with nations that opposed American policy. He called North Korea's leader a "tyrannical dictator" and said that life in that country was "a hellish nightmare" right before negotiators were to enter into talks to get North Korea to stop its nuclear weapons program.

Support for Bolton began to waver after senators on the Foreign Relations Committee learned more about his management style. One former State Department official called him both a "serial abuser" and a "kiss-up, kick-down sort of guy" who treats his bosses with respect while bullying subordinates. Two intelligence analysts accused Bolton of berating them and then trying to have them removed from their jobs for warning him that he was overstating the dangers of the Cuban and North Korean weapons programs. A former Bolton subordinate accused the nominee of treating visitors to his office as servants. In the most bizarre set of accusations, Bolton (who was working as a lawyer for a private contractor at the time) is said to have thrown a file folder and tape dispenser at an aid official who complained about his client. He then chased her through the halls of a Russian hotel. When the woman locked herself in her room, he continued to pound on the door, shout, and shove threatening letters under the door. Later he spread false rumors that she had misspent U.S. aid money.

Bolton's defenders argue that his intimidating style makes him just the right person to force the U.N. to make badly needed reforms. Critics have long complained that the international body is a bloated, corrupt bureaucracy. They believe that it will take a strong personality to help root out inefficiency, waste, and corruption and note that a lot of successful diplomats and U.S. senators can be abrasive. Secretary of State Condoleezza Rice stated that Bolton would make a "really great U.N. permanent representative. We make a mistake in that suddenly management style is part of the confirmation process."[1] However, GOP senator George Voinovich disagreed: "I think one's interpersonal skills and their relationship with their fellow man is a very important ingredient in anyone that works for me."[2] He broke ranks with his fellow Republicans and voted to delay the confirmation process. After failing to secure Bolton's confirmation, President Bush appointed him to the U.N. post when Congress was in recess.

DISCUSSION PROBES

1. Should Bolton have been appointed as U.N. ambassador? Why or why not?
2. Should management style be considered in the confirmation process for ambassador to the U.N.? When confirming judges and other officials?
3. Can an abusive management style ever be justified?
4. What accounts for the fact that many leaders who abuse power continue to be promoted and rewarded?
5. Have you ever worked for bullying boss? How did you respond? What advice would you give to others in the same situation?

NOTES

1. Harper (2005), p. A03.
2. Harper (2005), p. A03.

SOURCES

Boot, M. (2005, April 28). Nastiness is not the issue in Bolton's battle. *Financial Times,* p. 21.

Carney, J. (2005, May 2). Temper, temper, temper. *Time,* pp. 55–57.

Harper, T. (2005, April 21). Bolton's "a really creepy guy." *Toronto Star,* p. A03. Retrieved April 29, 2005, from LexisNexis Academic database.

Nichols, B. (2005, April 22). Tough bosses nothing new in Washington. *USA Today,* p. 4A.

Slavin, B. (2005, April 21). Woman accuses Bolton of harassing her in 1994. *USA Today,* p. 4A.

Endnotes

1. French, R. P., & Raven, B. (1959). The bases of social power. In D. Cartwright (Ed.), *Studies in social power* (pp. 150–167). Ann Arbor: University of Michigan, Institute for Social Research.

2. Yukl, G. (2002). *Leadership in organizations* (5th ed.). Upper Saddle River, NJ: Prentice Hall.

3. Hackman, M. Z., & Johnson, C. E. (2004). *Leadership: A communication perspective* (4th ed.). Prospect Heights, IL: Waveland Press, chap. 5; Yukl (2002).

4. Cruver, B. (2002). *Anatomy of greed: The unshredded truth from an Enron insider.* New York: Carroll & Graf.

5. Huffington, A. (2003). *Pigs at the trough: How corporate greed and political corruption are undermining America.* New York: Crown.

6. Fiske, S. T. (1993). Controlling other people: The impact of power on stereotyping. *American Psychologist, 48,* 621–628; Goodwin, S. A. (2003). Power and prejudice: A social-cognitive perspective on power and leadership. In D. van Knippenberg &

M. A. Hogg, *Leadership and power: Identity processes in groups and organizations* (pp. 138–152). London: Sage.

7. Kipnis, D., Schmidt, S. M., Swaffin-Smith, C., & Wilkinson, I. (1984). Patterns of managerial influence: Shotgun managers, tacticians, and bystanders. *Organizational Dynamics, 12,* 58–76.

8. Kanter, R. M. (1977). *Men and women of the corporation.* New York: Basic Books, chap. 7; Bennett, R. J. (1998). Perceived powerlessness as a cause of employee deviance. In R. W. Griffin, A. O'Leary-Kelly, & J. M. Collins (Eds.), *Dysfunctional behavior in organizations: Violent and deviant behavior* (pp. 221–239). Stamford, CT: JAI.

9. Block, P. (1993). *Stewardship: Choosing service over self-interest.* San Francisco: Berritt-Koehler; Greenleaf, R. K. (1977). *Servant leadership.* New York: Paulist Press.

10. Yukl (2002).

11. Bass, B. M. (1990). *Bass and Stogdill's handbook of leadership* (3rd ed.). New York: Free Press; Hackman & Johnson (2004).

12. Thomas, K. W., & Velthouse, B. A. (1990). Cognitive elements of empowerment: An "interpretive" model of intrinsic task motivation. *Academy of Management Review, 15,* 666–681; Spreitzer, G. M. (1996). Social structural characteristics of psychological empowerment. *Academy of Management Journal, 39,* 483–504; Spreitzer, G. M. (1995). Psychological empowerment in the workplace: Dimensions, measurement, and validation. *Academy of Management Journal, 38,* 1442–1485; Spreitzer, G. M., Kzilos, M. A., & Nason, S. W. (1997). A dimensional analysis of the relationship between psychological empowerment and effectiveness, satisfaction, and strain. *Journal of Management, 23,* 679–705.

13. Bandura, A. (1977). Self-efficacy: Toward a unifying theory of behavioral change. *Psychological Review, 84,* 191–215.

14. Kanter, R. M. (1979, July-August). Power failure in management circuits. *Harvard Business Review,* pp. 65–75.

15. Example taken from: Forrester, R. (2000). Empowerment: Rejuvenating a potent idea. *Academy of Management Executive, 14,* 67–80.

16. Randolph, W. A. (2000). Re-thinking empowerment: Why is it so hard to achieve? *Organizational Dynamics, 29,* 94–107.

17. Lincoln, N. D., Travers, C., Ackers, P., & Wilkinson, A. (2002). The meaning of empowerment: The interdisciplinary etymology of a new management concept. *International Journal of Management Reviews, 4,* 271–290.

18. Goffman, E. (1959). *The presentation of self in everyday life.* Garden City, NY: Doubleday. Schlenker, B. R. (1980). *Impression management: The self-concept, social identity, and interpersonal relations.* Monterey, CA: Brooks/Cole; Leary, M. R., & Kowalski, R. M. (1990). Impression management: A literature review and two-component model. *Psychological Bulletin, 107,* 34–47.

19. Rosenfeld, P., Giacalone, R. A., & Riordan, C. A. (1995). *Impression management in organizations: Theory, measurement, practice.* London: Routledge.

20. Gardner, W. L. (1992). Lessons in organizational dramaturgy: The art of impression management. *Organizational Dynamics, 21,* 33–47; Stevens, C. K., & Kristof, A. L. (1995). Making the right impression: A field study of applicant impression management during job interviews. *Journal of Applied Psychology, 80,* 587–606; Singh, V., Kumra, S., & Vinnicombe, S. (2002). Gender and impression management: Playing the promotion game. *Journal of Business Ethics, 37,* 77–89; Bratton, V. K., & Kacmar, K. M. (2004). Extreme careerism: The dark side of impression management. In W. Griffin and

K. O'Reilly (Eds.), *The dark side of organizational behavior* (pp. 291–308). San Francisco: Jossey-Bass.

21. Seabright, M. A., & Moberg, D. J. (1998). Interpersonal manipulation: Its nature and moral limits. In M. Schminke (Ed.), *Managerial ethics: Moral management of people and processes* (pp. 153–175). Mahwah, NJ: Lawrence Erlbaum; Kidwell, R. E. (2004). "Small" lies, big trouble: The unfortunate consequences of resume padding, from Janet Cooke to George O'Leary. *Journal of Business Ethics, 51*, 175–184; Padded resumes: Fake laurels that went unnoticed for years. (2003, January 13). *BusinessWeek*, p. 1C. Retrieved April 14, 2006, from Business Source Premier database.

22. Rosenfeld, Giacalone, & Riordan (1995).

23. This discussion of emotional labor is adapted from: Johnson, C. E. (2001, November). *Responding to the moral bind of positive emotional labor: Enacting bounded emotionality in the service encounter.* Paper presented at the National Communication Association convention, Atlanta, GA.

24. Hochschild, A. R. (1983). *The managed heart: Commercialization of human feeling.* Berkeley: University of California Press; Leidner, R. (1991). Selling hamburgers and selling insurance: Gender, work, and identity in interactive service jobs. *Gender & Society, 5*, 154–177. Leidner, R. (1993). *Fast food, fast talk: Service work and the routinization of everyday life.* Berkeley: University of California Press; Tracy, S. J. (2000). Becoming a character for commerce: Emotion labor, self-subordination, and discursive construction of identify in a total institution. *Management Communication Quarterly, 14*, 90–128; Tracy, S. J., & Tracy, K. (1998). Emotional labor at 911. *Journal of Applied Communication Research, 26*, 390–411; Van Maanen, J. (1991). The smile factory: Work at Disneyland. In P. J. Frost, L. F. Moore, M. R. Louis, C. C. Lundberg, & J. Martin (Eds.), *Reframing organizational culture* (pp. 58–76). Newbury Park, CA: Sage;

25. Yanay, N., & Sharar, G. (1998). Professional feelings as emotional labor. *Journal of Contemporary Ethnography, 27*, 345–373; Sutton, R. I. (1991). Maintaining norms about expressed emotions: The case of bill collectors. *Administrative Science Quarterly, 36*, 245–268.

26. Fineman, S. (1995). Stress, emotion and intervention. In T. Newton (Ed.), *Managing stress: Emotion and power at work* (pp. 120–136). London: Sage.

27. Steinberg, R. J., & Figart, D. M. (1999). Emotional labor since *The Managed Heart. Annals of the American Academy of Political and Social Sciences, 561*, 10-26.

28. Rafaeli, A., & Sutton, R. I. (1989). The expression of emotion in organizational life. In L. L. Cummings & B. M. Staw (Eds.), *Research in organizational behavior* (Vol. 2, pp. 1–42). Greenwich, CT: JAI.

29. Waldron, V. R. (1994). Once more, with feeling: Reconsidering the role of emotion at work. In S. A. Deetz (Ed.), *Communication Yearbook 17* (pp. 388–428). Thousand Oaks, CA: Sage; Sutton, R. I., & Rafaeli, A. (1988). Untangling the relationship between displayed emotions and organizational sales: The case of convenience stores. *Academy of Management Journal, 31*, 461–487.

30. Mumby, D. K., & Putnam, L. L. (1993). The politics of emotion: A feminist reading of bounded rationality. *Academy of Management Review, 17*, 465–486; Putnam, L. L., & Mumby, D. K. (1993). Organizations, emotion, and the myth of rationality. In S. Fineman (Ed.), *Emotion in organizations* (pp. 36–57). London: Sage.

31. Martin, J., Knopoff, K., & Beckman, C. (1998). An alternative to bureaucratic impersonality and emotional labor: Bounded emotionality at The Body Shop. *Administrative Science Quarterly, 43*, 429–469.

32. See, for example: Eden, D., & Shami, A. B. (1982). Pygmalion goes to boot camp: Expectancy, leadership, and trainee performance. *Journal of Applied Psychology, 67*, 194–199; Eden, D. (1984). Self-fulfilling prophecy as a management tool: Harnessing Pygmalion. *Academy of Management Review, 9*, 64–73; Eden, D. (1990). *Pygmalion in management.* Lexington, MA: Lexington Books/D.C. Heath; Eden, D. (1993). Interpersonal expectations in organizations. In P. D. Blanck (Ed.), *Interpersonal expectations: Theory, research, and applications* (pp. 154–178). Cambridge, UK: University of Cambridge Press; Rosenthal, R., & Jacobson. L. (1968). *Pygmalion in the classroom.* New York: Holt, Rinehart & Winston.

33. White, S. S., & Locke, E. A. (2000). Problems with the Pygmalion effect and some proposed solutions. *Leadership Quarterly, 11*, 389–415; McNatt, D. B. (2000). Ancient Pygmalion joins contemporary management: A meta-analysis of the result. *Journal of Applied Psychology, 85*, 314–322; Divir, T., Eden, D., & Banjo, M. L. (1995). Self-fulfilling prophecy and gender: Can women be Pygmalion and Galatea? *Journal of Applied Psychology, 80*, 253–270.

34. Oz, S., & Eden, D. (1994). Restraining the golem: Boosting performance by changing the interpretation of low scores. *Journal of Applied Psychology, 79*, 744–754.

35. Rosenthal, R. (1993). Interpersonal expectations: Some antecedents and some consequences. In P. D. Blanck (Ed.), *Interpersonal expectations: Theory, research, and applications* (pp. 3–24). Cambridge, UK: Cambridge University Press.

36. Good, T., & Brophy, J. (1980). *Educational psychology: A realistic approach.* New York: Holt, Rinehart & Winston.

37. White & Locke (2000).

Part IV

Transforming Group and Leadership Ethics

6

Improving Group Ethical Performance

Chapter Preview

Groups play a larger role than ever in the workplace. Most significant projects—creating a video game or film, building an apartment complex, opening a new market, raising money for a nonprofit—require the efforts of teams of people. Self-directed work groups are now charged with everything from organizing the assembly line to hiring and firing (see Chapter 5). Teams, not individuals, generally make important organizational decisions.

Groups tend to bring out the moral best and worst in us. If you're like me, some of your proudest moments are associated with small groups. Your team may have completed a service project for your local community or determined how to fairly distribute student fees to campus organizations. (See the Case Study in Box 6.1 for an example of extraordinary group moral performance.) At the same time, some of your most regrettable moments (like mine) may also relate to group experiences. Your team may have made poor moral choices and convinced you to engage in unethical activities.

CASE STUDY

Box 6.1 A Miracle of Cooperation

More than 35,000 Sri Lankans died when a tsunami, triggered by an earthquake off the Indonesian island of Sumatra, struck on the morning of December 26, 2004. A thousand of these victims were passengers and railroad workers on a commuter train traveling from the country's capital city of Colombo to the coastal town of Matara. Two giant waves toppled eight rail carriages and destroyed 80 miles of track.

At first it appeared as if the 77,000 passengers who ride the train daily would have to wait many months if not years for service to be restored. Government officials believed that it would take foreign experts and tens of millions of dollars of foreign aid to get the trains running again in a minimum of 6 months. Priyal de Silva, the general manager of the railways, thought different. He argued that the line could be rebuilt in 3 months. However, to accomplish the task would take the cooperation of the railroad's union. Union officials routinely clashed with management; they had led a 14-day strike in January 2004. Plans were underway for another walkout when the tsunami struck.

Fortunately for general manager de Silva and the Sri Lankan public, union leaders decided that they had a duty to the nation as well as a chance to improve the railway workers' public image as "an inefficient, lazy lot." They mobilized 1,000 volunteers to clear the tracks and within 3 days had removed fallen trees, bodies, and other debris. Engineers then surveyed the damage and the reconstruction began. Crews worked on four different sections of the track simultaneously so that restoration continued even when progress slowed on one portion of the project. April 13, the traditional Sri Lankan New Year, was set as the completion date.

Repairing the track was a massive effort requiring the cooperative efforts of union members and management alike. Workers toiled 12 hours a day or more, sleeping in makeshift camps or on the job site. Managers worked alongside their employees. According to one laborer: "Even the officials didn't pull rank. . . . Usually the higher officers don't do as much work, [but] they stayed by our sides without eating or drinking."[1] Crews dug through 2 feet of muck to salvage rail ties and other parts. At one point they replaced a bridge embankment by hand, stone by stone.

The rebuilding effort was completed in only 57 days (February 27), well ahead of schedule. One advisor to the project called it a "marvelous achievement." However, in light of the obstacles faced by de Silva and his team, this accolade seems like an understatement. "Miraculous" may better describe this accomplishment. Not only did two previously warring groups have to join forces, but they had to contend with shortages of supplies, materials, and money; the opposition of government officials who wanted to turn the project over to outsiders even as it neared completion; and the fact that many laborers were recovering from injuries suffered in the tidal wave at the same time that they were grieving for dead family members. The success of the project was even more remarkable given the failure of efforts to rebuild the rest of Sri Lanka. Over a year after the disaster, tens of thousands of residents remained in temporary wooden shelters.

DISCUSSION PROBES

1. What would have likely happened if the repair project had been turned over to foreigners?
2. What factors fostered cooperation in this situation? Can any of these factors be used to encourage a cooperative orientation in other settings?
3. Do you think this collaborative effort will permanently change union-management relations in Sri Lanka?
4. Have you ever been in a group that was highly successful due to the collaborative efforts of members? Did you exceed expectations?

NOTE

1. Wiseman, P. (2005), p. 16A.

SOURCE

Wiseman, P. (2005, December 9). On the train tracks in Sri Lanka, life does move on. *USA Today,* pp. 15A-16A.

Transforming our teams so that they spur us to higher, not lower, moral performance is the goal of this chapter. Achieving that end requires that we act as morally responsible group members and help our teams steer clear of ethical dangers.

Acting as a Morally Responsible Team Member

Group membership does not excuse us from our individual ethical responsibilities. Quite the contrary. In small groups, our behaviors can have a significant impact on the team's ethical success or failure.[1] We have a duty to apply the concepts and skills discussed in earlier chapters (ethical theories, character, moral reasoning, and ethical communication competencies) to the team setting. In addition, we need to adopt a cooperative orientation, do our fair share of the work, be open and supportive, and offer dissent.

ADOPTING A COOPERATIVE ORIENTATION

In Chapter 4 we noted that the outcome of interpersonal communication is dependent on the attitude we bring to our conversations. The same is true for our group interactions. Groups committed to cooperation can accomplish great things, as the case in Box 6.1 demonstrates. Conversely, if we lack this commitment to working together, our performance, as well as that of the team as a whole, is likely to suffer.

A cooperative orientation is based on the realization that an individual's success is dependent on the success of other team members.[2] To reach shared goals, everyone must do her or his part. This perspective stands in sharp contrast to individualistic and competitive points of view. Individualistic members rely on their own efforts to achieve their private agendas. For example, an individualist assigned to a class project group puts personal goals (developing a romantic relationship with someone else on the team, earning an A in another class) ahead of the collective goal of producing an excellent presentation. Competitive group members achieve their objectives at the expense of others. They want to earn the highest grade in the class, for instance, or get promoted ahead of other employees. In order to succeed, they may withhold information or claim too much credit for the group's success.

Individualism and competition are celebrated in Western culture but are counterproductive in small groups. In an analysis of the results of over 100 studies, brothers David and Roger Johnson and their colleagues found that in the vast majority of cases, cooperative groups had higher levels of achievement and productivity.[3] No matter what the subject matter (math, psychology, physical education), task (problem solving, retention and memory, categorization), and age group (elementary school through adult), cooperative groups are more successful. That's because cooperative team members are more likely to:[4]

- help one another
- support (reinforce) the identities of other group members
- be open to influence from others

- detect and correct errors in reasoning
- think clearly because they feel relaxed
- engage in healthy conflict that refines solutions
- develop positive relationships with other group members
- share accurate messages and accurately interpret messages from others
- provide positive feedback to other members which builds self-esteem
- value and accept differences
- demonstrate a positive attitude towards the task

In light of this evidence, we have an ethical duty to behave in a cooperative manner while encouraging others to do the same. We need to ask ourselves if we are committed to the success of the group and can put aside our desire to pursue personal agendas and to best others. If we can't answer in the affirmative, a change in attitude or withdrawing from the group is in order. We can foster cooperation through such communication behaviors as proposing compromises or concessions, carrying through on promises, pointing out the need to cooperate, asking for help, and accurately paraphrasing others' points of view.[5] The group as a whole needs to make sure that the team is pursuing a joint product, which fosters interdependence, and not a series of individual products, which encourage individualistic or competitive behavior. Collectively, members should divide the work fairly, reward the group as whole (not individual members), involve everyone in decision making, and emphasize shared values like a commitment to service or quality.

DOING YOUR FAIR SHARE (NOT LOAFING)

Many attempts at creating a cooperative climate falter because participants fail to do their fair share of the work. Researchers use the term *social loafing* to describe the tendency of individuals to reduce their efforts when working in a group. Social loafing is common in all kinds of teams, though women and people from Eastern cultures are less likely to reduce their efforts. (Complete the Self-Assessment in Box 6.2 to determine how much social loafing goes on in your group.)

Self-Assessment

Box 6.2 Social Loafing Scale

Instructions

This scale is written for the retail sales setting but can easily be adapted to other work contexts. Indicate how characteristic each of the

(Continued)

(Continued)

items is of the person you are rating: 1—Not at all characteristic; 2—Slightly characteristic; 3—Somewhat characteristic; 4—Characteristic; 5—Very characteristic.

Sum up the responses to the 10 items to come up with a score for each person (Range: 10–50). To come up with an overall score for the group, rate all the members (including yourself), add up the scores, and divide by the number of group members.

1. Defers responsibilities he or she should assume to other salespeople.
2. Puts forth less effort on the job when other salespeople are around to do the work.
3. Does not do his or her share of the work.
4. Spends less time helping customers if other salespeople are present to serve customers.
5. Puts forth less effort than other members of his or her work-group.
6. Avoids performing housekeeping tasks as much as possible.
7. Leaves work for the next shift which he or she should really complete.
8. Is less likely to approach a customer if another salesperson is available to do this.
9. Takes it easy if other salespeople are around to do the work.
10. Defers customer service activities to other salespeople if they are present.

Source: From George, J. M. (1995). Asymmetrical effects of rewards and punishments: The case of social loafing. *Journal of Occupational and Organizational Psychology, 68,* 327–338. Reprinted with permission from the *Journal of Occupational and Organizational Psychology,* © The British Psychological Society.

Social psychologists Steven Karau and Kipling Williams developed the Collective Effort Model (CEM) to identify the causes of social loafing.[6] They theorize that the motivation of group members depends on three factors: (1) *expectancy:* how much an individual expects that his or her effort will lead to high group performance; (2) *instrumentality:* the strength of the perceived relationship between personal and group effort and group achievement; and (3) *valence:* how desirable the outcome is for individual group members. Motivation drops when any of these factors is low. Individuals are more likely to slack off in collectives because the group can still succeed even if they do less (low expectancy). Participants may also believe that the group won't succeed (win a majority of its games, secure a contract) no matter how hard they and their fellow group members try (low instrumentality). Or participants may not value the group's goal or outcome (low valence).

Karau, Williams, and other investigators treat social loafing as undesirable, unethical behavior that undermines cooperation, encourages others to slack off for fear of being seen as "suckers," and diminishes the productivity of the group as a whole. They've identified ways to reduce or eliminate this phenomenon through the strategies outlined below. Each set of tactics is designed to address one of the three elements of motivation.[7]

Strategies for Increasing Expectancy

Reinforce the tie between individual efforts and successful group performance by

- careful selection of members and matching them to tasks
- providing training in needed skills
- setting challenging yet realistic goals
- supplying needed resources and support
- building feelings of self efficacy
- raising the visibility of individual tasks
- monitoring individual efforts

Strategies for Increasing Instrumentality

Link individual performance to group performance by

- making sure tasks are not too demanding
- reducing the size of the group so that members don't feel that their efforts are redundant
- pointing out that each member is making a unique, valuable contribution
- clarifying how individual efforts relate to the team's final product

Link group performance and outcomes by

- recognizing group work
- evaluating team products
- creating norms that emphasize high performance standards

Outcomes

Increase the positive value of the group's collective product to members by

- offering meaningful, interesting work that becomes intrinsically motivating
- providing tangible incentives like raises and bonuses
- encouraging members to identify with the group
- strengthening the social bonds between members
- creating norms which foster a sense of group pride and mutual obligation

DISPLAYING OPENNESS AND SUPPORTIVENESS

Ethical team members are both open and supportive.[8] Openness refers to an individual's willingness to surface issues and talk about problems while, at the same time, enabling others to do the same. Supportiveness describes the desire to help others succeed. Supportive group members encourage and defend others, help teammates overcome obstacles, and put the goals of the group first. These two characteristics work together. Openness by itself could pave the way for brutal honesty, insults, and sarcasm, so ethical issues must be discussed in a supportive manner. Otherwise, participants feel threatened and divert their attention from understanding and problem solving to defending themselves. Poorer ethical choices result.

Psychologist Jack Gibb identified six pairs of behaviors that promote either a defensive or supportive group climate.[9] Our moral duty as group members is to engage in supportive communication that contributes to a positive emotional climate and accurate understanding. At the same time, we need to draw attention to the comments of others that spark defensive reactions.

Evaluation Versus Description

Evaluative messages are judgmental. They can be sent through statements ("What a jerk!") or through such nonverbal cues as using a sarcastic tone of voice or rolling one's eyes. Those being evaluated put up their guard. Insecure group members are likely to respond by assigning blame ("You messed up"), by making judgments of their own ("At least my proposal didn't go over budget"), and by questioning the motives of the speaker. Descriptive messages, such as asking for information and reporting data and feelings, create a more positive environment.

Control Versus Problem Orientation

Controlling messages imply that the recipient is inadequate (uninformed, immature, stubborn, overly emotional) and needs to change. Control, like evaluation, can be communicated through both verbal (issuing orders, threats) and nonverbal (stares, threatening body posture) means. Problem-centered messages ("What will be your next step?") reflect a willingness to collaborate in defining and solving problems. They demonstrate that the sender has no predetermined solution and give the receiver permission to set his or her own direction.

Strategy Versus Spontaneity

Strategic communicators are seen as manipulators who try to hide their true motivations. They appear to be playing games, withholding data, or developing special sources of information. Worse yet, strategic communicators engage in "false spontaneity" by using gimmicks to disguise their intentions. Some supervisors solicit the input of employees in order to appear open-minded, for instance, when they have already made the decision. In contrast, behavior that is truly spontaneous (unplanned) and honest reduces defensiveness.

Neutrality Versus Empathy

Neutral messages like "Don't worry" and "Don't take it personally" communicate little warmth or caring. These low affect messages may be meant as supportive, but listeners come away feeling disconfirmed. Empathetic statements, such as "I can see why you would be worried" and "No wonder you were offended by the boss's comment," communicate reassurance and acceptance.

Superiority Versus Equality

Attempts at "one-upmanship," like claiming to be smarter or more knowledgeable, generally provoke such defensive responses as ignoring the message, competition, and jealousy. Those claiming superiority communicate that they don't want help or need feedback and may try to reduce the social standing of receivers. Status and power differences are less disruptive if participants indicate that they want to work with others on an equal basis. Supportive communicators treat others as partners worthy of respect and trust.

Certainty Versus Provisionalism

Dogmatic, inflexible individuals claim to have all the answers and are unwilling to change or to consider other points of view. They have little patience with those they consider "wrong." As a consequence, they appear more interested in being right than in solving the problem and maintaining group relationships. Gibb found that listeners often perceive the certainty of dogmatic individuals as a mask hiding their feelings of inferiority. Conversely, provisional individuals are willing to experiment and explore. They want to investigate issues instead of taking sides or controlling outcomes. These communicators gladly accept help from others as they seek information and answers.

BEING WILLING TO STAND ALONE

This final responsibility may be the toughest to assume. Being in the minority is never easy because it runs contrary to our strong desire to be liked and accepted by others. We can expect criticism, ridicule, and other forms of group pressure when we offer dissenting ideas that challenge the majority opinion.

The difficulty of standing alone should not be an excuse for keeping quiet instead of speaking up. As we'll see in the second half of the chapter, team members' willingness to take issue with the prevailing group opinion is essential if the team is to avoid moral failure. Further, minority opinion greatly increases a group's decision-making effectiveness even if the group doesn't change its collective mind.[10] Team members focus on one solution when there is no minority. They have little incentive to explore the problem in depth. As a result, they disregard novel solutions and converge on one position. Minorities cast doubt on group consensus, stimulating more thought about the dilemma. Members exert more effort because they must resolve the clash between the majority and minority solutions. They pay more attention to all aspects of the issue, consider more viewpoints, and use a wider variety of problem-solving strategies. Such divergent thinking leads to more creative, higher quality solutions. Responding to the dissenting views of minorities also encourages team members to resist conformity in other settings.[11]

Minorities are most influential when they consistently advocate for their positions. Others may initially reject dissenters and their ideas but, over time, forget the source of the arguments and focus instead on the merits of their proposals. This can gradually convert them to the minority viewpoint.[12]

Recognizing the importance of minority opinion should increase our motivation to play this role. We'll also need to exercise courage in order to accept the consequences for doing so. Teams can do their part to spark dissent by (a) making sure that members come from significantly different backgrounds and perspectives, and by (b) protecting rather than attacking those who disagree.

Responding to Ethical Danger Signs

Accepting our moral responsibilities is a good start to improving group ethical performance. However, we also need to be alert to moral pitfalls that arise during team interaction. These traps account for the ethical failure of a great many groups and their members. In this section I'll identify five signs that indicate that a team is in ethical danger—groupthink, mismanaged agreement, escalating commitment, excessive control, and moral exclusion—and provide some suggestions for responding to the risks posed by each.

GROUPTHINK

Earlier I noted that adopting a cooperative orientation is critical to group success. However, there is significant danger in making team unity the group's primary goal. Social psychologist Irving Janis popularized the term *groupthink,* which describes teams that put unanimous agreement ahead of reasoned problem solving.[13] Janis first noted faulty thinking in small groups of ordinary citizens. For example, he observed one group of heavy smokers meeting to kick the habit who decided that quitting was impossible. One member had stopped but the rest of the group pressured him back into smoking two packs a day.

The term groupthink became part of the national vocabulary largely based on Janis's analysis of major U.S. policy disasters like the failure to anticipate the attack on Pearl Harbor, the invasion of North Korea, the Bay of Pigs fiasco, and the escalation of the Vietnam War. In each of these incidents, some of the brightest (and presumably most ethically minded) political and military leaders in our nation's history made terrible choices. More recent examples of groupthink include the Challenger and Columbia shuttle disasters and the decision to storm the Branch Davidian compound in Waco Texas. Future scholars will have to determine if the decision to invade Iraq was also the product of groupthink among members of the second Bush administration.

Groups are more likely to fall victim to this syndrome when they (a) are highly cohesive; (b) find themselves insulated or isolated from other groups; (c) lack decision-making formats like those described in Chapter 3; (d) have highly directive leaders and members who push for a particular solution; and (e) are under stress with little hope of coming up with alternatives to the ideas offered by their leaders. These forces exert pressure on members to agree and produce the following symptoms, which I'll illustrate through examples taken from Janis's analysis of major policy disasters. The greater the number of these characteristics displayed by a group, the greater the likelihood that members have made cohesiveness their top priority.[14]

Signs of Overconfidence

1. *Illusion of invulnerability.* Members think they can do no wrong. They are overly optimistic and prone to take extraordinary risks. President Lyndon Johnson and his advisors kept escalating the war in Vietnam because they thought the North Vietnamese would back down. One policy maker later remarked: "We thought we had the golden touch."

2. *Belief in the inherent morality of the group.* Participants do not question the inherent morality of the group and therefore ignore the ethical consequences of their actions and decisions. In discussions of the Cuban Bay of Pigs operation (which resulted in the death or capture of all the invading troops), President Kennedy's policy group barely noted the ethical implications of attacking a small neighboring country or of lying to the American public about the invasion. Later, during the deliberations that safely ended the Cuban missile crisis, many of the same group members debated at length the morality of a surprise air attack. The team decided that this option was not in the best, moral American tradition.

Signs of Closed-Mindedness

1. Collective rationalization. Group members invent rationalizations to protect themselves from any feedback that would challenge their operating assumptions. In 1941, United States naval officers rationalized that any enemy carriers headed for Hawaii would be detected before attack. Warships anchored in Pearl Harbor would be safe from torpedo bombs because the water was too shallow.

2. Stereotypes of outside groups. Decision makers underestimate the capabilities of other groups (armies, citizens, teams), thinking that people in these groups are weak or stupid. Truman and his advisors fell victim to the belief that the Chinese wouldn't be able to respond to a United States invasion of North Korea. As a result of this miscalculation, China entered the Korean conflict and the war ended in a stalemate.

Signs of Group Pressure

1. Pressure on dissenters. Majority members coerce dissenters to go along with the prevailing opinion in the group. Former presidential advisor Bill Moyers felt the power of this pressure after taking issue with escalating the Vietnam War. When he arrived at one strategy discussion, President Johnson greeted him by saying: "Well, here comes Mr. Stop-the-Bombing."

2. Self-censorship. Individuals keep their doubts about group decisions to themselves. Perhaps because of being labeled as "Mr. Stop-the-Bombing," Moyers became a "domesticated dissenter" who only expressed reservations about a few details of the plan to ratchet up the war in Vietnam.

3. Illusion of unanimity. Since members keep quiet, the group mistakenly assumes that everyone agrees on a course of action. Historian Arthur Schlesinger, a participant in the Bay of Pigs planning sessions, had serious doubts about the project but he and others remained silent because they assumed the group had consensus.

4. Self-appointed mindguards. Certain members take it upon themselves to protect the leader and others from dissenting opinions that might disrupt the group's consensus. President Kennedy's brother Robert took this role during the Bay of Pigs decision. He told Schlesinger: "You may be right or you may be wrong, but the President has made his mind up. Don't push it any further. Now is the time for everyone to help him all they can."[15]

The symptoms of groupthink seriously disrupt the decision-making process. Members fail to consider all the alternatives, outline objectives, or gather additional information. They follow preconceived notions, are less likely to reexamine a course of action when it's not working, don't carefully weigh risks or work out contingency plans. While groupthink undermines all types of decisions, it is particularly destructive to ethical reasoning. This helps explain why, in the 1980s, Beech Nut employees decided to sell adulterated apple juice and E. F. Hutton officials defrauded financial institutions by writing checks before they had deposited the funds to cover them. Nearly everyone (including employees of these two firms) would agree that selling "phony" apple juice and bouncing checks is wrong. However, groupthink banished any moral considerations.[16]

Interest in the causes and prevention of groupthink remains high decades after Janis first offered his theory.[17] Contemporary researchers have discovered social cohesion is dangerous, while task cohesion (agreement about how to complete the group's work) is not. A group is in greatest danger when the leader actively promotes his or her agenda and when it doesn't have any procedures in place for solving problems. Investigators note that self-directed teams, which incorporate an estimated 40 percent of the workforce, are particularly vulnerable to groupthink. Members work under strict time limits and are often isolated and undertrained. They may fail at first and the need to function as a cohesive unit may blind them to ethical dilemmas.[18]

Janis and his successors offer the following suggestions for preventing groupthink:

- As a leader, don't express a preference for a particular solution; solicit ideas instead.
- Utilize a decision-making format.
- Divide the group regularly into subgroups and then bring the entire group back together to negotiate differences.
- Construct and then debate counterproposals.
- Bring in outsiders—experts or colleagues—to challenge the group's ideas.
- Appoint individuals to act as "devil's advocates" at each session to air doubts and objections.
- Realistically assess dangers and anticipate possible setbacks.
- Train members to speak up.
- Encourage dissenting points of view.
- Think through the ethical implications of options.
- Adopt an optimistic frame of mind, viewing obstacles as "opportunities" and envisioning success.
- Develop group norms that encourage critical thinking about reasoning, assumptions, and alternatives.
- Avoid isolation; keep the group in contact with other groups.
- Initiate role-play of the reactions of other groups and organizations to reduce the effects of stereotyping and rationalization.
- Once a decision has been made, give group members one last chance to express any remaining doubts about the decision.

MISMANAGED AGREEMENT

Groups frequently run into trouble when members publicly express their support for decisions that they oppose in private. Teams continue to pour time and money into new products that no one believes will succeed, for example, or engage in illegal activities that everyone in the group is uneasy about. George Washington University management professor Jerry Harvey refers to this phenomenon as mismanaged agreement or the Abilene Paradox.[19] He describes a time when his family decided to drive (without air conditioning) 100 miles across the Texas desert one hot July afternoon from their home in Coleman to Abilene so they could eat a bad meal at a rundown cafeteria. After returning home, family members discovered that no one had really wanted to make the trip. Each agreed to go to Abilene based on the assumption that everyone else in the group was enthusiastic about eating out.

Harvey believes failure to manage agreement, not failure to manage conflict, is the biggest problem facing organizations. Like his family, teams also take needless "trips":

> I now call the tendency for groups to embark on excursions that no group member wants "the Abilene Paradox." Stated simply, when organizations blunder into the Abilene Paradox, they take actions in contradiction to what they really want to do and therefore defeat the very purposes they are trying to achieve.[20]

Members of groups caught in the Abilene Paradox agree in private about the nature of the problem and what ought to be done about it. However, they fail to communicate their desires and beliefs, misleading others into believing that a consensus exists. Based on faulty assumptions, members act in counterproductive ways that undermine their purposes. These actions generate lots of anger and irritation and participants blame each other for the group's failures. The cycle of miscommunication and misunderstanding continues unless confronted.

Why do members publicly support decisions they privately oppose? Harvey offers the following five psychological factors to account for the Paradox.

1. Action Anxiety

Group members know what should be done but are too anxious to follow through on their beliefs. They choose to endure the negative consequences of going along (professional and economic failure) instead of speaking up.

2. Negative Fantasies

Action anxiety is driven in part by the negative fantasies members have about what will happen if they voice their opinions. These fantasies ("I'll be shunned or branded as disloyal") serve as an excuse for not attacking the problem, absolving the individual (in his or her own eyes) of any responsibility.

3. Real Risk

There are risks to expressing dissent—getting fired, lost income, damaged relationships. However, most of the time the danger is not as great as we think.

4. Fear of Separation

Separation, alienation, and loneliness constitute the most powerful force behind the Paradox. Ostracism is strong punishment. Group members fear being cut off or separated from others. To escape this fate, they cheat, lie, take bribes, use accounting tricks to boost earnings, and so forth.

5. Psychological Reversal of Risk and Certainty

In the Abilene Paradox, participants let their negative fantasies drive them into real dangers. Fearing that something bad may happen, decision makers act in a way that fulfills the fantasy. For instance, group members may support a project with no chance of success because they are afraid they will be fired or demoted if they don't. Ironically, they are likely to be fired or demoted anyway when the flawed project fails.

Harvey takes issue with proponents of groupthink who blame moral failure on group pressure. He contends that as long as we can blame our peers we don't have to accept personal responsibility. In reality, we always have a choice as to how we respond. He uses the Gunsmoke Myth to drive home this point. In this myth, the lone Western sheriff (Matt Dillon in the radio and television series) stands down a mob of armed townsfolk out to lynch his prisoner. If group tyranny is really at work, Harvey argues, Dillon stands no chance. After all, he is outnumbered 500 to 1 and could be felled with a single bullet from one rioter. The mob disbands because its members really didn't want to lynch the prisoner in the first place.

Breaking out of the Paradox begins with diagnosing its symptoms in your group or organization. Important indicators of mismanaged agreement include frustration and blaming, contradictions between privately and publicly expressed opinions, and the inability to solve problems. If you believe that the group is on its way to its own Abilene, call a meeting where you "own up" to your true feelings and invite feedback. The team may immediately come up with a better approach or engage in extended conflict that generates a more creative solution. You might suffer for your honesty, but you could be rewarded for saying what everyone else was thinking. In any case, you'll feel better about yourself for speaking up.

ESCALATING COMMITMENT

As we've seen, one of the products of mismanaged agreement is continuing in a failed course of action. Social psychologists refer to this phenomenon as the escalation of commitment.[21] Instead of cutting their losses, groups redouble their efforts, pouring in more resources. Costs continue to multiply up until the moment when the team finally admits defeat. Escalating commitment helps explain why bankers continue to loan money to problem borrowers, managers maintain support for failing employees, and investors put more money into declining stocks. Well-publicized cases of this phenomenon include creation of the automated baggage system at the Denver International Airport (which delayed its opening and never worked), the decision to introduce the New Coke, and the failed Shoreham Nuclear Power Plant. Costs for the Shoreham project on New York's Long Island ballooned from $75 million to over $5 billion over a 23-year period. The installation failed to produce a single kilowatt of electric power.

Teams may stay the course to justify their earlier choices, remain consistent, and retain their credibility. They often hope to recoup their "sunk costs" (previous investments). Setbacks are viewed as temporary; success is seen as just around the corner. Groups also have a tendency to take more risks than individuals ("risky shift"), which can encourage members to contribute more resources than they would on their own.[22]

Group members have a moral obligation to avoid escalation of commitment. Continuing to invest in doomed projects wastes resources that could go to better uses and puts the organization at risk. Often maintaining a failing course of action involves unethical behaviors like overstating potential benefits or hiding safety problems. We can take a number of steps to de-escalate commitment to destructive courses of action.[23] First, don't ignore negative feedback or external pressure. Combat the tendency to be overly optimistic by being alert to red flags like missed deadlines, cost overruns, and pressure from outsiders who take issue with the project. Second, bring new group members or leaders into the group who are less invested in the program. Third, hire an outside auditor to provide a "fresh set of eyes" to assess the severity of the problem and to provide alternative courses of action. Fourth, don't be afraid to withhold further funding until more information can be gathered. Fifth, look for opportunities to deinstitutionalize the project by separating it from the key goals of the organization or isolating it physically. Corporations frequently spin off troubled units, for example, and risky projects can be redefined as "experiments."

EXCESSIVE CONTROL

Members of newly formed self-directed work teams frequently find that the group exerts more control over their behavior than their former managers ever did. One team member at a small manufacturing company complained, for example, that his group had stricter rules about tardiness than his old boss and that he was more closely observed than before:

> [Now] I don't have to sit there and look for the boss to be around; [before] if the boss is not around, I can sit there and talk to my neighbor or do what I want. Now the whole team is around me and the whole team is observing what I'm doing.[24]

The experience of this employee illustrates the power of *concertive control.* Concertive control has replaced the traditional rules based bureaucracy in many organizations.[25] Groups empowered to direct their own behaviors exert control by agreeing on a common set of values, engaging in high levels of coordination, and creating their own enforcement mechanisms. Concertive control (sometimes referred to as *unobtrusive control*) is subtler than its bureaucratic predecessor and often goes unrecognized. This combination of high power and low visibility makes concertive influence particularly dangerous. Members can unwittingly exert excessive, unhealthy influence over one another.

Organizational communication expert James Barker describes how self-directed work teams transition from freeing to imprisoning their members.[26] In the first phase, newly formed groups develop their vision and values statements. These values then become the basis for making ethical decisions in the group. Members commit themselves to reaching shared goals and develop norms for putting their values into action. A group might implement its concern for customer service, for instance, by adopting the norm that it will do whatever it takes to ship products on time.

In the second phase, members turn their norms into specific behavioral rules like "You must stay late in order to meet shipping schedules." These rules are then used to regulate the behavior of new members. In phase 3, the rules are formalized. They are written down and used for evaluation. A member may be removed from the team if he or she doesn't work overtime to help ship products, for example. These rules can be stricter than those operating in a bureaucracy. Group members are thus imprisoned in an "iron cage" of regulations of their own making.

Barker is concerned that "concertive control is the next step on our long march toward totally organized lives."[27] Members pay a high price for remaining in good standing with the team, including burnout and the sacrifice of family and personal time. Teams can make sure that concertive control is put to constructive use by continually criticizing their own actions, according to Barker. They need to set aside regular times (perhaps an hour a month) to talk about their moral reasoning and the positive and negative effects of their practices. Some values and rules will be reaffirmed, while others will be modified. In such discussions it is critical that everyone be heard and that members engage in dialogue, working through their differences. This ongoing group analysis is the best way to ensure that a team creates a fair and reasonable system of norms and regulations to guide its members.

MORAL EXCLUSION

The worst examples of group behavior arise out of the process of moral exclusion. In moral exclusion, group and societal members set a psychological boundary around justice.[28] Those inside the boundary treat each other fairly, are willing to sacrifice for one another, and share collective resources. However, insiders treat outsiders much differently. Fairness is no longer a consideration. Those beyond the scope of justice (often members of low status groups) are seen as unimportant and expendable. Insiders don't feel remorse when outsiders are harmed but believe that the mistreatment is morally justified.

Mild forms of exclusion are part of everyday life and include, for example, acting in a patronizing manner, applying double standards to judge the behavior of different groups, and making unflattering comparisons to appear superior to others. An example of ordinary exclusion would be a work team that mocks other groups while excusing its own failings. Extreme forms of exclusion produce human rights violations, torture, genocide, and other atrocities. For instance, Japanese soldiers in World War II viewed the Chinese with contempt. Murdering them was no more troubling than "squashing a bug or butchering a hog."[29] Driven by this belief, they were willing to rape, torture, and slaughter civilians in the city of Nanking, killing approximately 300,000 residents. Similar exclusionary reasoning has been to justify genocide in Serbia and Guatemala, attacks on villages in the Darfur region of Sudan, and the abuse of prisoners at Iraq's Abu Ghraib prison (see the Chapter End Case).

Educational psychologist Susan Opotow believes that moral exclusion progresses through five stages or elements, which can reinforce one another. The presence of one or more of these elements serves as a warning that this danger is present.[30]

1. Conflicts of interest are salient.

Moral exclusion is more likely to occur during conflicts where one group wins at the expense of the other. As tensions increase, members separate themselves from their opponents, focusing on differences based on religion, education, ethnic background, social status, skin color, job functions, and other factors.

2. Group categorizations are salient.

The characteristics of members of the opposing group are given negative labels, dividing the world into those who deserve empathy and help and those who don't. These derogatory labels, like those used by the Japanese, excuse unfair treatment and negative outcomes.

3. Moral justifications are prominent.

Damaging behavior is justified and even celebrated as a way to strike a blow against a corrupt foe. Such exclusionary moral claims are self-serving, excuse wrongdoing, and set boundaries by denigrating outsiders. For instance, Hutu leaders in Rwanda whipped their followers into a murderous rage by playing on their resentments towards their higher status Tutsi neighbors.

4. Unjust procedures are described as expedient.

Harm is often disguised through policies and procedures, what some observers label "administrative evil."[31] In administrative evil, ordinary people commit heinous crimes while carrying out their daily tasks. The Holocaust demonstrates administrative evil in action. Extermination camps would not have been possible without the cooperation of thousands of civil servants who identified undesirables and seized their assets, managed the ghettos, built concentration camp latrines, and shipped prisoners to their deaths.

Procedures can be identified as unjust when they fail to serve the interests of those they are supposed to benefit. For example, government bureaucrats in the U.S. and Australia claimed to be helping Native peoples even as they stole their lands and tried to eradicate their cultures. Military officials in Japan believed that committing atrocities would ultimately benefit the Chinese because, once subjugated, they would prosper under Japanese rule.

5. Harmful outcomes occur.

The negative products of exclusion are both physical and psychological. Members of excluded groups may suffer physical harm and, at the same time, suffer from a loss of self-esteem and identity as they internalize the negative judgments of the dominant group. Perpetrators also pay a high price. They have to expend significant energy and resources dealing with conflicts, excusing their conduct, and maintaining exclusionary systems. The harm they cause overshadows any good that they do.

Opotow argues that adopting a pluralistic perspective—one that acknowledges the legitimacy of a variety of groups—can help us deter moral exclusion at each stage of its development.[32] This approach sees conflicts as opportunities to integrate the interests of all parties, not as win-lose battles. Members of pluralistic groups enlarge the definition of moral community by including people of all categories. Participants engage in critical analysis of moral justifications, calling into question suspect claims at the same time they develop equitable procedures for distributing resources. They also support dissenters.

Implications

- Your behavior will have a significant impact on your team's ethical success or failure.
- Recognize that your success in a group is dependent on the efforts of others. Adopt a cooperative orientation and encourage others to do the same.
- Do your fair share. Combat the tendency to engage in social loafing by strengthening connection between individual effort and group performance as well as between group performance and group success. Increase the positive value of the team's collective product to members.
- Be open and supportive. Talk about issues and help others to succeed. Promote a supportive climate by engaging in communication that is descriptive, problem oriented, spontaneous, empathetic, egalitarian, and provisional.
- Have the courage to stand alone. Expressing a minority opinion increases group decision-making effectiveness by encouraging additional problem analysis, divergent thinking, and resistance to conformity pressures.
- Reduce the likelihood of groupthink (putting unanimity ahead of careful problem solving) by (a) withholding your initial opinion, (b) dividing the group into subgroups, (c) bringing in outsiders, (d) keeping the group in contact with other groups, (e) role-playing the reactions of other teams, (f) and revisiting the decision.
- Mismanaged agreement (the Abilene Paradox) occurs when members publicly express support for decisions that they oppose in private. The group then acts in counterproductive ways that undermine its goals. "Owning up" to your doubts can stop the team from taking unwanted "trips."
- Groups trapped in escalating commitment pursue failed courses of action, continuing to pour in additional resources when they should go in another direction instead. You can de-escalate the situation by noting warning signs; bringing in new members or outside auditors; withholding funding; and deinstitutionalizing the project (making it less central to group goals and physically isolating it).
- Be aware of the power of concertive control in which teams manage the behavior of members by agreeing on a common set of values, engaging in high levels of coordination, and creating their own enforcement mechanisms. Such control is often more intrusive than traditional bureaucracy. However, you can put this form of group influence to constructive use by encouraging your team to regularly examine, criticize, and modify its values and rules.
- Resist the temptation to engage in moral exclusion—placing members of other groups outside the scope of justice where the rules of fairness do not apply. Deter moral exclusion by adopting a pluralistic perspective that respects the rights of all groups.

Application Projects

1. What was your best small group experience? Your worst? What accounts for the differences between these two experiences? How would your rate the moral behavior of each group?

2. Record a group discussion and then identify and categorize the defensive and supportive comments made by team members. What do you conclude about the communication climate of the group? Report your conclusions to the team you observe.

3. Rate your performance as a morally responsible group member. What behaviors do you demonstrate? Need to develop? What steps can you take to improve?

4. If you are part of an ongoing group, meet together to discuss members' tendencies to loaf and how the team exercises control over its members. Develop an action plan to address these issues.

5. Examine a significant conflict between groups that produced negative outcomes. Analyze the role played by moral exclusion in this situation. Provide examples of the five elements of exclusion in action. Write up your findings.

6. Which of the dangers described in the chapter does the most damage to the ethical performance of groups? Defend your choice.

CHAPTER END CASE

Moral Exclusion at Abu Ghraib

Images of prisoner abuse at Iraq's Abu Ghraib prison sickened viewers around the world when they were released in the spring of 2004 and again in 2005. The photos record soldiers of the 372nd Military Police Company unit subjecting detainees to physical and psychological abuse as well as sexual humiliation. Naked male prisoners cower before police dogs, pose in simulated sex acts, and form human pyramids. Smiling soldiers of both sexes stand by, flashing the thumbs-up sign, mocking the plight and the genitals of their victims. In the image that has come to symbolize Abu Ghraib, a hooded prisoner stands with his arms outstretched on a box, with electric wires attached to his hands, feet, and private parts.

Abu Ghraib demonstrates a failure of both individual and shared moral responsibility. Soldiers involved in the abuse were unwilling to stand alone. Specialist Jeremy Spivits admitted that all of the incidents of abuse were wrong but he went along because "I try to be friends with everyone."[1] Pfc. Lynndie

England (seen leading a naked prisoner around on a leash in one picture) told a judge that she had a choice not to participate but caved in to peer pressure.

Collectively, this small group fell victim to groupthink and mismanaged agreement. Conditions at Abu Ghraib made members highly susceptible to conformity pressures. The unit was isolated, and it was led by highly directive sergeants who initiated the abuse. Members of the team were under a great deal of stress as well. Not only were they overwhelmed by a sudden influx of prisoners, but the prison was under mortar attack. Military intelligence personnel pressured the soldiers to "soften up" their charges so they could extract more information. Participants kept their moral objections to themselves and operated under the assumption that everyone was eager to engage in the "fun."

Moral exclusion also played a role in scandal at Abu Ghraib. Following the events of 9/11, a small group of lawyers at the Justice Department's Office of Legal Counsel drafted a new set of policies dealing with the treatment of terrorists. They believed that saving Americans from further attacks justified extreme measures. White House counsel Alberto Gonzalez, who was later to become attorney general, advised the president that the Geneva Convention didn't apply to terrorists. According to Gonzalez, "the war on terrorism is a new kind of war . . . a new paradigm [that] renders obsolete Geneva's strict limitations on questioning of enemy prisoners and renders quaint some of its principles."[2]

Under the Geneva accord, prisoners of war (a category that includes members of the armed forces, militias, and resistance groups) can refuse to answer questions beyond name, rank, and serial number and are guaranteed humane treatment. No "physical or moral coercion" should be used to obtain information from civilians. Noncombatants are also protected from "outrages upon personal dignity, in particular, humiliating and degrading treatment." If there is any doubt as to who should be covered under the treaty, belligerents are protected by its provisions until a "competent tribunal" determines otherwise.[3]

President Bush followed the advice of the Legal Counsel lawyers and declared that terrorist suspects were "unlawful combatants" excluded from provisions that apply to prisoners of war. Suspects were then taken to Guantanamo Bay, where they were held without trial. Administration officials also narrowed the definition of torture to acts involving serious mental or physical damage (organ failure, for example). Under this new definition, interrogators were free to engage in variety of aggressive tactics, such as sleep deprivation, isolation, the use of dogs, stress positions, yelling, loud music, and light control. The revised interrogation guidelines were exported from Guantanamo to Abu Ghraib in the summer of 2003 after the Department of Defense grew frustrated by the lack of intelligence coming out of Iraq.

Guards at Abu Ghraib went far beyond anything sanctioned by the less restrictive interrogation guidelines. However, excluding terror suspects from the rule of international law made it easier to justify their mistreatment. Conflicts of interest and group categories were particularly salient at Abu Ghraib, where interrogators and guards were pitted against insurgents and detainees. Soldiers might have also shared a broader dislike for Iraqis, who some military personnel describe as "rag heads," "turbans," and "haji" (a derogatory term used like "gook" and "Charlie" during the Vietnam War). Tougher measures appeared justified in the face of a rising insurgency.

Members of the 372nd company appearing in the photos were tried and sentenced to jail. However, no high level officials were court-martialed for what happened. A later check of prison records revealed that military police at Abu Ghraib tortured innocent people. Many prisoners were criminals, not terrorists, and others were released without being charged.

Abu Ghraib highlights the dangers of moral exclusion, even when engaged in a cause as important as the War on Terrorism. Severe interrogation methods did elicit valuable information, such as details about the 9/11 plot and future Al Qaeda operations. This intelligence may help prevent future attacks like the one on the World Trade Center. However, tales of the abuse further fanned anti-American sentiment, making it easier to recruit new terrorists. The moral authority of the nation was undermined. Arab observers referred to the hooded detainee on the box as "the statue of liberty" and wondered how the U.S. could claim to model democracy even as it engaged in acts that are typically practiced in dictatorships. American military officers warned that violating the Geneva Convention put U.S. soldiers at risk. Future captured Americans may receive the same treatment that the U.S. is currently dishing out. Other governments may now use the terrorist label to excuse all kinds of injustice.

DISCUSSION PROBES

1. Is torture justified if it saves innocent lives from terrorist attacks? How do you reach this conclusion?
2. Should terrorists be treated like other prisoners of war, according to the provisions of the Geneva Convention?
3. Are the revised interrogation tactics used by the U.S. (sleep deprivation, loud music, dogs, light control) forms of torture? Why or why not?
4. What factors do you think contributed to the abuse at Abu Ghraib? How far up the chain of command does the responsibility extend?
5. What can be done to prevent abuses of military prisoners in the future?

NOTES

1. McGeary (2004), p. 44
2. Danner (2004), p. 42.
3. Barry, Hirsch, & Isikoff (2004), p. 29.

SOURCES

Badger, T. A. (2005, May 3). Soldier says peers pressed for abuse. *Oregonian,* pp. A1, A3.

Barry, J., Hirsh, M., & Isikoff, M. (2004, May 24). The roots of torture. *Newsweek,* pp. 26–34.

Danner, M. (2004). *Torture and truth: America, Abu Ghraib, and the war on terror.* New York: New York Review Books.

Herbert, B. (2005, May 2). From "gook" to "raghead." *New York Times,* p. A21. Retrieved June 14, 2005, from LexisNexis Academic database.

McGeary, J. (2004, May 24). Pointing fingers. *Time,* pp. 43–47, 50.

Murphy, D. (2004, June 4). Abu Ghraib holds mirror to Arabs. *Christian Science Monitor,* p. 1c. Retrieved March 23, 2005, from LexisNexis Academic database.

Riesen, J. (2004, May 3). The struggle for Iraq: Prisoners. *New York Times,* p. A1. Retrieved June 14, 2005, from LexisNexis Academic database.

Ripley, A. (2004, June 21). Redefining torture. *Time,* pp. 49–50.

Scelfo, J., & Nordland, R. (2004, July 19). Beneath the hoods. *Newsweek,* pp. 40–42.

Zernike, K. (2004, June 27). Defining torture: Russian roulette, yes. Mind-altering drugs, maybe. *New York Times,* p. 7. Retrieved June 27, 2004, from LexisNexis Academic database.

Endnotes

1. Locke, E. A., Tirnauer, D., Roberson, Q., Goldman, B., Lathan, M. E., & Weldon, E. (2001). The importance of the individual in an age of groupism. In M. E. Turner (Ed.), *Groups at work: Theory and research* (pp. 501–528). Mahwah, NJ: Lawrence Erlbaum.

2. Rothwell, J. D. (1998). *In mixed company: Small group communication* (3rd ed.). Fort Worth, TX: Harcourt Brace.

3. Johnson, D. W., Maruyama, G., Johnson, R., Nelson, D., & Skon, L. (1981). Effects of cooperative, competitive, and individualistic goal structures on achievement: A meta-analysis. *Psychological Bulletin, 82,* 47–62.

4. Tjosvold, D. (1984). Cooperation theory and organizations. *Human Relations, 37,* 743–767; Tjosvold, D. (1986). The dynamics of interdependence in organizations. *Human Relations, 39,* 517–540; Johnson, D. W., & Johnson, R. T. (1974). Instructional goal structure: Cooperative, competitive, or individualistic. *Review of Educational Research, 44,* 212–239; Milton, L. P., & Westphal, J. D. (2005). Identity confirmation networks and cooperation in work groups. *Academy of Management Journal, 48,* 191–212.

5. Johnson, D. W. (1974). Communication and the inducement of cooperative behavior in conflicts: A critical review. *Speech Monographs, 41,* 64–78; Rubin, J. Z., & Brown, B. R. (1975). *The social psychology of bargaining and negotiation.* New York: Academic Press.

6. Karau, S. J., & Williams, K. D. (2001). Understanding individual motivation in groups: The collective effort model. In M. E. Turner (Ed.), *Groups at work: Theory and research* (pp. 113–141). Mahwah, NJ: Lawrence Erlbaum; Karau, S. J., & Williams, K. D. (1993). Social loafing: A meta-analytic review and theoretical integration. *Journal of Personality and Social Psychology, 65,* 681–706.

7. Karau & Williams (2001). Sheppard, J. A. (2001). Social loafing and expectancy-value theory. In S. G. Harkins (Ed.), *Multiple perspectives on the effects of evaluation on performance: Toward an integration* (pp. 1–24). Boston: Kluwer; Sheppard, J. A. (1993). Productivity loss in performance groups: A motivation analysis. *Psychological Bulletin, 113,* 67–81.

8. LaFasto, F., & Larson, C. (2001). *When teams work best.* Thousand Oaks, CA: Sage.

9. Gibb, J. R. (1961). Defensive communication. *Journal of Communication, 11–12,* 141–148.

10. For summaries of research on minority influence process, see: Moscovici, S., Mugny, G., & Van Avermaet, D. (Eds.). (1985). *Perspectives on minority influence.* Cambridge, UK: Cambridge University Press; Mass, A., & Clark. R. D. (1984). Hidden impact of minorities: Fifteen years of minority influence research. *Psychological Bulletin, 95,* 428–450; Wood, W., Lundgren, S., Ouellette, J. A., Busceme, S., & Blackstone, T. (1994). Minority influence: A meta-analytic review of social influence processes. *Psychological Bulletin, 115,* 323–345; Moscovici, S., Mucchi-Faina, A., & Mass, A. (1994). *Minority influence.* Chicago: Nelson-Hall.

11. Nemeth, C. (1985). Dissent, group process and creativity: The contribution of minority influence research. In E. Lawler (Ed.), *Advances in group processes* (Vol. 2, pp. 57–75). Greenwich, CT: JAI; Nemeth, C., & Chiles, C. (1986). Modeling courage: The role of dissent in fostering independence. *European Journal of Social Psychology, 18,* 275–280.

12. Mugny, G., & Perez, J. A. (1991). *The social psychology of minority influence* (V. W. Lamongie, Trans.). Cambridge, UK: Cambridge University Press.

13. Janis, I. (1971, November). Groupthink: The problems of conformity. *Psychology Today,* pp. 271–279.; Janis, I. (1982). *Groupthink* (2nd ed.). Boston: Houghton Mifflin; Janis, I. (1989). *Crucial decisions: Leadership in policymaking and crisis management.* New York: Free Press.

14. Portions of this material were adapted from: Johnson, C. E., & Hackman, M.Z. (1995). *Creative communication: Principles and applications.* Prospect Heights, IL: Waveland Press, chap. 5.

15. Janis (1982), p. 40

16. Sims, R. R. (1992). Linking groupthink to unethical behavior in organizations. *Journal of Business Ethics, 11,* 651–662.

17. See, for example: Bernthal, P. R., & Insko, C. A. (1993). Cohesiveness without groupthink: The interactive effects of social and task cohesion. *Group & Organizational Management, 18,* 66–87; Chen, A., Lawson, R. B., Gordon, L. R., & McIntosh, B. (1996). Groupthink: Deciding with the leader and the devil. *Psychological Record, 46,* 581–590; Esser, J. K. (1998). Alive and well after 25 years: A review of groupthink research. *Organizational Behavior and Human Decision Processes, 73,* 116-141; Flippen, A. R. (1999). Understanding groupthink from a self-regulatory perspective. *Small Group Research, 30,* 139–165; Postmes, T., Spears, R., & Cihangir, S. (2001). Quality of decision-making and group norms. *Journal of Personality and Social Psychology, 80,* 918–930; Street, M. D. (1997). Groupthink: An examination of theoretical issues, Implications, and future research suggestions. *Small Group Research, 28,* 72–93; T'Hart, P. (1990). *Groupthink in government: A study of small groups and policy failure.* Baltimore, MD: Johns Hopkins University Press.

18. Moorhead, G., Neck, C. P., & West, M. S. (1998). The tendency toward defective decision making within self-managing teams: The relevance of groupthink for the 21st century. *Organizational Behavior and Human Decision Processes, 73,* 327–351; Manz, C. C., & Neck, C. P. (1995). Teamthink: Beyond the groupthink syndrome in self-managing work teams. *Journal of Managerial Psychology, 10,* 7–15.

19. Harvey, J. (1988). *The Abilene Paradox and other meditations on management.* Lexington, MA: Lexington Books; Harvey, J. (2001). The Abilene Paradox: The

management of agreement. *Organizational Dynamics, 33,* 17–34; Kanter, R. M. (2001). An Abilene defense: Commentary one. *Organizational Dynamics, 33,* 37–40.

20. Harvey (2001), p. 15.

21. See, for example: Staw, B. M. (1981). The escalation of commitment to a course of action. *Academy of Management Review, 6,* 577–587; Ross, J., & Staw, B. M. (1993). Organizational escalation and exit: Lessons from the Shoreham Nuclear Plant. *Academy of Management Journal, 36,* 701–732; Bobocel, D. R., & Meyer, J. P. (1994). Escalating commitment to a failing course of action: Separating the roles of choice and justification. *Journal of Applied Psychology, 79,* 360–363; McNamara, G., Moon, H., & Bromiley, P. (2002). Banking on commitment: Intended and unintended consequences of an organization's attempt to attenuate escalation of commitment. *Academy of Management Journal, 45,* 443–452.

22. Whyte, G. (1991). Diffusion of responsibility: Effects on the escalation tendency. *Journal of Applied Psychology, 76,* 408–415; Jones, P. E., & Roelofsma, P. H. M. P. (2000). The potential for social contextual and group biases in team decision-making: Biases, conditions and psychological mechanisms. *Ergonomics, 43,* 1129–1152.

23. Keil, M., & Montealegre, R. (2000, Spring). Cutting your losses: Extricating your organization when a big project goes awry. *Sloan Management Review*, pp. 55–58; Ross & Staw (1993).

24. Barker, J. R. (1993). Tightening the iron cage: Concertive control in self-managing teams *Administrative Science Quarterly, 38,* 408–437.

25. Tompkins, P. K., & Cheney, G. (1985). Communication and unobtrusive control in contemporary organizations. In R. D. McPhee & P. K. Tompkins (Eds.), *Organizational communication: Traditional themes and new directions* (pp. 179–210). Newbury Park, CA: Sage; Bullis, C. (1991). Communication practices as unobtrusive control: An observational study. *Communication Studies, 42/3,* 254–271.

26. Barker, J. R. (1999). *The discipline of teamwork: Participation and concertive control.* Thousand Oaks, CA: Sage; Barker (1993).

27. Barker (1999), p. 177.

28. Opotow, S. (1990). Moral exclusion and injustice: An introduction. *Journal of Social Issues, 46,* 1–20.

29. Chang, I. (1997). *The rape of Nanking: The forgotten holocaust of World War II.* New York: Basic Books, p. 218.

30. Opotow (1990).

31. Adams, G. B., & Balfour, D. L. (1998). *Unmasking administrative evil.* Thousand Oaks: CA: Sage.

32. Opotow, S. (1990). Deterring moral exclusion. *Journal of Social Issues, 46,* 173–182; Opotow, S. (1995). Drawing the line: Social categorization, moral exclusion, and the scope of justice. In B. B. Bunker & J. Z. Rubin (Eds.), *Conflict, cooperation, and justice: Essays inspired by the work of Morton Deutsch* (pp. 347–369). San Francisco: Jossey-Bass.

7

Leadership and Followership Ethics

Chapter Preview

Leaders are critical to the ethical transformation of any organization. They are largely responsible for determining mission and values, developing structure, and creating ethical climates. As a consequence, leaders deserve a good deal of credit for transforming ethics and a good deal of the blame when groups fall short. That's why names of prominent leaders are linked to well-publicized ethical successes (Malden Mills CEO Aaron Feuerstein, Starbucks

CEO Howard Schultz) and failures (Martha Stewart, former WorldCom CEO Bernie Ebbers, Enron's Ken Lay, Dennis Kowslowski of Tyco).

While leaders largely determine the ethical direction of organizations, this does not excuse followers from their moral responsibilities. Followers have a choice as to whether or not to follow a particular leader, to maintain the status quo or to work for change, to obey commands or to object, to draw attention to wrongdoing or to keep silent. How they respond to these alternatives will either promote or block transformation.

Both leaders and followers face unique ethical challenges. In the first portion of the chapter, I'll identify the ethical demands of the leadership and followership roles. In the second and third sections, I'll introduce theories and principles that will equip us to meet these moral responsibilities. So armed, we can better function as transforming agents, whether as leaders or as followers.

The Ethical Challenges of Leadership and Followership

Identifying the ethical challenges faced by leaders and followers begins with understanding the expectations associated with each role. Leadership is the exercise of influence in a group context.[1] Leaders engage in furthering the needs, wants, and objectives shared by leaders and followers alike.

Because leadership is exercised in the group context in pursuit of common goals, leaders and followers function collaboratively. They are relational partners who play complementary roles. Leaders take more responsibility for the overall direction of the group; followers are more involved in implementing plans and doing the work itself. Here's a short summary of the functions associated with each role:

Key Leader Functions	*Key Follower Functions*
Establishing direction	Carrying out tasks
Organizing	Generating task-related improvements
Assembling staff	Managing self and responsibilities
Initiating	Engaging in teamwork
Setting structure	Providing feedback
Coordinating activities and resources	Challenging policies and procedures
Motivating	Supplying information
Managing conflicts	Assisting leaders
Determining policies	Modifying policies and procedures

While leaders and followers work together, they face different sets of ethical demands based on the roles they play. We'll turn first to the ethical challenges faced by leaders and then examine the moral demands of followership.

THE ETHICAL CHALLENGES OF LEADERSHIP

Leaders, as noted earlier, exert greater influence and have broader responsibility for organizational outcomes. In light of these realities, they face the following challenges.

1. The Challenge of Power

I talked at length about power and influence in Chapter 5. However, it is worth noting that power is of greater concern to leaders because (a) they generally have more of it, and (b) power is the tool or currency that leaders use to exercise influence over the direction of the group. Leaders have to be particularly careful not to be corrupted by power. Media giant Viacom's CEO Sumner Redstone knows firsthand the seductive nature of power. He reportedly advised Disney CEO Michael Eisner (who was later removed from his post) to hang onto his job despite the efforts of stockholders who opposed him. Redstone told Eisner, "Once you've had this kind of power, Michael, let's face it, nobody wants to give it up."[2]

2. The Challenge of Privilege

Power and privilege generally operate in tandem. The more power a leader has, generally the greater the privileges he or she enjoys. Evidence of this fact can be found in the wide gulf between the nation's highest and lowest paid workers. The gap between the compensation packages of top executives and average workers in the U.S. is wider than ever. The average CEO in the United States makes $301 for every $1 paid to the typical employee, up from a $42 to $1 ratio in 1982.[3]

The appetites of some CEOs are insatiable. Ken Lay wasn't satisfied with being wealthy. He declared, "I don't want to be rich, I want to be world-class rich."[4] Martha Stewart was sentenced to jail and house arrest for lying about a stock sale which saved her $52,000, a tiny percentage of her billion dollar net worth.[5]

Leaders probably deserve higher salaries and more benefits because they shoulder greater responsibility for the success or failure of the organization as a whole. At the same time it is clear that far too many leaders are getting more than they deserve. Leaders must answer such questions as: How much should top managers be paid? How many additional privileges should they enjoy?

What should be the relative difference in pay and benefits between employees and supervisors? What can be done to narrow the current gap in wages and benefits between the top and bottom organizational layers?

3. The Challenge of Responsibility

Leaders are accountable for the entire group (a sports franchise, a nonprofit, a public relations agency), while followers are largely responsible for their own actions. Determining the extent of a leader's responsibility is difficult, however. That becomes evident when ethical standards are violated. Should Wal-Mart be held responsible for the actions of subcontractors who clean their stores using illegal workers making subminimum wages? Can we hold the editor of a newspaper responsible for reporters who plagiarize stories? What should be the penalty for military officers if they sanctioned prisoner abuse in Iraq and Afghanistan? Should they receive the same or harsher sentences than the soldiers who followed their orders? How do we respond to managers who fail to follow the codes of ethics they write for their employees? (See Box 7.1 for examples of leaders who reportedly have consistently failed to take their responsibilities seriously.)

CASE STUDY

Box 7.1 Clueless in the Boardroom

Prominent executives get most of the press when organizations misbehave, but boards of directors share much of the blame. Boards are charged with hiring and firing chief operating officers, shaping policies, monitoring financial performance, and representing the interests of shareholders and donors. Board members can prevent criminal activities if they take their duties seriously. Unfortunately, far too many do not. Directors at Enron, for example, failed to exercise proper oversight. Many members of the energy giant's board didn't seem to understand the company's operations or its numbers. They rarely challenged management decisions. In fact, the Enron directors helped doom the company by approving exceptions to Enron's code of ethics. These waivers allowed chief financial officer Andrew Fastow to create illegal off-the-books partnerships that ultimately led to bankruptcy.

Clueless might be the best adjective to describe Enron's board as well as the boards of other prominent organizations embroiled in scandal. Directors at Worldcom, like Enron, had no inkling of the company's imminent collapse until it was too late. The board of the New York Stock Exchange approved an outrageous pay and benefits package ($140 million as well as a car and driver, private club memberships, and private jet privileges) for former CEO Richard Grasso. However, some NYSE directors later claimed they had no knowledge of the details of the agreement.

A number of factors account for the irresponsible behavior of many boards, both business and nonprofit. In theory, boards are supposed to be independent, but many are beholden to the organization's CEO. They are stacked with friends and relatives of the chief executive who generally rubber-stamp his or her proposals and approve generous raises. For instance, NYSE's Grasso handpicked his compensation committee, which was chaired by Home Depot cofounder Ken Langone, a close friend. Far too many board members have financial ties to the organizations they are supposed to oversee, serving as consultants or suppliers. They don't want to endanger their lucrative arrangements by "rocking the boat" or they may use their board positions to enrich themselves further. Such appears to be the case at the Nature Conservancy. Conservancy board members have been accused of arranging lucrative land deals with the conservation group.

A lack of time and expertise also weakens board oversight. Those who serve on several boards don't have the time and energy to carry out their duties. Individuals lacking financial training often staff board compensation and accounting committees.

Efforts are underway to reform the boardroom. The SEC now requires companies to disclose if they have a financial expert on their audit committees. Firms listed on the New York Stock Exchange must have a majority of independent directors who have no connection to the firm. These directors must meet regularly without management present. A smaller, more independent board now governs the NYSE itself. In the future, the roles of president and chief executive officer may have to be separated. Congress has debated the wisdom of expensing stock options, which are used to reward top execs but aren't usually counted against company earnings. The IRS is taking a closer look at the generous pay packages given a number of nonprofit CEOs (see the Goodwill Case in the Introduction). State attorney generals are also investigating nonprofit boards that misappropriate donations.

Reforms will have limited impact unless those who serve as directors take their responsibilities seriously. They need to study the company's operations carefully, challenge management proposals, engage in vigorous debate, and act immediately when ethics are violated. The board at Apria Healthcare Group models this kind of activism. In less than a day after learning that CEO Philip Carter's wife had been hired for a company position, they demanded his resignation and rescinded her job offer.

DISCUSSION PROBES

1. Can you think of other factors that might encourage boards to act irresponsibly?
2. Which of the recent reforms will have the most positive impact on board performance? Why?

3. What other steps could be taken to reform boards of directors?
4. How would you rate the board of your college or university? Why?
5. Have you ever served on a board? Was the group clueless or active and informed? What elements contributed to its high or poor performance?

SOURCES

Borrus, A., McNames, M., Symonds, W., Byrnes, N., & Park, A. (2003, February 2). Reform: Business gets religion. *BusinessWeek,* pp. 40–41. Retrieved July 6, 2004, from EBSCOhost database.

Brooker, K. (2002, June 24). Fire the chairman of the bored. *Fortune,* pp. 72–73. Retrieved July 6, 2004, from EBSCOhost database.

Elkind, P. (2004, June 14). The trials of Eliot Spitzer. *Fortune,* pp. 33–35. Retrieved July 6, 2004, from EBSCOhost database.

Greed is bad. (2004, May 29). *Economist,* pp. 72–73. Retrieved July 6, 2004, from EBSCOhost database.

Hempel, J., & Borrus, A. (2004, June 21). Now the nonprofits need cleaning up. *BusinessWeek,* pp. 107–108. Retrieved July 6, 2004, from EBSCOhost database.

Lavelle, L. (2002, June 17). When directors join CEOs at the trough. *BusinessWeek,* p. 57. Retrieved July 16, 2002, from EBSCOhost database.

Lavelle, L. (2002, October 7). The best and worst boards. *BusinessWeek,* pp. 104–114.

Answers to these questions can vary depending on the particular situation. Nevertheless, there are some general expectations of leaders. Responsible leaders

- admit they have duties to followers
- take reasonable steps to prevent crimes and other follower abuses
- acknowledge and try to correct ethical problems
- take responsibility for the consequences of their orders and actions
- hold themselves to the same standards as their followers

4. The Challenge of Information Management

Leaders generally have access to more information than do followers. They network with other managers, participate in task forces, keep personnel files, receive financial data, get advance notice of new programs, and so forth. Being "in the know" is a mixed blessing. Leaders need lots of data to carry out their tasks. Yet, possessing knowledge raises some sticky ethical dilemmas. The most obvious is deciding whether or not to tell the truth or to conceal it. Leaders must also determine whether or not to reveal that they have important information, when to release that information, and to whom. Consider the case of the manager who gets early notice of increases in employee health insurance costs. He is asked to keep this knowledge to himself until the official announcement is made. In the meantime, his subordinates are angered by rumors that health coverage is going to be cut altogether. Does he let it slip that he knows what will happen? Does he immediately try to squelch the rumors or maintain his silence? Finally, how information is gathered is yet another concern. Librarians have protested against a provision of the Patriot Act that allows law enforcement agencies to spy on the reading habits of patrons without their knowledge. A number of consumers are uneasy about "courtesy cards" which enable Safeway, Albertsons, and other grocery stores to track the buying habits of individual shoppers.

We'll explore the topics of lying and invasion of privacy in the next chapter. In the meantime, you can use the following as signs that leaders are failing to meet the ethical challenge of information management:

- lying, particularly for selfish ends
- using information solely for personal benefit
- denying having knowledge that is in their possession
- gathering data in a way that violates privacy rights
- withholding information that followers legitimately need
- sharing information with the wrong people
- releasing information at the wrong time (too early or too late)
- putting followers in moral binds by insisting that they withhold information that others have a right to know

5. The Challenge of Consistency

In an ideal world, leaders would treat all followers equally and all followers would respond in an identical fashion. This is not the case, of course. All too often leaders act inconsistently, giving more favorable treatment (extra pay and time off, special attention, longer deadlines) to their friends and to their favorite subordinates. Followers react to leaders in a variety of ways because of diverse backgrounds, skill levels, and personalities. Those from individualistic cultures respond well to personal rewards, while members of collectivist groups (where group unity is prized) do not. Some followers are better at their tasks than others. In addition, tactics that motivate certain individuals will backfire on their colleagues. Wise coaches, for example, know that there are some players who work harder when yelled at in practice and others who get discouraged. The latter group responds better when quietly taken aside for private instruction.

Obviously, a one-size-fits-all approach to managing followers doesn't work. Throw in the fact that rules may have to bend to fit changing circumstances like weather emergencies and flu epidemics, and you can see why consistency puts ethical demands on leaders. They have to determine (a) how to adapt to individual needs while acting justly; (b) when to bend the rules and for whom; (c) how to adjust to the reality that some followers are going to be more competent than others; and (d) how to be fair to those who aren't as close to them.

Some degree of inconsistency appears inevitable, but leaders generate resentments when they seem to be acting arbitrarily and unfairly. Consistent leaders try their best to respond to the individual preferences of each constituent while supporting the principle that all followers deserve the same level of respect and attention. They go out of their way to treat "fringe" subordinates (those who are less skilled, less committed, and less connected to the leader) justly and compassionately, providing equal access to promotions and other benefits. Fair leaders also try to be evenhanded in their dealings with outsiders, treating their opponents as well as their friends with respect.

6. The Challenge of Loyalty

Leaders have to balance a variety of loyalties, weighing their commitments to employees, suppliers, families, investors, their professions, the larger society, and the environment. Model leaders put the needs of the larger community ahead of selfish interests (see Chapter 10). They reject decisions that benefit themselves and their organizations at the expense of such outside constituencies as consumers, neighborhoods, local governments, and fellow professionals. Leaders also face the challenge of honoring the loyalty that followers and others place in them. Followers trust leaders to act in their best interests and the public trusts leaders to act as responsible members of the community. Many organizational leaders fail to live up this challenge. Managers at the Imperial Food Products chicken-processing plant, for example, betrayed the trust of workers by padlocking exit doors and failing to install a sprinkler system. When fire broke out, 25 employees died and 56 were injured. Severely damaged, the plant closed down and the town of Hamlet, North Carolina, lost its largest employer.[6]

THE ETHICAL CHALLENGES OF FOLLOWERSHIP

Followers, like leaders, face a special set of demands or challenges based on the nature of the role they play. As we saw earlier, followers are charged with carrying out the work and implementing the directives of leaders. They have less power and status than leaders do. In light of these realities, here are important moral challenges confronted by followers.

1. The Challenge of Obligation

All followers have obligations to their leaders as well as to the institutions that provide them with paychecks, retirement plans, friendships, prestige, training, fulfilling work, and other benefits. Obligations don't end at the organizational door, however. Followers must frequently fulfill duties to external stakeholders. For instance, government employees "owe" it to taxpayers to use their money wisely by working hard and spending carefully. Members of a law firm owe their clients the best possible representation as well as accurate billing.

Determining minimal responsibilities is easier than deciding how far follower obligations should extend. At the very least, employees shouldn't rip off their employers by showing up late (or not at all), doing nothing, and stealing property. Yet some workers are asked to sacrifice too much for their organizations. Consider the case of technology and consulting firms that demand that employees travel constantly, work nights and weekends, and attend meetings instead of their kids' school events. Giving into the excessive demands of workaholic organizations generates stress and burnout, endangering mental health, marriages, and relationships with children. Volunteers must also determine what they owe their leaders and groups. Religious cults are criticized for demanding that followers devote long hours to the cause, turn over their paychecks to leaders, and cut off their connections to families and friends.

Every situation is different, so followers have to determine if they are meeting their ethical obligations or giving too little or too much. However, the following questions can serve as a guide to sorting out the obligations we owe as followers.

- Am I doing all I reasonably can to carry out my tasks and further the mission of my organization? What more could I do?
- Am I earning the salary and benefits I receive?
- Can I fulfill my organizational obligations and, at the same time, maintain a healthy personal life and productive relationships? If not, what can I do bring my work and personal life into balance?

2. The Challenge of Obedience

Followers must routinely obey orders and directives, even the ones they don't like. Deciding when to disobey is the challenge. There's no doubt that following authority can drive followers to engage in illegal and immoral activities that they would never participate in on their own. This point was driven home in experiments carried out by Stanley Milgram.[7] Students playing the role of teacher were asked to administer shocks to a learner when he answered incorrectly. Subjects continued to ramp up the voltage of the shocks at the request of the experimenter even though the learner (really an actor who received no shock at all) expressed more and more discomfort. Two thirds of the students obeyed the experimenter despite the pleas and screams of the learner.

Milgram's findings only confirm what has been repeated time and again in real life. Serbian soldiers charged with war crimes, members of Rwandan death squads, and Saddam Hussein's torturers committed atrocities because they were "following orders." However, following orders is no excuse. This is called the Nuremberg trials principle.[8] At the Nuremberg war crime trials following World War II, the tribunal rejected claims that atrocities were justified because German defendants were obeying authority. Based on this principle, the U.S. Army punishes those who follow illegal orders.

Every follower has to consider such factors as: (a) Does this order appear to call for unethical behavior? (b) Would I engage in this course of action if I weren't ordered to? (c) What are the potential consequences for others if these directions are followed? For myself? (d) Does obedience threaten the mission and health of the organization as a whole? (e) What steps should I take if I decide to disobey?

3. The Challenge of Cynicism

It's easy for followers to get cynical. They don't have much power, and they are often left out of the information loop and important decisions. Often the choices and actions of their leaders appear arbitrary if not stupid.

Cynicism can be justified (just look at what happened to thousands of loyal, hard-working employees at Enron, Worldcom, Arthur Andersen, and elsewhere). Nevertheless, cynicism acts like acid, reducing commitment levels, destroying trust, cutting off communication, and lowering organizational performance. Few of us give our best effort when we are skeptical about the organizations we've committed ourselves to. The more cynical we become, the more energy we put into critiquing and complaining and the less we devote to the task at hand. Followers must walk a fine line between healthy skepticism, which prevents them from being exploited, and unhealthy cynicism, which undermines their efforts and those of the group as a whole.

4. The Challenge of Dissent

Followers frequently take issue with policies, procedures, orders, working conditions, pay, benefits, values, and other factors. They can't make the changes themselves, so they must express their disagreement to those who can. At this point followers must make a number of strategic decisions. To begin, they have to determine when to speak up and when to keep silent. There may be several points of contention, but generally followers have to "pick their battles." Raising too many issues may turn leaders off and can label the follower as a whiner. On the other hand, silence can be immoral, as in the case of the engineer who discovers his company is shipping defective airplane parts but decides to keep this information to himself.

Once the decision to protest has been made, followers must then determine

- how to express dissent (when, what to say, through what channels)
- who to contact with their concerns (immediate supervisor, professional supervisor, etc.)
- how to respond if their opinions are rejected
- when to go outside the organization with concerns and complaints

5. The Challenge of Bad News

Few of us have a problem with telling our superiors what they want to hear. For example, we've reached our goals, sales are up, the project is under budget, and the software implementation will be done on time. Delivering bad news is much riskier. Telling our bosses what they don't want hear can incur their wrath, bring penalties, and seriously damage our standing in the organization. The risk is highest when we are directly at fault. No wonder that researchers report that subordinates routinely keep negative information from their superiors, including feedback about leader behaviors that could be undermining the group's success.[9]

Organizations can pay a high price when followers hide or cover over bad news, deny responsibility, or shift blame. Leaders can't take corrective steps if they don't know a problem exists. Their failure to address serious deficiencies like safety hazards and accounting fraud can destroy an organization. Further, leaders who don't get feedback about their ineffective habits can't change these patterns. Teachers who use lots of ums and ahs in their lectures, for example, need feedback about their speech behaviors from students if they are to eliminate these language features. Finally, denying accountability and shifting blame undermines trust and focuses people on defending themselves instead of on solving the problem.

Declaring that ethical followers should faithfully deliver bad news and accept responsibility for their actions is easier than doing so ourselves. Being the bearer of bad tidings takes courage, as we'll see later in the chapter. The challenge is not so much in determining what to do but in following through. As in delivering all messages, selecting the right time, place, and channel is critical. Significant problems should be brought to light as soon as possible, when the receiver is most receptive, and delivered face-to-face, not through e-mail and other less personal channels.

William J. LeMessuier provides an excellent example of someone who didn't hesitate to deliver bad news that revealed his errors. LeMessuier was the lead structural engineer for the Citicorp Tower in New York City that was completed in 1979. After the building was complete, he discovered that the structure's design and braces made it susceptible to wind damage. The building would likely collapse in a violent storm that might occur every 16 years.

LeMessuier could have kept silent. Instead, he put his professional reputation on the line and admitted his mistakes to the architect and top Citicorp officers. Working together, LeMessuier and company officials developed a plan to fix the brace problem. In 3 months the mistake was fixed. The project manager for the project described the incident and LeMessurier this way: "It started with a guy who stood up and said, 'I got a problem, I made the problem, let's fix the problem.'"[10]

Meeting the Moral Demands of Leadership: Normative Leadership Theories

Normative leadership theories tell leaders how to act. They are designed to help us manage our ethical duties when we take on the leadership role. While specifically focused on the leader-follower relationship, these approaches draw heavily from general ethical perspectives, character ethics, and other material presented in earlier chapters.

TRANSFORMATIONAL LEADERSHIP

Since the late 1970s, the transformational approach has emerged as the dominant perspective in leadership studies. Former presidential advisor, political scientist, and historian James MacGregor Burns laid the groundwork for this approach in his book *Leadership*. Burns identified two forms of leadership he labeled as transactional and transformational. Transactional leadership is based on leader-member exchange. Leaders trade money, benefits, and recognition for the labor and obedience of followers. They emphasize values that make routine transactions go smoothly—responsibility, fairness, and honesty. The underlying system remains unchanged. Transformational leadership is more powerful and inspiring. Transformational leaders speak to higher level needs—the need to belong, to feel good about oneself, and to reach one's full potential. They spotlight values that are more likely to mobilize and energize followers like equality, liberty, justice, freedom.[11] In the process, these leaders change the very nature of the group, the organization or the society.

Burns sketched the broad outline of transformational leadership; it was up to other researchers to fill in the details. Bernard Bass, Bruce Avolio, and their colleagues identified seven dimensions of transactional and transformational leadership.[12] Transactional leaders rely on *contingent reward* and *management-by-exception*. They provide rewards and recognition for acceptable performance while disciplining followers who fall below performance standards. The poorest transactional leaders are *passive-avoidant* or *laissez-faire*. They are inactive, failing to provide goals or standards or to clarify expectations.

Transformational leaders engage in the following:

1. Idealized Influence

Transformational leaders serve as admired role models for followers. They put the needs of others first; share risks with followers; and act in a way that is consistent with the group's values and principles.

2. Individualized Consideration

Transformational leaders act as coaches and mentors, continually encouraging follower development. They provide learning opportunities along with a supportive climate. Their coaching, mentoring, and teaching efforts are tailored to the personal concerns of each follower.

3. Inspirational Motivation

Transforming leaders motivate and inspire through providing meaning and challenge to the work of followers. They are enthusiastic and optimistic, arousing team spirit and focusing follower attention on desirable organizational visions.

4. Intellectual Stimulation

Transformational leaders foster creativity and innovation in followers by questioning assumptions, reframing situations, and tackling old problems in new ways. They don't criticize mistakes or new approaches. At the same time, they are open to creative ideas that may challenge their opinions.

Burns believed that leaders were either transactional or transformational, but later investigators found that highly effective leaders use *both* transactional and transformational tactics. Transformational leaders may inspire, but they aren't afraid to set standards and monitor performance as well as to issue rewards and punishments.

Transforming leadership has attracted so much attention largely because it generates outstanding results. Transformational leaders are more successful than their transactional counterparts in a variety of settings—sales organizations, military units, schools, large corporations.[13] However, Burns left no doubt that transforming leadership rests on an ethical foundation. "Such leadership," stated Burns, "occurs when one or more persons engage with others in such a way that leaders and followers raise one another to higher levels of motivation and morality."[14]

Burns argued that transforming leaders are moral leaders because they produce higher moral standards and performance. However, he apparently overlooked the fact that individuals can use transformational tactics to reach immoral ends. When it comes to idealized influence, some leaders appear to be honest and supportive of their people, but privately they are unreliable and all too willing to sacrifice their followers for their own goals. They engage in inspirational motivation by appealing to the worst in people—their fears, anger, and insecurities. Their approach to intellectual stimulation relies on false assumptions and appeals to their own authority instead of reason and dialogue. Instead of coaching and mentoring followers into leaders, the individualized attention they give followers encourages dependency and blind obedience.

Bernard Bass adopts the terms *authentic* and *pseudo-transformational* to distinguish between ethical and unethical transformational leaders.[15] Authentic transformational leaders are altruistic, genuinely concerned for others and the purposes of the organization as a whole. They channel their energies in constructive ways to serve the greater good. They permit their followers free choice in the hope that the followers will voluntarily commit themselves to worthy moral principles. Pseudo-transformational leaders provide a sharp contrast. They are ultimately self-centered. Instead of caring for others, they may secretly despise them. They use power to manipulate others for personal ends instead of on behalf of shared objectives.

Debate over whether or not there is a distinction between ethical and unethical transformational leaders continues. Nevertheless, if you want to become a more effective, ethical leader, transformational leadership has a lot to offer. The goal of this approach is to raise the level of morality of the group or organization, encouraging those in both leadership and followership roles to set and to meet higher ethical standards. In the process of pursuing this objective, employees engage in higher level moral reasoning and the moral climate and culture of the entire organization improves.[16] Workers achieve higher results at the same time that they generate higher ethical standards. The fact that transforming leadership consists of a set of behaviors means that anyone can act as a transformational leader by adopting these practices. You can employ these behaviors in a variety of contexts (work, sports, the family, volunteer activities). In addition, transforming leadership appears to have universal appeal. A study conducted in 62 countries found that effective leaders in all of these cultures exhibit transformational behaviors. They have high integrity, demonstrate foresight, and inspire others by being positive, dynamic, encouraging and by building their confidence.[17]

SERVANT LEADERSHIP

The servant leadership model is based on the premise that leaders should put the needs of followers before their own needs. This approach has its roots in both Eastern and Western thought. Taoist philosophers encouraged leaders to act like children and humble valleys instead of mountains.[18] Jesus told his disciples, "Whoever wants to become great among you must be your servant, and whoever wants to be first must be slave of all."[19]

Current interest in leaders as servants can be traced back to management expert Robert Greenleaf. He coined the term *servant-leader* in 1970 to describe those whose primary concern is the growth and development of their followers.[20] Greenleaf later founded a nonprofit organization to promote servant-leadership. A number of businesses (Toro Company, TD Industries, Synovus), nonprofit groups, and community leadership programs have adopted this approach. Other notable advocates of servant leadership include James Autry, Margaret Wheatley, Max DePree, and Peter Block.

Practicing servant leadership discourages unethical behavior. Leaders who put concerns of followers first are less likely to accumulate power and privilege for themselves, lie to followers, take advantage of them, or act inconsistently or irresponsibly.

Larry Spears, director of the Greenleaf Center for Servant Leadership, identifies ten characteristics of the servant-leader drawn from Greanleaf's writings.[21] These qualities include:

1. Listening

Servant-leaders put a high priority on listening. They listen intently to others to identify and clarify the needs of the group. They listen to themselves by hearing their inner voices and analyzing what their bodies, minds, and spirits are communicating. Listening to the self, combined with periods of reflection, promotes personal growth.

2. Empathy

Servant-leaders seek both to understand and to empathize with followers. They accept coworkers as unique human beings and assume that others act out of good intentions. However, at the same time, servant leaders refuse to accept destructive behavior or poor performance.

3. Healing

Servant-leaders bring followers to wholeness, helping them recover from emotional injury and to experience the personal ethical development described in Chapter 2.

4. Awareness

Servant-leaders are attuned to elements of a situation as well as to their own thoughts and emotions. Such awareness heightens their sensitivity to the ethical dimension of situations.

5. Persuasion

Servant-leaders rely on persuasion rather than on positional power when making decisions in the organizational setting. While authoritarian leadership relies on coercion, servant leadership builds group consensus.

6. Conceptualization

Servant-leaders master the day-to-day operations but also engage in big picture, long range thinking. They create an attractive long-term vision for the organization.

7. Foresight

Servant-leaders can foresee or anticipate the likely outcome of a situation, such as the possible negative consequences of an ethical choice or marketing plan. This ability also enables them to understand the lessons of the past and the realities of the present.

8. Stewardship

Servant-leaders act as stewards who "hold something in trust for another." Greenleaf believed that CEOs, executive staffs, and boards of directors are particularly responsible for holding their institutions in trust for the greater good of society as a whole. Stewardship is a key element of servant leadership because it focuses on serving the needs of others.

9. Commitment to the Growth of People

Servant-leaders believe in the intrinsic value of people that extends beyond their roles as workers. They seek to promote the personal, professional, and spiritual growth of all employees through, for instance, providing development funds, soliciting suggestions from everyone, and involving workers in the decision-making process

10. Building Community

Servant-leaders recognize that the influence of organizations has supplanted that of local communities. They seek, as a result, to build communities of employees. In this way, a sense of community is rebuilt in society as a whole, one organization at a time.

Advocates of servant leadership have much in common with virtue ethicists. They believe that ethical choices should be based on character rather than codes of conduct. "What you do as a leader," argues management consultant James Autry, "will depend on who you are."[22] Autry uses the phrase "ways of being" to describe the character traits of servant-leaders. If you want to become an ethical leader, you must (a) *be authentic* (be who you are whatever situation you find yourself in); (b) *be vulnerable* (be open about doubts, fears, concerns, and mistakes); (c) *be accepting* (accept ideas as valid for discussion and don't attack others); (d) *be present* (remain wholly focused on the issues at hand and be available to others in the midst of problems and crises); (e) *be useful* (act as a resource for followers). You can develop these characteristics by engaging in the kind of self-listening and reflection described above.

RELATIONAL LEADERSHIP

Relational scholars believe that popular leadership theories are too person centered. Success in the transformational approach, for example, depends almost entirely upon the skill of a leader who sets direction, exercises influence, encourages commitment, helps the group adapt to change, and so on. Relational theorists argue that leadercentric approaches are ill suited to an increasingly complex, interconnected global society. Successful leadership in the postindustrial 21st century will be based on collaboration, consensus, diversity, dealing with ambiguity, and participation. These characteristics emerge, not from the qualities or behaviors of individual leaders, but out of the relationships between leaders and followers that enable them to get things done.

James Rost highlights the partnership between leaders and followers in his definition of leadership. Leadership, he says, "is an influence relationship among leaders and followers who intend real changes that reflect their mutual purposes."[23] Influence in the leadership relationship is noncoercive and flows in many different directions (leaders to followers, followers to leaders, followers to followers, and leaders to leaders). Followers are active partners with leaders. Even though leaders have more power to influence, they work together with constituents. The parties in the relationship work to bring about substantial changes and come to a common agreement about what they hold to be important.

Rost sums up the ethical challenges of leadership by focusing on the interaction between leaders and followers. He argues that leaders need to generate ethical *products* or content (decisions, policies, programs) as they follow ethical *processes.* Influence in the leader-follower relationship should be based on persuasion, not coercion (physical force, psychological intimidation, obedience to authority), and followers must be free to choose whether or not to participate. Goals ought to be jointly created through discussion and argument. Rost concludes by offering the following ethical standard: "The leadership process is ethical if the people in the relationship (the leaders and followers) *freely* agree that the intended changes *fairly* reflect their mutual purposes."[24]

Relational theorists put a high moral value on shared understanding. According to Wilfred (Bill) Drath of the Center for Creative Leadership, people with very different but equally valid worldviews (beliefs, attitudes, values) must accomplish leadership tasks together in the postindustrial or postmodern world.[25] They do so through relational dialogue—talk aimed at the goal of people's understanding each other's experience. (Turn to Chapter 4 for an in-depth look at dialogue.) Together, members of groups and organizations open conversations that make sense of new subjects. Organizational and community members meet to develop a common language to identify and to describe problems before attempting to solve them. For example, the concept of sustainable development, which I'll discuss in Chapter 10, emerged out of earlier conflict between conservationists and economic developers.

Advocates of relational leadership reject many popular ethical perspectives as well as the idea that there is one objective truth or reality. Rost objects to Utilitarianism, Kant's Categorical Imperative, and other popular ethical perspectives on the grounds that they are too individualistic. Instead, he believes that leaders and followers must work together to develop ethical standards by which to judge their actions. He advocates a Communitarian approach, shifting the focus from individual choices to those made by the community and arguing that leaders and followers should pursue the common good. For his part, Drath acknowledges that some worldviews are unworthy because they destroy life and try to dominate other perspectives. However, in general, he believes that there are many different ways of understanding the world, each as useful and valid as the other.

Meeting the Moral Demands of Followership: Principles and Strategies

This final section of the chapter introduces key concepts and tactics designed to help you master the ethical duties of the followership role. To be an ethical, effective follower, you will need to act in an exemplary manner, demonstrate courage, and determine when to bring organizational misconduct to the attention of outsiders.

EXEMPLARY FOLLOWERSHIP

Business professor, consultant, and author Robert Kelley believes that servant followership is more important than servant leadership. He points out that most people spend most of their time in follower roles and that followers contribute the most to organizational success. From an ethical perspective, seeking to be a follower rather than a leader reduces the destructive competition and conflict that occurs when individuals compete against each other for leadership positions. Servant-followers are more likely to build trust and keep the focus on organizational goals. They avoid the temptation to adopt authoritarian, self-centered styles when they do land in leader roles.[26]

Kelley uses the term *exemplary* to describe ideal servant-followers. The best followers score high in two dimensions—independent, critical thinking and active engagement. They think for themselves and, at the same time, take initiative. Outstanding followers contribute innovative ideas and go beyond what is required. Leaders can count on them to take on new challenges, follow through on projects without much supervision, disagree constructively, and think through the implications of their actions.

Kelley contrasts exemplary followers with their less effective counterparts based on two dimensions: independent thinking and engagement (see the Self-Assessment in Box 7.2). *Passive followers* demonstrate little original thought or commitment. They rely heavily on leaders for directions and only meet minimal expectations. Kelley compares them to sheep because they follow herd instincts: "They can be trained to perform necessary simple tasks and then wander around while awaiting further directions."[27] *Conformist followers* are more enthusiastic than their passive coworkers but still depend on leaders to tell them what to do. They follow exactly what the leader says and only tell the leader what he or she wants to hear. Not surprisingly, insecure leaders prefer this type of subordinate.

Self-Assessment

Box 7.2 Followership Styles

Followership Questionnaire

For each statement, think of a followership situation and how you acted. Choose a number from 0 to 6 to indicate the extent to which the statement describes you. 0 indicates rarely applies and 6 indicates almost always.

_____ 1. Does your work help you fulfill some societal goal or personal dream that is important to you?

_____ 2. Are your personal work goals aligned with the organization's priority goals?

(Continued)

(Continued)

_____ 3. Are you highly committed to and energized by your work and organization, giving them your best ideas and performance?

_____ 4. Does your enthusiasm also spread to and energize your co-workers?

_____ 5. Instead of waiting for or merely accepting what the leader tells you, do you personally identify which organizational activities are most critical for achieving the organization's priority goals?

_____ 6. Do you actively develop a distinctive competence in those critical activities so that you become more valuable to the leader and the organization?

_____ 7. When starting a new job or assignment, do you promptly build a record of successes in tasks that are important to the leader?

_____ 8. Can the leader give you a difficult assignment without the benefit of much supervision, knowing that you will meet your deadline with highest-quality work and that you will "fill in the cracks" if need be?

_____ 9. Do you take the initiative to seek out and successfully complete assignments that go above and beyond your job?

_____ 10. When you are not the leader of a group project, do you still contribute at a high level, often doing more than your share?

_____ 11. Do you independently think up and champion new ideas that will contribute significantly to the leader's or the organization's goals?

_____ 12. Do you try to solve the tough problems (technical or organizational), rather than look to the leader to do it for you?

_____ 13. Do you help out co-workers, making them look good, even when you don't get any credit?

_____ 14. Do you help the leader or group see both the upside potential and downside risks of ideas or plans, playing the devil's advocate if need be?

_____ 15. Do you understand the leader's needs, goals, and constraints, and work hard to help meet them?

_____ 16. Do you actively and honestly own up to your strengths and weaknesses rather than put off evaluation?

_____ 17. Do you make a habit of internally questioning the wisdom of the leader's decision rather than just doing what you are told?

_____ 18. When the leader asks you to do something that runs contrary to your professional or personal preferences, do you say "no" rather than "yes"?

_____ 19. Do you act on your own ethical standards rather than the leader's or the group's standards?

_____ 20. Do you assert your views on important issues, even though it might mean conflict with your group or reprisals from the leader?

Finding Your Followership Style

Use the scoring key below to score your answers to the questions.

Independent Thinking Items		*Active Engagement Items*	
Question 1.	______	Question 2.	______
5.	______	3.	______
11.	______	4.	______
12.	______	6.	______
14.	______	7.	______
16.	______	8.	______
17.	______	9.	______
18.	______	10.	______
19.	______	13.	______
20.	______	15.	______
Total Score	______	Total Score	______

Add up your scores on the Independent Thinking items. Record the total on a vertical axis, as in the graph below. Repeat the procedure for the Active Engagement items and mark the total on a horizontal axis. Now plot your scores on the graph by drawing perpendicular lines connecting your two scores.

The juxtaposition of these two dimensions forms the basis upon which people classify followership styles.

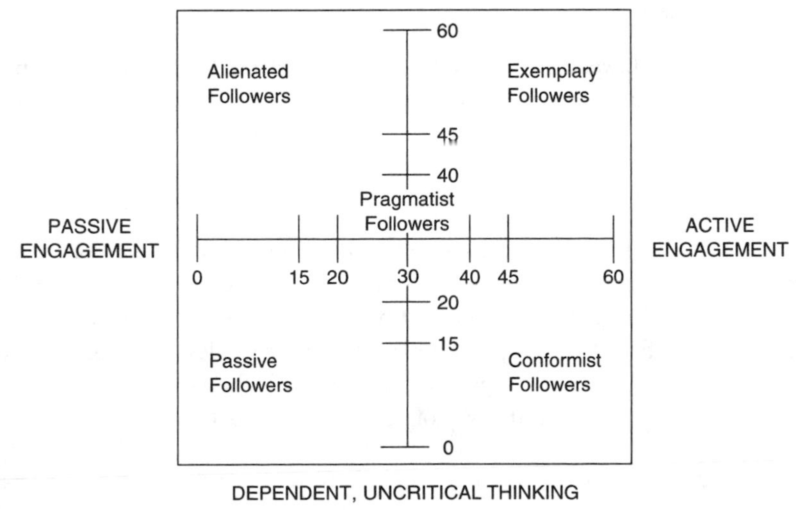

(Continued)

(Continued)

Followership Style	*Independent Thinking Score*	*Active Engagement Score*
EXEMPLARY	High	High
ALIENATED	High	Low
CONFORMIST	Low	High
PRAGMATIST	Middling	Middling
PASSIVE	Low	Low

Source: From *The Power of Followership* by Robert E. Kelley, copyright © 1992 by Consultants to Executives and Organizations, Ltd. Used by permission of Doubleday, a division of Random House, Inc.

Alienated followers are highly independent thinkers who are only minimally committed to their roles and organizations. They put their energies into fighting the leader or organization instead of into reaching shared goals. Alienated followers are highly cynical. They may have started out as exemplary followers but become disillusioned with the leader and/or the group as a whole. *Pragmatic followers* fall in the middle of the independent thinking and engagement continua. Pragmatists often have been victimized by frequent layoffs, restructurings, and leadership changes. They are more interested in surviving than serving.

Kelley outlines five behavior patterns that you need to follow if you hope to become an exemplary follower.

1. Leading Yourself

Excellent followers know how to lead themselves. They step up to their responsibilities and view their work as equal in importance to that of leaders because they recognize that implementation is critical to success.

2. Commit and Focus

Exemplary followers are committed to ideas and causes bigger than themselves. They look beyond their personal careers and needs to serve an elevating purpose like fighting illness or protecting the environment. Because they're committed to a broad principle, exemplary followers feel less need for status or titles. They consider leaders as part of the team and will take steps to keep the leader's ego from getting in the way of achieving the goal.

3. Develop Competence and Credibility

Enthusiastic commitment is not enough. Or, as Kelley tells his students and clients: "Highly committed and motivated incompetence is still incompetence."[28] Exemplary followers set high personal standards which are more strenuous than those set by the leader or the organization as a whole. They are proactive, taking advantage of continuing education and performance development opportunities. Outstanding followers also know their weaknesses and take steps to compensate either by acquiring the necessary skills or by stepping aside to let others complete the task.

4. Use Your Courageous Conscience

Exemplary followers are very concerned about the ethics of their actions even if their leaders are not. Such followers serve as ethical watchdogs. They refuse to abandon personal principles but challenge immoral directives instead (see the discussion of courageous followership in the next section).

5. Disagree Agreeably

Exemplary followers recognize that their job is to make the job of the leader easier, not harder. They work cooperatively with the leader. However, when conflicts arise and decisions must be challenged, outstanding followers disagree using the following strategies:

- Be proactive. Assume that the leader wants the best and operate from that assumption. Sometimes leaders slip because they lack information or are out of touch with followers.
- Gather the facts. Gathering solid evidence makes it easier to disagree and to object in good conscience.
- Seek wise counsel. Find others, most often outsiders, who can provide good advice and test the strength of your position.
- Play by the rules. Exemplary followers want to be seen as part of the community and do so by working within established guidelines whenever possible.
- Persuade by speaking the language of the organization. Proactive followers draw upon the purpose and values of the organization to make their case.
- Prepare your courage to go over heads when absolutely necessary. Exemplary followers don't just go along but test their courage regularly by challenging small ethical breaches.
- Take collective action or plan well to stand alone. Chances of success are greater if you work with others but prepare to step out on your own. Develop contingency plans (other job prospects, savings accounts) when acting individually.

COURAGEOUS FOLLOWERSHIP

Government and business consultant Ira Chaleff believes that followership requires courage.[29] He defines courage as accepting a higher level of risk. It's risky for a camp counselor to confront a camp director who is demeaning children, for a shift supervisor to oppose new work rules developed by the plant manager, or for a member of the cabinet to challenge the decision of the President of the United States. (For an outstanding example of follower courage, turn to the Chapter End Case.) Acting courageously is easier if followers recognize that their ultimate allegiance is to the purpose and values of the organization and not to the leader.

1. The Courage to Assume Responsibility

The first dimension of courageous followership specifically addresses the challenge of obligation. Courageous followers assume responsibility for themselves and the organization as a whole. They assess their own performance, elicit feedback from others, seek opportunities for personal growth, manage their tasks, and maintain a healthy personal life. At the same time, they are passionate about the work of the organization as a whole, taking initiative to challenge the status quo by modifying the culture, challenging rules and mindsets, and improving processes.

2. The Courage to Serve

Courageous followers actively support their leaders, often by working behind the scenes. This service takes form in

- helping leaders conserve their energies by focusing their attention on the most important tasks
- organizing communication flow from and to the leader
- controlling and allowing access to the leader
- screening out unsubstantiated criticism of the leader and defending the leader from unjust criticism
- relaying a leader's messages in an accurate, effective manner
- acting on behalf of the leader when appropriate
- shaping a leader's public image
- focusing the creative leader on the most fruitful ideas
- presenting options during decision making
- encouraging the leader to develop healthy peer relationships
- preparing for and preventing crises
- helping the leader and the group cope with the leader's illness
- mediating conflicts between leaders
- promoting performance reviews for leaders

3. The Courage to Challenge

Inappropriate behavior threatens the leader-follower relationship and the entire organization. Leaders may engage in petty theft, scream at or use demeaning language with employees, display an arrogant attitude, and engage in sexual harassment. Such behavior needs to be confronted immediately, before it becomes a habit. In some instances, a gentle, indirect approach will do, as in questioning the wisdom of a policy or focusing attention on the idea or program rather than on the personal shortcomings of the leader. In more extreme cases, followers will need to directly challenge or disobey orders.

4. The Courage to Participate in Transformation

Unchecked, negative behavior patterns can lead to a leader's destruction. But changing ingrained habits is a long, difficult process. Leaders often deny the need to change or justify their behavior. They may claim that anger is an effective management tool or that misleading investors boosts company profits. To modify their behavior, leaders must admit they have a problem, accept responsibility, and desire to change. They are more likely to persist in the change process if they can visualize positive outcomes like more productive employees, better health, restored relationships, and higher self-esteem. Followers play a critical role in the transformation process by (a) drawing attention to what needs to be changed (and not reinforcing dysfunctional behavior), (b) providing honest feedback, (c) suggesting resources and outside facilitators, (d) creating a supportive climate, (e) modeling openness to change and empathy, (f) helping contain abusive behavior, and (g) providing positive reinforcement when the leader adapts effective new patterns.

5. The Courage to Leave

There are lots of reasons to leave an organization. A new setting may offer more opportunities for personal growth, leaving may help the group as a whole, and followers may be experiencing exhaustion and burnout. However, leaving for principled reasons takes the most courage because it may mean the loss of a job, career, or reputation. Followers should resign when they fail to fulfill the organization's purpose or violate an important trust. They may also withdraw their support when those in authority continue their abuse, violate their professed values, serve their own agendas, and ask followers to engage in unethical and illegal behavior.

WHISTLE-BLOWING

Whistle-blowers are organizational members who decide to remain in the organization but take their concerns about abuses (for example, bid rigging, bribery, unsafe products, substandard working conditions) to outsiders in the hope of correcting the problem.[30] They often begin by expressing their dissent through organizational channels but end up making problems public when their concerns are ignored. Prominent whistle-blowers have become national heroes in recent years. The film *The Insider* profiled scientist Jeffrey Wigand's decision to turn over tobacco company documents to *60 Minutes.* These records and his courtroom testimony revealed that tobacco executives knew about the health risks of cigarettes despite sworn testimony to the contrary. Three whistle-blowers—FBI agent Colleen Rowley, WorldCom auditor Cynthia Cooper, and Enron vice-president Sherron Watkins—were named *Time* magazine's Persons of the Year in 2002.[31]

All the favorable publicity given to famous whistle-blowers could give the impression that going public with concerns is easy and rewarding. Nothing could be further from the truth. Even successful whistle-blowers pay a steep price for speaking up. Wigand lost his high-paying job and his marriage at the same time that his character was attacked in the press. Fellow officers criticized agent Rowley for being disloyal and threatened her with criminal charges for publicizing the FBI's failure to monitor some of the 9/11 highjackers. Cooper was screamed at and shunned by some of her fellow employees. Not one senior WorldCom executive has ever thanked her or her internal audit team that brought the company's accounting scandal to light. Watkins was demoted and given little to do after warning Enron CEO Kenneth Lay about the company's shaky finances.

After conducting a national survey of past whistle-blowers, Terrence Miethe concludes: "Most whistleblowers discover that exposing organizational misconduct is a low-reward and high-risk activity."[32] Dissenters can expect to be attacked instead of supported, despite federal and state laws designed to protect those who come forward and support groups for those who do. They will likely be abandoned by coworkers, criticized or humiliated by superiors, denied promotions, relegated to meaningless positions, cut off from neighbors, and on and on. As a consequence, the majority of employees who learn of organizational transgressions fail to report them.[33]

The experience of Mike Quint illustrates the negative consequences of whistle-blowing. Quint was an engineer assigned to inspect construction of the Los Angeles Metro Rail Project between 1987 and 1991.[34] Quint noted a number of problems on the project that could pose safety hazards to riders, including missing reinforcement bars, poor inspection procedures, and violations of structural codes. After his concerns were ignored, Quint notified a variety of government officials and the local press. Later the Army Corps of Engineers confirmed his allegations and the problems were corrected. Nonetheless, Quint was transferred and terminated, blacklisted from getting another inspection job. He reports feeling depressed, isolated and distrustful, and in poorer physical health.

In light of the risks, blowing the whistle on organizational wrongdoing takes a great deal of courage. Yet courage by itself is not enough. Whistle-blowers must also engage in careful ethical reasoning. They have to determine where their ultimate loyalty should rest, and whether the disruption they will cause is justified. When the whistle blows, everyone in the organization suffers. Workers lose their jobs, the credibility of the organization is damaged, stock prices decline, and so forth.

Ethicist Sissela Bok divides the act of whistle-blowing into three parts to help ethical decision makers weigh the moral implications of exposing misbehavior to outsiders.[35] Each element of the process raises ethical questions, which are summarized by R. A. Johnson in Box 7.3. *Dissent* addresses the relative benefits of going public. Most whistle-blowers believe that their actions will benefit society as a whole. Before going forward, they need to determine if this is indeed the case. Whistle-blowers break their *loyalty* to fellow members and to the group as a whole. Therefore whistle-blowing should only be used as a last resort when time is limited and internal channels aren't an option. Whistle-blowers bring serious charges against individuals in public. *Accusation* highlights the fact that dissenters are ethically obligated to consider such issues as fairness, the public's right to know, anonymity, and their personal motives.

Box 7.3 The Whistle-Blower Checklist

Dissent: When whistle-blowers claim their dissent will achieve a public good, they must ask:

- ✓ What is the nature of the promised benefit?
- ✓ How accurate are the facts?
- ✓ How serious is the impropriety?
- ✓ How imminent is the threat?
- ✓ How closely linked to the wrongdoing are those accused?

Loyalty: When whistle-blowers breach loyalty to their organization, they must ask:

- ✓ Is whistle-blowing the last and only alternative?
- ✓ Is there no time to use routine channels?
- ✓ Are internal channels corrupted?
- ✓ Are there no internal channels?

Accusation: When whistle-blowers are publicly accusing others, they must ask:

- ✓ Are the accusations fair?
- ✓ Does the public have a right to know?

(Continued)

(Continued)

✓ Is the whistle-blower *not* anonymous?
✓ Are the motives *not* self-serving?

Source: Johnson, R. A. (2003). *Whistle-blowing: When it works—and why*. Boulder, CO: Lynne Rienner, p. 30.

Implications

- The ethical challenges of leaders and followers are a product of their complementary roles. As a leader, you will have power, broader authority, and more responsibility for the overall direction of the group. As a follower, you are accountable for implementing plans and carrying out the work.
- The six moral demands you'll face as a leader include: (1) the challenge of power; (2) the challenge of privilege; (3) the challenge of information management; (4) the challenge of consistency; (5) the challenge of loyalty; and (6) the challenge of responsibility.
- The moral demands you'll face as a follower are the challenge of obligation, the challenge of obedience, the challenge of cynicism, the challenge of dissent, and the challenge of delivering bad news.
- To be a transformational leader means speaking to the higher level needs of followers and raising the ethical standards of the organization. This requires practicing idealized influence, individualized consideration, inspirational motivation, and intellectual stimulation.
- Servant-leaders avoid the ethical pitfalls of the leadership role by putting the needs of followers first. You can put servant leadership into practice by acting as a steward, fulfilling obligations, partnering with followers, and exercising moral character.
- As a leader, keep in mind that you accomplish shared goals together with followers. Your goal is to generate ethical products (decisions, policies, procedures) through ethical processes that encourage free choice and participation.
- In order to act as an exemplary follower, you'll need to practice service to your leaders and organizations by exercising independent, critical thought and by becoming actively engaged in organizational affairs.
- You will need to demonstrate courage if you are to fulfill your ethical duties as a follower. Dimensions of courage include: (a) the courage to assume responsibility; (b) the courage to serve; (c) the courage to challenge; (d) the courage to participate in transformation; and (e) the courage to leave.
- Whistle-blowing, bringing wrongdoing to the attention of outsiders, should only be considered as a last resort. Not only will you need courage to be a whistle-blower, but you'll also have to engage in careful moral reasoning, weighing the relative benefits of going public, breaking loyalties, and publicly accusing others.

Application Projects

1. In a group, identify additional ethical demands on leaders and followers that you would add to those in the chapter.
2. Create a case study that illustrates how a leader or follower responded to one of the ethical challenges.
3. Which ethical challenge is the most difficult to resolve? Write up your conclusions.
4. Apply the characteristics of transformational leadership to a leader of your choice. Determine if this person is transactional or transformational. Defend your conclusion.
5. Identify the strengths and weaknesses of each of the normative leadership theories presented in the chapter. Which one do you find most useful and helpful?
6. Have you had to display any of the dimensions of courageous followership? Share your story in a small group.
7. Rate yourself as a follower. Into which category do you fall? What can you do to become a more exemplary follower? Write up your analysis.
8. Analyze the actions of a whistle-blower using Bok's checklist. Was this person justified in coming forward?

CHAPTER END CASE

Courage Under Fire: Hugh Thompson at My Lai

The massacre of 500 unarmed civilians at the Vietnamese village of My Lai is one of the darkest moments in U.S. military history. On the morning of March 16, 1968, troops from Task Force Barker entered the village of My Lai in South Vietnam. American soldiers expected stiff resistance from a large contingent of Vietcong reportedly in the area. Task force members were in a vengeful mood, bitter at local residents who had failed to warn them about booby traps and mine-fields. When they encountered no Vietcong, soldiers turned on innocent villagers—women, elderly men, children, and babies—instead. For several hours, members of Charlie Company, under the direction of Lieutenant William Calley, went on a murderous rampage. They threw fragmentation grenades into houses, gunned down villagers who were trying to surrender, slit the throats of some of their victims, and raped others.

In the midst of this evil, one small group of men acted with courage. Army helicopter pilot Hugh Thomson and crewmembers Lawrence Colburn and Glenn Andreotta were assigned to fly over the village to draw enemy fire. When they came back from refueling, what they saw didn't make sense. The ground was littered with the bodies of civilians and water buffalo. They saw a teenage girl, seriously injured, lying on her back in a rice field. They marked her location with a smoke flare and radioed for help. An American soldier walked up, nudged her with his foot, and then shot her.

After confirming that the Americans were killing unarmed villagers, Thompson landed his helicopter between a band of soldiers and a group of Vietnamese huddled in a bunker. Thompson told Colburn to shoot if they began to fire at the civilians. He warned the commanding officer: "You see my guns? If you open up, they open up."[1] The pilot was able to get 10 people out of the bunker and safely to a bigger chopper for evacuation.

Andreotta noticed movement on their last pass over an irrigation ditch containing many of the victims. Thompson set the helicopter down and, covered by the weapons of his fellow crewmembers, Androetta rescued a 4-year-old boy. The child was covered with blood but otherwise unhurt. Thompson then flew back to base and confronted his superiors. However, the story of My Lai didn't become public until 18 months later when Ron Ridenhour, a GI who heard about My Lai from buddies in Task Force Barker, brought the story to the attention of *New York Times* writer Seymour Hirsch and government officials.

Nearly 80 soldiers participated in the killing and subsequent cover up. Twenty-five stood trial but just one, William Calley, was convicted. Calley was seen as a scapegoat by both supporters and opponents of the war and eventually served only 3 years of house arrest. For his part, Thompson received death threats for testifying about the crime. It took 30 years for Thompson and Colburn to be officially acknowledged for their heroics. In 1998 they were given the highest noncombat military honor—the Soldiers Medal—despite resistance from some at the Pentagon. (Andreotta died during the war.) That same year the former pilot and his crewmember returned to My Lai to be reunited with the little boy they had rescued from the killing fields.

Thompson labels what happened at My Lai "premeditated murder." He told a My Lai symposium, "It did not take a rocket scientist to realize it was wrong."[2] The chief prosecutor for the My Lai courts-martial sums up Thompson's heroics this way: "When you have evil, sometimes, in the midst of it, you will have incredible, selfless good. And that's Hugh Thompson."[3]

DISCUSSION PROBES

1. How do you account for Thompson's courage and that of his crew?
2. Can you think of other examples of followers who risked their lives in the face of evil?
3. What parallels do you see between the massacre at My Lai and prisoner abuse in Iraq and Afghanistan?

4. Why do you think so few were punished for their actions at My Lai?

5. Why is it so difficult for organizations to admit their guilt?

6. How can the military and other organizations encourage followers to act with moral courage?

NOTES

1. Thompson (1999).
2. Berry (1995), p. 11
3. Boyce (2001), p. 33.

SOURCES

Belknap, M. R. (2002). *The Viet Nam war on trial: The My Lai massacre and the court martial of Lieutenant Calley*. Lawrence: University of Kansas Press.

Berry, J. (1995, February 24). My Lai massacre was an American tragedy. *National Catholic Reporter*, pp. 10–11. Retrieved June 23, 2004, from EBSCOhost database.

Boyce, N. (2001, August 20). Hugh Thompson. *U.S. News and World Report*, pp. 33–34. Retrieved June 23, 2004, from Academic Source Premier database.

Hitchens, C. (2001, May 28). Leave no child behind? *The Nation*, pp. 9-10. Retrieved June 23, 2004, from EBSCOhost database.

Thompson, H. (1999, March 8). The massacre at My Lai. *Newsweek*, p. 64. Retrieved June 23, 2004, from EBSCOhost database.

Vistica, G. L. (1997, November 24). A quiet war over the past. *Newsweek*, p. 41. Retrieved June 23, 2004, from EBSCOhost database.

Endnotes

1. Yukl, G. (2002). *Leadership in organizations* (5th ed.). Upper Saddle River, NJ: Prentice Hall, chap. 1.

2. Sellers, P. (2005, August 22), Retire? No Way! *Fortune*, p. 18. Retrieved January 2, 2006, from EBSCOhost database.

3. Fonda, D., & Kadlec, D. (2004, May 31). The rumble over executive pay. *Time*, pp. 62–64.

4. Cruver, B. (2002). *Anatomy of greed: The unshredded truth from an Enron insider*. New York: Carroll & Graf, p. 23.

5. Naughton, K., & Gimbel, B. (2004, March 14). Martha's fall. *Newsweek*, pp. 28–36.

6. Wright, J. P., Cullen, F. T., & Blankenship, M. B. (2002). Chained factory fire exits: Media coverage of a corporate crime that killed 25 workers. In M. D. Ermann & R. J. Lundman (Eds.), *Corporate and governmental deviance* (6th ed., pp. 262–276). New York: Oxford University Press.

7. Milgram, S. (1974). *Obedience to authority*. New York: Harper & Row.

8. Chaleff, I. (1995). *The courageous follower: Standing up to and for our leaders.* San Francisco: Berritt-Koehler, p. 162.

9. Roloff, M. E., & Paulson, G. D. (2001). Confronting organizational transgressions. In J. M. Darley, D. M. Messick, & T. R. Tyler (Eds.), *Social influences on ethical behavior in organizations* (pp. 53–68). Mahwah, NJ: Lawrence Erlbaum.

10. Susskind, L., & Field, P. (1996). *Dealing with an angry public.* New York: Free Press, p. 223.

11. Burns, J. M. (1978). *Leadership.* New York: Harper & Row; Burns, J. M. (2003). *Transforming leadership: A new pursuit of happiness.* New York: Atlantic Monthly Press.

12. Avolio, B. J. (1999). *Full leadership development: Building vital forces in organizations.* Thousand Oaks, CA: Sage; Bass, B. M., Avolio, B. J., Jung, D. I., Berson, Y. (2003). Predicting unit performance by assessing transformational and transactional leadership. *Journal of Applied Psychology, 88,* 207–218; Bass, B. M. (1996). *A new paradigm of leadership: An inquiry into transformational leadership.* Alexandria, VA: Army Research Institute for the Behavior and Social Sciences.

13. Lowe, K. B., & Kroeck, K. G. (1996). Effectiveness correlates of transformational and transactional leadership: A meta-analytic review. *Leadership Quarterly, 7,* 385–425.

14. Burns (1978), p. 20.

15. Bass, B. M. (1995). The ethics of transformational leadership. In J. Ciulla (Ed.), *Ethics: The heart of leadership* (pp. 169–192). Westport, CT: Praeger; Bass, B. B, & Steidlmeier, P. (1999). Ethics, character, and authentic transformational leadership behavior. *Leadership Quarterly, 10,* 181–227.

16. For empirical evidence that transformational leadership raises ethical standards for both leaders and followers, see: Turner, N., Barling, J., Epitropaki, O., Butcher, V., & Milner, C. (2002). Transformational leadership and moral reasoning. *Journal of Applied Psychology, 87,* 304–311; Graham, J. (1995). Leadership, moral development, and citizenship behavior. *Business Ethics Quarterly, 5,* 43–54.

17. House, R. J., Hanges, P. J., Javidan, M., Dorfman, P. W., & Gupta, V. (2004). *Culture, leadership, and organizations: The GLOBE study of 62 societies.* Thousand Oaks, CA: Sage.

18. Johnson, C. E. (2000). Taoist leadership ethics. *Journal of Leadership Studies, 7,* 82–91.

19. Matthew 20:26 in *The Holy Bible: New International Version* (1973). Grand Rapids, MI: Zondervan.

20. Greenleaf, R. K. (1977). *Servant leadership.* New York: Paulist Press; Ruschman, N. L. (2002). Servant-leadership and the best companies to work for in America. In L. C. Spears & M. Lawrence (Eds.), *Focus on leadership: Servant-leadership for the twenty-first century* (pp. 123–139). New York: John Wiley.

21. Spears, L. (2002). Introduction: Tracing the past, present and future of servant-leadership. In L. Spears & M. Lawrence (Eds.), *Focus on leadership: Servant-leadership for the twenty-first century* (pp. 1–18). New York: John Wiley.

22. Autry, J. A. (2001). *The servant leader.* New York: Crown.

23. Rost, J. (1991). *Leadership for the twenty-first century.* New York: Praeger, p. 102. See also: Rost, J. (1993). Leadership in the new millennium. *Journal of Leadership Studies, 1,* 92–110.

24. Rost (1991), p. 109.

25. Drath, W. (2001). *The deep blue sea: Rethinking the source of leadership.* San Francisco: Jossey-Bass.

26. Kelley, R. E. (1998). Followership in a leadership world. In L. C. Spears (Ed.), *Insights on leadership* (pp. 170–184). New York: John Wiley. See also: Kelley, R. E. (1992). *The power of followership: How to create leaders people want to follow and followers who lead themselves.* New York: Doubleday/Currency.

27. Kelley (1998), p. 175.

28. Kelley (1998), p. 178.

29. Chaleff (1995).

30. Johnson, R. A. (2003). *Whistle-blowing: When it works and why.* Boulder, CO: Lynne Rienner.

31. Lacoay, R., & Ripley, A. (2003, January 6). Persons of the year. *Time,* pp. 30–60.

32. Miethe, T. D. (1999). *Whistleblowing at work: Tough choices in exposing fraud, waste, and abuse on the job.* Boulder, CO: Westview Press, p. 209.

33. Roloff, M. E., & Paulson, G. D. (2001). Confronting organizational transgressions. In J. M. Darley, D. M. Messick, & T. R. Tyler (Eds.), *Social influences on ethical behavior in organizations* (pp. 53–68). Mahwah, NJ: Lawrence Erlbaum.

34. Miethe (1999).

35. Bok, S. (1980). Whistleblowing and professional responsibilities. In D. Callahan & S. Bok (Eds.), *Ethics teaching in higher education* (pp. 277–295). New York: Plenum Press.

Part V

Transforming the Ethics of Organizational Systems

8

Combating Destructive Behavior

Chapter Preview

Violence, sexual harassment, lies, racist comments, insults, and other destructive actions are an unpleasant fact of life in far too many workplaces. Like the dangerous aspects of ourselves, the shadow side of organizations must be acknowledged and confronted. There is little hope of transforming organizational systems unless we first address the behaviors that undermine any change effort. The good news is that understanding what motivates and encourages such behavior can lead to prevention. In the pages to come we'll examine six types of misbehaviors with the goal of reducing their frequency (in ourselves and in others) and minimizing their damage.

Confronting Problematic Behaviors

Problematic behaviors earn that label because, while they are generally undesirable, they can be morally justified under certain circumstances. Deception and invasion of privacy are two such behaviors. We need to acknowledge the damage they cause. Yet, at the same time, we need to recognize that they are not universally condemned. In this section we'll take a closer look at the ethical dilemmas posed by deception and invasion of privacy as well as guidelines for resolving these issues.

DECEPTION

All forms of deceit involve knowingly misleading other people. Lies are the most obvious example of messages designed to convince others of something we ourselves don't believe. Liars are (a) aware that the information is false, and (b) knowingly deliver a message with (c) the intent of misleading someone else. Deception can also occur when parties keep secrets or reveal only part of the truth (see the Case Study in Box 8.1).

CASE STUDY

Box 8.1 This Train Isn't Leaving the Station

Consider the case of the public relations director for a popular regional historic site. The park's restored village completely recreates an earlier era, showing home life and skilled craftspeople working their trades. The most visible attraction, though, and the one most clearly identified with the site, is an authentic restored railroad train, which visitors not only tour, but can also ride for an hour-long trip through the surrounding countryside.

It's time to begin promotion of the upcoming season. With minor adjustments of times or fees, the announcement of the park's opening has been largely the same year after year. One thing, though, is different this year: The popular train will not be operating at all this season, because it is undergoing extensive maintenance and repair work. It will be on the grounds for outside viewing, but visitors will not be able to board it. One concern, of course, is that many people will not visit the site if the most prominent attraction is not operating. This will be a loss for the visitors, because they will miss out on the wonderful experiences they can gain from the other attractions. But it is also true that lower attendance could affect the finances of the park.

The PR director's considered course of action is to simply issue a news release similar to ones of earlier years, giving the factual information about the season. There will be even fuller descriptions of the other attractions, but there will be no mention of the train not operating. Before they pay their admission, visitors arriving at the park will be advised by a large sign that the train is not operating.

DISCUSSION PROBES

1. What is the potential harm to the public if the director withholds the information that the train isn't running in the news release? The potential benefit?
2. What is the potential benefit to the PR director and organization of withholding information about the train's repairs? The potential cost?
3. Is withholding information justified in this case? Why or why not? Would your answer be different if the director was buying ad space instead of sending a press release?
4. What alternative courses of action would you suggest to the public relations manager to the one that he or she is considering?

SOURCE

Schick (1994). From *Public Relations Quarterly* by Hudson, Howard Penn. Copyright © 1994 by *Public Relations Quarterly*. Reproduced with permission of *Public Relations Quarterly* in the format Textbook via Copyright Clearance Center.

Most moral thinkers concur that lying is wrong.[1] Deontological theorists (and some theologians) generally prohibit lying on the basis that such behavior violates moral law or duty. If everyone lied, we would lose our confidence in verbal commitments and in the value of speech itself. Many Utilitarians point out that lies typically cause more harm than good. Even if the benefits of a particular lie outweigh the harm (telling "white" lies to protect the feelings of a coworker, for example), the practice of lying generates more costs than benefits. Virtue ethicists note the damage done to the character of the person who lies. Habitual lying becomes second nature, driving out such virtues as honesty, consistency, and integrity.

Researchers who study lying in the organizational context also take a dim view of the practice. They note that lying is costly to organizational performance. Lies not only undermine trust, they corrupt the flow of information essential to organizational decisions and coordination. Deception damages the reputation of the organization, lowers job satisfaction, drives out ethical employees, and encourages further dishonesty.[2]

While the preponderance of evidence suggests that lying and related forms of deception are unethical, there are a number of exceptions to this general rule. The law allows police officers to lie to suspects in order to obtain confessions, for instance, and we applaud investigators who go undercover to uncover fraud and corruption. Organizations maintain trade secrets and nations attempt to dupe each other during war.

Ethicist Sissela Bok offers the *principle of veracity* as a way to affirm our commitment to the truth while acknowledging that deceit may be justified in special circumstances.[3] She contends that truth should function as the moral standard. Liars must assume the burden of proof if they want to violate this standard, establishing that deceit is justified. In particular, they need to look at the lie from the target's point of view. Deception might be justified from the liar's vantage point, but it's much more difficult to defend lying when taking the other person's perspective. Targets of deception typically feel victimized even by well-intentioned lies.

What special circumstances might permit lying? Bok doesn't offer a definitive list but suggests that deception might be justified when (1) there is significant threat to life and safety; (2) society has publicly agreed that certain forms of deceit can be used, like unmarked patrol cars, surprise audits, and random drug tests; and (3) both parties acknowledge that the situation calls for mutual deceit (a poker game, bargaining at a foreign bazaar).

The principle of veracity would outlaw many common lies and other forms of deception, like overstating a company's income, offering an unrealistically optimistic status report on a project, or padding resumes and expense accounts. Salespeople would have a duty to tell the entire truth about their products (including possible hazards) and refuse to steer customers toward purchases that might harm them.[4]

You may think Bok's guideline is too restrictive. Or you may hold a deontological position that outlaws any exceptions to total honesty. Nevertheless, the principle of veracity does address the need for truth telling while acknowledging that lying can pose complex ethical dilemmas. It also encourages us to take a closer look at how we might promote truthfulness in organizational relationships.

Explanations for the causes of organizational lying generally fall into two categories: self-interest and role conflict.[5] Members lie for personal benefit—to cover up a mistake, save money, further a career, or avoid conflict with the boss. They also lie in order to relieve tension between the various roles they play. For example, a contractor who is unable to complete two remodeling projects at the same time may falsely claim to be waiting for materials in order to placate one homeowner while working at the other job site.

The combination of role conflict and self-interest is more likely to result in deceit than is either factor on its own. Role conflict acts as a stimulus, providing the reason to lie; rewards then provide the motivation or encouragement to engage in lying. The contractor in our example feels caught between two sets of role obligations, and his lie pays off by buying him more time to complete (and to get paid for) both tasks.

As a manager you can reduce the frequency of deception because you determine both the roles that employees play and the rewards they receive. Reduce the pressure of role conflicts through clarifying expectations and chains of command, opening up lines of communication to resolve role issues, and making sure that you don't set unreasonably high expectations that tempt workers to lie. "Teach" employees that honesty pays by rewarding integrity while punishing offenders. Further, make honesty a core value, highlighting it in mission statements while promoting truthful interactions with all constituencies.

INVASION OF PRIVACY

Privacy refers to setting limits or boundaries on what we reveal about the self—our thoughts, for example, or our medical records and family history. The right to privacy empowers us to set these limits and resist intrusion from peers, employers, the government, and others. Violations of privacy occur when outsiders gain unauthorized access to personal information. These violations can be just as damaging to trust as deception. We feel betrayed when we learn that our manager has been secretly videotaping our workplace or that a coworker has been rifling through our desk drawers.

Business ethicist Richard DeGeorge identifies six kinds of privacy in businesses and other organizations. These categories overlap, but they help us identify some of the key issues that arise in workplace and volunteer settings.[6]

Space privacy refers to limiting access to particular locations like a file cabinet, cubicle, or office. Intrusion can take the form of physically entering the space or through listening to private conversations and peeking in.

Body/mental privacy. Bodily modesty requires that certain parts of the body be covered, and that certain bodily functions be carried out in private. Employers violate this norm when urine samples are given in the presence of drug testers. Mental privacy refers to the right to keep certain thoughts and feelings secret unless we choose to make them public.

Personal information privacy describes the privilege of keeping information about us from public view. While much is public record, we still want to keep certain data from others in the organization. This might include, for instance, our tastes in music and videos, political affiliation, sexual orientation, and credit score.

Communication privacy covers the interaction between people. Laws forbid tampering with the mail or tapping into phone conversations without good cause. However, courts have allowed organizations a good deal of leeway in monitoring communication channels. Messages produced on company property (computer files, e-mail) belong to the organization and can serve as grounds for termination.

Personal privacy limits the extent of control the organization can exert over the private lives of employees. Off-the-job behavior (hobbies, voting, dating relationships, church attendance or nonattendance) that doesn't relate to job performance should not be factored into promotion and retention decisions.

Cyber privacy refers to the gathering and use of information from the Internet. Companies routinely collect and share data on our Web use—the sites we visit, what we buy. For example, Amazon.com gathers information not only on what its customers purchase but also on what they browsed for or recommended to others. The company uses those data to recommend purchases and then shares the information with companies it partners with.[7]

Much of the ongoing debate about privacy rights in the workplace has been sparked by technological developments.[8] Advances in computer, video, and audio technology enable managers to monitor employee behavior more closely than ever before. A number of large firms track worker productivity through spy ware that records computer keystrokes. Spyzone.com markets mini audio systems and cameras to managers. Another firm sells Hygiene Guard, a product which tracks whether employees are using soap dispensers and washing their hands in the restroom. If they don't, the device flashes or beeps to alert supervisors!

Moral justification for privacy rights is largely based on the values of autonomy and respect for persons.[9] Respecting someone's privacy is a way to recognize his or her value as a person, one of Kant's key principles. According to the Categorical Imperative, individuals are ends in and of themselves, not means to some other ends. They have the right to determine what they want to reveal about themselves. Within their self-imposed boundaries, they can pursue their own goals, experiment with new behaviors and identities, and relax. Unwanted intrusion is disrespectful and denies the individual's dignity and worth. In addition, happiness and well-being are dependent on privacy. The right to own property, the right to free speech, the right to be safe from harm, and the right to move about as one pleases are all based on the fundamental value of privacy.

Arrayed against privacy rights is the organization's right to gather information about its members. Employers are held liable for the sexist and racist messages sent through their e-mail systems, for instance. They have an interest in gathering data to track and improve performance (how telephone operators treat callers, how quickly restaurant patrons are served), and to meet government regulations. Organizations also prevent employee fraud and theft by conducting investigations.

Information privacy expert Laura Hartman suggests that the tension between the member's right to privacy and the employer's right to know can be resolved by implementing two values: integrity and accountability.[10] Integrity refers to consistency in organizational values. Any choice to infringe upon employee privacy must be consistent with the values of the firm. Monitoring must fulfill the mission statement and reflect the organization's priorities. If it doesn't, the practice should be discontinued.

When gathering information is consistent with the group's values, the next step is to ensure it is done in a way that is accountable to those being observed. Accountability means notifying employees of the intent to monitor, why monitoring is necessary, and how the process will be carried out (video cameras, telephone recording devices, random drug tests, GPS tracking). Supervisors should also indicate how frequently they intend to gather information and allow employees some freedom in blocking observation. For instance, a beep can be added to remind workers when telephone monitoring is taking place and they could be allowed to prevent monitoring of personal calls.

Hartman suggests that the following checklist be used to determine if your decision to gather information is ethical. If you answer "yes" to any of these questions, then your choice (or that of your organization) ought to be reconsidered.

- Does the collection of data involve physical or psychological harm?
- Does the technique cross a personal boundary without permission?
- Could the collection produce invalid results?
- Are you being more intrusive than necessary?
- Is the data subject prohibited from appealing or changing the information recorded?
- Are there negative effects on those beyond the data subject?
- Is the link between the information collected and the goal sought unclear?
- Are the data being used in such a way as to cause a disadvantage to the subject?

Reducing Antisocial Behavior

Antisocial interpersonal behaviors are deliberate attempts to inflict harm on others and/or the organization as a whole.[11] Unlike deception and invasion of privacy, antisocial actions are always unethical and self-centered. Perpetrators are driven to meet their own needs at the expense of other individuals and the group.

We'll focus on four forms of interpersonal misbehavior in this section of the chapter: incivility, aggression, sexual harassment, and discrimination. Such behaviors can't be eliminated entirely, but they can be controlled. To this end, I'll describe each misbehavior, identify its consequences and causes, and then offer prevention strategies based on research findings.

INCIVILITY

Incivility consists of rude, discourteous actions which disregard others and violate norms for respect.[12] These are the mildest of all antisocial behaviors and are also the only ones that can be either intentional or unintentional. I may deliberately ignore a coworker, for example, or just fail to notice him when I come into the office. As a result, the target of the behavior (in this case the fellow employee I failed to acknowledge) is not clear as to how to interpret the intent behind my message.

Incivility appears to be rampant in the workplace. In a series of studies involving 2,400 employees in the U.S. and Canada, management professors Christine Pearson, Lynne Andersson, and Christine Porath found that 10 to 25 percent of their sample witnessed incivility daily and 20 to 50 percent were the targets of uncivil messages every week.[13] Examples of workplace incivility include leaving a mess for custodians to clean up, sending a "flaming" e-mail, making a sarcastic comment about a peer in front of coworkers, and claiming credit for someone else's work. (To measure your experience of incivility at your workplace, complete the Self-Assessment in Box 8.2.)

Self-Assessment

Box 8.2 Workplace Incivility Scale

Respond to the following items to determine the amount of incivility you encounter at your workplace.

During the past year while employed at _____________, have you been in a situation where any of your superiors or coworkers . . .

Put you down or was condescending to you?
Paid little attention to your statement or showed little interest in your opinion?
Made demeaning or derogatory remarks about you?
Addressed you in unprofessional terms, either publicly or privately?
Ignored or excluded you from professional camaraderie?
Doubted your judgment on a matter over which you have responsibility?
Made unwanted attempts to draw you into a discussion of personal matters?

Source: Cortina, L. M., Magley, V. I., Hunter Williams, J., & Langhout, R. D. (2001). Incivility in the workplace: Incidence and impact. *Journal of Occupational Health Psychology, 6*, 64-80, p. 70.

Incivility has both direct and indirect negative effects. Direct effects include lower job satisfaction; reduced motivation, performance, organizational loyalty, and creativity; and more resistance to helping others. Indirect effects include the erosion of shared values and cooperation as well as the escalation of conflict spirals. Incivility sets the stage for more aggressive, damaging behaviors.

Incivility may be on the rise because of increasing job demands, downsizing and outsourcing which reduce organizational loyalty, and the spread of the "casual" workplace that deemphasizes rules of conduct. Based on their research, Pearson and Porath offer the following suggestions for curtailing incivility and reducing its costly effects.

1. Set a zero-tolerance policy.

Executives need to communicate that employee-to-employee incivility will not be tolerated and repeat this message on a regular basis, both verbally and in writing. Such statements set a baseline for evaluating and correcting behavior. For example, Boeing requires that workers "treat each other with respect." Southwest Airlines states that employees will be treated with the "same concern, respect, and caring attitude" that they are expected to display to customers.

2. Take an honest look in the mirror.

Managers and executives must live by the civility standard they set. Employees follow the example set by their leaders. If mid and upper level managers behave uncivilly, their subordinates are much more likely to do the same.

3. Weed out trouble before it enters your organization.

Some individuals are repeat offenders, leaving a trail of disrespectful behaviors in their wake. Often they are shuttled from department to department, organization to organization. Try to screen out those offenders through thorough reference checks that go beyond the contacts provided by the candidate.

4. Teach civility.

Introduce training designed to improve listening, confirmation, and conflict management skills. Tie performance evaluations and career advancement to the use of these competencies. Reduce the stress that may drive people to act poorly and emphasize that there is always enough time to be "nice."

5. Put your ear to the ground and listen carefully.

Collect feedback to identify repeat offenders and to keep them from poisoning their colleagues. Anonymous feedback from employees can help reveal if managers are being uncivil to subordinates while they are presenting a positive image to superiors. Provide channels (human relations departments, open door policies) for employees who want to report disrespectful behavior.

6. When incivility occurs, hammer it.

Since incivility breeds further incivility, such behavior needs to be curtailed immediately, even at the lowest level of the organization. Failure to punish incivility signals that such behavior is sanctioned and enables perpetrators to advance their careers.

7. Heed warning signals.

Porath and her colleagues note that "incivility thrives in environments where input from employees is squelched." Therefore, managers must take action when informed of abuse and protect those who report problems. Employees will keep silent if leaders fail to investigate and correct uncivil patterns or if they fear retaliation.

8. Don't make excuses for powerful instigators.

All violators, no matter how powerful or talented, must be confronted. Managers must be required to discipline instigators who report to them, despite the temptation to rationalize their behavior. They must also refuse to transfer troublemakers, because violators will continue to cause problems in their new locations.

9. Invest in postdeparture interviews.

Incivility can be hard to track because victims don't leave immediately but often remain in their current positions until they can land new jobs in other organizations. Targets are often reluctant to give the true reason for their departure, believing that the organization doesn't really care or for fear that they will appear weak if they do speak up. Conduct postdeparture interviews with former employees who have been gone for some time to determine if incivility was a factor in their decision to leave.

AGGRESSION

In contrast to incivility, there can be no doubt as to the intent of aggressive behavior. Interpersonal aggression consists of conscious actions that hurt or injure. Such behavior can take a variety of forms, ranging from refusing to return phone calls to screaming at employees to murder. One widely used typology categorizes aggression along three dimensions: (1) physical-verbal (destructive words or deeds); (2) active-passive (doing harm by acting or by failing to act); and (3) direct-indirect (doing harm directly to the individual or indirectly through an intermediary and by attacking something the individual values).[14] Examples of behaviors that fit into each of these categories can be found in Box 8.3.

Box 8.3 Forms of Aggressive Behavior

Type of Aggression	*Examples*
Physical-active-direct	Punching, kicking, stabbing, shooting another person
Physical-active-indirect	Sabotaging a piece of equipment so that another person will be hurt, removing tools and supplies
Physical-passive-direct	Physically preventing another person from obtaining a desired goal or performing a desired act (e.g., by failing to move out of the person's way when asked to do so)
Physical-passive-indirect	Refusing to perform necessary tasks (e.g., refusing to provide information or help needed by a coworker)
Verbal-active-direct	Insulting or derogating another person in some manner
Verbal-active-indirect	Spreading malicious rumors or gossip about another person
Verbal-passive-direct	Refusing to speak to another person or refusing to answer questions posed by this person
Verbal-passive-indirect	Failing to speak up in another person's defense when he or she is unfairly criticized

Source: Adapted from Baron, R. A. (2004). Workplace aggression and violence: Insights from basic research. In R. W. Griffin & A. M. O'Leary-Kelly (Eds.), *The dark side of organizational behavior*, p. 29. Reprinted by permission of John Wiley & Sons, Inc.

Interpersonal workplace aggression is all too prevalent.[15] An estimated 2 million U.S. workers are physically assaulted yearly and 16 million are threatened with violence; homicide is one of the leading causes of death on the job. In Canada, assault rates are higher than in the U.S. While violence attracts the most media attention, milder forms of workplace aggression are far more common. Studies conducted in Europe and the U.S. indicate that, for every physical assault, there are several instances of less serious aggression like being shouted at, insulted, and receiving threatening gestures. Thirty percent of European men and 55 percent of European women surveyed said that they had been victims of these milder aggressive behaviors during the last year. Twenty-seven percent of Michigan residents in one poll reported that they had been mistreated at work during the prior 12-month period.

Not surprisingly, aggression can do extensive damage to both individuals and the organization as a whole. Victims may be injured, experience higher stress levels leading to poor health, become fearful or angry or depressed, lose the ability to concentrate, and feel less committed to their jobs. Observers who witness aggressive incidents may suffer some of the same negative outcomes. They, too, experience more anxiety and a lowered sense of well-being and commitment. At the organizational level, performance drops as a result of aggressive actions. Workplace aggression is correlated with lower productivity, higher absenteeism and turnover rates, lawsuits and negative publicity.

Aggressive behavior is the product of a number of factors—personal, social, and situational—outlined below.[16]

Personal Causes of Aggression

Type A personality. Type A behavior pattern people are extremely competitive, generally in a hurry, and highly irritable. Such individuals are more likely to engage in hostile actions both on and off the job (child and spouse abuse, for instance).

Hostile attributional bias. Those with this perceptual bias tend to assume the worst in others. They believe that peers and subordinates are out to hurt them and then respond accordingly. For example, an employee with a hostile perspective who doesn't get notice of an important meeting will assume that his boss deliberately snubbed him even if this omission was a harmless oversight. He may refuse to answer questions from his supervisor the next time they meet.

Inflated (or deflated) self-esteem. Those who hold extremely high views of themselves are particularly sensitive to negative feedback which threatens their self-image. They are more likely to respond with anger and nurse grudges. Individuals with low self-esteem are more prone to revenge.

Low self-monitoring. High self-monitors pay close attention to situational cues and then modify their behavior to act appropriately. Low self-monitors, on the other hand, pay more attention to their inner attitudes and feelings. As a result, they are more likely to escalate conflict and misinterpret motives.

Social Causes of Aggression

Frustration. Interference with the pursuit of goals produces anger and hostility. Frustration is most likely to cause aggression when the interference is seen as illegitimate. An employee turned down for a promotion, for instance, will be more upset if he thinks that the job went to a much less qualified candidate.

Direct provocation. Aggression begets further aggression. Most people respond to verbal and physical assaults by retaliating with more extreme measures of their own.

Displaced aggression. If it's too dangerous or costly for a member to retaliate against someone who provokes her (the boss, for example), she may then take frustrations out on someone else (subordinates, friends, family members).

Triggered displaced aggression. Sometimes a weak provocation will trigger a strong aggressive response. This may occur because the individual recently experienced a much stronger provocation. For instance, an employee may lash out at a peer who suggests minor modifications to a project after being subjected to severe criticism about the same project from her supervisor.

Aggressive models. Aggressive individuals act as role models for other organizational members. Observers learn new ways to aggress which are often more subtle, like "playing politics" or quietly sabotaging the work of another department. Seeing aggression also "primes" hostile thoughts. Coworkers begin to think about the wrongs they have suffered at the hands of others. Finally, role models demonstrate that aggression is a legitimate means for dealing with frustration or provocation. Soon an organizational culture of aggression emerges.

Contextual Causes of Aggression

Oppressive supervision. Employees are more likely to strike out against their supervisors when they (a) sense that they have little influence over the workload and work pace, (b) are the victims of bullying bosses, and (c) feel overly controlled (given little power, monitored extremely closely).

Job stressors. Layoffs, demanding performance standards, role ambiguity, conflicts, increasing competition, and other job factors produce stress that can sow the seeds of aggression.

Use of alcohol. Alcohol weakens resistance to anger and aggression. Intoxicated people can still restrain themselves but are more likely to go along with suggestions to harm others and to attack helpless victims.

Perceived unfairness. Individuals are more likely to retaliate when they perceive that they have been treated unjustly. They may take issue with how resources are distributed (distributive injustice) and how decisions are reached (procedural injustice). However, being treated with disrespect (interactional or informational injustice) appears to be the strongest determinant of aggression.

Unpleasant working conditions. Extremely high or low temperatures, crowding, noise, and other uncomfortable environmental factors generate negative emotions and increase aggressive behavior. As a result, attempts to save money by cutting back on the quality of the work environment (shutting down the air conditioning, lowering the thermostat in the winter, removing carpet) often backfire, lowering productivity while producing more aggression.

Strategies for reducing aggression must address its personal, social and contextual origins. Careful screening of potential employees is a good place to start. Try to weed out those individuals with aggressive tendencies and strong Type A personalities through interviews, testing, and reference checks. Ask applicants how they responded when unfairly treated or what they would do in a difficult job-related situation. Careful reference checks can identify individuals who should not be hired because of their patterns of abusive behavior. For current employees, provide training in social skills. Some workers get caught up in aggressive interactions because they unwittingly provoke others. They may not understand that their behavior irritates their peers and generates negative feelings.

Next, address social factors. To reduce frustration, establish legitimacy for decisions and actions by providing background information and rationale to your employees. Short-circuit the development of a climate of aggression by eliminating aggressive role models and punishing offenders. Effective punishment is prompt, highly certain, strong, and justified.

Finally, reduce negative contextual factors. Cut back on tight supervision, eliminate unnecessary rules, and avoid intrusive monitoring practices like the hand-washing monitoring technology described earlier in the chapter. Give your employees more control over how they complete their tasks and outlaw drinking on the job (even over lunch). Reduce the impact of stressors by lowering work demands, by providing physical and emotional outlets (recreation areas, nap rooms, office celebrations), and by supplying stress management training. Create pleasant working environments with adequate space, comfortable temperatures, soundproofing, attractive furnishings, and so on. Prevent perceptions of injustice by treating others with respect using the communication skills described in Chapter 4.

SEXUAL HARASSMENT

Sexual harassment is a distinctive form of aggression that is overwhelmingly directed at women and prohibited by law. Title VII of the Civil Rights Act of 1964 forbids discrimination in employment based on "race, color, religion, sex, or national origin." The Equal Employment Opportunity Commission (EEOC) enforces this statute, as do the Americans with Disabilities Act and Equal Pay Act. State laws also apply to harassment cases.

According to the EEOC and a number of court decisions, there are two types of sexual harassment.[17] The first is called *quid pro quo,* which is a legal term roughly meaning "something for something." Plaintiffs in quid pro quo cases claim that they were coerced into providing sexual favors to their supervisors in return for keeping their jobs or getting promotions and raises. This constitutes discriminatory behavior because victims were required to submit to conditions not placed on other workers. The second type of harassment involves the creation of a "hostile work environment." Plaintiffs in hostile work environment cases claim that working conditions interfered with their job performance. While the law is still evolving, the following have been identified as components of a hostile work environment:

- *Harassment aimed at one gender.* For example: comments or slurs directed only at one gender, not the other.
- *Severe and sustained negative behavior.* Generally a pattern of behavior must be established, like a series of lewd comments and offensive gestures, not just one isolated remark.
- *Negative effects of behavior on the receiver.* Behavior is considered harassing when it offends the recipient regardless of the expressed intent of the perpetrator. A male worker may put up a sexual poster "for fun," for instance, but this display is illegal because it makes his female coworkers uncomfortable.
- *Violation of the "reasonable woman" standard.* The behavior must violate what the typical woman would see as appropriate. A business lunch between a male and female colleague would not be seen as harassment under this standard. Harassment would occur, however, if a supervisor kept asking a subordinate for a date despite her repeated refusals.
- *Significant damages.* Claimants must establish that the behavior had a significant negative impact (caused discomfort, lowered work performance).
- *Unwelcome behavior.* Consensual behavior is not illegal, but unwanted behavior is. Researchers have discovered that men and women often interpret the

> same behavior differently. Males see "friendly" behavior on the part of women as sexual in nature. They are more likely to be flattered by sexual attention, whereas females find it offensive. Conversely, men are less likely than women to define teasing sexual remarks, jokes, and suggestive looks and gestures as harassing behavior. (Turn to Scenario B in the Chapter End Case to determine your response to a situation that may or may not involve harassment.)

Sexual harassment, while unique, does have elements in common with other forms of workplace aggression. Like other aggressive behavior, it occurs with distressing frequency. An analysis of 55 surveys involving over 86,000 women found that 58 percent had experienced potentially harassing behaviors at work.[18] Harassment is most frequent in male-dominated blue collar jobs (construction worker, machinist), but female doctors, lawyers, and other professionals are not immune from such behavior. Neither are women students. The rate of harassment among female college students is roughly that of female workers, with approximately 50 percent reporting being targeted for such harassing actions as insulting remarks, propositions, bribes, threats, and sexual assault.[19]

The costs of sexual harassment mirror those of other aggressive behaviors. The work performance of targets suffers due to stress, decreased morale, damaged relationships, withdrawal, and career changes. Many victims quit their jobs or are fired for filing complaints. Targets experience headaches, sleep loss, weight loss or gain, nausea, sexual dysfunction, and eating and gastrointestinal disorders. Negative psychological effects include depression, a sense of helplessness and loss of control, fear, detachment, and decreased motivation.[20]

Many of the same personal, social, and contextual factors that promote other forms of aggression also contribute to harassment. Offenders are more likely to harbor hostility and be low self-monitors. Men may be frustrated because women as a group appear to be taking away their privileges and they retaliate as a result. Perpetrators also take their cue from others who model harassing behavior.

In addition to these general factors, there are unique determinants of harassment:[21] First, male sexual aggressors hold more traditional (less egalitarian) views of females. They expect women to function in nurturing roles and believe that some professions should be closed to females. Harassment punishes those who violate these prescriptions and victimizes women while reinforcing the masculine image of the perpetrator. Second, violators hope to win sexual favors and other payoffs, like reduced competition for jobs. Third, rates of sexual harassment are substantially higher in organizations that don't take complaints seriously, fail to investigate charges or punish offenders, and retaliate against whistle-blowers. Fourth, harassment preserves male-dominated organizational systems that give men power over women.

You can take a number of steps to prevent sexual harassment, beginning with creating a zero-tolerance organizational climate. Adopt a written policy that condemns such actions, spells out what types of behavior qualify as harassing, encourages victims to come forward, identifies penalties, and prohibits retaliation. Then back up the policy with an effective investigation procedure using an impartial third party who interviews all participants. Attack gender stereotypes through training which also encourages men to understand how women perceive behavior that men interpret as harmless. Increase the proportion of women in the organization to reduce the likelihood of harassment.

University of Arkansas business professor Anne O'Leary-Kelly suggests that paying more attention to the moral dimension of sexual harassment would also reduce its frequency.[22] Clearly, such behavior, which is harmful, selfish, and unfair, is unethical as well as illegal. The stronger the employees' sense that harassment has a moral component (the higher its degree of *moral intensity*), the more likely that those workers will avoid sexually aggressive actions and intervene when they observe harassment. Professor O'Leary-Kelly suggests that you can increase the moral intensity of sexual harassment through the following:

1. Make aggressors aware of the effects of their actions.

Some individuals, as noted earlier, aren't aware that their actions are harmful. Others may think they are only hurting the target of their sexual advances or remarks. Perpetrators need to learn that their actions are destructive, not only to the target, but to other women, the work team, and the entire organization. This is particularly important in light of the fact that the majority of victims do not file complaints for fear of retaliation. Offenders therefore get the mistaken notion that their behavior is not destructive.

2. Encourage consensus about the definition and immorality of sexual harassment.

Social consensus is still emerging as to what constitutes a hostile working environment. Create a shared understanding of what harassment might be in your particular organization and develop clear standards of behavior that highlight the unethical nature of harassing actions. Promote discussion about situations that make participants uncomfortable.

3. Shorten the time between conduct and consequences.

Moral intensity drops when there is a substantial delay between a behavior and its consequences. Immediate response is difficult in hostile environment harassment cases since a pattern of behavior must be established. Offenders feel distanced from their harmful actions as a result. Try to shorten this psychological distance by investigating and responding promptly. Begin investigations immediately after complaints surface and come to a quick resolution.

4. Emphasize similarities.

Our sense of moral obligation is highest when we perceive similarities between others and ourselves. Even though harassment is based on the differences between agents and targets, build a sense of similarity by emphasizing shared organizational goals and values. Provide opportunities for men and women to discuss their similar personal values, goals, and dreams.

5. Promote individual responsibility.

Moral intensity is heightened by acknowledgment of personal accountability. Harassers will more likely desist if they stop trying to diffuse responsibility by blaming the work environment or the behavior of their colleagues. Highlight the fact that sexual harassment damages the character of the perpetrator and is inconsistent with such personal values as equality, respect, and concern for others.

DISCRIMINATION

Discriminatory behavior puts members of another group at a disadvantage. Racism and sexism are the best-known examples of discrimination, but members of almost any group can be victimized—older workers, the poor, homeless people, homosexuals.

Due to the passage of civil rights laws and changes in societal values, employment discrimination is more likely to be covert than overt. Racial slurs and jokes, demeaning comments about disabled employees, and other blatant behaviors have been replaced with subtler forms of discrimination like downplaying the abilities of minorities and females, hiring and promoting those of similar backgrounds, and avoiding members of low status groups. For example, many whites express their racism indirectly by claiming that blacks are overly demanding, receive preferential treatment, and have nothing to complain about because discrimination is over.

Discriminatory behavior may be taking indirect forms, but it still inflicts significant damage in the workplace. In 2002, the unemployment rate for whites was 4.2 percent as compared to 7.7 for blacks, 6.1 percent for Hispanics, and 8.7 percent for disabled workers. Once on the job, the disparities continue. Minorities and women continue to earn less than white males, for example, and are less likely to be in management positions. Few females or persons of color make it to the highest organizational levels (president, CEO, board member).[23]

On a personal level, discrimination is the product of stereotypes and prejudice. Stereotypes are generalized beliefs about other people. Common stereotypes include: women can't handle hard physical labor; Asians make excellent technical employees but poor managers; those over 65 find it difficult to learn new skills. These categorizations, which we start to learn as children, become self-confirming by shaping perceptions and reactions. Take the case of bankers who believe that blacks are more likely to default on commercial loans. Not only will they be reluctant to make such loans, but they may also charge higher interest rates and refuse to extend further credit. As a result, more black businesses default on their loans.[24]

Perceptual bias makes it hard to shake negative stereotypes. We tend to blame our failings on external factors while assuming that members of the target group were in control of their actions. For instance, if we shout at subordinates, we excuse our behavior (we were under pressure or provoked). However, when members of low status groups engage in the same behavior, we believe that they were in command of their choices (they are abusive and controlling). The opposite happens when it comes to positive behaviors. We claim that our hard work is a natural extension of who we are. But the same effort is seen as exceptional in those groups we stereotype as lazy. These attributional errors pose a significant obstacle to organizational advancement. A woman is often less likely to be promoted because her success is attributed to outside factors like luck and preferential treatment, while a man's success is credited to his innate talent and abilities.

Prejudice describes negative emotional responses to members of other groups. It arises out of the negative stereotypes described above as well as[25]

- conflicts of interest between groups. Nothing creates an "us vs. them" mentality quicker than conflict over scarce resources and competing goals. Perceived interference generates feelings of anger, frustration, anxiety, and fear.
- threats to social identity. Group members want to maintain the positive image or identity of the group. They do so by viewing themselves favorably and by being less generous in their evaluations of outsiders. They also strive to differentiate themselves from members of out-groups. Prejudice increases when one group threatens another group's identity.
- relative deprivation. This refers to the sense that one's group isn't doing as well as it should when compared to other groups. Such perceptions ("women have an unfair advantage," "white males are an endangered species") produce a sense of injustice, which, as we've seen, results in anger and frustration.

Group and organizational factors can inflame stereotypes and prejudice that result in discriminatory behavior. In order to fit in and avoid criticism, members tend to go along with sexual harassment, racial slurs, giving favorable treatment to majority members, and other discriminatory behavior. Many organizations emphasize competitive rewards, which pits group members against each other, increasing hostility and prejudice. They also send mixed messages about the importance of equality. Management may set a nondiscrimination policy (treat all customers equally) but, at the same time, require participants to discriminate in order to do their jobs (charge inner city residents more for goods and services).

There are several attitudinal tactics you can use to combat discrimination. One is to resist the temptation to lump people into broad stereotypical categories (see the discussion of mindfulness in Chapter 4). Making finer distinctions prevents you from assuming that all retirees, disabled employees, and Hispanics are alike. Another is acting with dignity. Dignity ought to characterize all of our interactions with people of other groups. We maintain our own dignity by confronting others who engage in prejudicial comments or actions; we maintain the dignity of others by respecting their views, even when we disagree.[26] Our moral obligation is to intervene in clear cases of sexual harassment and when peers make sexist and racist comments. If we don't speak out, these practices will continue.

Increased contact is another strategy for reducing discrimination at both the personal and group level. More contact between groups diminishes stereotyping and prejudice if you make sure it occurs under these conditions: (a) support from those in authority; (b) sustained contact that permits the development of relationships; (c) equal status between group members; and (d) cooperation in order to achieve shared goals.

You may also need to undertake organizational diversity initiatives, which are proactive efforts to reduce discrimination through increased contact by recruiting, retaining, and promoting more minority group members. The most effective diversity programs adopt an integration-and-learning perspective that identifies differences as valuable organizational assets.[27] Managers recognize that drawing upon the insights of diverse members can dramatically change the way their organizations operate—helping them think in new ways about markets, products, services, goals, and strategies. This approach stands in sharp contrast to the diversity paradigms adopted by the leaders of most organizations. Executives in some groups treat diversity initiatives solely as a way to provide equal opportunity; they strive to treat everyone the same way and try to ignore cultural and other differences rather than building on them. Executives in other groups value minorities solely as marketing agents who can sell to their ethnic groups. Diversity programs limited to equality or marketing concerns have little impact on the way that organizations conduct their core operations and do little to tie members together in pursuit of shared goals.

Implications

- Truth telling should be the norm, to be violated only under exceptional circumstances. The burden of proof is on you as the liar to justify your deception. You can encourage truth telling as a manager by reducing role conflicts that prompt lying and by making sure that employees aren't rewarded for engaging in this behavior.

- The tension between privacy rights and the organization's right to know can be reconciled by emphasizing integrity and accountability. The information you gather must support the group's goals and values, and employees must be informed as to the purpose and form of the monitoring process.
- Deal promptly with incivility—rude, discourteous actions that disregard others and violate norms for respect. These are the mildest form of antisocial behaviors, but they damage both the individual and working relationships. Incivility sets the stage for conflict spirals and aggression.
- Aggressive acts are designed to hurt others and/or the organization. Your strategies for reducing aggression must address its personal, social, and contextual origins: (1) Screen out potential offenders. (2) Provide interpersonal skills training for employees. (3) Share your rationale for decisions. (4) Punish offenders and eliminate aggressive role models. (5) Cut back on intrusive management practices. (6) Reduce stressors. (7) Empower workers. (8) Create pleasant working conditions.
- You can prevent quid pro quo and hostile environment sexual harassment by creating a zero-tolerance climate, training, hiring more women, and raising awareness that this type of behavior is immoral.
- Be alert to subtle discrimination in the workplace that puts members of groups at a disadvantage. Overcome the stereotypes (generalized beliefs) and prejudice (negative emotional responses) that produce discrimination through changing your attitudes, encouraging increased contact between groups, and supporting organizational diversity initiatives.

Application Projects

1. Under what circumstances is lying justified? See if you can reach a consensus in a small group and report your conclusions to the rest of the class.
2. Evaluate the right to privacy in your organization. How does information gathering match up to the standards of integrity and accountability to employees?
3. Is incivility a problem in your organization? Why or why not? What are the costs of rude behavior? Would the suggestions outlined in the chapter eliminate this kind of behavior?
4. Create a case study dealing with workplace violence. What factors contributed to this incident and how could they be reduced or eliminated?
5. Have you ever been the victim of aggression or sexually harassing behaviors? How did you feel and respond? What suggestions would you make to others who might be victims? Write up your conclusions.
6. How is subtle discrimination expressed at your school or workplace? What steps can be taken to reduce its effects?

CHAPTER END CASE

Antisocial Behavior Scenarios

SCENARIO A: SPARKS OF AGGRESSION

Pedro, a clerk at a credit union, became angry with one of his fellow employees, a college student working there as a summer fill-in. He informed the student that he knew he was out to get him, was spreading false rumors about him, and was trying to sabotage his career. When the student strongly denied these charges, Pedro became verbally abusive, cursing him loudly in front of other employees and accusing him of receiving special treatment because he was related to a high official at the credit union. A supervisor stepped in and ended this episode, but the next day Pedro loudly accused the student and a female employee, who had previously rebuffed Pedro's romantic overtures, of "making fun of him" as they conversed. They vigorously denied this accusation, stating that they were talking about a totally unrelated topic, but Pedro refused to believe them and threatened to "make them pay" for their actions. The situation reached a climax about a week later on a suffocatingly hot day when the credit union's air conditioning failed. During that steamy afternoon, Pedro informed the student that this was the day on which he would get his revenge and teach him that he could not treat people from his country this way. That evening, Pedro followed the student home on public transportation, muttering curses and grimacing all the way. He kept fingering his pocket, and the student was certain that Pedro was carrying a weapon. Fortunately, the student had arranged for several friends to meet him, and they were standing on the train station platform when he got off. When Pedro saw them, he shook his fist but retreated. That night, he was arrested for assaulting and seriously wounding a neighbor. He never returned to the credit union.

What factors contributed to Pedro's aggressive behavior?

Source

Folger, R., & Baron, R. A. (1996). Violence and hostility at work: A model of reactions to perceived injustice. In G. VandenBos and E. Q. Bulato (Eds.), *Violence on the job: Identifying risks and developing solutions* (pp. 51–85). Washington, DC: American Psychological Association, p. 56. Used by permission.

SCENARIO B: A CASE OF SEXUAL HARASSMENT?

As the only woman sales associate in her company, Ellen broke all records for newcomers. She was invited to the company's annual dinner and presented with an award. Each sales associate was called to the podium and thanked by the president. Words bestowed on the men were, "terrific job, "wonderful results," "thanks for your solid contributions." Remarks the first year were not directed to Ellen, but to the crowd in attendance: "What a surprise! I just can't believe how this woman can do this! Can you?" as he handed her the award. After doubling her sales the second year and facing the same award celebration, remarks to the men had not changed. Remarks to the crowd about Ellen had changed only slightly, "She never ceases to amaze me!"[1]

Do you consider the remarks of the company president to be offensive? Why or why not?

Note

1. Seventy percent of the women surveyed by McCann and McGinn (1992) found this behavior mildly offensive.

Source

McCann, N. D., & McGinn, T. A. (1992). *Harassed: 100 women define inappropriate behavior in the workplace*. Homewood IL: BusinessIrwin, p. 38. Used by permission.

SCENARIO C: TAKING OFFENSE AT INDIAN MASCOTS (OR NOT)

The National Collegiate Athletic Association (NCAA) recently announced it would ban the use of American Indian mascots and logos by sports teams participating in postseason tournaments. The rule forbids displays of "hostile or abusive" references on the uniforms of teams, cheerleaders, and bands. Institutions with such mascots or imagery would be prohibited from hosting championship competitions. Eighteen colleges and universities were originally deemed to have offensive mascots, including Florida State (Seminoles), Utah (Utes), Illinois (Illini), North Dakota (Fighting Sioux), and Central Michigan (Chippewas). Florida State got the ban lifted by demonstrating that it has a long-standing relationship with the Seminole tribe, providing internships, scholarships, and classes on tribal history and culture.

Not surprisingly, the NCAA's action has aroused the ire of alumni and students. They argue that these mascots are a cherished tradition and a source of pride. Opponents point out that nicknames like Warriors and Braves honor the bravery of Native peoples rather than demean them. Evidence on how Native tribes respond to the issue is mixed. A 2002 survey, conducted by *Sports Illustrated*, found that 53 percent of Native Americans on reservations did not find the images discriminatory. A 2003 poll conducted by *Indian Country Today* generated a very different response. Eighty-one percent found the images disparaging to Native Americans and 75 percent believed that they violated antidiscrimination laws.

Are Native American mascots "hostile and abusive"? If you were enrolled in one of the colleges covered by the ban, what advice would you give to your administration about how to respond to this edict?

Sources

Fears, D. (2005, August 14). Indian mascots: Matter of pride or prejudice? Even tribes are divided as NCAA issues edict. *Washington Post*, p. A03. Retrieved October 4, 2005, from LexisNexis Academic database.

Shore, J. (2005, August 27). Play with our name. *New York Times*, p. A13. Retrieved October 4, 2005, from LexisNexis Academic database.

Wieberg, S. (2005, August 8). Mascot policy will be tough to overcome. *USA Today*, p. 9C.

Endnotes

1. Solomon, R. C. (1993). What a tangled web: Deception and self-deception in philosophy. In M. Lewis & C. Saarni (Eds.), *Lying and deception in everyday life* (pp. 30–58). New York: Guilford Press.

2. Grover, S. L. (1997). Lying in organizations: Theory, research, and future directions. In R. A. Giacalone & J. Greenberg (Eds.), *Antisocial behavior in organizations* (pp. 68–84). Thousand Oaks, CA: Sage; Cialdini, R. B., Petrova, P. K., & Goldstein, N. J. (2004, Spring). The hidden costs of organizational dishonesty. *MIT Sloan Management Review*, pp. 67–73.

3. Bok, S. (1978). *Lying: Moral choice in public and private life.* New York: Pantheon Books; Bok, S. (1989). *Secrets: On the ethics of concealment and revelation.* New York: Random House.

4. Carson, T. (2001). Deception and withholding information in sales. *Business Ethics Quarterly, 11*, 275–306.

5. Grover, S. (1993). Lying, deceit, and subterfuge: A model of dishonesty in the workplace. *Organization Science, 4*, 478-494; Grover (1997); Ross, W. T., & Robertson, D. C. (2000). Lying: The impact of decision context. *Business Ethics Quarterly, 10*, 409–440; Sims, R. L. (2000). The relationship between employee attitudes and conflicting expectations for lying behavior. *Journal of Psychology, 134*, 619–633; Aquino, K. (1998). The effects of ethical climate and the availability of alternatives on the use of deception during negotiation. *International Journal of Conflict Management, 9*, 195–217.

6. De George, R. T. (2003). *The ethics of information technology and business.* Malden, MA: Blackwell, chap. 2.

7. Linn, A. (2005, March 28). Amazon.com knows clientele, which worries privacy backers. *Oregonian*, pp. B1–B2.

8. Moore, A. (2000). Employee monitoring and computer technology: Evaluative surveillance v. privacy. *Business Ethics Quarterly, 10*, 697–709; Marx, G. T. (1998). Ethics for the new surveillance. *Information Society, 14*, 171–185; Werhane, P. H. (1985). *Persons, rights and corporations.* Englewood Cliffs, NJ: Prentice Hall; De George (2003).

9. Hubbartt, W. S. (1998). *The new battle over workplace privacy.* New York: AMACOM.

10. Hartman, L. P. (2001). Technology and ethics: Privacy in the workplace. *Business and Society Review, 106*, 1–26; Hartman, L. P., & Bucci, G. (1999). The economic and ethical implications of new technology on privacy in the workplace. *Business and Society Review, 102/103*, 1–23.

11. Giacalone, R. A., & Greenberg, J. (1997). *Antisocial behavior in organizations.* Thousand Oaks, CA: Sage.

12. Carter, S. L. (1998). *Civility: Manners, morals, and the etiquette of democracy.* New York: HarperCollins.

13. Pearson, C. M., & Porath, C. L. (2005). On the nature, consequences and remedies of workplace incivility: No time for "nice"? Think again. *Academy of Management Executive, 19,* 7–18; Pearson, C. M., & Porath, C. L. (2004). On incivility, its impact, and directions for future research. In R. W. Griffin & A. M. O'Leary-Kelly (Eds.), *The dark side of organizational behavior* (pp. 23–61). San Francisco: Jossey-Bass; Pearson, C. M., Andersson, L. M., & Porath, C. L. (2000). Assessing and attacking workplace incivility. *Organizational Dynamics, 29,* 123–137; Andersson, L. M., & Pearson, C. M. (1999). Tit for tat? The spiraling effect of incivility in the workplace. *Academy of Management Review, 24,* 452–471.

14. Buss, A. H. (1961). *The psychology of aggression.* New York: John Wiley.

15. Information on the prevalence of workplace violence and aggression taken from Glomb, T. M., & Hui, L. (2003). Interpersonal aggression in work groups: Social influence, reciprocal, and individual effects. *Academy of Management Journal, 46,* 486–496; O'Leary-Kelly, A. M., Griffin, R. W., & Glew, D. J. (1996). Organization-motivated aggression: A research framework. *Academy of Management Review, 21,* 225–253; Depre, K. E., & Barling, J. (2003). Workplace aggression. In A. Sagie, S. Stashevsky, & M. Koslowsky (Eds.), *Misbehaviour and dysfunctional attitudes in organizations* (pp. 13–32). Hampshire, UK: Palgrave Macmillan; Neuman, J. H. (2004). Injustice, stress, and aggression in organizations. In R. W. Griffin & A. M. O'Leary-Kelly (Eds.), *The dark side of organizational behavior* (pp. 62–102). San Francisco: Jossey-Bass.

16. Baron, R. A. (2004). Workplace aggression and violence: Insights from basic research. In R. W. Griffin & A. M. O'Leary-Kelly (Eds.), *The dark side of organizational behavior* (pp. 23–61). San Francisco: Jossey-Bass; Neuman, J. H., & Baron, R. A. (1997). Aggression in the workplace. In R. A. Giacalone & J. Greenberg (Eds.) *Antisocial behavior in organizations* (pp. 37–67). Thousand Oaks, CA: Sage; O'Leary-Kelly, Griffin, & Glew (1996); Douglas, S. C., & Martinko, M. J. (2001). Exploring the role of individual differences in the prediction of workplace aggression. *Journal of Applied Psychology, 86,* 547–559; Barling, J. (1996). The prediction, experience, and consequences of workplace violence. In G. R. VandenBos & E. Q. Bulato (Eds.), *Violence on the job: Identifying risks and developing solutions* (pp. 29–49). Washington, DC: American Psychological Association; Folger, R., & Baron, R. A. (1996). Violence and hostility at work: A model of reactions to perceived injustice. In G. R. VandenBos & E. Q. Bulato (Eds.), *Violence on the job: Identifying risks and developing solutions* (pp. 51–85). Washington, DC: American Psychological Association.

17. Levy, A. C., & Paludi, M. A. (2002). *Workplace sexual harassment* (2nd ed.). Upper Saddle River, NJ: Prentice Hall.

18. Ilies, R., Hauserman, N., Schwochau, S., & Stibal, J. (2003). Reported incidence rates of work-related sexual harassment in the United States: Using meta-analysis to explain reported rate disparities. *Personnel Psychology, 56,* 607–651.

19. Fitzgerald, L. F. (1993). Sexual harassment: Violence against women in the workplace. *American Psychologist, 48,* 1070–1076.

20. Levy & Paludi (2002); Fitzgerald (1993).

21. See, for example: Fitzgerald, L. F., Drasgow, F., Hulin, C. L., Gelfand, M. J., & Magley, V. (1997). Antecedents and consequences of sexual harassment in organizations:

A test of an integrated model. *Journal of Applied Psychology, 82,* 578–589; Offermann, L. R., & Malamut, A. B. (2002). When leaders harass: The impact of target perceptions of organizational leadership and climate on harassment reporting and outcomes. *Journal of Applied Psychology, 87,* 885–893; O'Leary-Kelly, A. M., Paetzold, R. L., & Griffin, L. W. (2000). Sexual harassment as aggressive behavior: An actor-based perspective. *Academy of Management Review, 25,* 372–388; Wiener, R. L., & Gutek, B. A. (1999). Advances in sexual harassment research, theory, and policy. *Psychology, Public Policy and Law, 5,* 597–518; Wilson, F., & Thompson, P. (2001). Sexual harassment as an exercise of power. *Gender, Work and Organization, 8,* 61–83.

22. O'Leary-Kelly, A. M. (2001). Sexual harassment as unethical behavior: The role of moral intensity. *Human Resource Management Review, 11,* 73–92; Bowes-Sperry, L., & O'Leary-Kelly, A. M. (2005). To act or not to act: The dilemma faced by sexual harassment observers. *Academy of Management Review, 30,* 288–306.

23. Dipboye, R. L., & Halverson, S. K. (2004). Subtle (and not so subtle) discrimination in organizations. In R. W. Griffin & A. M. O'Leary-Kelly (Eds.), *The dark side of organizational behavior* (pp. 131–158). San Francisco: Jossey-Bass.

24. Loury, G. C. (2002). *The anatomy of racial inequality.* Cambridge, MA: Harvard University Press.

25. Brown, R. (1995). *Prejudice: Its social psychology.* Oxford, UK: Blackwell; Fiske, S. T. (1998). Stereotyping, prejudice, and discrimination. In D. T. Gilbert, S. T. Fiske, & G. Lindzey (Eds.), *The handbook of social psychology* (Vol. 2, pp. 357–411). Boston: McGraw-Hill.

26. Gudykunst, W. B., & Kim, Y. Y. (1997). *Communicating with strangers: An approach to intercultural communication* (3rd ed.). New York: McGraw-Hill.

27. Thomas, D. A., & Ely, R. D. (1996, September-October). Making differences matter: A new paradigm for managing diversity. *Harvard Business Review,* pp. 79–90; Ely, R. D., & Thomas, D. A. (2001). Cultural diversity at work: The effects of diversity perspectives on work group processes and outcomes. *Administrative Science Quarterly, 46,* 229–273.

9

Building an Ethical Workplace

Chapter Preview

In the last chapter we were on the defensive, looking at ways to prevent destructive behavior. In this chapter we go on the offensive, focusing on how we can intentionally create ethical work organizations. We'll see how building ethical workplaces requires (a) understanding the components of ethical culture, and (b) engaging in successful cultural change efforts.

Components of Ethical Culture

Scholars from a variety of fields borrow the concept of culture from the field of anthropology to describe how organizations create shared meanings. As members meet and interact, they develop common beliefs, values, and assumptions, which are expressed through architecture, ceremonies, rituals, dress, and other visible artifacts. Culture binds the organization together and, at the same time, greatly influences the behavior of individuals. What members wear and drive to work, the way they carry out their tasks and organize their time, and whom they socialize with at lunch are all products of shared culture. Ethicists are particularly interested in how cultural elements, both formal and informal, promote or discourage moral action. Formal cultural components include structure, codes of ethics, reward and evaluation systems, core values, and mission statements. Informal components include language, norms, rituals, and stories.[1] In this section I'll describe each of these elements and its relationship to ethical behavior. I will also outline ways that you can use each component to contribute to the formation of an ethical environment.

FORMAL ELEMENTS

1. Structure

Structure influences moral behavior through the creation of authority relationships, delineation of lines of accountability, and allocation of decision-making rights.[2] As we saw in Chapter 7, leaders are granted a great deal of power over the lives of followers. Their power is enhanced by the fact that people appear "programmed" to obey authority.[3] The greater the demand for obedience, the higher the likelihood that employees will engage in unethical activities and keep silent about the ethical violations they observe.[4]

Lines of accountability are blurred in many large, complex organizations, diffusing responsibility for choices and actions. The result can be an increase in immoral behavior. Managers may deliberately keep themselves in the dark about illegal activities so that they can maintain "plausible deniability" if this wrongdoing ever comes to light. Division of labor and compartmentalization can blind employees to the consequences of their choices. One department can develop a drug, for example, and expect that another department will test it for side effects. At the same time another unit will market the drug, assuming that the medication is safe. However, the testing group may fail to communicate that there is no way to accurately determine side effects. A harmful drug (like thalidomide, which caused serious birth defects) is released as a result.[5] Individuals may also shift ethical responsibilities from themselves to their roles. They use their jobs as cover by claiming that (a) they had no choice but to engage in unethical behavior, or that (b) there was little that they could do to stop immoral and/or illegal activities.

Allocation of decision-making rights is another important structural determinant of moral behavior. Empowered employees are more likely to make better ethical choices (see Chapter 5). Those closest to the problem are best equipped to solve it and are more likely to be sensitive to ethical issues.

Denying decision-making authority to such knowledgeable workers can be costly. This was vividly illustrated in the Challenger and Columbia shuttle disasters. In both cases, managers overruled lower level engineers who had safety concerns.

Implementation guidelines. Try to modify structural defects that contribute to immoral behavior. As a leader, encourage others to challenge and, at times, disobey orders. Help your employees recognize how their activities relate to the organization's overall direction and to consider how their actions affect others. Ensure that those closest to the ethical dilemma have significant input into how it is resolved.

2. Codes of Ethics

Codes of ethics are among the most common ethics tools. Over 90 percent of all major corporations have them, along with a great many government departments, professional associations, social service agencies, and schools.[6] Codes typically address these six areas:[7]

Conflicts of interest. Conflict provisions deal with cases where employees benefit at the expense of the organization or where an individual's judgment might be compromised. Cases of conflicts of interest include accepting gifts from suppliers or diverting contracts to relatives. Former Enron CFO Andrew Fastow provides one blatant example of conflict of interest. While working for Enron, he set up partnerships that generated millions in fees for him at the company's expense.

Records, funds, and assets. All chartered and tax-exempt organizations must keep accurate financial records. Under the Sarbanes-Oxley accounting act, large corporations now submit more extensive documentation than ever before. Publicly traded firms must also follow Security and Exchange regulations as well as state and local laws and their own bylaws.

Information. For-profit organizations try to keep information from competitors. Revealing such data (even to family members) can result in legal action. Public sector organizations, on the other hand, may have codes that encourage compliance to "sunshine laws" that require the release of information.

Outside relationships. Relationships with suppliers, competitors, government agencies, and others have legal and ethical ramifications. Members must avoid behaviors ranging from collusion, price-fixing, and insider trading to gossiping about the competition.

Employment practices. Employment provisions deal with discrimination, drug use, sexual harassment, aggression, and related issues.

Other practices. This category incorporates statements about employee health and safety, the use of technology, treatment of the environment, political activities, overseas conduct, and other topics. One provision found in many codes forbids the use of organizational assets for personal benefit. According to Coca-Cola's code of ethics, such assets include work time, work products, equipment, vehicles, computers and software, as well as the company's information, trademarks, and name.[8]

Despite their popularity, formal ethics statements are controversial. Skeptics argue that they are vague public relations documents designed to improve an organization's image. Few employees know what the codes say and their provisions are rarely enforced. Worse yet, critics say, codes are ineffectual. These documents do nothing to improve ethical behavior.

Defenders of ethical codes point out that such documents describe an organization's ethical position both to insiders and outsiders. They are particularly important to newcomers learning about the work group's ethical standards and potential moral problems they may face. Referring to a code can encourage employees, both new and old, to resist unethical group and organizational pressures. In the case of wrongdoing, an organization can point to the code as evidence that the immoral behavior is not official policy. Most importantly, ethics codes can have a direct, positive influence on ethical behavior. Students who sign honors codes, for example, are significantly less likely to plagiarize and cheat on tests.[9] Codes influence ethical perceptions even when organizational members don't remember exactly what is in them. Those in organizations with codes judge themselves and their coworkers more ethical than those in organizations without codes. They believe that their organizations are more supportive of ethical behavior and they are more satisfied with their group's moral decisions. These employees feel freer to act ethically and are more committed to their organizations.[10]

Implementation guidelines. While adopting a code doesn't guarantee moral improvement, the evidence cited above demonstrates that codes can play an important role in fostering an ethical environment. You need to encourage your organization to develop a formal set of ethical guidelines. Standards will have most impact when senior executives make them a priority and follow their provisions while, at the same time, rewarding followers who do the same. Back your code up with enforcement. Create procedures for interpreting the code and applying sanctions. Set up systems for reporting problems, investigating charges, and reaching conclusions.[11]

3. Reward and Performance Evaluation Systems

Organizational members determine what actions are measured and rewarded. They then engage in those activities, moral or otherwise. That fact makes reward systems a powerful determinant of ethical or unethical behavior. Unfortunately, ethical behavior often goes unnoticed and unrewarded. (Who gets praised for NOT padding expense accounts or NOT inflating earnings?)[12] Organizations often reward immoral behavior instead. For instance, auditors at Arthur Andersen (who were supposed to act as watchdogs) were rewarded for turning a blind eye to accounting fraud at Enron, Qwest, and WorldCom so the accounting firm could continue to sell these clients lucrative consulting services.[13]

Focus on ends to the exclusion of means is another problem with many reward and performance appraisal systems. Consumed with the bottom line, leaders set demanding performance goals but intentionally or unintentionally ignore how these objectives are to be reached. They pressure employees to produce sales and profits by whatever means possible. Followers then feel powerless and alienated, becoming estranged from the rest of the group. Sociologists use the term *anomie* to refer to this sense of normlessness and unease that results when rules lose their force.[14] Anomie increases the likelihood that group members will engage in illegal activities, and reduces their resistance to demands from authority figures who want them to break the law. Loss of confidence in the organization encourages alienated employees to retaliate against coworkers and the group as a whole.

Implementation guidelines. Use the following strategies to help insure that reward and performance systems in your organization reinforce rather than undermine ethical behavior:

- *Catch people doing good (reward moral behavior that might otherwise go unappreciated).* Publicly acknowledge workers who offer outstanding customer service, government departments that spend taxpayer money wisely, and so on.
- *Evaluate current and proposed reward and performance systems to insure that they are not reinforcing undesirable behavior.* In particular, take note of possible unintended consequences. Take the case of teacher performance standards based on student test scores. Such standards are supposed to improve learning but can encourage teachers to cheat (provide too much assistance to pupils) in order to boost test results.
- *Avoid a bottom line mentality.*[15] Financial returns (profits, donations) are critical to business and nonprofits alike. Yet, focusing solely on the bottom line blinds decision makers to other important responsibilities like supporting workers and the community. Develop other measures of performance, such as civic involvement and work-family balance. (We'll take an in-depth look at alternative performance scorecards in the next chapter.)

- *Evaluate based on processes as well as on results.* Measuring how individuals achieve their goals should be part of any performance review process. Provide incentives for moral behavior and disincentives for unethical actions. Punish salespeople who lie about delivery times or exaggerate the features of products, for instance. Resist the temptation to forgive organizational "stars" who generate great results while bending the rules. To reinforce the importance of ethical process, the army's chief recruiting officer held a daylong "values stand down." He took this action after recruiters were accused of making their enlistment quotas by helping unqualified applicants cheat (pass drug tests, hide criminal records). During the stand down recruiters viewed a video on army values, reviewed their oaths of office and correct procedures, and discussed current recruiting challenges.[16]

4. Core Values

Core values serve as enduring, guiding principles. Most organizations have between three and five such values, which are central to their collective identities.[17] Leaders at the Sealed Air Corporation (the makers of bubble wrap) consider their "bedrock values" to be personal accountability, respect for the individual, truth, and fair dealing. They take these values seriously. Concern for truth and fair dealing, for example, prevents company sales people from slamming the competition. Independent energy producer AES incorporated the following values in the prospectus for its initial public offering: (1) integrity (wholenesss, honoring commitments, adhering to the truth, consistency); (2) fairness to all stakeholders and just rewards; (3) fun (creating an enjoyable work atmosphere); (4) social responsibility—doing a good job of fulfilling the company's purpose and doing something extra for society.[18]

Organizations run into trouble when they either fail to identify and communicate their core values or fail to live up to them. Some groups have never taken the time and effort to isolate those principles that set them apart; others have clearly defined values but don't put enough effort into publicizing them. To shape behavior, values must be continually reinforced through training, public meetings, annual reports, corporate videos, brochures, and other means. In addition, leaders must "walk the talk," living out the values through their performance.

Implementation guidelines. There is no universal set of correct organizational core values. Instead, the key is to determine what members find intrinsically valuable in your work group regardless of what outsiders think. Bring members from around the organization together to consider such questions as: "If we were penalized for holding this core value, would we still hold on to it?" "Would we want to keep this value no matter how the world around us changes in the next 10 years?" "What are the very best attributes of our organization?"[19]

Once they have been selected, incorporate these values into decision-making processes and evaluation systems; continually communicate them. Hold your leaders as well as followers to these standards.

5. Mission (Purpose) Statements

A mission statement identifies an organization's reason for being, which reflects the ideals of its members. This statement combines with core values to form what management experts James Collins and Jerry Porras refer to "core ideology."[20] Core ideology is the central identity or character of an organization. Collins and Porras found that the character of the outstanding companies they studied remained constant even as those firms continued to learn and adapt. Some examples of purpose statements are found in Box 9.1.

Box 9.1 Sample Mission Statements

To make a positive difference in the lives of children and youth. (Big Brothers/Big Sisters)

A human relations organization dedicated to fighting bias, bigotry and racism in America. (National Conference of Christians and Jews)

To solve unsolved problems innovatively. (3M)

To offer competitive advantages to our customers worldwide by providing them with the capability required for the rapid design and volume production of electronic systems. (LSI Logic Corporation)

To be a leader in the distribution and merchandising of food, health, personal care, and related consumable products and service. (The Kroger Company)

To serve the needs of investors. (Charles Schwab)

Dedication to the highest quality of Customer Service delivered with a sense of warmth, friendliness, individual pride, and Company Spirit. (Southwest Airlines)

To be the best by offering the most innovative, highest quality products to advance the health and well-being of people around the world. (Warner-Lambert)

(Continued)

(Continued)

To collect the proper amount of tax revenue at the least cost; serve the public by continually improving the quality of our products and services; and perform in a manner warranting the highest degree of public confidence in our integrity, efficiency, and fairness. (Internal Revenue Service)

To become the leading premium ice cream company in America. (Dreyers Grand Ice Cream)

To provide products and services which increase the efficiency and profitability of the world's farmers. (Pioneer Hi-Bred International)

To be the world standard for quality and performance in general aviation, related products, and services. (Beechcraft)

To produce, distribute, and market a variety of high-quality beers in a manner that meets or exceeds the expectations of our customers. (Stroh Brewery)

To be the information partner of choice in each market we serve—helping people gain the knowledge they need to work, live and govern themselves. (Times Mirror)

Sources:

Abrahams, J. (1999). *The mission statement book: 301 corporate mission statements from America's top companies.* Berkeley, CA: Ten Speed Press.

Collins, J. C., & Porras, J. I. (1996, September-October). Building your company's vision. *Harvard Business Review,* pp. 65–77.

Radtke, J. M. (1998). *Strategic communications for nonprofit organizations: Seven steps to creating a successful plan.* NewYork: John Wiley.

Many mission statements fail to guide and inspire or promote moral conduct. "Maximize shareholder wealth" is a purpose that provides minimal guidance or inspiration to members. Not only does it fail to distinguish a company from its competitors, but also few people get excited about increasing earnings per share. Pursuing this objective may promote such unethical activities as overstating earnings, hiding expenses, lying to investors, and shipping shoddy products. In contrast, pursuing such goals as "to advance the health and well-being of people around the world" (Warner-Lambert) and "helping people gain the knowledge they need to work, live and govern themselves" (Times Mirror) is likely to inspire employees and encourage them to produce quality goods and services which benefit others.

Like core values, mission statements must be continually communicated and reinforced. They, too, can be undermined by inconsistent behavior. Lofty official goals do little to promote morality when leaders and followers ignore them in order to pursue their personal agendas.

Implementation guidelines. To create your organizational mission statement, try to identify what members of your organization are passionate about and capture this passion in your document. In the case of a business, ask what purpose would keep employees working for the group even if they had enough money to retire. Evaluate the mission statement on how well it guides, inspires, and promotes moral behavior.

INFORMAL ELEMENTS

1. Language

Informal language is the type of talk used in daily organizational conversations. Such talk often inhibits ethical behavior. Ethics officers report that the word *ethical* is "charged" and "emotional" for some workers.[21] These employees become defensive if their decisions are challenged. They're more comfortable using words like *shared values, mission,* and *integrity* instead. The fact that many employees are uneasy with ethical terminology, coupled with the fact that many managers are morally mute (see Chapter 3), makes it less likely that members will identify the ethical implications of their choices. They decide based on efficiency, profitability, convenience, or other criteria instead of on moral principles. Unethical choices are more likely to result.

Not only do organizational members avoid ethical terminology, they sometimes invent euphemisms to avoid thinking about the true ethical implications of their choices. It is easier to send troops on a military "mission" than a full fledged war, for example, or to "counsel someone out of an organization" instead of firing this individual.

Implementation guidelines. You and your colleagues need to become comfortable with moral terminology to encourage ethical behavior. Employ such vocabulary when discussing routine decisions and behaviors. Further, you need to be alert to euphemisms, rejecting terms that hide the moral dimension of activities.

2. Norms

Norms are widely accepted standards of behavior that reveal how an organization "really works."[22] Some norms ("Deal honestly with suppliers"; "Pitch in to help team members") support ethical conduct. Others ("Do whatever it takes to get the lowest price"; "Do as little as you can") encourage immoral behavior instead. Norms generally exert more influence over individual behavior than formal rules and policies, which helps explain why some codes of ethics are ineffectual. Members will generally do what is expected and accepted even if it is officially forbidden.

Implementation guidelines. Your organization's norms should be aligned with its ethical codes and policies. Identify important informal standards and then determine if these norms support your organization's stated rules, mission, and values. If they don't, consider how they might be modified (see Application Project 3 on page 257).

3. Rituals

Rituals are organizational dramas that are repeated at regular intervals. Actors follow carefully planned scripts in front of selected audiences; costumes and props may be involved. At one metal foam manufacturer, for instance, managers and employees gathered daily for "pour time." At this critical juncture in the manufacturing process, they don white smocks, safety glasses, and asbestos mitts to pour molten metal into a large cylinder. Flames shoot out of the cylindrical vessel, which are doused. The container is then sealed for cooling. Pour time is a particularly dramatic ritual because any mistake will cause an expensive failure and participants could be injured by molten metal and fire.[23]

Rituals serve many functions, some more obvious than others. The manifest or stated function of the pour time ritual is to complete the manufacturing process and demonstrate just how difficult it is. Latent or hidden functions of this rite might include reinforcing the importance of teamwork, boosting the importance of employees (the top manager steps aside during the process), and building commitment to the organization.

Harrison Trice and Janice Beyer provide the most popular typology of organizational rites based on their functions. These six rituals include:[24]

Rites of passage. These dramas mark important changes in roles and statuses. One of the most dramatic rites of passage is military boot camp. New recruits are stripped of their civilian identities and converted into soldiers with new haircuts, uniforms, and prescribed ways of speaking, standing, and walking. Rites of passage impart important values and enforce behaviors. In military boot camps, recruits learn the importance of obeying authority. In company boot camps in Japan, new employees develop loyalty to their firms.

Rites of degradation. Degradation rituals lower the status of organizational members, as when an officer is stripped of rank or when a player is kicked off the team. These routines identify punishable behaviors and signal how willing the organization is to stand behind its values (see the case in Box 9.2).

CASE STUDY

Box 9.2 Sending Mixed Signals at Boeing

The board of directors at Boeing Company faced a series of difficult choices in March 2005. Upon arriving for a semiannual meeting, members learned of written allegations that married CEO Harry Stonecipher was carrying on a consensual affair with a vice-president in the firm's Washington office. Stonecipher was accused of helping his lover's career and using company resources (including the corporate jet) to pursue the relationship.

The board initially responded by confronting Stonecipher, who admitted to the affair, and by confronting the vice-president. It hired an outside investigator to determine if the CEO had abused his power or company funds. The outside counsel determined that he had not. However, a series of potentially embarrassing e-mails came to light during the investigation.

The board then had to determine whether or not to fire Stonecipher who, like Boeing's other 160,000 workers, had signed a pledge stating, "Employees will not engage in conduct or activity that may raise questions as to the company's honesty, impartiality, reputation or otherwise cause embarrassment to the company."[1] The company's strict code of ethics was instituted after the firm was caught stealing secrets from competitor Lockheed Martin and offering an Air Force procurement official a job in return for federal contracts. Boeing was banned from bidding on Air Force rocket launching contracts as punishment.

CEO Stonecipher was brought out of retirement to help clean up the company's image and restore the firm's stock price. His efforts were largely successful. By the time of the board meeting, the Department of Defense was leaning toward lifting the bidding ban, airplane orders were up, and the firm's stock price was recovering.

Consensual affairs are not specifically banned in the Boeing code of ethics. Nonetheless, board members were disappointed that the CEO had engaged in such behavior while the firm was under intense ethical scrutiny. They determined that they had to protect Boeing's image. In explaining the board's decision to fire Stonecipher, board chair Lewis Platt said, "The CEO must set a standard for unimpeachable, professional and personal behavior."[2] He noted that the board's investigation had revealed "some things that we thought reflected poorly on Harry's judgment and would impair his ability to lead the company going forward."[3]

Boeing's board offered Stonecipher a generous severance package. They decided to pay him a $2.1 million bonus for 2004, provide him with financial counseling, pay an additional 6 weeks of salary, and allow him to use the company car. He was prevented from using the company jet without the permission of the board chair, however, and was declared ineligible for any future bonuses and employee benefits. The woman involved in the affair resigned and forfeited all employment benefits.

If the board of directors at Boeing hoped to send a clear signal about the importance of ethics, it failed. Observers cheered the company for firing Stonecipher but noted that his compensation package undercut the board's attempts to punish misbehavior. According to a military analyst at Taxpayers for Common Sense: "At the beginning of the week, it looked like the Boeing board was getting tough on unethical behavior. By the end of the week, they were giving Harry Stonecipher millions of dollars. This lush compensation package hurts any efforts of the board to make Boeing look better."[4] Employees wondered if Stonecipher had been fired for having sex or for writing about it in his e-mails. After all, other Boeing executives (including past CEOs) had engaged in affairs and remained on the job. They doubted that Stonecipher would have been fired if Boeing had not been under the "ethical microscope."

DISCUSSION PROBES

1. Evaluate the decisions made by Boeing's board of directors. What did members do right? Wrong?

2. What course of action would you have recommended if you were a member of the Boeing board?

3. What messages did the board send through its handling of this incident? Do you agree that board members sent mixed signals?

4. Do you think the board would have acted differently if the company wasn't under ethical scrutiny because of previous ethical and legal problems?

5. Should executives be fired for engaging in office romances?

NOTES

1. Holt (2005).
2. Holt (2005).
3. Wayne (2005, March 8).
4. Wayne, (2005, March 11).

SOURCES

Gates, D. (2005, March 8). Boeing faces CEO dilemma. *Seattle Times,* p. A1. Retrieved July 27, 2005, from LexisNexis Academic database.

Holt, S. (2005, March 8). Personal lives of executives under scrutiny. *Seattle Times,* p. C1. Retrieved July 27, 2005, from LexisNexis Academic database.

Mundy, A. (2005, March 8). The board took 8 days to decide CEO had to go. *Seattle Times,* p. A1. Retrieved July 27, 2005, from LexisNexis Academic database.

Norris, F. (2005, March 8). Moving from scandal to scandal, Boeing finds its road to redemption paved with affairs great and small. *New York Times,* p. C5. Retrieved July 27, 2005, from LexisNexis Academic database.

Wayne, L. (2005, March 8). Boeing chief is ousted after admitting affair. *New York Times,* p. A1. Retrieved July 27, 2005, from LexisNexis Academic database.

Wayne, L. (2005, March 11). Ousted chief of Boeing gets $2.1 million bonus for 2004. *New York Times*, p. C6. Retrieved July 27, 2005, from LexisNexis Academic database.
Wayne, L. (2005, March 19). Executive involved with chief has resigned, Boeing says. *New York Times*, p. C10. Retrieved July 27, 2005, from LexisNexis Academic database.
Westneat, D. (2005, March 11). Boeing's message puzzling. *Seattle Times*, p. B1. Retrieved July 27, 2005, from LexisNexis Academic database.

Rites of enhancement. In contrast to rites of degradation, rites of enhancement raise the standing of organizational members. Giving vacation trips to top salespeople, announcing the university's teacher of the year, and identifying the team's most valuable player are examples of this type of ritual. Recipients become positive role models, illustrating how members can get ahead in the organization.

Rites of renewal. These rituals strengthen and improve the current system. Examples include team-building exercises, Six Sigma quality processes, and organizational development (OD) programs. The manifest function of such rituals is to bring about improvement. However, they also have hidden consequences, like reassuring members that the organization is dealing with problems and focusing attention toward some issues and away from others.

Rites of conflict reduction. Organizations develop rituals for releasing tension and managing conflicts. Common conflict resolution rituals are collective bargaining sessions and committee meetings. In collective bargaining, union and management representatives engage in such ritualistic behavior as presenting demands and proposals, talking long hours, and threatening to walk out. In committees, members try to resolve differences between competing interests and cooperate to solve problems. The formation of a task force or committee signals that organizational leaders are serious about addressing issues.

Rites of integration. Integration dramas tie members into larger systems, reinforcing feelings of commitment and belonging. The pour time ritual described earlier brings members of different departments of the metal manufacturer together for an important shared activity. Other companies hold Christmas parties and picnics where members of all ranks mix informally. Integration ceremonies also bind individuals to regional, national, and international associations. Annual conventions and conferences connect professors, lawyers, and doctors to larger professional communities.

Rites of passage, degradation, and enhancement have manifest ethical functions. They reinforce important values, provide role models, and identify desirable and undesirable behaviors. In contrast, rites of renewal, conflict reduction, and integration have latent moral effects. One of the latent ethical effects of renewal rites is the highlighting of important organizational priorities. For example, a company may focus on cost cutting while ignoring diversity issues. Rites of conflict reduction send indirect yet important messages about how an organization values its people. Most airlines are locked into hostile relationships with their unions, for instance. Not so at Southwest Airlines. It treats unions as partners, thus reinforcing the firm's emphasis on building quality relationships.[25] Integration rituals, which are designed to increase feelings of belonging, also have the latent effect of tying members to the values and codes of conduct of larger groups.

Implementation guidelines. Since every ritual has an impact on ethical behavior, direct or indirect, you will need to carefully analyze each one. Some questions to consider include: What values and behaviors are being reinforced? What priorities are being communicated? Are these values, behaviors, and priorities desirable and ethical? Are important ethical issues being ignored? What might be the unintended ethical consequences of this ritual?

Trice and Beyer suggest modifying rituals rather than eliminating them. Discontinuing rituals can be risky since they are important events in the life of the organization. Instead, change current rites and add new ones. Open your firm's books to union personnel during negotiations instead of shutting them out, for example. Introduce an ethics award to your company's annual gathering or reward teams of salespeople rather than individuals.

4. Stories

One way to determine an organization's ethical stance is to examine its stories. Narratives, as noted in Chapter 2, provide meaning, impart values, and promote desired behavior. A tale qualifies as an organizational story when (1) many people know it, not just a few individuals, (2) the narrative focuses on one sequence of events rather than an extended history of a person or organization, (3) central characters are organization members, and (4) the story is supposedly true.

Joanne Martin of Stanford University divides organizational stories into two parts: the narrative itself and the interpretations or morals of the story that follow.[26] Both the narrative and its meaning will vary depending on the storyteller, audience, and organizational context. Martin provides three examples of a common story, which illustrate how the same basic narrative pattern can send different ethical messages. In the first version of the story, a security guard refused to let IBM chair Thomas Watson enter a restricted area without the proper badge. Instead of firing her, Watson sent someone off to get his badge. In the second version, an assembly-line worker ordered the president of another company to leave the work area and return with his safety glasses. He apologized and obeyed, impressed with the fact that she was not intimidated by his organizational rank.

These two accounts demonstrate the importance of upholding the rules regardless of status. In both cases, the high-ranking official complied, thus reinforcing the behavior of the employee. The third variation of the story is quite different, and paints a much more negative picture of corporate values. At the Revlon Company, everyone was to sign in when they arrived in the morning. One morning company founder Charles Revson arrived and picked up the sign-in sheet. The receptionist, who was new, refused to let him take the sheet because she was under "strict orders that no one is to remove the list." Revson then asked her, "Do you know who I am?" She replied that she did not. "Well," Revson said, "when you pick up your final paycheck this afternoon, ask 'em to tell ya."[27]

Heroes play a particularly important role in organizational narratives. They embody organizational values while modeling desirable behaviors. IBM's Thomas Watson was one such figure. Watson's response to the lowly security guard demonstrated how important it was to obey the rules and to treat others with respect. Stories about Watson are still told at IBM and continue to guide behavior. Of course, not all those cast as heroes truly deserve that label. Enron's Ken Skilling and top trader Lou Pai created a fictional trading floor to impress financial analysts during a 1998 meeting. Visitors were escorted into what was called the Enron Energy Services war room. During their 10-minute tour they "beheld the very picture of a sophisticated, booming business: a big open room bustling with people, all busily working the telephones and hunched over computer terminals, seemingly cutting deals and trading energy."[28] In reality, it was all a ruse. The room was filled with secretaries and other employees who were brought in for the demonstration and coached to look busy. One administrative assistant reports that she was told to bring her personal pictures to make it look like she worked at the desk where she sat. The analysts (who were charged with evaluating the financial health of the firm) were completely fooled. Skilling and his accomplices were seen as heroes, which helped foster the climate of deception that led to the firm's collapse.

Implementation guidelines. Your most pressing task may be to reduce the damage done by stories currently being told in your work group. Take the case of a tale of an abusive executive, for instance. This narrative, which illustrates how poorly the company treats its employees, can be reframed. If you fire the abuser, the tale serves as an example of how the organization has changed. Lay the groundwork for more positive stories by modeling moral behavior, which can become the basis for future tales. Strive to find heroes who embody worthy values and provide positive role models.

Cultural Change Efforts

Every component of culture contributes to the formation of an ethical organizational environment. However, by focusing on each element, it is easy to lose sight of the reality that cultures function as interrelated systems. If you want to change an organization's ethical culture, you must simultaneously address all the components described in the previous section. In fact, introducing piecemeal changes can backfire. Members can become more entrenched in their current behavior patterns when, for example, managers create a new values statement without also changing the way that employees are rewarded and evaluated. Disillusioned workers conclude that management isn't really serious about moral behavior. They greet future ethics initiatives with skepticism.

Highly ethical organizations make sure that cultural components align or support one another.[29] Ethical codes are backed by norms, stories reflect core values, structure supports individual initiative, and so forth. These collectives also demonstrate ethical consistency. All units and organizational levels share a commitment to high moral standards. Ethical values are factored into every organizational activity, whether planning and goal setting, spending, gathering and sharing of information, or marketing. Further, constituents are encouraged and equipped to make ethical choices following core principles.

ETHICAL DRIVERS

Ethical drivers are factors that play a particularly significant role in promoting or driving systematic ethical change. Without them, any change effort is likely to fail. These drivers include ethical diagnosis, engaged leadership, targeted socialization processes, ethics training, and continuous ethical improvement.

Driver #1: Ethical Diagnosis

Determining the organization's current ethical condition should be the first step in any systematic change initiative. Diagnosis surfaces moral strengths and weaknesses, areas of misalignment, the criteria for making ethical choices, and shared perceptions of the organization's moral health. These data should then drive the rest of the change effort.

Auditing the cultural components described earlier is one way to diagnose your workplace's current ethical condition. The ethical culture audit probes both formal and informal systems using the self-assessment questions listed in Box 9.3. When conducting the audit, use surveys, interviews, observation, and analysis to gather information. You could also ask these questions when applying for jobs to assess the ethical status of prospective employers.

Self-Assessment

Box 9.3 Ethics Audit Questions

Use the following set of questions to evaluate the ethical culture of your current organization or one that you would like to join.

Selected Questions for Auditing the Formal System

1. How are organizational leaders perceived in terms of their integrity? Is ethics part of the leadership agenda?
2. How are ethics-related behaviors modeled by organizational leaders?
3. Are workers at all levels encouraged to take responsibility for the consequences of their behavior? To question authority when they are asked to do something that they consider to be wrong? How?
4. Does a formal code of ethics and/or values exist? Is it distributed? How widely? Is it used? Is it reinforced in other formal systems such as reward and decision-making systems?
5. Are whistle-blowers encouraged and are formal channels available for them to make their concerns known confidentially?
6. Is misconduct disciplined swiftly and justly in the organization, no matter what the organizational level?
7. Are people of integrity promoted? Are means as well as ends important?
8. Is integrity emphasized to recruits and new employees?
9. Are managers oriented to the values of the organization in orientation programs? Are they trained in ethical decision making?
10. Are ethical considerations a routine part of planning and policy meetings, new venture reports? Is the language of ethics taught and used? Does a formal committee exist high in the organization for considering ethical issues?

Selected Questions for Auditing the Informal System

1. Identify informal organizational norms. Are they consistent with formal rules and polices?
2. Identify the organization's heroes. What values do they represent? Given an ambiguous ethical dilemma, what decision would they make and why?
3. What are some important organizational rituals? How do they encourage or discourage ethical behavior? Who gets the awards,

(Continued)

(Continued)

people of integrity who are successful or individuals who use unethical methods to attain success?

4. What ethical messages are sent to new entrants into the organization—must they obey authority at all costs, or is questioning authority acceptable or even desirable?
5. Does analysis of organizational stories and myths reveal individuals who stand up for what's right despite pressure, or is conformity the valued characteristic? Do people get fired or promoted in these stories?
6. Does acceptable language exist for discussing ethical concerns? Is this language routinely incorporated and encouraged in business (organizational) decision making?
7. What informal socialization processes exist and what norms for ethical or unethical behavior do they promote? Are these different for different organizational subgroups?

Conclusion

What is your overall evaluation of this organization's ethical culture? What are its areas of strength and weakness?

Source: Trevino, L. K., & Nelson, K. A. (2004). *Managing business ethics: Straight talk about how to do it right.* Hoboken, NJ: John Wiley, p. 259. Reprinted by permission of John Wiley & Sons, Inc.

Climate analysis is another way to measure moral performance. *Ethical climate* refers to the "shared perceptions of what is ethically correct behavior and how ethical issues should be handled in the organization."[30] Management ethicists Bart Victor and John Cullen developed the Ethical Climate Questionnaire (ECQ) to measure these perceptions. The ECQ classifies moral climates according to (a) the ethical principles that members use to make moral choices, and (b) the groups that members refer to when making ethical determinations. Members out to maximize their self-interest are guided by egoism. Individuals may also seek to benefit others (benevolence) or act according to universal standards (principle). To determine what is ethically correct, they may rely on their own judgments, refer to local organizational standards, or look to outside groups for help.

Victor and Cullen identify five climate types. *Instrumental* climates encourage self-serving (egoistic) behavior, which is often economically driven. *Caring* climates emphasize concern for others and the organization as a whole, even at the cost of meeting individual needs. *Rules* climates are governed by the policies, rules, and procedures (principles) developed within the organization. *Law and code* climates turn to external criteria or principles like professional codes of conduct or state laws for guidance. *Independence* climates are also principled but encourage individuals to make choices based on their personal values and ethics.

Victor and Cullen suggest that an organization's ethical orientation might make it more susceptible to some forms of unethical behavior and shape its response to change efforts. For instance, members of caring organizations may break laws in order to help others. A written code of ethics is likely to receive a better reception in a rules or law and code climate than in a caring or independence environment.

Investigators continue to probe the relationship between climate types and ethical behavior, but so far they've discovered that[31]

- ethical climates often vary between departments and locations within an organization
- rates of immoral behavior are highest in instrumental climates
- organizational commitment is greatest in caring climates and lowest in instrumental climates
- for-profit climates are more likely to be driven by self-interest, while nonprofit climates are more likely to be founded on benevolence
- an emphasis on obeying the law and adhering to professional codes reduces unethical behavior
- employees are more satisfied when they work for organizations with ethical climates that reflect their personal preferences
- professionals prefer to work for organizations with rule or law and code climates

According to these findings, self-interest poses the greatest threat to ethical performance, and you need to confront this attitude, whether at the unit or organizationwide level. Creating a more caring environment in your work group can pay off in higher trust and commitment levels, referring to rules and codes can decrease immoral behavior. Finally, match the person (yourself or potential hires) with the climate. Employees are more satisfied and are less likely to leave if their personal ethical preferences match those of the organization.

Driver #2: Engaged Leadership

Significant cultural change is extremely difficult without the buy-in of top leadership.[32] We've already noted how leaders are largely responsible for shaping organizations, play a key role in curbing or promoting destructive behaviors, reinforce or undermine values and standards, and so on. The acronym CEO could stand for "Chief Ethics Officer."

Organizational psychologist Edgar Schein outlines six primary mechanisms that you can use in a leadership role to establish, maintain, and change ethical culture.[33]

1. Attention. Followers will pick up on your priorities through what you pay attention to, measure, and control. Ethics won't be taken seriously unless you consistently talk about the importance of ethical behavior, act ethically, measure moral performance, and punish those who fall short of standards. Systematically and persistently emphasize core values and mission.

2. Reactions to critical incidents. The way you respond to stressful events sends important messages about underlying organizational values. Some firms, which value efficiency, handle financial setbacks through layoffs, for example. Others, which value cooperation, cut costs by asking everyone to work fewer hours. Major crises quickly reveal the true ethical character of a leader and his or her organization. Johnson and Johnson CEO James Burke is a case in point. He earned widespread praise for his response to the Tylenol product-tampering crisis. Under his leadership, the company cooperated with authorities, voluntarily recalled the product, admitted when it released faulty information, and developed new packaging. (Turn to the Chapter End Case to read about another leader who effectively handled a crisis.) In contrast, the leaders of Bridgestone/Firestone waited months after learning of problems with its Wilderness tires before issuing a recall. The company then wanted to stagger the replacement schedule, forcing some customers to risk their lives as they waited their turn for safer tires.[34]

3. Resource allocation. How an organization spends its money is a key indicator of its values and priorities. What types of projects get supported? How much money is devoted to ethics programs and training? Does the organization invest in the health and well-being of its employees? Does it support their personal development? The process of budgeting also reveals underlying moral assumptions. The greater the organization's commitment to empowering its members, the more likely it is to involve people from all levels of the organization in setting financial targets. Because resource allocation and budgeting send strong cultural signals, think carefully about what you want to communicate when deciding how to create the departmental or organizational spending plan.

4. Role modeling. Acting as a role model is more than setting an example; it also means developing others. Become a coach and teacher to others, particularly to those who report directly to you. Help them identify and manage ethical issues and develop their ethical problem-solving skills.

5. *Rewards.* Rewards, discussed earlier in the chapter as an element of performance and evaluation systems, also go hand-in-hand with attention mechanisms. Use them to draw attention to important goals, shared values, and desirable and undesirable behaviors.

6. *Selection.* Organizations tend to perpetuate current cultural components by hiring people who fit into the current system. If you want to reform the culture, recruit members who share the new ethical standards rather than the old ones. Promote those who support the group's mission values and, if necessary, remove those who don't.

Driver #3: Targeted Socialization Processes

Socialization describes the process of becoming a group member. To make this transition, individuals have to learn how to perform their individual roles and, at the same time, absorb information about the organization's culture.[35] There are several reasons why socialization can play a key role in driving ethical change. First, new members are most susceptible to influence and open to instruction about ethical behavior. Their values and perceptions are being formed and they are anxious to learn how to behave in a new environment. Second, discussion of ethics can be incorporated into existing socialization programs. Third, the values learned during the socialization process will shape an employee's behavior throughout her or his career with the organization. Fourth, when newcomers become ethical veterans, they then communicate and model important values to new generations of members.

Socialization begins even before a member joins a new organization or organizational unit. Job applicants typically have expectations about the prospective organization gathered from recruitment brochures, Web sites, and other channels. The employment interview plays a particularly significant role in shaping these expectations. Applicants come away with an image of what the organization is like, which may be unrealistic. This can lead to dissatisfaction and a quick exit after they join.

Formal socialization mechanisms kick in when newcomers begin their membership. As they "learn the ropes," rookies participate in training and orientation sessions designed to integrate them into the organization. They also come under the influence of socializing agents. Important socializing agents include: (a) veteran coworkers who serve as day-to-day guides and sounding boards; (b) respected senior peers who guide by example and impart organizational standards and values; (c) supervisors who act as official guides to policies and procedures; and (d) mentors and/or advisors who model core organizational values and philosophy.

Socialization concludes when newcomers become accepted members of the group. It should be noted that new members aren't merely sponges, soaking up cultural information. They also help to shape the culture by introducing new values and practices.

Unfortunately, socialization processes may contribute to immoral behavior. New members can be corrupted through co-option, incrementalism, and compromise.[36] In *co-option,* the organization uses rewards to reduce newcomers' discomfort with unethical behaviors. Targets may not realize that these incentives are skewing their judgment, making it easier to rationalize poor behavior. For example, brokers who are rewarded for pushing certain stocks may convince themselves that these picks are outstanding investments. *Incrementalism* gradually introduces new members to corrupt practices, leading them up the "ladder of corruption." Newcomers are first persuaded to engage in a practice that is only mildly unethical. They turn to the rationalizations offered by their peers ("Everybody does it"; "Nobody was really hurt"; "They deserved it") to relieve the cognitive dissonance produced by this act. After the first practice becomes normal, acceptable behavior, individuals are then encouraged to move on to increasingly more corrupt activities. In the end, they find themselves participating in acts that they would have rejected when they first joined the organization. *Compromise* "backs" members into corruption as they strive to solve dilemmas and conflicts. Politicians, for instance, enter into lots of compromises in order to keep and expand their power. Cutting deals and forming networks makes it harder for them to take ethical stands.

The danger of dysfunctional socialization is greatest when newcomers join a social cocoon. A social cocoon is a strong culture in which norms and values are very different from those in the rest of the organization or society. In cocoons, members highly prize their membership in the group and tend to compartmentalize their lives, holding one set of values outside work and another on the job. At a prestigious law firm, a cocoon may develop as new attorneys strive to become partners. Veterans of the firm (whom newcomers admire) may encourage rookies to overbill for services and to neglect their families by working extremely long hours. The recent law school graduates put aside their misgivings about these patterns, blaming themselves for their doubts rather than blaming the firm for encouraging unhealthy practices.

As a change agent, target the socialization process in your work group to promote positive ethical change rather than reinforcing corrupt behavior. Start with clearly describing your organization's values and ethical climate in the employment interview. Paint a truthful picture of conditions in your organization. Ensure that ethics is a top priority in orientation and training sessions. Communicate core values and mission statements, present the code of ethics, highlight potential ethical dilemmas, introduce ethics officers and procedures, and engage in ethics discussions. Then place newcomers with socializing agents who reinforce rather than undermine values and standards. Provide channels for new hires to express their concerns about ongoing practices. Puncture the social cocoon by training employees to think about the perspectives of outsiders and by bringing in external change agents (new leaders, consultants, speakers).

Driver #4: Ethics Training

Formal ethics training, as we've seen, should be part of the socialization process. However, the need for ethics education doesn't end when members are assimilated into the group. Ongoing training can play an important role in creating and maintaining ethical environments. Training sessions can increase moral sensitivity and moral judgment, make it easier to use moral vocabulary, reduce destructive behaviors, prevent scandals, reinforce mission and values, and integrate ethical considerations into the fabric of organizational life.

Of course, offering ethics training is not a panacea. There is no guarantee that those who attend will make better decisions or change their behaviors; poorly designed training programs can actually increase resistance to change. Nonetheless, effective ethics training can make a positive difference in your organization. Effective training does the following:[37]

1. *Focuses on your organization's unique ethical problems.* The most useful training addresses the dilemmas encountered by group members. Issues that professors face (grading, academic freedom, tenure decisions) will be different than those encountered by physicians (managed care, patient privacy, malpractice), for example. Help your organization's employees identify potential ethical issues that may be hidden at first. Introduce examples drawn directly from the organization, industry, and profession. Equip trainees with the tools they need to solve these dilemmas.

2. *Allows plenty of time for discussion and interaction.* Key concepts can be presented in lectures and handouts, but spend most of your class time in dyad, small group, and large group discussion. Introduce case studies; raise questions, and debate issues. Trainees can also interact about ethical issues outside of class via the Internet.

3. *Taps into the experiences of participants.* Ask your trainees to provide dilemmas and insights drawn from their own experiences. Participants then become the instructors, "teaching" one another. They also receive feedback that enables them to better handle their dilemmas.

4. *Is integrated into the entire curriculum.* The stand-alone ethics workshop or class promotes moral reasoning but is easily disconnected from the rest of the organization's activities. Whenever possible, you should integrate ethics

discussion into other subjects like sales skills, leadership development, conflict management, and supervision.

Implications

- Both the formal and informal components of your organization's culture will influence the ethical behavior of employees. You need to address all of these elements to foster an ethical workplace.
- Structure shapes behavior through the creation of authority relationships, delineation of lines of accountability, and the allocation of decision-making rights. Encourage employees to challenge orders when necessary, help them understand how their actions impact others, and empower them to resolve the dilemmas they face.
- Codes of ethics can play a vital role in improving an ethical climate. Your organization's ethical guidelines need to have the backing of senior managers who consistently enforce them.
- To promote moral behavior, acknowledge ethical performance, reward desirable (not undesirable) activities, and make sure goals are reached through ethical means.
- Core values serve as enduring, guiding principles which reflect what organizational members find intrinsically valuable. However, to have a positive influence on behavior, your group's collective values must be clearly identified, continually reinforced, and modeled by leaders.
- Create a powerful mission or purpose statement that reflects the ideals of your members while inspiring and promoting ethical behavior.
- Use moral vocabulary even when making routine decisions and avoid euphemisms which hide the ethical implications of your choices.
- Create norms (widely accepted standards of behavior) that support, not undermine, your formal codes and policies.
- Analyze rituals to determine the behaviors, values, and priorities they promote. Modify those rites that poison the ethical climate.
- Turn negative organizational stories into positive ones by reframing them, modeling desired behaviors, and identifying worthy heroes.
- Your attempts to change the ethical culture must be systematic, simultaneously addressing multiple components. Cultural elements should align (support) one another and consistently demonstrate ethical values.
- Diagnosis should be the first step in any ethical change initiative. Use an ethics audit to measure the relationship of cultural components and ethical behavior.
- Conduct an ethical climate analysis to determine how members perceive what is ethically correct behavior and how they believe the organization deals with ethical issues.
- As a leader, be actively engaged in creating, maintaining, and changing ethical culture through (1) attention, (2) your reaction to critical incidents, (3) resource allocation, (4) role modeling, (5) rewards, and (6) selection.
- Communicate positive moral values and standards to newcomers through employment interviews, formal orientation programs, and socializing agents.

- Focus your ongoing ethics training on your organization's unique ethical problems, allow plenty of time for trainees to discuss issues, tap into the experiences of participants, and integrate discussion of ethics into the entire curriculum.

Application Projects

1. List the core values of your organization. How well are they publicized? How well are they supported by the behavior of organizational leaders?
2. Evaluate the effectiveness of the mission statements in Box 9.1 or, as an alternative, collect and evaluate your own examples. How well do these statements guide, inspire, and promote ethical behavior? What characteristics separate the effective statements from their ineffective counterparts?
3. With your fellow employees, volunteers, or students, identify a list of norms in your organization. Compare these norms with the group's formal code of ethics, core values, and mission statement. Do the norms support the formal cultural components? Brainstorm strategies for bringing them into alignment. Report your findings to a significant organizational decision maker.
4. Do an in-depth analysis of an important organizational ritual. Identify its manifest and latent ethical functions. Write up your findings.
5. Complete the Self-Assessment in Box 9.3 to analyze your organization's ethical culture. Record your answers to each question. Conclude with an overall evaluation of the group's moral condition and suggestions for improvement. If you can, distribute the ethics audit questions to others and discuss your findings as a group.
6. Analyze your socialization experience from an ethical vantage point. How well did the organization communicate its values and standards? What could be done to improve the process?
7. Attend an ethical training program and evaluate its effectiveness using the guidelines in the chapter.
8. Create a case study based on an organization's attempt to change its ethical culture. Outline what can be learned from this group's experience.

CHAPTER END CASE

Cleaning Up the Mess at Waste Management

Enron wasn't the first Houston-based company to engage in massive accounting fraud. In 1998, garbage hauler Waste Management was accused of overstating over a billion dollars in earnings between 1992 and 1997, triggering the largest accounting restatement to that point in U.S. history. Company officials were later convicted of collecting close to $29 million through ill-gotten bonuses and insider trading. The company went through five CEOs between 1996 and 1999 and its stock lost $25 billion in value.

Maurice (Marty) Myers was hired in November 1999 to help reverse the company's fortunes and save it from ruin. Myers had previously directed the turnarounds of America West Airlines and Yellow Corporation trucking. However, Waste Management posed by far the greatest challenge.

CEO Myers took a "relentlessly hands-on" approach to dealing with the crisis. Before joining the firm, he spent a day interviewing employees and continued the practice for the first few weeks on the job. According to Myers, "there is not a company in the world whose problems are not known by the people who work for it."[1] He worked hard to regain the trust of workers, visiting them when their paychecks were shortchanged and improving employee benefits in response to complaints. To boost morale, he drove a garbage truck on stage for an employee meeting. Weekends were spent recruiting new staff (he interviewed 140 candidates to select 14 new executives).

Myers concerned himself with both ethical and operational issues. To highlight the importance of organizational integrity, he created an anonymous hotline to receive reports of immoral behavior. The hotline logged over 4,600 calls in a 2-year period, resulting in the terminations of 60 employees and disciplinary actions for many others. These measures were then reported in the weekly company newsletter. The CEO also reinstituted the position of the ethics officer. The person in this role trains the board as well as the workforce.

At the same time that he was addressing Waste Management's ethical culture, Myers was also focused on its profitability. He moved quickly to settle a class action lawsuit for $547 million that was a drag on the firm's stock price. Waste Management improved its billing system, began to track customer concerns and accident rates, sold its overseas operations, negotiated lower prices with truck manufacturers, and developed more efficient pick up schedules using global positioning system (GPS) technology. CEO Myers was careful not to oversell the company's progress to financial analysts, however, emphasizing steady results instead. He sought to underpromise and overdeliver because with companies tainted by scandal, "everybody is watching you. You just can't mess up."[2]

By the middle of 2003, the firm had experienced a remarkable recovery. Its debt was down by a third and cash flow had increased 30 percent. Income had risen and the stock price had jumped 85 percent. Even more importantly, the company was no longer seen as a corporate villain. Myers stepped down as CEO in November 2004, leaving his successor (whom he had recruited to help in the turnaround) a transformed organization.

DISCUSSION PROBES

1. Would Myers have succeeded if he had been less "hands on" in his approach?
2. What elements of ethical culture did CEO Myers address? Why was he so successful?

3. What change mechanisms did Myers use to change Waste Management's ethical culture?
4. How much credit for the turnaround should go to Myers? How much to the rest of the management team and employees?
5. Can you think of other examples of ethical turnarounds. What do they have in common with this case?

NOTES

1. Cleaning up the mess (2001).
2. Creswell (2003), p. 129.

SOURCES

Cleaning up the mess. (2001, June 30). *Economist,* p. 64. Retrieved July 25, 2005, from Business Source Premier database.

Creswell, J. (2003, July 7). Scandal hits—now what? *Fortune,* pp. 127–129.

Hensel, B. (2004, April 4). Business Q & A: Not a garbage guy, CEO talks about the turnaround. *Houston Chronicle,* Business section, p. 1. Retrieved July 25, 2005, from Business Source Premier database.

Endnotes

1. Trevino, L. K. (1990). A cultural perspective on changing and developing organizational ethics. In W. A. Pasmore & R. W. Woodman (Eds.), *Research in organizational change and development* (Vol. 4). Greenwich, CT: JAI; Trevino, L. K., & Nelson, K. A. (2004). *Managing business ethics: Straight talk about how to do it right* (3rd ed.). Hoboken, NJ: John Wiley.

2. Harvey, S. J., Jr. (2000). Reinforcing ethical decision making through organizational structure. *Journal of Business Ethics, 28,* 43–58.

3. Cialdini, R. B. (2001). *Influence. Science and practice* (4th ed.). Boston: Allyn & Bacon.

4. Trevino, L. K., Weaver, G. R., Gibson, D. G., & Toffler, B. L. (1999). Managing ethics and legal compliance: What works and what hurts. *California Management Review, 41,* 131–151.

5. Darley, J. M. (1996). How organizations socialize individuals into evildoing. In D. M. Messick & A. E. Tenbrunsel (Eds.), *Codes of conduct: Behavioral research into business* ethics (pp. 13–43). New York: Russell Sage Foundation.

6. Adams, J. S., Tashchian, A., & Shore, T. H. (2001). Codes of ethics as signals for ethical behavior. *Journal of Business Ethics, 29,* 199–211.

7. Hoppen, D. (2002, Winter). Guiding corporate behavior: A leadership obligation, not a choice. *Journal for Quality & Participation, 25,* 15–19.

8. Barth, S. R. (2003). *Corporate ethics: The business code of conduct for ethical employees.* Boston: Aspatore Books.

9. McCabe, D., & Trevino, K. L. (1993). Academic dishonesty: Honor codes and other contextual influences. *Journal of Higher Education, 64,* 522–569.

10. Adams, Tashchian, & Shore (2001); Valentine, S., & Barnett, T. (2003). Ethics code awareness, perceived ethical values, and organizational commitment. *Journal of Personal Selling & Sales Management, 23,* 359–367.

11. Brandl, P., & Maguire, M. (2002, Winter). Codes of ethics: A primer on their purpose, development and use. *Journal for Quality & Participation, 25,* 9–12; Johannesen, R. L. (2002). *Ethics in human communication* (5th ed.). Prospect Heights, IL: Waveland Press, chap. 10.

12. Trevino (1990).

13. Toffler, B. (2003). *Final accounting: Ambition, greed and the fall of Arthur Andersen.* New York: Broadway Books.

14. Cohen, D. V. (1993). Creating and maintaining ethical work climates: Anomie in the workplace and implications for managing change. *Business Ethics Quarterly, 3,* 343–358.

15. Estes, R. (1996). *Tyranny of the bottom line.* San Francisco: Berritt-Koehler.

16. Lumpkin, J. L. (2005, May 11). One day halt called in Army recruiting. *Associated Press.* Retrieved June 10, 2005, from LexisNexis Academic database.

17. Collins, J. C., & Porras, J. I. (1996, September-October). Building your company's vision. *Harvard Business Review,* pp. 65–77.

18. Paine, L S. (2003). *Value shift: Why companies must merge social and financial imperatives to achieve superior performance.* New York: McGraw-Hill.

19. Collins & Porras (1996).

20. Collins, J. C., & Porras, J. I. (1994). *Built to last: Successful habits of visionary companies.* New York: HarperBusiness.

21. Trevino & Nelson (2004).

22. Trevino & Nelson (2004).

23. Martin, J. (2002). *Organizational culture: Mapping the terrain.* Thousand Oaks, CA: Sage.

24. Beyer, J. M., & Trice, H. M. (1987). How an organization's rites reveal its culture. *Organizational Dynamics,* 15, 5–24; Trice, H. M., & Beyer, J. M. (1984). Studying organizational cultures through rites and ceremonials. *Academy of Management Review, 9,* 653–699.

25. Gittell, J. H. (2003). *The Southwest Airlines way.* New York: McGraw-Hill.

26. Martin (2002).

27. Tobias, A. (1976). *Fire and ice.* New York: William Morrow, pp. 98–99.

28. McLean, B., & Elkind, P. (2003). *The smartest guys in the room: The amazing rise and fall of Enron.* New York: Portfolio.

29. Trevino & Nelson (2004); Paine, L. S. (1996, March-April). Managing for organizational integrity. *Harvard Business Review,* pp. 106–117.

30. Victor, B., & Cullen, J. B. (1988). The organizational bases of ethical work climates. *Administrative Science Quarterly, 33,* 101–125; Victor, B., & Cullen, J. B. (1990). A theory and measure of ethical climate in organizations. In W. C. Frederic & L. E. Preston (Eds.), *Business ethics: Research issues and empirical studies* (pp. 77–97). Greenwich, CT: JAI.

31. See, for example: Brower, H. H., & Shrader, C. B. (2000). Moral reasoning and ethical climate: Not-for-profit vs. for-profit boards of directors. *Journal of Business Ethics, 26,* 147–167; Sims, R. L., & Keon, T. L. (1997). Ethical work climate as a factor in the development of person-organization fit. *Journal of Business Ethics, 16,* 1095–1105; Peterson, D. K. (2002). The relationship between unethical behavior and the dimensions

of the Ethical Climate Questionnaire. *Journal of Business Ethics, 41,* 313–326; Fritzche, D. J. (2000). Ethical climates and the ethical dimension of decision making. *Journal of Business Ethics, 24,* 125–140; Trevino, L. K., Butterfield, K. D., & McCabe, D. L. (1998). The ethical context in organizations: Influences on employee attitudes and behaviors. *Business Ethics Quarterly, 8,* 447–476; Wimbush, J. C., Shepard, J. M., & Markham, S. E. (1997). An empirical examination of the relationship between ethical climate and ethical behavior from multiple levels of analysis. *Journal of Business Ethics, 16,* 1705–1716; Cullen, J. B., Parboteeah, K. P., & Victor, B. (2003). The effects of ethical climates on organizational commitment: A two-study analysis. *Journal of Business Ethics, 46,* 127–141; Victor, B., Cullen, J. B., & Boynton, A. (1993). Toward a general framework of organizational meaning systems. In C. Conrad (Ed.), *Ethical nexus* (pp. 193–216). Norwood, NJ: Ablex.

32. Gellerman, S. W. (1989, Winter). Managing ethics from the top down. *Sloan Management Review,* pp. 73–79; Longnecker, J. G. (1985). Management priorities and management ethics. *Journal of Business Ethics, 4,* 65–70; Trevino, L. K., Hartman, L. P., & Brown, M. (2000). Moral person and moral manager: How executives develop a reputation for ethical leadership. *California Management Review, 42,* 128–142; Weaver, G. R., Trevino, L. K., & Cochran, P. L. (1999). Corporate ethics programs as control systems: Influence of executive commitment and environmental factors. *Academy of Management Journal, 42,* 41–57.

33. Schein, E. H. (1992). *Organizational culture and leadership* (2nd ed.). San Francisco: Jossey-Bass.

34. Eisenberg, D., Szczesny, J. R., Forster, P., Larimer, T., Eskenazi, M., & Greenwald, J. (2000, September 18). Firestone's rough road. *Time,* pp. 38–40.

35. Albrecht, T. L, & Bach, B. W. (1997). *Communication in complex organizations: A relational approach.* Fort Worth, TX: Harcourt Brace.

36. Anand, V., Ashforth, B. E., & Joshi, M. (2004). Business as usual: The acceptance and perpetuation of corruption in organizations. *Academy of Management Executive, 18,* 39–53.

37. Heames, J. T., & Service, R. W. (2003). Dichotomies in teaching, application, and ethics. *Journal of Education for Business, 79,* 118–122; Rice, D., & Dreilinger, C. (1990, May). Rights and wrongs of ethics training. *Training and Development Journal,* pp. 103–108; Piper, T. R., Gentile, M. C., & Parks, S. D. (1993). *Can ethics be taught? Perspectives, challenges, and approaches at Harvard Business School.* Boston: Harvard Business School Press; Hartog, M., & Frame, P. (2004). Business ethics in the curriculum: Integrating ethics through work experience. *Journal of Business Ethics, 54,* 399–409; Mintzberg, H. (2004). *Managers, not MBAs.* San Francisco: Berritt-Koehler; Rest, J. R. (1994). Background: Theory and research. In J. R. Rest & D. Narvaez (Eds.), *Moral development in the professions: Psychology and applied ethics* (pp. 1–25). Hillsdale, NJ: Lawrence Erlbaum.

10

Promoting Organizational Citizenship in a Global Society

In this final chapter we'll look beyond the borders of our organizations to focus on the role that our employers should play in local, national, and international communities. Our individual responsibility is to equip our work groups to act as socially responsible citizens in a world marked by rapid globalization. Section one offers frameworks for promoting and evaluating organizational citizenship. Section two describes the demands of global citizenship and introduces strategies for meeting these challenges.

The Organization as Citizen

"To whom much has been given, much will be expected." That saying encapsulates the relationship between organizations and Western society over the past several decades. Organizations wield more power than ever before. The decline of the extended family, urbanization, industrialization, and other factors have increased our reliance on corporations, governments, schools, nonprofit agencies, and other institutions. At the same time, societal expectations of organizations have greatly expanded. We now demand that organizations, even for-profit entities, be socially responsible. As evidence of this trend, consider the following:[1]

- Seventy-nine percent of Americans believe that businesses should support social causes.
- Eighty-nine percent of U.S. respondents reported they would switch brands to one associated with a worthy cause if price and quality were similar.
- A survey of citizens in 23 countries found that 90 percent of respondents wanted firms to focus on more than profits.
- Over 2 trillion dollars is invested in socially conscious mutual funds that screen out "sin stocks" like tobacco companies, distillers, and weapons manufacturers.
- America's Most Admired Companies earn that label, in part, because they are concerned about the community and the environment.
- Watchdog groups regularly monitor the financial status and effectiveness of charities.
- AIDS activists, disability advocates, environmentalists, and other groups are quick to bring suit against governments and businesses that don't fulfill their social duties.

The term *organizational citizenship* best describes what society expects from businesses, governments, and nonprofits. Good citizens acknowledge their obligations to their communities. These responsibilities are economic, legal, ethical, and philanthropic. A corporation, for example, should seek to be profitable, obey the law, do what is right and just, and contribute to the community. Organizational citizens also develop ongoing processes for anticipating and responding to societal pressures. They continually scan the environment for emerging issues and actively engage their critics in dialogue. Finally, they back up their convictions with concrete actions—treating workers fairly, reducing manufacturing waste, sending volunteers to local schools, promoting cancer awareness, and so on.[2]

PROMOTING ORGANIZATIONAL CITIZENSHIP

Encouraging our organizations to become active citizens is easier if we can offer them principles and strategies for doing so. Three perspectives—the stakeholder framework, the stewardship approach, and the sustainability standard—provide valuable insights into the "whys" and "hows" of organizational citizenship.

The Stakeholder Framework

The stakeholder framework first developed as an alternative way to define the relationship between large businesses and society but since has been extended to organizations of all types—partnerships, small businesses, governments, and nonprofits.[3] Traditionally, corporate executives have been viewed as agents who act on behalf of the company's owners. According to this perspective (called *agency theory*), the manager's primary ethical obligation is to promote the interests of stockholders. Companies that operate efficiently and profitably benefit the community through the creation of jobs and wealth as well as through higher tax revenues.

Stakeholder theorists challenge the notion that a manager's sole moral duty is to company owners.[4] They note that the pursuit of corporate wealth doesn't benefit everyone. When a major retailer forces its suppliers to cut costs, for example, lots of groups suffer. Employees manufacturing the goods see their wages and benefits cut and jobs are lost. Local businesses and economies decline. Also, shareholders aren't the only groups with a stake in what the company does. Governments charter corporations based in part on the expectation that they will provide benefits to society. They invest in businesses by supplying them with cheap land, building access roads, and offering tax breaks.

Advocates of stakeholder theory argue that organizations of all kinds have an ethical obligation to "heed the needs, interests, and influence of those affected by their policies and operations."[5] (See Box 10.1 for a list of the possible stakeholders of one organization.) Drawing from Kant's Categorical Imperative, some proponents believe that all stakeholders have intrinsic value.[6] It is wrong to use any group of people as a means to organizational ends. The interests of diverse stakeholder groups are valid and worthy of respect. Other supporters of this approach draw upon Justice as Fairness Theory to emphasize that outside groups and individuals need to be treated fairly by the organization.[7] Still others adopt a communitarian perspective to point out that serving stakeholders, not just stockholders, is more likely to promote cooperation and the development of relationships that contribute to the common good of society.[8]

Box 10.1 Organizational Stakeholders

Stakeholder	*Nature of the Stakeholder Claim*
Shareholders	Participation in distribution of profits, additional stock offerings, assets on liquidation; vote of stock; inspection of company books; transfer of stock; election of board of directors; and such additional rights as have been established in the contract with the corporation.
Employees	Economic, social, and psychological satisfaction in the place of employment. Freedom from arbitrary and capricious behavior on the part of company officials. Share in fringe benefits, freedom to join union and participate in collective bargaining, individual freedom in offering up their services through an employment contract. Adequate working conditions.
Customers	Service provided with the product; technical data to use the product; suitable warranties; spare parts to support the product during use; R&D leading to product improvement; facilitation of credit.
Creditors	Legal proportion of interest payments due and return of principal from the investment. Security of pledged assets; relative priority in event of liquidation. Management and owner prerogatives if certain conditions exist with the company (such as default of interest payments).
Suppliers	Continuing source of business; timely consummation of trade credit obligations; professional relationship in contracting for, purchasing, and receiving goods and services.
Unions	Recognition as the negotiating agent for employees. Opportunity to perpetuate the union as a participant in the business organization.
Competitors	Observation of the norms of competitive conduct established by society and the industry. Business statesmanship on the part of peers.
Governments	Taxes (income, property, and so on); adherence to the letter and intent of public policy dealing with the requirements of fair and free competition; discharge of legal obligations of businesspeople (and business organizations); adherence to antitrust laws.

Local communities	Place of productive and healthful environment in the community. Participation of company officials in community affairs, provision of regular employment, fair play, reasonable portion of purchases made in the local community, interest in and support of local government, support of cultural and charitable projects.
The general public	Participation in and contribution to society as a whole; creative communications between governmental and business units designed for reciprocal understanding; assumption of fair proportion of the burden of government and society. Fair price for products and advancement of the state-of-the-art technology that the product line involves.

Source: From Sims, R. R., *Ethics and corporate social responsibility: Why giants fall*, copyright © 2003. Reprinted with permission of the Greenwood Publishing Group, Inc.

Recognizing the concerns of multiple stakeholders has strategic as well as ethical implications. Identifying the needs of stakeholders should be part of any major decision, like entering additional markets, establishing a new social service program, or changing an investment strategy. You will want to engage in stakeholder management in order to improve organizational performance at the same time that you respond to your moral responsibilities. According to business ethicists Archie Carroll and Ann Buchholtz, stakeholder management means answering five key questions:[9]

1. Who are our stakeholders? Categorizing stakeholders can make it easier to answer this question. Those with an interest in the organization can be classified as primary or secondary stakeholders. Primary stakeholders (customers, investors, employees, suppliers) have a direct stake in the organization's success or failure and thus exert significant influence. Their interests generally are given priority. Secondary stakeholders (social pressure groups, media, trade bodies) have an indirect stake in the organization. Accountability to these groups is therefore less.

2. What are our stakeholders' stakes? As Box 10.1 illustrates, stakeholder groups have different interests, concerns, and demands. Some of these stakes are more legitimate than others. Owners, for example, have a legal interest in a corporation, while suppliers do not. Further, some groups have more power than others. The board of trustees of a university system typically wields more power than the faculty or students.

3. What opportunities and challenges do our stakeholders present? Opportunities allow organizations to build cooperative, productive relationships with stakeholder groups. An inner city church, for instance, might view other religious groups, local merchants, civic associations, and government agencies as potential allies in combating neighborhood blight. Challenges take the form of demands from groups who believe that the organization is at fault. These must be handled carefully or they may result in significant damage. Home Depot faced such a challenge from the Rainforest Action Network.[10] The retailer pulled old growth lumber from the shelves after the Network threatened to picket if it did not.

4. What responsibilities does the firm have to its stakeholders? These include the economic, legal, ethical, and environmental factors described earlier.

5. What strategies or actions should management take to best handle stakeholder challenges and opportunities? Organizations can take the offensive or go on the defensive when dealing with stakeholders, decide to accommodate or negotiate, use one strategy or a combination of several, and so on. One consideration is the potential for cooperation or threat posed by a particular group. Typically, the best strategy is to become involved with groups that are currently supportive or could be cooperative in the future and to defend against those who pose a significant threat.

In addition to managing ongoing relationships with stakeholders, organizations also need to identify and respond to changing social and ethical conditions. This process is called *issues management.* Ethical sensitivities and moral customs continually evolve. Smoking, which once was allowed nearly everywhere in this country, is now banned from many indoor public spaces, for instance. Fast food outlets now have to contend with charges that they contribute to the nation's obesity epidemic.

Issues management is a function of public relations departments at major corporations. S.C. Johnson & Sons credits its issues management program for the firm's decision to eliminate fluorocarbon from aerosol sprays 3 years before federal regulations took effect. Sears noted the potential dangers of flammable nightwear early on and quickly removed these products before federal regulations were passed.[11] Despite these successes, it would be wrong to make issues management solely a public relations function. All employees have a responsibility to be on the lookout for future trends through scanning and monitoring. Scanning refers to surveying the environment to identify potential issues that might impact your organization. Read a wide variety of issues-oriented publications (*The Nation, Mother Jones, The Standard*), for example, and surf the Web, monitor news sources and talk shows, and dialogue with stakeholder groups. Once an issue is identified, actively monitor it. Track its progress and work with others to develop a response.[12]

One model of the stages of issue development is found in Box 10.2. You can monitor the progress of any issue using this format. Take the issue of global warming, for example. At first only a few environmental groups were aware of this problem, and evidence of its existence was scarce. Next, the issue began to grab political and media attention and some businesses began to take note. Currently this concern appears to be moving from the consolidating to the institutionalized stage with increasing recognition of the ethical dimension of the problem. A number of nations have signed the Kyoto Treaty to reduce greenhouse admissions, and businesses around the world have joined in the effort. While federal officials in the U.S. have resisted pressure to sign the Kyoto Accord and to enact stricter pollution emission standards, many American corporations recognize that they could be condemned as immoral for contributing to global warming.

Box 10.2 The Four Stages of Issue Maturity

Pharmaceutical company Novo Nordisk created a scale to measure the maturity societal issues and the public's expectations around the issues. An adaptation of the scale appears below and can be used by any organization facing any number of societal issues.

Stage	*Characteristics*
Latent	• Activist communities and NGOs (Non-Government Organizations) are aware of the societal issue. • There is weak scientific or other hard evidence. • The issue is largely ignored or dismissed by the business community.
Emerging	• There is political and media awareness of the societal issue. • There is an emerging body of research, but data are still weak. • Leading businesses experiment with approaches to dealing with the issue.
Consolidating	• There is an emerging body of business practices around the societal issue. • Sectorwide and issue-based voluntary initiatives are established. • There is litigation and an increasing view of the need for legislation. • Voluntary standards are developed, and collective action occurs.

(Continued)

(Continued)

Institutionalized	• Legislation or business norms are established. • The embedded practices become a normal part of a business-excellence model.

Source: Zadek, S., 2004, December, The path to corporate responsibility, *Harvard Business Review,* p. 128. Used by permission.

The Stewardship Approach

Stewardship, as we noted in our discussion of servant leadership in Chapter 7, means acting on behalf of others. Stewards seek to serve the interests of the organization and outsiders rather than pursuing selfish concerns. Stewardship theory shifts the focus from stakeholders to managers. It operates on the premise that virtuous managers will meet the needs of internal and external stakeholders and society as a whole. By seeking long-term organizational benefits or goals, stewards are better able to serve the needs of all stakeholders and the common good.

Several characteristics set stewards apart from their managerial colleagues.[13] First, they are intrinsically motivated. They seek such intangible rewards as personal growth, affiliation, achievement, and self-actualization rather than tangible rewards like bonuses and company cars. Second, stewards identify themselves with the goals, mission, and vision of their organizations. They take credit for the group's success and blame for its failure when it falls short. Third, stewards rely on personal power instead of on positional forms of power (see Chapter 5).

Covenantal relationships play an important role in the stewardship approach.[14] Unlike traditional, transactional contracts, which are based on exchanges between parties (labor for money, money for products), covenantal relationships are based on the commitment of parties to each other and loyalty to shared values. Stakeholders realize that they may not benefit from every decision but remain committed to the relationship. Covenants are directly tied to social responsibility. Covenantal relationships between workers and employers are more likely to develop in organizations that invest in social welfare. Employees are more likely buy into the ideology of groups that promote community interests.

Stewardship theory is not as fully developed as the stakeholder model. At first glance, it seems idealistic. Serving the organizational good doesn't always benefit society, for instance, and it may be difficult to establish covenantal relationships with outsiders. Nonetheless, if you place collective interests over selfish concerns, you are less likely to engage in such ethical abuses as excessive executive compensation and lying to boost short-term profits. Acting as a steward, you are more likely to be a committed, productive organizational member who reaches out to help your colleagues and outsiders.

The Sustainability Standard

Sustainability serves as the primary standard or guideline for corporate citizenship in Europe and other parts of the world. The most cited definition of the term, developed by the World Commission on Environment and Development (WCED), defines *sustainability* as "development that meets the needs of the present without compromising the ability of future generations to meet their own needs."[15] Sustainability means preserving the natural environment while, at the same time, creating long-lasting economic and social value. Sustainable organizations adopt a long-term perspective, hoping to create conditions that foster decades of economic health and social responsibility.

Sustainability is a lofty standard that calls for continuous improvement. For instance, manufacturers seeking to boost their environmental records go through three stages on the way to enhanced performance.[16] In the first stage they move from pollution control to pollution prevention. Instead of cleaning up messes after they occur, they try to prevent them from happening in the first place by reducing smokestack emissions and waste. Such tactics can greatly reduce the costs of disposing of toxic substances. In stage two, manufacturers shift their focus from minimizing pollution to considering all the possible environmental impacts over the life cycle of a product. They create goods that are easier to recover, recycle, or reuse. Xerox took this approach by taking parts from leased copiers and reconditioning them for use in new machines. In stage three, corporations invest in clean technology that is environmentally sustainable. Hybrid gas and electric cars are a step in this direction. So are BMW cars that are built to be easier to disassemble when they leave the road for good.

You can promote organizational sustainability by adopting sustainable practices yourself and by encouraging others to do the same. Participate in recycling and energy reduction programs, drive less, develop ways to reduce pollution in production processes, build products that last, cut back on packaging, put the long-term health of the community above short-term profits, address the problems that lead to overexploitation of resources, and so forth.

MEASURING SOCIAL PERFORMANCE

Social performance—translating intentions into action—is the "bottom line" of organizational citizenship. Measuring such performance is critical for evaluating the ethical behavior of organizations, addressing weaknesses, and developing strategies for ongoing improvement. You can use motivational tests and social audits to determine how well your organization is fulfilling it citizen role.

Motivational Measures

Motivational tests look at the source and level of organizational commitment to social concerns. One such approach contrasts instrumental and intrinsic social activities.[17] Some organizations hope to be seen as responsible citizens but act out of less than noble motives. They promote worthy causes (e.g. breast cancer research, providing school supplies for children), make contributions to charity, and send employees out to work in soup kitchens to boost profits and public image. In this *instrumental* approach, the motivation is to enhance shareholder value. Ethical obligations take a backseat to promoting the interests of the group.

Instrumental motivations drive most socially responsible corporate activities. While there's no doubt that such initiatives produce a great deal of benefit, doing good for selfish reasons is another example of the decoupled approach to ethics I described in the Introduction to this text. Such efforts have little impact on the key operations of the organization and are easily jettisoned if public attitudes shift or when funds run short. In contrast, transformed organizations take an *intrinsic* approach to social responsibility. They recognize that their fundamental ethical responsibilities extend beyond their members. These groups pursue a course of action because it's the right thing to do, not because it will pay off. Commitment to society and the environment flows out of the group's core values and purpose. (See Box 10.3 for an example of an organization that takes an intrinsic approach to its social responsibilities.)

CASE STUDY

Box 10.3 Social Responsibility at Starbucks

Starbucks is one of the world's best-known and best-liked brands. The growth of the Seattle-based coffee retailer has been nothing short of phenomenal. Since 1981 the firm has mushroomed from 100 shops to over 7,600 outlets worldwide employing over 70,000. Starbucks opens three new stores daily and believes it can expand to 25,000 locations. Twenty-five million people visit Starbucks locations every day and loyal customers return 18 times a month. The company's stock increased in value over 2,200 percent in 10 years, outstripping such corporate giants as Wal-Mart, Coca-Cola, Microsoft, and General Electric. Starbucks has appeared on the list of the Most Admired Companies in the U.S., the list of 100 Best Companies to Work For, and the list of 100 Best Corporate Citizens.

Starbucks' commitment to social causes is one reason why the company is widely respected. These obligations are woven into the company's mission and values. Starbucks' stated mission is "To establish Starbucks as the premier purveyor of the finest coffee in the world while maintaining our uncompromising principles as we grow." Its corporate values (called Guiding Principles) are well publicized, showing up in its stores as well as in its press releases and annual reports. Employees are encouraged to contact headquarters if the firm seems to fall short on one or more of these guidelines:

- respect and dignity for partners
- embracing diversity
- sustaining coffee communities
- enthusiastically satisfied customers
- contributing positively to communities and the environment
- ensuring profitability

To measure company compliance to its values, Starbucks commissions a Corporate Social Responsibility Annual Report called "Living Our Values." The results of the report, which have been independently verified, indicate that the company is reaching its social goals. Eighty-two percent of its partners reported being satisfied or very satisfied with the company in 2003, for example.

Starbucks' commitment to doing good takes a number of forms. The company is the only major food and beverage chain to offer health benefits to both full- and part-time employees. "Partners" are also eligible for stock options in the company called "Bean Stock." Each store can determine which local charities to promote through volunteer hours, store products, and cash contributions, while the corporation as a whole supports literacy programs and international relief. In recent years the firm has strengthened its outreach to minority communities and to coffee producers. Sixty-three percent of its employees are women and 24% are people of color. Thirty-two percent of executives at the vice-president level and above are women and 9% are minorities. In order to deal more equitably with coffee suppliers, Starbucks pays premium prices for beans, encourages sustainable production of coffee, invests in the educational and health projects in coffee communities, and purchases more organic and shade-grown beans.

Starbucks, while admirable, is far from perfect. Detractors complain about the firm's predatory policies (it saturates markets and pays higher than market rents to drive out competitors), the threat it poses to local businesses and distinctive neighborhoods, and the firm's reluctance to sell organic coffees (these blends make up only a small portion of total sales). To critics of globalization, Starbucks epitomizes global economic imperialism.

The coffee giant faces significant challenges to its social concern. Rapid growth is a constant threat to ethical consistency. Maintaining commitment to core values becomes harder as the number of stores multiplies. Stockholders may pressure the firm to reduce its social emphasis in order to increase profits and stock price.

DISCUSSION PROBES

1. Is the success of Starbucks tied in part to its commitment to social responsibility?
2. Do you consider yourself more of a supporter or more of a critic of the company? Why?
3. What ethical dangers does rapid expansion pose to Starbucks?
4. Do you think Starbucks can maintain its values as it grows?
5. Can you think of other companies that integrate social responsibility into their core mission and values?

SOURCES

Anderson, R. (2003, April 30). Starbucks: Just getting started. *Seattle Weekly,* p. 11. Retrieved May 24, 2004, from LexisNexis Academic database.
Batsell, J. (2004, March 28). A bean counter's dream. *Seattle Times,* p. E1.
Clark, T. (2004, May 26). Thoroughly Starbucked. *Willamette Week,* pp. 18–19, 21, 23–25.
Daniels, C. (2003, April 14). Mr. Coffee. *Fortune,* pp. 139–140.
ElBoghdady, D. (2002, August 25). Pouring it on. *Washington Post,* p. H01. Retrieved May 24, 2004, from LexisNexis Academic database.
Holmes, S., Bennett, D., Carlisle, K., & Dawson, C. (2002, September 9). Planet Starbucks. *BusinessWeek,* pp. 100–106. Retrieved May 24, 2004, from LexisNexis Academic database.
Schultz, H., & Yang, D. J. (1997). *Pour your heart into it: How Starbucks built a company one cup at a time.* New York: Hyperion.
Starbucks recognized as one of the most valued global brands. (2004, March 30). *Business Wire.* Retrieved May 24, 2004, from LexisNexis Academic database.
Sullivan, J. (2003, August 13). Call it Starbucking, the fine art of hating your local outlet of the Seattle coffeehouse chain. *San Francisco Chronicle,* p. D1. Retrieved May 24, 2004, from LexisNexis Academic database.

The second motivational measure looks at the principles that underlie social activities to determine the depth of an organization's commitment to citizenship.[18]

At the lowest level are those organizations motivated by *social obligation.* Managers at these organizations engage in "negative duties (thou-shalt-nots)" like avoiding racial discrimination in hiring or granting parental leave as required by law. They view social contributions as largely the responsibility of individuals, not the organization as a whole.

Organizations at the intermediate level of commitment are *socially responsible.* They try to live up to societal expectations. Managers at these organizations voluntarily assume social responsibilities, going beyond the letter of the law or anticipating changes in legal statutes. They try to reduce pollution at their plants and offices even if they meet current environmental guidelines, for instance.

Socially responsive organizations demonstrate the highest level of commitment. They take a proactive response, trying to identify and respond to emerging social issues and problems. Managers at these organizations serve as industry leaders. The 3M Company is such a leader in the environmental field. 3M's policy commits the firm to exceeding compliance standards and assisting regulatory agencies concerned with environmental issues.

Social Audits

Social audits are standardized procedures for evaluating social and environmental impact.[19] An audit can be sponsored by outside groups or by the organization itself. Charity Navigator hopes to equip donors to make wiser choices and to improve the efficiency of charities by ranking and comparing their performance.[20] Evaluators examine seven categories: (1) program expenses; (2) administration expenses; (3) fundraising expenses; (4) fundraising efficiency (the percentage of the budget spent on raising money); (5) primary revenue growth (the ability to sustain income over time); (6) program expenses growth (the ability to expand programs); and (7) working capital (the ability to survive a short downturn in revenue).

A number of companies sponsor their self-audits, which are conducted by outside auditors. Starbucks' annual "Living Our Values" report is one such example. The Values Audit of The Body Shop is another. In the case of The Body Shop, the audit team evaluated the firm's performance in relation to major stakeholder groups as well as its commitment to social change and needy communities. Results were made available to the public. The firm then followed up with a plan to address areas of low performance. Another example of a self-audit—the Sustainability Portfolio—is found in the Self-Assessment in Box 10.4.

Self-Assessment

Box 10.4 Sustainability Portfolio

The Sustainability Portfolio

	Clean Technology	*Sustainability Vision*
Tomorrow	Is the environmental performance of our products limited by our existing competency base?	Does our corporate vision direct us toward the solution of social and environmental problems?
	Is there potential to realize major improvements through new technology?	Does our vision guide the development of new technologies, markets, products, and processes?
	Pollution Prevention	*Product Stewardship*
Today	Where are the most significant waste and emission streams from our current operations?	What are the implications for product design and development if we assume responsibility for a product's entire life cycle?
	Can we lower costs and risks by eliminating waste at the source or by using it as useful input?	Can we add value or lower costs while simultaneously reducing the impact of our products?
	Internal	*External*

This simple diagnostic tool can help any company determine whether its strategy is consistent with sustainability and can be adapted to non-profits as well. First, assess your company's capability in each of the four quadrants by answering the questions in each box. Then rate yourself on the following scale for each quadrant: 1–nonexistent; 2–emerging; 3–established; or 4–institutionalized.

Most companies will be heavily skewed toward the lower left-hand quadrant, reflecting investment in pollution prevention. However, without investments in future technologies and markets (the upper half of the portfolio), the company's environmental strategy will not meet evolving needs.

Unbalanced portfolios spell trouble: a bottom-heavy portfolio suggests a good position today but future vulnerability. A top-heavy portfolio indicates a vision of sustainability without the operational or analytical skills needed to implement it. A portfolio skewed to the left side of the chart indicates a preoccupation with handling the environmental challenge through internal process improvements and technology-development initiatives. Finally, a portfolio skewed to the right side, although highly open and public, runs the risk of being labeled a "greenwash" because the underlying plant operation and core technology still cause significant environmental harm.

Source: Hart, S. L., 1997, January/February. Beyond greening: Strategies for a sustainable world, *Harvard Business Review*, p. 74. Used by permission of the publisher.

Organizations can also sponsor standardized audits like Social Accountability 8000, which was designed to measure labor practices at overseas suppliers.[21] A firm must meet measurable, verifiable performance standards in nine areas to be certified. These standards forbid child labor, forced labor, coercion, discrimination, unlimited overtime, and substandard wages. The Global Reporting Initiative, which has been adopted by such organizations as Baxter International, Canon, Deutsche Bank, and Ford Motor, is the most popular standardized measure of sustainability.[22] This instrument examines three sets of performance indicators. Economic indicators look at an organization's direct and indirect impacts on stakeholders and local, national, and global economic systems. These include such elements as wages, pensions and benefits, payments to suppliers, taxes, and subsidies received. Environmental indicators reveal an organization's impacts on natural systems. They cover energy, material and water use, greenhouse gases and waste generation, hazardous materials, recycling, pollution, and fines and penalties for environmental violations. Social indicators concern an organization's influence on social systems and cluster around labor practices (diversity, health and safety), human rights (child labor, for example), and other social issues (bribery and corruption, community relations).

Social auditing is gaining popularity but still is plagued with a number of problems.[23] Standardized social performance instruments are relatively new and they aren't as universally accepted as financial audits. There are questions about who is qualified to conduct social audits, what they should cover, how data should be collected, who should have access to the results, and how to draw comparisons between organizations. Self-audits are particularly prone to abuse. Firms may use them as public relations tools, limiting the analysis to just a few areas of strength or only reporting favorable findings. However, despite these concerns, the use of social audits is likely to continue to increase in the years to come.

Ethical Global Citizenship

Globalization is having a dramatic impact on life in the 21st century. We inhabit a global society knit together by free trade, international travel, immigration, satellite communication systems, and the Internet. In this interconnected world, ethical responsibilities extend beyond national boundaries. Decisions about outsourcing, farm subsidies, investments, marketing strategies, safety standards, and energy use made in one country have ramifications for residents of other parts of the world.

To act as ethical global citizens, organizations must confront and master the dangers of globalization and the dilemmas of ethical diversity. In this section I'll describe these obstacles and offer tactics for responding to such challenges.

THE DARK SIDE OF GLOBALIZATION AND THE DILEMMAS OF ETHICAL DIVERSITY

The benefits of living in a global economy are obvious: lower labor costs, higher sales and profits, cheaper goods and services, instant communication to anywhere on earth, increased information flow, and cross-cultural contact. What's often hidden is the downside of globalization. Of particular concern is the growing divide between the haves and have-nots. The richest 20 percent of the global population controls over 85 percent of the world's assets and income. Governments of wealthy nations appear more interested in promoting the sale of their goods than in opening up their markets to poor countries.[24] Lumber, minerals, and oil are extracted from poor regions and consumed in privileged areas, leaving environmental damage behind.

Critics also note that global capitalism frequently promotes greed rather than concern for others. Ethical and spiritual values have been shunted aside in favor of the profit motive. Few industrialized countries give even the suggested minimum of .07 of gross national product (70 cents of every $100 produced by the economy) to alleviate global poverty.[25] Local cultural traditions are being destroyed in the name of economic progress.

The big winners in globalization are multinational corporations. Fueled by international trade, the hundred biggest companies combined have annual revenue greater than the gross domestic product of half of the world's nations.[26] If Wal-Mart were a country, for instance, its economy would rank 15th among free market democracies.[27] So far many multinationals have pursued free trade at the cost of human rights and the environment. They have employed sweatshop and slave labor, stood by as repressive regimes tortured their citizens, and plundered local resources. (Turn to the Chapter End Case to see how one multinational corporation is responding to charges that it has failed to act as a responsible global citizen.)

Along with the potential moral pitfalls of globalization, organizations also face the challenges of ethical diversity. Nations, tribes, ethnic groups, and religions approach moral dilemmas differently. What members of one group accept as right may raise serious ethical concerns for another. Consider, for example, the variety of responses to the following ethical issues.[28]

Contracts

In Germany, contracts are highly detailed and strictly enforced. In Egypt, contracts spell out guidelines for business deals rather than specific requirements. Egyptians expect to renegotiate and revise contracts and there is no moral stigma attached to violating a signed agreement. In Mexico, honoring a contract is based on the signer's personal ethics. There is little legal recourse if a contract is violated.

Bribery

In South American countries it is nearly impossible to move goods through customs without making small payments to cut through red tape. At the other extreme, Malaysia executes corporate officials who offer and accept bribes. U.S. corporations are prevented from exchanging money or goods for favors or services under the Foreign Corrupt Practices Act of 1977. However, in recognition of the fact that petty bribery is common in some parts of the world, small payments to facilitate travel and business are permitted under the statute.

Intellectual Property Rights

Copyright laws are strictly enforced in many Western nations but are less binding in many Asian countries. In fact, intellectual piracy is legal in Thailand, Indonesia, and Malaysia.

False Information

Americans lie to protect their privacy; Mexicans are more likely to lie to protect the group or family. Germans express their disagreement directly, not hesitating to say "No" directly to another party. Japanese may answer by saying "That will be difficult" rather than by offering an out-and-out refusal. This indirect strategy (often seen as deceptive by Westerners) is designed to save the "face" or image of the receiver.

The challenges posed by globalization and ethical diversity can undermine ethical decision making. For some organizations it is business as usual. Interested only in making a profit or expanding their influence, they fail to weigh the possible negative consequences of their choices in the global environment. Leaders faced with ethical diversity sometimes behave as ethical imperialists by imposing their personal moral standards on members of other cultures. Or they may opt for cultural relativism by always following local customs ("When in Rome, do as the Romans do"). Nevertheless, being in a new culture or working with a diverse group of followers doesn't excuse managers from careful ethical deliberation. Standards from one culture can't be blindly forced upon another and, conversely, just because a culture has adopted a practice doesn't make it right. For example, trafficking in humans takes place in some parts of the world, but most societies condemn this practice.

Fortunately, you can develop your cross-cultural ethical competence and help your organizations to do the same. To achieve this goal, you must first wrestle with ethnocentrism. Next, you have to identify universal moral principles that should govern behavior in every cultural setting and employ guidelines for sorting through conflicts between competing ethical norms.

COMING TO GRIPS WITH ETHNOCENTRISM

Overcoming the challenges of globalization and ethical diversity is impossible if we fall victim to ethnocentrism. Ethnocentrism is viewing the world from our cultural group's point of view, which makes our customs and values the standard by which the rest of the world is judged. Our ways are "right," while their ways fall short. A certain degree of ethnocentrism is probably inevitable, helping a group to band together and survive in the face of outside threats. Nevertheless, high levels of ethnocentrism can lead to reduced contact with outsiders, racial slurs, insensitivity to strangers, pressure on other groups to conform, justification for violence and war, and other negative outcomes.[29]

A number of the ethical communication competencies introduced earlier in the text can be used to confront ethnocentrism. Pursue dialogue in cross-cultural conversations by treating members of other cultures as equal partners and by trying to understand their point of view (Chapter 4). Mindfulness is particularly important in diverse cultural settings because the scripts we follow in our own groups don't work when we find ourselves in another culture. Adopt a pluralistic perspective that acknowledges the legitimacy of other groups and customs in order to avoid moral exclusion (Chapter 8).

Personal virtues (Chapter 3) can help undermine ethnocentric attitudes and, at the same time, lay the groundwork for meeting the challenges of globalization and ethical diversity. Philosopher and theologian Michael Novak identifies four cardinal or hinge virtues essential to encouraging global cooperation: cultural humility, truth, dignity, and solidarity.[30] Cultural humility means acknowledging the shortcomings of our own cultures as well as our personal biases. A commitment to truth allows for reasoned argument based on evidence and logic. Recognition of human dignity forbids using others as a means to an end. Solidarity is being aware that each individual lives in communion with others and has responsibility for their welfare.

FINDING MORAL COMMON GROUND

As I noted earlier, some organizations and their members respond to ethical diversity by practicing ethical relativism. Ethical relativism avoids the problem of ethnocentrism while simplifying the decision-making process. We never have to pass judgment and can concentrate on fitting in with the prevailing culture. However, this approach is fraught with difficulties. Without shared standards, there is little hope that people of the world can come together to tackle global problems. There is no basis upon which to condemn the actions of governments (like that of Sudan, for example) engaged in genocide and torture or to criticize businesses that exploit their employees and the environment. Cultural relativism obligates us to follow (or as least not to protest against) abhorrent local practices like female circumcision. Without universal rights and wrongs, we have no grounds for contesting such practices.

There appears to be a growing consensus that ethical common ground can be found. In fact, the existence of common moral standards has enabled the world community to punish crimes against humanity in Germany, Serbia, and Rwanda. Responsible multinational corporations like Starbucks, The Body Shop, and Proctor and Gamble adhere to widely held moral principles as they do business in a variety of cultural settings. Activist groups use these same guidelines to condemn irresponsible firms.

Identifying universal principles can help us address the dark side of globalization while managing ethical diversity. I'll describe four different approaches to universal ethics, any one of which could serve as a worldwide standard. You'll note a number of similarities between the lists. Decide for yourself which approach or combination of approaches best captures the foundational values of humankind (see Application Project 5 on page 288).

United Nations Universal Declaration of Human Rights

Human rights are granted to individuals based solely on their status as persons. Such rights protect the inherent dignity of every individual regardless of background. Rights violations are unethical because they deny human value and potential.[31]

The most influential list of basic human rights was adopted by the United Nations immediately following World War II, a conflict fought in large part to protect human freedoms. Among the key rights spelled out in the Universal Declaration are the following:[32]

Article 4. No one shall be held in slavery or servitude; slavery and the slave trade shall be prohibited in all their forms.

Article 5. No one shall be subjected to torture or to cruel, inhuman or degrading treatment or punishment.

Article 9. No one shall be subjected to arbitrary arrest, detention or exile.

Article 13. Everyone has the right to freedom of movement and residence.

Article 17. Everyone has the right to own property alone as well in association with others.

Article 19. Everyone has the right to freedom of thought, conscience and religion.

Article 25. Everyone has the right to a standard of living adequate for the health and well-being of himself [or herself] and of his [or her] family.

Article 26. Everyone has the right to education.

In 2000 the U.N. launched a program called the Global Compact to encourage multinational corporations to honor human rights, labor rights, and the environment. Members agree to the principles outlined in Box 10.5 and specify how they are complying with these guidelines. Nonprofit watchdog groups meet regularly with corporate representatives to talk about their firms' performance. Membership in the Global Compact has grown rapidly. It is now the largest voluntary corporate citizen group in the world, with over 1,700 members.[33]

Box 10.5 United Nations Secretary General: The Global Compact

The Nine Principles

Human Rights

Principle 1: Businesses should support and respect the protection of international human rights within their sphere of influence; and

Principle 2: make sure their own corporations are not complicit in human rights abuses.

Labour

Principle 3: Businesses should uphold the freedom of association and the effective recognition of the right to collective bargain;

Principle 4: the elimination of all forms of forced and compulsory labour;

Principle 5: the effective abolition of child labour; and

Principle 6: the elimination of discrimination in respect of employment and occupation.

Environment

Principle 7: Businesses should take a precautionary approach to environmental challenges;

Principle 8: undertake initiatives to promote greater environmental responsibility; and

Principle 9: encourage the development and diffusion of environmentally friendly technologies.

Source: Mares, R. (Ed.) (2004). *Business and Human Rights: A Compilation of Documents,* p. 95. Used by permission of BRILL NV.

A Global Ethic

Religions get blamed for many of the world's conflicts in the Middle East, India, Northern Ireland, and elsewhere. Yet, despite their differences, religious traditions share common values that can lay the foundation for international cooperation. For example, 6,500 representatives from a wide range of religious faiths reached agreement on a global ethic.[34] A council of former heads of state and prime ministers then ratified this statement. Delegates of both groups agreed on two universal principles. First, all people must be treated humanely regardless of language, skin color, mental ability, political beliefs, or national or social origin. Every person and group, no matter how powerful, must respect the dignity of others. Second, "what you wish done to yourself, do to others." Some version of this principle (referred to as the Golden Rule) is found in most religious and ethical traditions. Following this guideline prevents a wide variety of destructive behaviors, like stealing, murder, torture, and oppression.

Treating others humanely and obeying the Golden Rule lead to these ethical directives or imperatives:

- commitment to a culture of nonviolence (seek peace) and respect for all life (human, animal, plant)
- commitment to a culture of solidarity and a just economic order (do not steal, deal fairly and honestly with others, distribute the world's wealth fairly, reject greed)
- commitment to a culture of tolerance and a life of truthfulness (seek and serve the truth)
- commitment to a culture of equal rights and partnership between men and women (avoid immorality; respect and love members of both genders)

Eight Global Values

Rushworth Kidder and his colleagues at the Institute for Global Ethics identify eight core values that appear to be shared the world over. They isolated these values after conducting interviews with 24 international "ethical thought leaders."[35] Kidder's sample included former heads of states, professors, activists, business executives, writers, and religious figures drawn from such nations as Vietnam, Mozambique, New Zealand, Bangladesh, Britain, the U.S., China, Japan, Sri Lanka, Costa Rica, and Lebanon. Each interview ran from 1 to 3 hours and began with this question: "If you could help create a global code of ethics, what would be on it?" These global standards emerged:[36]

1. *Love.* Spontaneous concern for others; compassion that transcends political and ethnic differences.
2. *Truthfulness.* Achieving goals through honest means; keeping promises; being worthy of the trust of others.
3. *Fairness (justice).* Fair play, even-handedness, equality.
4. *Freedom.* The pursuit of liberty; right of individual conscience, free expression and action.
5. *Unity.* Seeking the common good; cooperation, community, solidarity.
6. *Tolerance.* Respect for others and their ideas; empathy; appreciation for variety.
7. *Responsibility.* Care for self and others, the community and future generations; responsible use of force.
8. *Respect for life.* Reluctance to kill through war and other means.

Kidder admits that there are few surprises on this list. Yet, the common-sense nature of these values is good news, signaling that these standards are widely shared:

> This is not . . . an off-the-wall, unique, bizarre list. It may even strike us as familiar, ordinary, and unsurprising. That's a comforting fact. Codes of ethics, to be practicable, need to have behind them a broad consensus. The originality of the list matters less than its consistency and universality.[37]

The Caux Principles

The Caux Round Table is made up of corporate executives from the U.S., Japan, and Europe who meet every year in Caux, Switzerland. Round Table members believe that businesses should improve economic, social, and environmental conditions and hope to set a world standard by which to judge business behavior. Their principles are based on twin ethical ideals. The first is the Japanese concept of *kyosei*, which refers to living and working together for the common good. The second is the Western notion of human dignity, the sacredness and value of each person as an end rather than as a means to someone else's end.[38] The Caux standards, perhaps because they were written by corporate executives from around the world, have gained widespread support. Business schools in Latin America, Asia, Europe, and the U.S. have endorsed them, and a number of international firms have used them as a guide when developing their own mission statements and ethics codes.

Principle 1. The Responsibilities of Corporations: Beyond Shareholders Toward Stakeholders.[39] Businesses should have goals that extend beyond economic survival. Corporations have a responsibility to improve the lives of everyone they come in contact with, starting with employees, customers, shareholders, and suppliers, and then reaching out to local, national, regional, and global communities.

Principle 2. The Economic and Social Impact of Corporations: Toward Innovation, Justice and World Community. Companies operating in foreign countries not only should create jobs and wealth but should also foster human rights, better education and social welfare. Multinational corporations have an obligation to enrich the world community through the wise use of resources, fair competition, and innovation.

Principle 3. Corporate Behavior: Beyond the Letter of Law Toward a Spirit of Trust. Businesses ought to promote honesty, transparency, integrity and keeping promises. These behaviors make it easier to conduct international business and to support a global economy.

Principle 4. Respect for Rules: Beyond Trade Friction Toward Cooperation. Leaders of international firms must respect both international and local laws in order to reduce trade wars, to ensure fair competition, and to promote the free flow of goods and services. They also need to recognize that some behaviors may be legal but still have damaging consequences.

Principle 5. Support for Multilateral Trade: Beyond Isolation Toward World Community. Firms should support international trading systems and agreements and eliminate domestic measures that undermine free trade.

Principle 6. Respect for the Environment: Beyond Protection Toward Enhancement. Corporations ought to protect and, if possible, improve the physical environment through sustainable development and by cutting back on the wasteful use of natural resources.

Principle 7. Avoidance of Illicit Operations: Beyond Profit Toward Peace. Global business managers must ensure that their organizations aren't involved in such forbidden activities as bribery, money laundering, supporting terrorism, and drug and arms trafficking.

After spelling out general principles, the Caux accord applies them to important stakeholder groups. Organizations following these standards seek to (a) treat customers and employees with dignity, (b) honor the trust of owners/investors, (c) create relationships with suppliers based on mutual respect, (d) interact fairly with competitors, and (e) work for reform and human rights in host communities.

RESOLVING ETHICAL CONFLICTS: INTEGRATED SOCIAL CONTRACTS THEORY

So far we've established that (1) there are significant differences between cultures in how they respond to ethical issues, and (2) there are universal moral principles that apply across cultural boundaries. Reconciling these two facts when making ethical decisions is not easy. How do we respect ethical diversity while remaining true to global moral principles, for example? What do we do when two competing ethical perspectives appear to be equally valid? What set of standards should have top priority—those of the host nation or those of the international organization? Business ethicists Thomas Donaldson and Thomas Dunfee developed the Integrated Social Contracts Theory (ISCT) to help us answer questions like these.[40]

ISCT is based on the notion of social contracts, which are agreements that spell out the obligations or duties of institutions, communities, and societies. The model is integrative because it incorporates two kinds of contracts. The first kind of contract (*macrosocial*) sets the groundwork or standards for social interaction. Examples of ideal contracts include the requirement that governments respect the rights of people and help the poor. The second type of contract (*microsocial*) governs the relationships between members of particular communities (nations, regions, towns, professions, industries). These contracts are revealed by the norms of the group. Community contracts are considered authentic or binding if (a) members of the group have a voice in the creation of the norms, (b) members can exit the group if they disagree with prevailing norms, and (c) the norms are widely recognized and practiced by group members.

According to ISCT, universal principles (called *hypernorms*) act as the ultimate ethical standard when making choices. Communities have a great deal of latitude or *moral free space* to create their own rules, however, as long as these local norms do not conflict with hypernorms. Victim compensation provides one example of norms arising out of moral free space. In Japan (where the victim compensation system is unreliable), airline officials go in person to offer compensation to victims' families after an accident. In the U.S. (where the compensation system is more reliable), payments are determined through court decisions.

Dunfee and Donaldson offer a number of guidelines for determining which norms should take priority. Three of these rules of thumb are particularly important. One, determine if the local practice is authentic (widely shared) and legitimate (in harmony with hypernorms). If it's not, it should be rejected. Second, follow the legitimate local customs of the host community whenever possible. To return to our earlier compensation example, a U.S. airline official stationed in Japan should distribute compensation directly to crash victims' families instead of relying on the Japanese court system. Third, give more weight to norms generated by larger communities. A norm embraced by a nation as a whole, for instance, should generally take precedence over the norm of a region. The U.S. government followed this guideline in overturning laws promoting racial discrimination in the South. A similar argument can be made for choosing the norm of gender equality (which has broad international acceptance) over the norms of a particular nation that discriminate against women.

Implications

- Encourage your organization to act as a responsible citizen that acknowledges its obligations to outside communities, develops processes for anticipating and responding to societal pressures, and backs up its convictions with concrete actions.
- Your organization has a moral obligation to respond to groups affected by its policies and operations. Engage in stakeholder management by responding to five questions: (1) Who are our stakeholders? (2) What are our stakeholders' stakes? (3) What opportunities and challenges do our stakeholders present? (4) What responsibilities does the firm have to its stakeholders? (5) What strategies or actions should management take to best handle stakeholder challenges and opportunities?
- You have an ethical duty as a steward to act on behalf of others and to seek the long-term benefit of the organization. In so doing, you also serve the interests of stakeholders and society.
- Adopt the sustainability standard to promote corporate citizenship. This goal encourages your organization to meet current needs while preserving the environment and creating long-term economic and social value.
- Measure the social performance of your organization. You can do so through motivational tests, which look at the source and level of commitment to social concerns, or through social audits, which are standardized procedures for evaluating social and environmental impact.

- Recognize the dangers of globalization, which include the growing gap between the world's rich and poor, greed, the concentration of economic power in large corporations, and the destruction of local cultures.
- Cultural groups reach different conclusions about how to resolve ethical issues, but resist the temptation to practice cultural relativism. Instead, look for ethical common ground found in such universal principles as the U.N. Universal Declaration of Human Rights, the eight global values, the Global Ethic, and the Caux Principles.
- Overcome ethnocentrism, the tendency to see the world from your cultural group's point of view, through dialogue, mindfulness, adopting a pluralistic perspective, and adopting personal virtues that promote global cooperation.
- Integrated Social Contracts Theory (ISCT) can help you balance universal principles and ethical diversity. Keep three key decision-making guidelines in mind: (1) local customs must conform to global standards or hypernorms; (2) give priority to the authentic, legitimate norms of the host country; (3) whenever possible, give more weight to norms generated by larger communities.

Application Projects

1. In a group, identify the important stakeholders of your college or university. What ethical responsibilities does your institution have to each group?

2. What are the strengths and weaknesses of stakeholder theory?

3. Identify an ethical issue that could pose a challenge to your college or university. Track its stage of development. How should your school respond?

4. Use the Sustainability Portfolio to measure the performance of an organization. Write up your findings.

5. Is there a common morality that peoples of all nations can share? Which of the global codes described in the chapter best reflects these shared standards and values? If you were to create your own declaration of global ethics, what would you put on it?

6. Develop a case study based on the conflict between the norms of different countries. Resolve the conflict using the guidelines provided by Integrated Social Contracts Theory.

CHAPTER END CASE

Nike Becomes a Global Citizen

In 1962 Stanford University student Phil Knight came up with the idea to create one of the world's first "virtual companies," a manufacturing firm with no physical assets. According to Knight's business plan, the company would cut costs by outsourcing all manufacturing and then pour the savings into marketing. Knight followed this formula to make Nike into the dominant athletic apparel manufacturer with an internationally recognized brand name.

Key to Nike's growth was the aggressive pursuit of low cost labor. When labor costs began to rise, Nike urged its suppliers to move to lower cost regions. The firm's first contracts were with Japanese manufacturers but then migrated to South Korea and Taiwan as production expenses increased. When costs in these nations soared, Nike contracted with facilities in China and Indonesia.

By the early 1990s, critics began to take note of conditions at Nike's suppliers. They documented inadequate pay (sometimes below legal minimums), dangerous working conditions, sexual harassment and physical abuse by supervisors, forced overtime, and the hiring of underage workers. The high profile company made a tempting target for the Asian-American Free Labor Association and other human rights groups.

At first Nike denied that it had any responsibility for conditions in its contractors' factories. One Nike manager responded to criticism in 1991 by claiming, "It's not within our scope to investigate. . . . I don't know that I need to know."[1] Pressure on the firm continued to increase, however. In 1992, *Harper's* magazine published a pay stub from an Indonesian factory, comparing workers' wages and Michael Jordan's Nike endorsement contract. It would have taken the average Indonesian worker 44,492 years to make what Jordan earned by promoting the company's sneakers. Later CBS interviewed Indonesian workers who were paid 19 cents an hour and found that women employees could only leave the company barracks on Sunday afternoons with a special letter of permission from management. In 1996, *Life* magazine published a photo of a 12-year-old Pakistani boy stitching a Nike soccer ball.

Nike abandoned its hands-off policy in response to public criticism and began to address working conditions at its suppliers. The firm drafted a set of standards, hired Ernst & Young to conduct formal audits of overseas factories, sent former ambassador Andrew Young overseas to evaluate its Code of Conduct, and established a Labor Practices department. Activists and the public were skeptical about these efforts. In particular, they questioned the validity of the audits, which were sponsored by Nike. These evaluations were poorly designed and ignored key issues like factory wages.

The year 1998 was a watershed year for Nike. The company's earnings dropped dramatically, due to changing tastes and anti-Nike campaigns. Knight announced a series of reforms, including (1) raising the minimum age of all sneaker workers to 18 and apparel employees to 16, (2) implementing OSHA (Occupational Safety and Health Administration) clean air standards in all of its factories, (3) expanding educational programs for workers, and (4) making micro loans to employees. Nike then helped create an oversight organization with other apparel groups (the Fair Labor Association), and Knight was the only U.S. CEO at the formation of the U.N. Global Compact.

By 2004 Nike had completed the transition from corporate pariah to a socially responsible industry leader. That year representatives from the human rights, international labor development, and environmental communities (often highly critical of the Swoosh brand) gathered at the company's headquarters to discuss issues facing international workers. That same year Nike's corporate responsibility report contained the names and addresses of 705 contract factories operating in 50 countries along with audit results. This marked the first time that any major U.S. apparel company had released such details to the public.

Nike admits that a great many of its factories could stand improvement (only 15 percent earned top ratings in its corporate responsibility report). Some activists argue that the multinational has yet to adequately address the biggest problem—low wages. Nevertheless, the experience of Nike demonstrates that organizations can learn from their mistakes and transform themselves into global citizens.

DISCUSSION PROBES

1. Why do you think Nike was so resistant at first to taking responsibility for working conditions at its factories?
2. Do you think Nike would have changed its policy towards its international workers if it hadn't suffered significant financial losses in 1998?
3. What risks did Nike take in meeting with its critics? In releasing the names and addresses of its overseas suppliers? Were these risks justified?
4. Do you think other apparel companies will follow Nike's lead and release details about their overseas manufacturing sites? Why or why not?
5. Would you consider Nike an ethical role model when it comes to overseas labor practices? Why or why not?

NOTE

1. Paine (2003), p. 121.

SOURCES

Paine, L. S. (2003). *Value shift: Why companies must merge social and financial imperatives to achieve superior performance*. New York: McGraw-Hill.

Phatak, A. V., Bhagat, R. S., & Kashlak, R. J. (2005). *International management: Managing in a diverse and dynamic global environment*. Boston: McGraw-Hill Irwin, pp. 543–561.

Rafter, M. V. (2005, May). Nike opens a window on overseas factories. *Workforce Management, 84*, 17. Retrieved July 25, 2005, from Business Source Premier database.

Ritson, M. (2005, April 20). Nike shows way to return from the wilderness. *Marketing* (UK), p. 21. Retrieved July 25, 2005, from Business Source Premier database.

Zadek, S. (2004, December). The path to corporate responsibility. *Harvard Business Review*, pp. 125–132.

Endnotes

1. Carroll, A. B., & Buchholtz, A. K. (2003). *Business and society: Ethics and stakeholder management* (5th ed.). Mason, OH: South-Western; Kottler, P., & Lee, N. (2005). *Corporate social responsibility*. Hoboken, NJ: John Wiley.
2. Carroll & Buchholtz (2003); Carroll, A. B. (1979). A three-dimensional conceptual model of corporate performance. *Academy of Management Review, 4*, 497–508.
3. Philips, R. (2003). *Stakeholder theory and organizational ethics*. San Francisco: Berritt-Koehler.
4. Freeman, E. (1984). *Strategic management*. Marshfield, MA: Pitman; Freeman, R. E. (1994). The politics of stakeholder theory: Some future directions. *Business Ethics Quarterly, 4*, 409–421; Freeman, R. E. (1995). Stakeholder thinking: The state of the art. In J. Nasi (Ed.), *Understanding stakeholder thinking* (pp. 35–73). Helsinki, Finland: LSR-Julkaisut Oy; Sims, R. R. (2003). *Ethics and corporate social responsibility: Why giants fall*. Westport, CT: Praeger.
5. Buchholz, R. A., & Rosenthal, S. B. (2005). Toward a conceptual framework for stakeholder theory. *Journal of Business Ethics, 58*, 137–148.
6. Donaldson, T., & Preston, L. E. (1995). The stakeholder theory of the corporation: Concepts, evidence, and implications. *Academy of Management Review, 20*, 65–91; Cooper, S. (2004). *Corporate social performance: A stakeholder approach*. Burlington, VT: Ashgate; Goodpaster, K. E. (1991). Business ethics and stakeholder analysis. *Business Ethics Quarterly, 1*, 53–72.
7. Phillips (2003).
8. Arandona, A. (1998). The stakeholder theory and the common good. *Journal of Business Ethics, 17*, 1093–1102.
9. Carroll & Buchholz (2003).
10. Carroll & Buchholz (2003).
11. Carroll & Buchholz (2003).
12. Guth, D. W., & Marsh, C. (2006). *Public relations: A values-driven approach* (3rd ed.). Boston: Pearson; Seitel, F. P. (1997). *The practice of public relations* (7th ed.). Upper Saddle River, NJ: Prentice Hall.
13. Davis, J. H., Schoorman, F. D., & Donaldson, L. (1997). Toward a stewardship theory of management. *Academy of Management Review, 22*, 20–47.
14. Caldwell, C., & Karri, R. (2005). Organizational governance and ethical systems: A covenantal approach to building trust. *Journal of Business Ethics, 58*, 249–259; Caldwell, C., Bishchoff, S. J., & Karri, R. (2002). The four umpires: A paradigm for ethical leadership. *Journal of Business Ethics, 36*, 153–163; Barnett, T., & Schubert, E. (2002). Perceptions of the ethical work climate and covenantal relationships. *Journal of Business Ethics, 36*, 279–290.
15. Wheeler, D., Coalbert, B., & Freeman, R. E. (2003). Focusing on value: Reconciling corporate social responsibility, sustainability and a stakeholder approach in a network world. *Journal of General Management, 28*, 1–28.
16. Hart, S. L. (1997, January-February). Beyond greening: Strategies for a sustainable world. *Harvard Business Review*, pp. 66–76.
17. Martin, R. L. (2003). The virtue matrix: Calculating the return of corporate responsibility. *Harvard Business Review on Corporate Responsibility* (pp. 83–104). Boston: Harvard Business School Press.

18. Sethi, S. P. (1975). Dimensions of corporate social performance: An analytical framework. *California Management Review, 17,* 58–64.

19. Johnson, H. H. (2001). Corporate social audits—this time around. *Business Horizons, 44,* 29–36.

20. Charity navigator (www.charitynavigator.org).

21. Social Accountability International. (2005). *Overview of SA8000.* Retrieved August 10, 2005, from http//:www.sa-intl.org

22. Global Reporting Initiative. (2002). *The 2002 sustainability reporting guidelines.* Retrieved April 13, 2006, from http//:www.globalreporting.org/

23. See, for example: Norman, W., & MacDonald, C. (2004). Getting to the bottom of "triple bottom line." *Business Ethics Quarterly, 14,* 243–262; Adams, C. A., & Evans, R. (2004). Accountability, completeness, credibility and the audit expectations gap. *Journal of Corporate Citizenship, 14,* 97–115; Boele, R., & Kemp, D. (2005, Spring). Social auditors: Illegitimate offspring of the audit family? Finding legitimacy through a hybrid approach. *Journal of Corporate Citizenship,* 109–119.

24. Singer, P. (2002). *One world: The ethics of globalization.* New Haven, CT: Yale University Press; Lacey, M. (2003, September 10). Africans' burden: West's farm subsidies. *New York Times,* p. A9; Muzaffar, C. (2002). Conclusion. In P. F. Knitter & C. Muzaffar (Eds.), *Subverting greed: Religious perspectives on the global economy* (pp. 154–172). Maryknoll, NY: Orbis Books; Harvesting poverty: Inching toward trade fairness [Editorial]. (2003, August 15). *New York Times,* p. A28. Retrieved September 15, 2003, from LexisNexis Academic database.

25. Singer (2002).

26. Robinson, M. (2000). Internalizing human rights in corporate business practices. *UN Chronicle, 37,* 38–39.

27. Nielsen, S. (2003, November 2). At Wal-Mart, a world power runs the sale bins. *Oregonian,* pp. E1–E2.

28. Mitchell, C. (2003). *International business ethics: Combining ethics and profits in global business.* Novato, CA: World Trade Press; Carroll, S. J., & Gannon, M. J. (1997). *Ethical dimensions of management.* Thousand Oaks, CA: Sage.

29. Gudykunst, W. B., & Kim, Y. Y. (1997). *Communicating with strangers: An approach to intercultural communication* (3rd ed.) New York: McGraw-Hill.

30. Novak, M. (2003). A universal culture of human rights and freedom's habits: Caritapolis. In J. H. Dunning (Ed.), *Making globalization good: The moral challenges of global capitalism* (pp. 253–279). Oxford, UK: Oxford University Press.

31. Humphrey, J. (1989). *No distant millennium: The international law of human rights.* Paris: UNESCO; Donnelly, J. (1989). *Universal human rights in theory and practice.* Ithaca, NY: Cornell University Press.

32. Mares, R. (Ed.). (2004). *Business and human rights: A compilation of documents.* Leiden, the Netherlands: Martinus Nijhoff, pp. 2–7.

33. Engardio, P. (2004, July 12). Global Compact, little impact. *BusinessWeek,* pp. 86–87; Engardio, P. (2004, July 20). Two views of the Global Compact. *BusinessWeek Online.* Retrieved September 3, 2005, from Academic Source Premier database.

34. Kung, H. (1998), *A global ethic for global politics and economics.* New York: Oxford University Press; Kung, H. (1999). A global ethic in an age of globalization. In G. Enderle (Ed.), *International business ethics: Challenges and approaches* (pp. 109–127). Notre Dame, IN: University of Notre Dame Press; Kung, H. (2003). An ethical framework for the global market economy. In J. H. Dunning (Ed.), *Making globalization good:*

The moral challenges of global capitalism (pp. 146–158). Oxford, UK: Oxford University Press; Kung, H., & Kuschel, K. J. (Eds.). (1993). *A global ethic: The declaration of the parliament of the world's religions.* New York: Continuum.

35. Kidder, R. M. (1994). *Shared values for a troubled world: Conversations with men and women of conscience.* San Francisco: Jossey-Bass; Kidder, R. M. (1994, July-August). Universal values: Finding an ethical common ground. *Futurist,* pp. 8–13.

36. Kidder (1994, July-August), pp. 8-11.

37. Kidder (1994), p. 312.

38. Caux Round Table. (2004). The Caux Round Table principles for business, 1994. In R. Mares (Ed.), *Business and human rights: A compilation of documents* (pp. 288–292). Leiden, the Netherlands: Brill; Caux Round Table. (2000). Appendix 26: The Caux Principles (pp. 384–388). In O. F. Williams, *Global codes of conduct: An idea whose time has come.* Notre Dame, IN: Notre Dame University Press.

39. Caux Round Table (2000), pp. 384–388.

40. Donaldson, T., & Dunfee, T. W. (1994). Toward a unified conception of business ethics: Integrative social contracts theory. *Academy of Management Review, 19,* 252–284. Donaldson, T., & Dunfee, T. W. (1999). *Ties that bind: A social contracts approach to business ethics.* Boston: Harvard Business School Press; Dunfee, T. W., & Donaldson, T. (1999). Social contract approaches to business ethics: Bridging the "is-ought" gap. In R. E. Frederick (Ed.), *A companion to business ethics* (pp. 38–52). Malden, MA: Blackwell.

References

Abrahams, J. (1999). *The mission statement book: 301 corporate mission statements from America's top companies.* Berkeley, CA: Ten Speed Press.

Adams, C. A., & Evans, R. (2004). Accountability, completeness, credibility and the audit expectations gap. *Journal of Corporate Citizenship, 14,* 97–115.

Adams, G. B., & Balfour, D. L. (1998). *Unmasking administrative evil.* Thousand Oaks, CA: Sage.

Adams, J. S., Tashchian, A., & Shore, T. H. (2001). Codes of ethics as signals for ethical behavior. *Journal of Business Ethics, 29,* 199–211.

Adler, A., Underwood, A., Scelfo, J., Juarez, V., Johnson, D., Shenfeld, H., Reno, J., Murr, A., Breslau, K., & Raymond, J. (2004, December 20). Toxic strength. *Newsweek,* pp. 44–52.

Albrecht, T. L., & Bach, B. W. (1997). *Communication in complex organizations: A relational approach.* Fort Worth, TX: Harcourt Brace.

Anand, V., Ashforth, B. E., & Joshi, M. (2004). Business as usual: The acceptance and perpetuation of corruption in organizations. *Academy of Management Executive, 18,* 39–53.

Anderson, R. (2003, April 30). Starbucks: Just getting started. *Seattle Weekly,* p. 11. Retrieved May 24, 2004, from LexisNexis Academic database.

Andersson, L. M., & Pearson, C. M. (1999). Tit for tat? The spiraling effect of incivility in the workplace. *Academy of Management Review, 24,* 452–471.

Aquino, K. (1998). The effects of ethical climate and the availability of alternatives on the use of deception during negotiation. *International Journal of Conflict Management, 9,* 195–217.

Arandona, A., (1998). The stakeholder theory and the common good. *Journal of Business Ethics, 17,* 1093–1102.

Aristotle. (1962). *Nicomachean ethics* (Martin Ostwald, Trans.). Indianapolis, IN: Bobbs Merrill. (Original work published 350 B.C.E.)

Arnett, R. C. (1986). *Communication and community: Implications of Martin Buber's dialogue.* Carbondale: Southern Illinois University Press.

Arnett, R. C., & Arneson, P. (1999). *Dialogic civility in a cynical age: Community, hope, and interpersonal relationships.* Albany: State University of New York Press.

Autry, J. A. (2001). *The servant leader.* New York: Crown.

Avolio, B. J. (1999). *Full leadership development: Building vital forces in organizations.* Thousand Oaks, CA: Sage.

Badger, T. A. (2005, May 3). Soldier says peers pressed for abuse. *Oregonian,* pp. A1, A3.

Baker, S. (1997). Applying Kidder's ethical decision-making checklist to media ethics. *Journal of Mass Media Ethics, 12*(4), 197–210.

Bandura, A. (1977). Self-efficacy: Toward a unifying theory of behavioral change. *Psychological Review, 84,* 191–215.

Bardi, A., & Schwartz, S. H. (2003). Values and behavior: Strength and structure of relations. *Journal of Personality and Social Psychology, 29,* 1207–1220.

Barker, J. R. (1993). Tightening the iron cage: Concertive control in self-managing teams. *Administrative Science Quarterly, 38,* 408–437.

Barker, J. R. (1999). *The discipline of teamwork: Participation and concertive control.* Thousand Oaks, CA: Sage.

Barker, L., & Watson, K. (2000). *Listen up: How to improve relationships, reduce stress, and be more productive by using the power of listening.* New York: St. Martin's Press.

Barlett, D. L, Steele, J. B., Karmatz, L., Kiviat, B., & Levinstein, J. (2004, February 2). Why we pay so much for drugs. *Time,* pp. 44–52.

Barling, J. (1996). The prediction, experience, and consequences of workplace violence. In G. R. VandenBos & E. Q. Bulato (Eds.), *Violence on the job: Identifying risks and developing solutions* (pp. 29–49). Washington, DC: American Psychological Association.

Barnett, T., & Schubert, E. (2002). Perceptions of the ethical work climate and covenantal relationships. *Journal of Business Ethics, 36,* 279–290.

Baron, R. A. (2004). Workplace aggression and violence: Insights from basic research. In R. W. Griffin & A. M. O'Leary-Kelly (Eds.), *The dark side of organizational behavior* (pp. 23–61). San Francisco: Jossey-Bass.

Barry, J., Hirsh, M., & Isikoff, M. (2004, May 24). The roots of torture. *Newsweek,* pp. 26–34.

Barry, V. (1978). *Personal and social ethics: Moral problems with integrated theory.* Belmont, CA: Wadsworth.

Barth, S. R. (2003). *Corporate ethics: The business code of conduct for ethical employees.* Boston: Aspatore Books.

Bass, B. (1990). *Bass and Stogdill's handbook of leadership* (3rd ed.). New York: Free Press.

Bass, B. M. (1995). The ethics of transformational leadership. In J. Ciulla (Ed.), *Ethics: The heart of leadership* (pp. 169–192). Westport, CT: Praeger.

Bass, B. M. (1996). *A new paradigm of leadership: An inquiry into transformational leadership.* Alexandria, VA: Army Research Institute for the Behavior and Social Sciences.

Bass, B. M., & Avolio, B. J. (1994). Transformational leadership and organizational culture. *International Journal of Public Administration, 17,* 541–554.

Bass, B. M., Avolio, B. J., Jung, D. I., & Berson, Y. (2003). Predicting unit performance by assessing transformational and transactional leadership. *Journal of Applied Psychology, 88,* 207–218.

Bass, B. M., & Steidlmeier, P. (1999). Ethics, character, and authentic transformational leadership behavior. *Leadership Quarterly, 10,* 181–227.

Batsell, J. (2004, March 28). A bean counter's dream. *Seattle Times,* p. E1.

Batson, C. D., Van Lange, P. A. M., Ahmad, N., & Lishner, D. A. (2003). Altruism and helping behavior. In M. A. Hogg & J. Cooper (Eds.), *The Sage handbook of social psychology* (pp. 279–295). London: Sage.

Belknap, M. R. (2002). *The Viet Nam war on trial: The My Lai massacre and the court martial of Lieutenant Calley*. Lawrence: University of Kansas Press.

Belluck, P. (2005, April 15). DNA test leads, at last, to arrest in Cape Cod case. *New York Times*, p. A6. Retrieved October 8, 2005, from LexisNexis Academic database.

Benjamin, M. (2002, April 22). Honest opinions. *U.S. News & World Report*, p. 47.

Bennett, R. J. (1998). Perceived powerlessness as a cause of employee deviance. In R. W. Griffin, A. O'Leary-Kelly, & J. M. Collins (Eds.), *Dysfunctional behavior in organizations: Violent and deviant behavior* (pp. 221–239). Stamford, CT: JAI.

Bennis, W. G., & Thomas, R. J. (2002). *Geeks and geezers: How era, values and defining moments shape leaders*. Boston: Harvard Business School Press.

Bentham, J. (1948). *An introduction to the principles of morals and legislation*. New York: Hafner.

Bernthal, P. R., & Insko, C. A. (1993). Cohesiveness without groupthink: The interactive effects of social and task cohesion. *Group & Organizational Management, 18*, 66–87.

Berry, J. (1995, February 24). My Lai massacre was an American tragedy. *National Catholic Reporter*, pp. 10–11. Retrieved June 23, 2004, from EBSCOhost database.

Beuchner, F. (1973). *Wishful thinking: A theological ABC*. New York: HarperCollins.

Beyer, J. M., & Trice, H. M. (1987). How an organization's rites reveal its culture. *Organizational Dynamics, 15*, 5–21.

Biemann, A. D. (Ed.). (2002). *The Martin Buber reader: Essential writings*. New York: Palgrave Macmillan.

Bird, F. B. (1996). *The muted conscience: Moral silence and the practice of ethics in business*. Westport, CT: Quorum Books.

Bloch, D. P., & Richmond, L. J. (Eds.). (1997). *Connections between spirit & work in career development*. Palo Alto, CA: Davies-Black.

Block, P. (1993). *Stewardship: Choosing service over self-interest*. San Francisco: Berritt-Koehler.

Blocker, H. G., & Smith, E. H. (Eds.). (1980). *John Rawls' theory of justice: An introduction*. Athens: Ohio University Press.

Bobocel, D. R., & Meyer, J. P. (1994). Escalating commitment to a failing course of action: Separating the roles of choice and justification. *Journal of Applied Psychology, 79*, 360–363.

Boele, R., & Kemp, D. (2005, Spring). Social auditors: Illegitimate offspring of the audit family? Finding legitimacy through a hybrid approach. *Journal of Corporate Citizenship*, 109–119.

Bok, S. (1978). *Lying: Moral choice in public and private life*. New York: Pantheon Books.

Bok, S. (1980). Whistleblowing and professional responsibilities. In D. Callahan & S. Bok (Eds.), *Ethics teaching in higher education* (pp. 277–295). New York: Plenum Press.

Bok, S. (1989). *Secrets: On the ethics of concealment and revelation*. New York: Random House.

Boot, M. (2005, April 28). Nastiness is not the issue in Bolton's battle. *Financial Times*, p. 21.

Borrus, A., McNames, M., Symonds, W., Byrnes, N., & Park, A. (2003, February 2). Reform: Business gets religion. *BusinessWeek*, pp. 40–41. Retrieved July 6, 2004, from EBSCOhost database.

Boule, M. (2005, January 9). She doesn't want to sit in her chair of anger any longer. *Oregonian*, p. L1.

Boule, M. (2005, February 27). Woman's "anger chair" got lighter each day, until it was time to let go. *Oregonian*, pp. L1, L3.

Bowes-Sperry, L., & O'Leary-Kelly, A. M. (2005). To act or not to act: The dilemma faced by sexual harassment observers. *Academy of Management Review, 30,* 288–306.

Boyce, N. (2001, August 20). Hugh Thompson. *U.S. News and World Report,* pp. 33–34. Retrieved June 23, 2004, from Academic Source Premier database.

Brandl, P., & Maguire, M. (2002, Winter). Codes of ethics: A primer on their purpose, development and use. *Journal for Quality & Participation, 25,* 9–12.

Bratton, V. K., & Kacmar, K. M. (2004). Extreme careerism: The dark side of impression management. In W. Griffin and K. O'Reilly (Eds.), *The dark side of organizational behavior* (pp. 291–308). San Francisco: Jossey-Bass.

Brehony, K. A. (1999). *Ordinary grace: Lessons from those who help others in extraordinary ways.* New York: Riverhead Books.

Brockner, J., Siegel, P. A., Daly, J. P., Tyler, T., & Martin, C. (1997). When trust matters: The moderating effect of outcome favorability. *Administrative Science Quarterly, 42,* 558–583.

Brooker, K. (2002, June 24). Fire the chairman of the bored. *Fortune,* pp. 72–73. Retrieved July 6, 2004, from EBSCOhost database.

Brower, H. H., & Shrader, C. B. (2000). Moral reasoning and ethical climate: Not-for-profit vs. for-profit boards of directors. *Journal of Business Ethics, 26,* 147–167.

Brown, C. T., & Keller, P. W. (1994). Ethics. In R. Anderson, K. N. Cissna, & R. C. Arnett (Eds.), *The reach of dialogue: Confirmation, voice, and community* (pp. 284–290). Cresskill, NJ: Hampton Press.

Brown, J., & Isaacs, D. (1995). Building corporations as communities: The best of both worlds. In K. Gozdz (Ed.), *Community building: Renewing spirit & learning in business* (pp. 69–83). San Francisco: Sterling & Stone.

Brown, R. (1995). *Prejudice: Its social psychology.* Oxford, UK: Blackwell.

Brownell, J. (2002). *Listening: Attitudes, principles, and skills* (2nd ed.). Boston: Allyn & Bacon.

Brownell, J. (2003, November 22). *The skills of listening-centered communication.* Paper presented at the National Communication Association convention, Miami, FL.

Buber, M. (1965). *The knowledge of man: Selected essays* (M. Friedman, Ed.). New York: Harper & Row, pp. 67–68.

Buber, M. (1970). *I and thou.* (R. G. Smith, Trans.). New York: Scribner's.

Buchholz, R. A., & Rosenthal, S. B. (2005). Toward a conceptual framework for stakeholder theory. *Journal of Business Ethics, 58,* 137–148.

Bullis, C. (1991). Communication practices as unobtrusive control: An observational study. *Communication Studies, 42/3,* 254–271.

Burns, J. M. (1978). *Leadership.* New York: Harper & Row.

Burns, J. M. (2003). *Transforming leadership: A new pursuit of happiness.* New York: Atlantic Monthly Press.

Buss, A. H. (1961). *The psychology of aggression.* New York: John Wiley.

Caldwell, C., Bishchoff, S. J., & Karri, R. (2002). The four umpires: A paradigm for ethical leadership. *Journal of Business Ethics, 36,* 153–163.

Caldwell, C., & Karri, R. (2005). Organizational governance and ethical systems: A covenantal approach to building trust. *Journal of Business Ethics, 58,* 249–259.

Callahan, D. (2004). *The cheating culture.* Orlando, FL: Harcourt.

Carney, J. (2005, May 2). Temper, temper, temper. *Time,* pp. 55–57.

Carroll, A. B. (1979). A three-dimensional conceptual model of corporate performance. *Academy of Management Review, 4,* 497–508.

Carroll, A. B., & Buchholtz, A. K. (2003). *Business and society: Ethics and stakeholder management* (5th ed.). Mason, OH: South-Western.

Carroll, S. J., & Gannon, M. J. (1997). *Ethical dimensions of management.* Thousand Oaks, CA: Sage.

Carson, T. (2001). Deception and withholding information in sales. *Business Ethics Quarterly, 11,* 275–306.

Carter, S. L. (1998). *Civility: Manners, morals, and the etiquette of democracy.* New York: HarperCollins.

Caruso, D. R., & Salovey, P. (2004). *The emotionally intelligent manager: How to develop and use the four key emotional skills of leadership.* San Francisco: Jossey-Bass.

Caux Round Table. (2000). Appendix 26: The Caux Principles. In O. F. Williams, *Global codes of conduct: An idea whose time has come* (pp. 384–388). Notre Dame, IN: Notre Dame University Press.

Caux Round Table. (2004). The Caux Round Table principles for business, 1994. In R. Mares (Ed.), *Business and human rights: A compilation of documents* (pp. 288–292). Leiden, the Netherlands: Brill.

Chaleff, I. (1995). *The courageous follower: Standing up to and for our leaders.* San Francisco: Berritt-Koehler.

Chang, I. (1997). *The rape of Nanking: The forgotten holocaust of World War II.* New York: Basic Books.

Charan, R., & Tichy, N. (1988). *Every business is a growth business: How your company can prosper year after year.* New York: Random House.

Chen, A., Lawson, R. B., Gordon, L. R., & McIntosh, B. (1996). Groupthink: Deciding with the leader and the devil. *Psychological Record, 46,* 581–590.

Christians, C. G., Rotzell, K. B., & Fackler, M. (1990). *Media ethics* (3rd ed.). New York: Longman.

Cialdini, R. B. (2001). *Influence: Science and practice* (4th ed.). Boston: Allyn & Bacon.

Cialdini, R. B., Petrova, P. K., & Goldstein, N. J. (2004, Spring). The hidden costs of organizational dishonesty. *MIT Sloan Management Review,* pp. 67–73.

Cissna, K. N., & Anderson, R. (1994). Communication and the ground of dialogue. In R. Anderson, K. N. Cissna, & R. C. Arnett (Eds.), *The reach of dialogue: Confirmation, voice, and community* (pp. 9–30). Cresskill, NJ: Hampton Press.

Cissna, K. N., & Sieburg, E. (1990). Patterns of interactional confirmation and disconfirmation. In J. Stewart (Ed.), *Bridges not walls: A book about interpersonal communication* (5th ed., pp. 237–246). New York: McGraw-Hill.

Clark, T. (2004, May 26). Thoroughly Starbucked. *Willamette Week,* pp. 18–19, 21, 23–25.

Cleaning up the mess. (2001, June 30). *Economist,* p. 64. Retrieved July 27, 2005, from Business Source Premier database.

Cohen, D. V. (1993). Creating and maintaining ethical work climates: Anomie in the workplace and implications for managing change. *Business Ethics Quarterly, 3,* 343–358.

Coles, R. (2001). *Lives of moral leadership.* New York: Random House.

Collins, J. C., & Porras, J. I. (1994). *Built to last: Successful habits of visionary companies.* New York: HarperBusiness.

Collins, J. C., & Porras, J. I. (1996, September-October). Building your company's vision. *Harvard Business Review*, pp. 65–77.

Cooper, S. (2004). *Corporate social performance: A stakeholder approach.* Burlington, VT: Ashgate.

Cooper, T. L. (1992). Prologue: On virtue. In T. L. Cooper & N. D. Wright (Eds.), *Exemplary public administrators: Character and leadership in government* (pp. 1–8). San Francisco: Jossey-Bass.

Cooper, T. L., & Wright, N. D. (1992). *Exemplary public administrators: Character and leadership in government.* San Francisco: Jossey-Bass.

Cortina, L. M., Magley, V. I., Hunter Williams, J., & Langhout, R. D. (2001). Incivility in the workplace: Incidence and impact. *Journal of Occupational Health Psychology, 6,* 64–80.

Covey, S. R. (1989). *The seven habits of highly effective people.* New York: Simon & Schuster.

Creswell, J. (2003, July 7). Scandal hits—now what? *Fortune,* pp. 127–129.

Cruver, B. (2002). *Anatomy of greed: The unshredded truth from an Enron insider.* New York: Carroll & Graf.

Cullen, J. B., Parboteeah, K. P., & Victor, B. (2003). The effects of ethical climates on organizational commitment: A two-study analysis. *Journal of Business Ethics, 46,* 127–141.

Czubaroff, J. (2000). Dialogic rhetoric: An application of Martin Buber's philosophy of dialogue. *Quarterly Journal of Speech, 2,* 168–189.

Daniels, C. (2003, April 14). Mr. Coffee. *Fortune,* pp. 139–140.

Danner, M. (2004). *Torture and truth: America, Abu Ghraib, and the war on terror.* New York: New York Review Books.

Darley, J. M. (1996). How organizations socialize individuals into evildoing. In D. M. Messick & A. E. Tenbrunsel (Eds.), *Codes of conduct: Behavioral research into business ethics* (pp. 13–43). New York: Russell Sage Foundation.

Davis, J. H., Schoorman, F. D., & Donaldson, L. (1997). Toward a stewardship theory of management. *Academy of Management Review, 22,* 20–47.

Day, L. A. (2003). *Ethics in media communications: Cases and controversies* (4th ed.). Belmont CA: Thomson/Wadsworth.

De George, R. T. (1995). *Business ethics* (4th ed.). Englewood Cliffs, NJ: Prentice Hall.

De George, R. T. (2003). *The ethics of information technology and business.* Malden, MA: Blackwell.

Denson, B., & Kosseff, J. (2005, December 20). Goodwill chief agrees to pay cut. *Oregonian,* p. A1. Retrieved January 25, 2006, from NewsBank database.

Depre, K. E., & Barling, J. (2003). Workplace aggression. In A. Sagie, S. Stashevsky, & M. Koslowsky (Eds.), *Misbehaviour and dysfunctional attitudes in organizations* (pp. 13–32). Hampshire, UK: Palgrave Macmillan.

Devettere, R. J. (2002). *Introduction to virtue ethics: Insights of the ancient Greeks.* Washington, DC: Georgetown University Press.

Dipboye, R. L., & Halverson, S. K. (2004). Subtle (and not so subtle) discrimination in organizations. In R. W. Griffin & A. M. O'Leary-Kelly (Eds.), *The dark side of organizational behavior* (pp. 131–158). San Francisco: Jossey-Bass.

Dirks, K. T. (1999). The effects of interpersonal trust on work group performance. *Journal of Applied Psychology, 84,* 445–455.

Dirks, K. T., & Ferrin, D. L. (2002). Trust in leadership: Meta-analytic findings and implications for research and practice. *Journal of Applied Psychology, 87*, 611–628.

Divir, T., Eden, D., & Banjo, M. L. (1995). Self-fulfilling prophecy and gender: Can women be Pygmalion and Galatea? *Journal of Applied Psychology, 80*, 253–270.

Donaldson, T., & Dunfee, T. W. (1994). Toward a unified conception of business ethics: Integrative social contracts theory. *Academy of Management Review, 19*, 252–284.

Donaldson, T., & Dunfee, T. W. (1999). *Ties that bind: A social contracts approach to business ethics.* Boston: Harvard Business School Press.

Donaldson, T., & Preston, L. E. (1995). The stakeholder theory of the corporation: Concepts, evidence, and implications. *Academy of Management Review, 20*, 65–91.

Donnelly, J. (1989). *Universal human rights in theory and practice.* Ithaca, NY: Cornell University Press.

Dotlich, D. L., Noel, J. L., & Walker, N. (2004). *Leadership passages: The personal and professional transitions that make or break a leader.* San Francisco: Jossey-Bass.

Douglas, S. C., & Martinko, M. J. (2001). Exploring the role of individual differences in the prediction of workplace aggression. *Journal of Applied Psychology, 86*, 547–559.

Drath, W. (2001). *The deep blue sea: Rethinking the source of leadership.* San Francisco: Jossey-Bass.

Dunfee, T. W., & Donaldson, T. (1999). Social contract approaches to business ethics: Bridging the "is-ought" gap. In R. E. Frederick (Ed.), *A companion to business ethics* (pp. 38–52). Malden, MA: Blackwell.

Dwyer, J., & Flynn, K. (2005). *102 minutes: The untold story of the fight to survive inside the Twin Towers.* New York: Times Books.

Eberly, D. E. (1998). *America's promise: Civil society and the renewal of American culture.* Lanham, MD: Rowman & Littlefield.

Eden, D. (1984). Self-fulfilling prophecy as a management tool: Harnessing Pygmalion. *Academy of Management Review, 9*, 64–73.

Eden, D. (1990). *Pygmalion in management.* Lexington, MA: Lexington Books/D.C. Heath.

Eden, D. (1993). Interpersonal expectations in organizations. In P. D. Blanck (Ed.), *Interpersonal expectations: Theory, research, and applications* (pp. 154–178). Cambridge, UK: University of Cambridge Press.

Eden, D., & Shami, A. B. (1982). Pygmalion goes to boot camp: Expectancy, leadership, and trainee performance. *Journal of Applied Psychology, 67*, 194–199.

Eisenberg, D., Szczesny, J. R., Forster, P., Larimer, T., Eskenazi, M., & Greenwald, J. (2000, September 18). Firestone's rough road. *Time*, pp. 38–40.

Eisenberg, N. (2000). Emotion, regulation, and moral development. *Annual Review of Psychology, 51*, 665–697.

Ekman, P. (2003). *Emotions revealed: Recognizing faces and feelings to improve communication and emotional life.* New York: Times Books.

ElBoghdady, D. (2002, August 25). Pouring it on. *Washington Post*, p. H01. Retrieved May 24, 2004, from LexisNexis Academic database.

Elkind, P. (2004, June 14). The trials of Eliot Spitzer. *Fortune*, pp. 33–35. Retrieved July 6, 2004, from EBSCOhost database.

Ellis, K. (2000). Perceived teacher confirmation: The development of validation of an instrument and two studies of the relationship to cognitive and affective learning. *Human Communication Research, 26*, 264–291.

Ellis, K. (2004). The impact of perceived teacher confirmation on receiver apprehension, motivation, and learning. *Communication Education, 53*, 1–20.

Ely, R. D., & Thomas, D. A. (2001). Cultural diversity at work: The effects of diversity perspectives on work group processes and outcomes. *Administrative Science Quarterly, 46*, 229–273.

Engardio, P. (2004, July 12). Global Compact, little impact. *BusinessWeek*, pp. 86–87.

Engardio, P. (2004, July 20). Two views of the Global Compact. *BusinessWeek Online.* Retrieved September 3, 2005, from Academic Source Premier database.

Enright, R. D., Freedman, S., & Rique, J. (1998). The psychology of interpersonal forgiveness. In R. D. Enright & J. North (Eds.), *Exploring forgiveness* (pp. 46–62). Madison: University of Wisconsin Press.

Esser, J. K. (1998). Alive and well after 25 years: A review of groupthink research. *Organizational Behavior and Human Decision Processes, 73*, 116–141.

Estes, R. (1996). *Tyranny of the bottom line.* San Francisco: Berritt-Koehler.

Etzioni, A. (1993). *The spirit of community: The reinvention of American society.* New York: Simon & Schuster.

Etzioni, A. (Ed.). (1995a). *New Communitarian thinking: Persons, virtues, institutions, and communities.* Charlottesville: University Press of Virginia.

Etzioni, A. (Ed.). (1995b). *Rights and the common good: A Communitarian perspective* (pp. 271–276). New York: St. Martin's Press.

Etzioni, A. (1996). *The new golden rule: Community and morality in a democratic society.* New York: Basic Books.

Etzioni, A. (2000). Epilogue. In E. W. Lehman (Ed.), *Autonomy and order: A communitarian anthology* (pp. 219–236). Lanham, MD: Rowman & Littlefield.

Etzioni, A., Volmart, A., & Rothschild, E. (2004). *The Communitarian reader: Beyond the essentials.* Lanham, MD: Rowman & Littlefield.

Ever farther, ever faster, ever higher? (2004, August 7). *Economist*, pp. 20–22. Retrieved January 5, 2005, from EBSCOhost database.

Fears, D. (2005, August 14). Indian mascots: Matter of pride or prejudice? Even tribes are divided as NCAA issues edict. *Washington Post*, p. A03. Retrieved October 4, 2004, from LexisNexis Academic database.

Ferrell, O. C., & Gardiner, G. (1991). *In pursuit of ethics: Tough choices in a world of work.* Springfield, IL: Smith Collins.

Fineman, S. (1995). Stress, emotion and intervention. In T. Newton (Ed.), *Managing stress: Emotion and power at work* (pp. 120–136). London: Sage.

Fiske, S. T. (1993, June). Controlling other people: The impact of power on stereotyping. *American Psychologist, 48*, 621–628.

Fiske, S. T. (1998). Stereotyping, prejudice, and discrimination. In D. T. Gilbert, S. T. Fiske, & G. Lindzey (Eds.), *The handbook of social psychology* (Vol. 2, pp. 357–411). Boston: McGraw-Hill.

Fitzgerald, L. F. (1993). Sexual harassment: Violence against women in the workplace. *American Psychologist, 48*, 1070–1076.

Fitzgerald, L. F., Drasgow, F., Hulin, C. L., Gelfand, M. J., & Magley, V. (1997). Antecedents and consequences of sexual harassment in organizations: A test of an integrated model. *Journal of Applied Psychology, 82*, 578–589.

Flippen, A. R. (1999). Understanding groupthink from a self-regulatory perspective. *Small Group Research, 30*, 139–165.

Folger, J., Poole, M., & Stutman, R. (1993). *Working through conflict.* New York: HarperCollins.

Folger, R., & Baron, R. A. (1996). Violence and hostility at work: A model of reactions to perceived injustice. In G. VandenBos & E. Q. Bulato (Eds.), *Violence on the job: Identifying risks and developing solutions* (pp. 51–85). Washington, DC: American Psychological Association.

Fonda, D., & Kadlec, D. (2004, May 31). The rumble over executive pay. *Time,* pp. 62–64.

Forrester, R. (2000). Empowerment: Rejuvenating a potent idea. *Academy of Management Executive, 14,* 67–80.

Fowler, J. W. (1984). *Becoming adult, becoming Christian: Adult development and the Christian faith.* San Francisco: Harper & Row.

Fowler, J. W. (1991). *Weaving the new creation: Stages of faith and the public church.* San Francisco: HarperSanFrancisco.

Freeman, E. (1984). *Strategic management.* Marshfield, MA: Pitman.

Freeman, R. E. (1994). The politics of stakeholder theory: Some future directions. *Business Ethics Quarterly, 4,* 409–421.

Freeman, R. E. (1995). Stakeholder thinking: The state of the art. In J. Nasi (Ed.), *Understanding stakeholder thinking* (pp. 35–73). Helsinki, Finland: LSR-Julkaisut Oy.

French, R. P., & Raven, B. (1959). *The bases of social power.* In D. Cartwright (Ed.), Studies in social power (pp. 150–167). Ann Arbor: University of Michigan, Institute for Social Research.

Fritzche, D. J. (2000). Ethical climates and the ethical dimension of decision making. *Journal of Business Ethics, 24,* 125–140.

Gardner, W. L. (1992). Lessons in organizational dramaturgy: The art of impression management. *Organizational Dynamics, 21,* 33–47.

Gates, D. (2005, March 8). Boeing faces CEO dilemma. *The Seattle Times,* p. A1. Retrieved July 27, 2005, from LexisNexis Academic database.

Gaudine, A., & Thorne, L. (2001). Emotion and ethical decision-making in organizations. *Journal of Business Ethics, 31,* 175–187.

Gellerman, S. W. (1989, Winter). Managing ethics from the top down. *Sloan Management Review,* pp. 73–79.

George, J. M. (1995). Asymmetrical effects of rewards and punishments: The case of social loafing. *Journal of Occupational and Organizational Psychology, 68,* 327–338.

Gergen, D. (2000). *Eyewitness to power: The essence of leadership.* New York: Simon & Schuster.

Giacalone, R. A., & Greenberg, J. (1997). *Antisocial behavior in organizations.* Thousand Oaks, CA: Sage.

Gibb, J. R. (1961). Defensive communication. *Journal of Communication, 11–12,* 141–148.

Gittell, J. H. (2003). *The Southwest Airlines way.* New York: McGraw-Hill.

Gladwell, M. (2005). *Blink: The power of thinking without thinking.* New York: Little, Brown.

Global Reporting Initiative. (2002). *The 2002 sustainability reporting guidelines.* Retrieved April 13, 2006, from http://www.globalreporting.org/

Glomb, T. M., & Hui, L. (2003). Interpersonal aggression in work groups: Social influence, reciprocal, and individual effects. *Academy of Management Journal, 46,* 486–496.

Goffman, E. (1959). *The presentation of self in everyday life.* Garden City, NY: Doubleday.

Good, T., & Brophy, J. (1980). *Educational psychology: A realistic approach.* New York: Holt, Rinehart & Winston.

Goodpaster, K. E. (1991). Business ethics and stakeholder analysis. *Business Ethics Quarterly, 1,* 53–72.

Goodwin, S. A. (2003). Power and prejudice: A social-cognitive perspective on power and leadership. In D. van Knippenberg & M. A. Hogg (Eds.), *Leadership and power: Identity processes in groups and organizations* (pp. 138–152). London: Sage.

Graham, G. (2004). *Eight theories of ethics.* London: Routledge.

Graham, J. (1995). Leadership, moral development, and citizenship behavior. *Business Ethics Quarterly, 5,* 43–54.

Greed is bad. (2004, May 29). *Economist,* pp. 72–73. Retrieved July 6, 2006, from EBSCOhost database.

Greenleaf, R. K. (1977). *Servant leadership.* New York: Paulist Press.

Grover, S. (1993). Lying, deceit, and subterfuge: A model of dishonesty in the workplace. *Organization Science, 4,* 478–494.

Grover, S. L. (1997). Lying in organizations: Theory, research, and future directions. In R. A. Giacalone & J. Greenberg (Eds.), *Antisocial behavior in organizations* (pp. 68–84). Thousand Oaks, CA: Sage.

Gudykunst, W. B., & Kim, Y. Y. (1997). *Communicating with strangers: An approach to intercultural communication* (3rd ed.). New York: McGraw-Hill.

Guth, D. W., & Marsh, C. (2006). *Public relations: A values-driven approach* (3rd ed.). Boston: Pearson.

Hackman, M. Z., & Johnson, C. E. (2004). *Leadership: A communication perspective* (4th ed.). Long Grove, IL: Waveland Press.

Hall, C. S., & Nordby, V. J. (1973). *A primer of Jungian psychology.* New York: New American Library.

Hardy, L. (1990). *The fabric of this world: Inquiries into calling, career choice, and the design of human work.* Grand Rapids, MI: Eerdmans.

Harper, T. (2005, April 21). Bolton's "a really creepy guy." *Toronto Star,* p. A03. Retrieved April 29, 2005, from LexisNexis Academic database.

Hart, D. K. (1994). Administration and the ethics of virtue. In T. C. Cooper (Ed.), *The handbook of administrative ethics* (pp. 107–123). New York: Marcel Dekker.

Hart, S. L. (1997, January/February). Beyond greening: Strategies for a sustainable world. *Harvard Business Review,* pp. 66–76.

Hartman, E. (1996). *Organizational ethics and the good life.* New York: Oxford University Press.

Hartman, L. P. (2001). Technology and ethics: Privacy in the workplace. *Business and Society Review, 106,* 1–26.

Hartman, L. P., & Bucci, G. (1999). The economic and ethical implications of new technology on privacy in the workplace. *Business and Society Review, 102/103,* 1–23.

Hartog, M., & Frame, P. (2004). Business ethics in the curriculum: Integrating ethics through work experience. *Journal of Business Ethics, 54,* 399–409.

Harvesting poverty: Inching toward trade fairness [Editorial]. (2003, August 15). *New York Times,* p. A28. Retrieved September 15, 2003, from LexisNexis Academic database.

Harvey, J. (1988). *The Abilene Paradox and other meditations on management.* Lexington, MA: Lexington Books.

Harvey, J. (2001). The Abilene Paradox: The management of agreement. *Organizational Dynamics, 33,* 17–34.

Harvey, S. J., Jr. (2000). Reinforcing ethical decision making through organizational structure. *Journal of Business Ethics, 28,* 43–58.

Hauerwas, S. (1981). *A community of character.* Notre Dame, IN: University of Notre Dame Press.

Heames, J. T., & Service, R. W. (2003). Dichotomies in teaching, application, and ethics. *Journal of Education for Business, 79,* 118–122.

Hempel, J., & Borrus, A. (2004, June 21). Now the nonprofits need cleaning up. *Business-Week,* pp. 107–108. Retrieved July 6, 2004, from EBSCOhost database.

Hensel, B. (2004, April 4). Business Q & A: Not a garbage guy, CEO talks about the turn-around. *Houston Chronicle,* Business section, p. 1. Retrieved July 25, 2005, from Business Source Premier database.

Herbert, B. (2005, May 2). From "gook" to "raghead." *New York Times,* p. A21. Retrieved June 14, 2005, from LexisNexis Academic database.

Hicks, D. A. (2003). *Religion and the workplace: Pluralism, spirituality, and leadership.* Cambridge, UK: Cambridge University Press.

Hiestand, M., & Mihoces, G. (2004, December 29). Apnea common for NFL linemen. *USA Today,* p. 1C.

Hinken, T. R., & Schreisheim, C. A. (1989). Development and application of new scales to measure the French and Raven (1959) Bases of Social Power. *Journal of Applied Psychology, 74,* 561–567.

Hitchens, C. (2001, May 28). Leave no child behind? *The Nation,* pp. 9–10. Retrieved June 23, 2004, from EBSCOhost database.

Hochschild, A. R. (1983). *The managed heart: Commercialization of human feeling.* Berkeley: University of California Press.

Holland, J. L. (1997). *Making vocational choices* (3rd ed.). Odessa, FL: Psychological Assessment Resources.

Holmes, S., Bennett, D., Carlisle, K., & Dawson, C. (2002, September 9). Planet Starbucks. *BusinessWeek,* pp. 100–106. Retrieved May 24, 2004, from LexisNexis Academic database.

Holt, S. (2005, March 8). Personal lives of executives under scrutiny. *Seattle Times,* p. C1. Retrieved July 27, 2005, from LexisNexis Academic database.

Hoppen, D. (2002, Winter). Guiding corporate behavior: A leadership obligation, not a choice. *Journal for Quality & Participation, 25,* 15–19.

Hosmer, L. T. (1995). Trust: The connecting link between organizational theory and philosophical ethics. *Academy of Management Review, 20,* 279–403.

House, R. J., Hanges, P. J., Javidan, M., Dorfman, P. W., & Gupta, V. (2004). *Culture, leadership, and organizations: The GLOBE study of 62 societies.* Thousand Oaks, CA: Sage.

Hubbartt, W. S. (1998). *The new battle over workplace privacy.* New York: AMACOM.

Huffington, A. (2003). *Pigs at the trough: How corporate greed and political corruption are undermining America.* New York: Crown.

Humphrey, J. (1989). *No distant millennium: The international law of human rights.* Paris: UNESCO.

Ilies, R., Hauserman, N., Schwochau, S., & Stibal, J. (2003). Reported incidence rates of work-related sexual harassment in the United States: Using meta-analysis to explain reported rate disparities. *Personnel Psychology, 56*, 607–651.

Isenhart, M. W., & Spangler, M. (2000). *Collaborative approaches to resolving conflict.* Thousand Oaks, CA: Sage.

James, H. S. (2000). Reinforcing ethical decision making through organizational structure. *Journal of Business Ethics, 28*, 43–58.

Janis, I. (1971, November). Groupthink: The problems of conformity. *Psychology Today*, pp. 271–279.

Janis, I. (1982). *Groupthink* (2nd ed.). Boston: Houghton Mifflin.

Janis, I. (1989). *Crucial decisions: Leadership in policymaking and crisis management.* New York: Free Press.

Jarett, J. L. (1991). *The teaching of values: Caring and appreciation.* London: Routledge.

Jaska, J. A., & Pritchard, M. S. (1994). *Communication ethics: Methods of analysis.* Belmont, CA: Wadsworth.

Johannesen, R. L. (2002). *Ethics in human communication* (5th ed.). Prospect Heights, IL: Waveland Press.

Johnson, C. E. (2000). Emerging perspectives in leadership ethics. *Proceedings of the International Leadership Association*, pp. 48–54. College Park, MD: International Leadership Association.

Johnson, C. E. (2000). Taoist leadership ethics. *Journal of Leadership Studies, 7*, 82–91.

Johnson, C. E. (2001, November). *Responding to the moral bind of positive emotional labor: Enacting bounded emotionality in the service encounter.* Paper presented at the National Communication Association convention, Atlanta, GA.

Johnson, C. E. (2003, November). *Aural space violations and unwanted intimacy: The ethics of cell phone use.* Paper presented at the National Communication Association convention, Miami Beach, FL.

Johnson, C. E., & Hackman, M. Z. (1995). *Creative communication: Principles and applications.* Prospect Heights, IL: Waveland Press.

Johnson, D. W. (1974). Communication and the inducement of cooperative behavior in conflicts: A critical review. *Speech Monographs, 41*, 64–78.

Johnson, D. W., & Johnson, R. T. (1974). Instructional goal structure: Cooperative, competitive, or individualistic. *Review of Educational Research, 44*, 212–239.

Johnson, D. W., Maruyama, G., Johnson, R., Nelson, D., & Skon, L. (1981). Effects of cooperative, competitive, and individualistic goal structures on achievement: A meta-analysis. *Psychological Bulletin, 82*, 47–62.

Johnson, H. H. (2001). Corporate social audits—this time around. *Business Horizons, 44*, 29–37.

Johnson, R. A. (1993). *Owning your own shadow: Understanding the dark side of the psyche.* San Francisco: Harper & Row.

Johnson, R. A. (2003). *Whistle-blowing: When it works—and why.* Boulder, CO: Lynne Rienner.

Jones, P. E., & Roelofsma, P. H. M. P. (2000). The potential for social contextual and group biases in team decision-making: Biases, conditions and psychological mechanisms. *Ergonomics, 43*, 1129–1152.

Kalwies, H. H. (1989). Ethical leadership: The foundation for organizational growth. *Howard Journal of Communications, 1*, 113–130.

Kant, I. (1964). *Groundwork of the metaphysics of morals* (H. J. Ryan, Trans.). New York: Harper & Row.

Kanter, R. M. (1977). *Men and women of the corporation.* New York: Basic Books.

Kanter, R. M. (1979, July-August). Power failure in management circuits. *Harvard Business Review,* pp. 65–75.

Kanter, R. M. (2001). An Abilene defense: Commentary one. *Organizational Dynamics, 33,* 37–40.

Kanungo, R. N., & Conger, J. A. (1993). Promoting altruism as a corporate goal. *Academy of Management Executive, 7,* 37–49.

Karau, S. J., & Williams, K. D. (1993). Social loafing: A meta-analytic review and theoretical integration. *Journal of Personality and Social Psychology, 65,* 681–706.

Karau, S. J., & Williams, K. D. (2001). Understanding individual motivation in groups: The collective effort model. In M. E. Turner (Ed.), *Groups at work: Theory and research* (pp. 113–141). Mahwah, NJ: Lawrence Erlbaum.

Keil, M., & Montealegre, R. (2000, Spring). Cutting your losses: Extricating your organization when a big project goes awry. *Sloan Management Review,* pp. 55–58.

Kelley, R. E. (1992). *The power of followership: How to create leaders that people want to follow and followers who lead themselves.* New York: Doubleday/Currency.

Kelley, R. E. (1998). Followership in a leadership world. In L. C. Spears (Ed.), *Insights on leadership* (pp. 170–184). New York: John Wiley.

Kidder, R. M. (1994). *Shared values for a troubled world: Conversations with men and women of conscience.* San Francisco: Jossey-Bass.

Kidder, R. M. (1994, July-August). Universal values: Finding an ethical common ground. *Futurist,* pp. 8–13.

Kidder, R. M. (1995). *How good people make tough choices.* New York: Simon & Schuster.

Kidwell, R. E. (2004). "Small" lies, big trouble: The unfortunate consequences of resume padding, from Janet Cooke to George O'Leary. *Journal of Business Ethics, 51,* 175–184.

Kipnis, D., Schmidt, S. M., Swaffin-Smith, C., & Wilkinson, I. (1984). Patterns of managerial influence: Shotgun managers, tacticians, and bystanders. *Organizational Dynamics, 12,* 58–76.

Kirkpatrick, W. K. (1992). Moral character: Story-telling and virtue. In R. T. Knowles & G. F. McLean (Eds.), *Psychological foundations of moral education and character development: An integrated theory of moral development* (pp. 169–184). Washington, DC: Council for Research in Values and Philosophy.

Kohlberg, L. A. (1984). *Essays on moral development: Vol. 2. The psychology of moral development: The nature and validity of moral stages.* San Francisco: Harper & Row.

Kohlberg, L. A. (1986). A current statement on some theoretical issues. In S. Modgil & C. Modgil (Eds.), *Lawrence Kohlberg: Consensus and controversy* (pp. 485–546). Philadelphia: Falmer Press.

Kosseff, J. (2004, March 14). Charity Inc. *Oregonian,* pp. A1, A11.

Kosseff, J. (2004, March 14). Goodwill gives, gets hand from disabled. *Oregonian,* p. A10.

Kottler, J. A. (2000). *Doing good: Passion and commitment for helping others.* Philadelphia: Brunner-Routledge.

Kottler, P., & Lee, N. (2005). *Corporate social responsibility.* Hoboken, NJ: John Wiley.

Kung, H. (1998). *A global ethic for global politics and economics.* New York: Oxford University Press.

Kung, H. (1999). A global ethic in an age of globalization. In G. Enderle (Ed.), *International business ethics: Challenges and approaches* (pp. 109–127). Notre Dame, IN: University of Notre Dame Press.

Kung, H. (2003). An ethical framework for the global market economy. In J. H. Dunning (Ed.), *Making globalization good: The moral challenges of global capitalism* (pp. 146–158). Oxford, UK: Oxford University Press.

Kung, H., & Kuschel, K. J. (Eds.). (1993). *A global ethic: The declaration of the parliament of the world's religions.* New York: Continuum.

Lacey, M. (2003, September 10). Africans' burden: West's farm subsidies. *New York Times,* p. A9.

Lacoay, R., & Ripley, A. (2003, January 6). Persons of the year. *Time,* pp. 30-60.

LaFasto, F., & Larson, C. (2001). *When teams work best.* Thousand Oaks, CA: Sage.

Laing, R. D. (1994). Confirmation and disconfirmation. In R. Anderson, K. N. Cissna, & R. C. Arnett (Eds.), *The reach of dialogue: Confirmation, voice, and community* (pp. 73–78). Cresskill, NJ: Hampton Press.

Langer, E. J. (1989). *Mindfulness.* Reading, MA: Addison-Wesley.

Langer, E. J. (1989). Minding matters: The consequences of mindlessness-mindfulness. *Advances in Experimental Social Psychology, 22,* 137–173.

Langer, E. J. (1997). *The power of mindful learning.* Reading, MA: Addison-Wesley.

Lavelle, L. (2002, June 17). When directors join CEOs at the trough. *BusinessWeek,* p. 57. Retrieved July 16, 2002, from EBSCOhost database.

Lavelle, L. (2002, October 7). The best and worst boards. *BusinessWeek,* pp. 104–114.

Leary, M. R., & Kowalski, R. M. (1990). Impression management: A literature review and two-component model. *Psychological Bulletin, 107,* 34–47.

Leidner, R. (1991). Selling hamburgers and selling insurance: Gender, work, and identity in interactive service jobs. *Gender & Society, 5,* 154–177.

Leidner, R. (1993). *Fast food, fast talk: Service work and the routinization of everyday life.* Berkeley: University of California Press.

Lemonick, M. D., & Novak, V. (2005, July 11). The power broker. *Time,* pp. 30–33.

Leslie, L. Z. (2000). *Mass communication ethics: Decision-making in postmodern culture.* Boston: Houghton Mifflin.

Levoy, G. (1997). *Callings: Finding and following an authentic life.* New York: Three Rivers Press.

Levy, A. C., & Paludi, M. A. (2002). *Workplace sexual harassment* (2nd ed.). Upper Saddle River, NJ: Prentice Hall.

Lewicki, R. J., & Bunker, B. B. (1996). Developing and maintaining trust in work relationships. In R. M. Kramer & T. R. Tyler (Eds.), *Trust in organizations: Frontiers of theory and research* (pp. 114–139). Thousand Oaks, CA: Sage.

Lincoln, N. D., Travers, C., Ackers, P., & Wilkinson, A. (2002). The meaning of empowerment: The interdisciplinary etymology of a new management concept. *International Journal of Management Reviews, 4,* 271–290.

Lindsay, R. M., & Irvine, V. B. (1996). Instilling ethical behavior in organizations: A survey of Canadian companies. *Journal of Business Ethics, 15,* 393–407.

Linn, A. (2005, March 28). Amazon.com knows clientele, which worries privacy backers. *Oregonian,* pp. B1-B2.

Lisman, C. D. (1996). *The curricular integration of ethics: Theory and practice.* Westport, CT: Praeger.

Locke, E. A., Tirnauer, D., Roberson, Q., Goldman, B., Lathan, M. E., & Weldon, E. (2001). The importance of the individual in an age of groupism. In M. E. Turner (Ed.), *Groups at work: Theory and research* (pp. 501–528). Mahwah, NJ: Lawrence Erlbaum.

Loe, T. W., Ferrell, L., & Mansfield, P. (2000). A review of empirical studies assessing ethical decision making in business. *Journal of Business Ethics, 25*, 185–204.

Longnecker, J. G. (1985). Management priorities and management ethics. *Journal of Business Ethics, 4*, 65–70.

Loury, G. C. (2002). *The anatomy of racial inequality*. Cambridge, MA: Harvard University Press.

Lowe, K. B., & Kroeck, K. G. (1996). Effectiveness correlates of transformational and transactional leadership: A meta-analytic review. *Leadership Quarterly, 7*, 385–425.

Lumpkin, J. L. (2005, May 11). One day halt called in Army recruiting. *Associated Press*. Retrieved June 10, 2005, from LexisNexis Academic database.

MacIntyre, A. (1984). *After virtue: A study in moral theory* (2nd ed.). Notre Dame, IN: University of Notre Dame Press.

Mahan, B. J. (2002). *Forgetting ourselves on purpose: Vocation and the ethics of ambition*. San Francisco: Jossey-Bass.

Manz, C. C., & Neck, C. P. (1995). Teamthink: Beyond the groupthink syndrome in self-managing work teams. *Journal of Managerial Psychology, 10*, 7–15.

Mares, R. (Ed.). (2004). *Business and human rights: A compilation of documents*. Leiden, the Netherlands: Martinus Nijhoff.

Martin, J. (2002). *Organizational culture: Mapping the terrain*. Thousand Oaks, CA: Sage.

Martin, J., Knopoff, K., & Beckman, C. (1998). An alternative to bureaucratic impersonality and emotional labor: Bounded emotionality at The Body Shop. *Administrative Science Quarterly, 43*, 429–469.

Martin, R. L. (2003). The virtue matrix: Calculating the return of corporate responsibility. *Harvard Business Review on Corporate Responsibility* (pp. 83–104). Boston: Harvard Business School Press.

Marx, G. T. (1998). Ethics for the new surveillance. *Information Society, 14*, 171–185.

Mass, A., & Clark. R. D. (1984). Hidden impact of minorities: Fifteen years of minority influence research. *Psychological Bulletin, 95*, 428–450.

Mattoon, M. A. (1981). *Jungian psychology in perspective*. New York: Free Press.

Mayhall, C. W., & Mayhall, T. B. (2004). *On Buber*. Belmont, CA: Wadsworth-Thomson Learning.

Mayer, J. D. (1986). How mood influences cognition. In N. Sharkey (Ed.), *Advances in cognitive science* (pp. 290–314). Chichester, UK: Ellis Horwood.

Mayer, J. D., Caruso, D. R., & Salovey, P. (2000). Emotional intelligence meets traditional standards for an intelligence. *Intelligence, 27*, 267–298.

Mayer, J. D., & Salovey, P. (1993). The intelligence of emotional intelligence. *Intelligence, 17*, 433–442.

Mayer, J. D., & Salovey, P. (1995). Emotional intelligence and the construction and regulation of feelings. *Applied and Preventive Psychology, 4*, 197–208.

Mayer, J. D., & Salovey, P. (1997). What is emotional intelligence? In P. Salovey & D. J. Sluyter (Eds.), *Emotional development and emotional intelligence: Educational implications* (pp. 3–31). New York: Basic Books.

Mayer, R. C., & Davis, J. H. (1995). An integrative model of organizational trust. *Academy of Management Review, 29*, 709–734.

McAllister, D. J. (1995). Affect- and cognition-based trust as foundations for interpersonal cooperation in organizations. *Academy of Management Journal, 38*, 24–61.

McCabe, D., & Trevino, K. L. (1993). Academic dishonesty: Honor codes and other contextual influences. *Journal of Higher Education, 64*, 522–569.

McCann, N. D., & McGinn, T. A. (1992). *Harassed: 100 women define inappropriate behavior in the workplace.* Homewood IL: BusinessIrwin.

McGeary, J. (2004, May 24). Pointing fingers. *Time*, pp. 43–47, 50.

McGee-Cooper, A., & Trammell, D. (2002). From hero-as-leader to servant-as-leader. In L. C. Spears & M. Lawrence (Eds.), *Focus on leadership: Servant-leadership for the 21st century* (pp. 145–146). New York: John Wiley.

McKinnon, C. (1999). *Character, virtue theories, and the vices.* Ontario: Broadview Press.

McLean, B., & Elkind, P. (2003). *The smartest guys in the room: The amazing rise and fall of Enron.* New York: Portfolio.

McNamara, G., Moon, H., & Bromiley, P. (2002). Banking on commitment: Intended and unintended consequences of an organization's attempt to attenuate escalation of commitment. *Academy of Management Journal, 45*, 443–452.

McNatt, D. B. (2000). Ancient Pygmalion joins contemporary management: A meta-analysis of the result. *Journal of Applied Psychology, 85*, 314–322.

Messick, D. M., & Bazerman, M. H. (1996, Winter). Ethical leadership and the psychology of decision making. *Sloan Management Review*, pp. 9–23.

Michalos, A. C. (1995). *A pragmatic approach to business ethics.* Thousand Oaks, CA: Sage.

Miethe, T. D. (1999). *Whistleblowing at work: Tough choices in exposing fraud, waste, and abuse on the job.* Boulder, CO: Westview Press.

Milgram, S. (1974). *Obedience to authority.* New York: Harper & Row.

Miller, W. A. (1981). *Make friends with your shadow.* Minneapolis, MN: Augsburg.

Milton, L. P., & Westphal, J. D. (2005). Identity confirmation networks and cooperation in work groups. *Academy of Management Journal, 48*, 191–212.

Mintzberg, H. (2004). *Managers, not MBAs.* San Francisco: Berritt-Koehler.

Mishra, A. K. (1996). Organizational responses to crisis: The centrality of trust. In R. M. Kramer & T. R. Tyler (Eds.), *Trust in organizations: Frontiers of theory and research* (pp. 261–287). Thousand Oaks, CA: Sage.

Mitchell, C. (2003). *International business ethics: Combining ethics and profits in global business.* Novato, CA: World Trade Press.

Mitroff, I. I., & Denton, E. A. (1999). *A spiritual audit of corporate America.* San Francisco: Jossey-Bass.

Mitroff, I. I., & Denton, E. A. (1999, Summer). A study of spirituality in the workplace. *Sloan Management Review*, pp. 83–92.

Moore, A. (2000). Employee monitoring and computer technology: Evaluative surveillance vs. privacy. *Business Ethics Quarterly, 10*, 697–709.

Moore, T. (1992). *Care of the soul: A guide to cultivating depth and sacredness in everyday life.* New York: HarperCollins.

Moore, T. (1995). Caring for the soul in business. In B. Defoore & J. Renesch (Eds.), *Rediscovering the soul of business: A renaissance of values* (pp. 341–356). San Francisco: Sterling & Stone.

Moorhead, G., Neck, C. P., & West, M. S. (1998). The tendency toward defective decision making within self-managing teams: The relevance of groupthink for the 21st century. *Organizational Behavior and Human Decision Processes, 73*, 327–351.

Moscovici, S., Mucchi-Faina, A., & Mass, A. (1994). *Minority influence.* Chicago: Nelson-Hall.

Moscovici, S., Mugny, G., & Van Avermaet, D. (Eds.). (1985). *Perspectives on minority influence.* Cambridge, UK: Cambridge University Press.

Moxley, R. S. (2004). Hardships. In C. D. McCauley, R. S. Moxley, & E. Van Velsor (Eds.), *Handbook of leadership development* (2nd ed., pp. 183–204). San Francisco: Jossey-Bass.

Mugny, G., & Perez, J. A. (1991). *The social psychology of minority influence* (V. W. Lamongie, Trans.). Cambridge, UK: Cambridge University Press.

Mulhall, S., & Swift, A. (1992). *Liberals and communitarians.* Oxford, UK: Blackwell.

Mumby, D. K., & Putnam, L. L. (1993). The politics of emotion: A feminist reading of bounded rationality. *Academy of Management Review, 17*, 465–486.

Mundy, A. (2005, March 8). The board took 8 days to decide CEO had to go. *Seattle Times*, p. A1. Retrieved July 27, 2005, from LexisNexis Academic database.

Murphy, D. (2004, June 4). Abu Ghraib holds mirror to Arabs. *Christian Science Monitor*, p. 1C. Retrieved March 23, 2005, from LexisNexis Academic database.

Muzaffar, C. (2002). Conclusion. In P. F. Knitter & C. Muzaffar (Eds.), *Subverting greed: Religious perspectives on the global economy* (pp. 154–172). Maryknoll, NY: Orbis Books.

Nash, L. (1990). *Good intentions aside: A manager's guide to resolving ethical problems.* Boston: Harvard Business School Press.

Naughton, K., & Gimbel, B. (2004, March 14). Martha's fall. *Newsweek*, pp. 28–36.

Nemeth, C. (1985). Dissent, group process and creativity: The contribution of minority influence research. In E. Lawler (Ed.), *Advances in group processes* (Vol. 2, pp. 57–75). Greenwich, CT: JAI.

Nemeth, C. & Chiles, C. (1986). Modeling courage: The role of dissent in fostering independence. *European Journal of Social Psychology, 18*, 275–280.

Neuman, J. H. (2004). Injustice, stress, and aggression in organizations. In R. W. Griffin & A. M. O'Leary-Kelly (Eds.), *The dark side of organizational behavior* (pp. 62–102). San Francisco: Jossey-Bass.

Neuman, J. H., & Baron, R. A. (1997). Aggression in the workplace. In R. A. Giacalone & J. Greenberg (Eds.), *Antisocial behavior in organizations* (pp. 37–67). Thousand Oaks, CA: Sage.

Newstrom, J. W., & Davis, K. (1993). *Organizational behavior: Human behavior at work* (9th ed.). New York: McGraw-Hill.

Nichols, B. (2005, April 22). Tough bosses nothing new in Washington. *USA Today*, p. 4A.

Nielsen, S. (2003, November 2). At Wal-Mart, a world power runs the sale bins. *Oregonian*, pp. E1-E2.

Norman, W., & MacDonald, C. (2004). Getting to the bottom of "triple bottom line." *Business Ethics Quarterly, 14*, 243–262.

Norris, F. (2005, March 8). Moving from scandal to scandal, Boeing finds its road to redemption paved with affairs great and small. *New York Times*, p. C5. Retrieved July 27, 2005, from LexisNexis Academic database.

Novak, M. (2003). A universal culture of human rights and freedom's habits: Caritapolis. In J. H. Dunning (Ed.), *Making globalization good: The moral challenges of global capitalism* (pp. 253–279). Oxford, UK: Oxford University Press.

Nutt, P. (2002). *Why decisions fail.* San Francisco: Berritt-Koehler.

O'Connor, E. S. (1997). Compelling stories: Narrative and the production of the organizational self. In O. F. Williams (Ed.), *The moral imagination: How literature and films can stimulate ethical reflection in the business world* (pp. 185–202). Notre Dame, IN: University of Notre Dame Press.

Offermann, L. R., & Malamut, A. B. (2002). When leaders harass: The impact of target perceptions of organizational leadership and climate on harassment reporting and outcomes. *Journal of Applied Psychology, 87,* 885–893.

O'Leary-Kelly, A. M. (2001). Sexual harassment as unethical behavior: The role of moral intensity. *Human Resource Management Review, 11,* 73–92.

O'Leary-Kelly, A. M., Griffin, R. W., & Glew, D. J. (1996). Organization-motivated aggression: A research framework. *Academy of Management Review, 21,* 225–253.

O'Leary-Kelly, A. M., Paetzold, R. L., & Griffin, L. W. (2000). Sexual harassment as aggressive behavior: An actor-based perspective. *Academy of Management Review, 25,* 372–388.

Opotow, S. (1990). Deterring moral exclusion. *Journal of Social Issues, 46,* 173–182.

Opotow, S. (1990). Moral exclusion and injustice: An introduction. *Journal of Social Issues, 46,* 1–20.

Opotow, S. (1995). Drawing the line: Social categorization, moral exclusion, and the scope of justice. In B. B. Bunker & J. Z. Rubin (Eds.), *Conflict, cooperation, and justice: Essays inspired by the work of Morton Deutsch* (pp. 347–369). San Francisco: Jossey-Bass.

Organ, D. W. (1988). *Organizational citizenship behavior: The good soldier syndrome.* Lexington, MA: Lexington Books.

Oz, S., & Eden, D. (1994). Restraining the golem: Boosting performance by changing the interpretation of low scores. *Journal of Applied Psychology, 79,* 744–754.

Padded resumes: Fake laurels that went unnoticed for years. (2003, January 13). *BusinessWeek,* p. 1C. Retrieved April 14, 2006, from Business Source Premier database.

Paine, L. S. (1996, March-April). Managing for organizational integrity. *Harvard Business Review,* pp. 106–117.

Paine, L. S. (2000). Does ethics pay? *Business Ethics Quarterly, 10,* 319–330.

Paine, L. S. (2003). *Value shift: Why companies must merge social and financial imperatives to achieve superior performance.* New York: McGraw-Hill.

Pauchant, T. C. (2002). Introduction: Ethical and spiritual management addresses the need for meaning in the workplace. In T. C. Pauchant (Ed.), *Ethics and spirituality at work* (pp. 1–27). Westport, CT: Quorum Books.

Pearson, C. M., Andersson, L. M., & Porath, C. L. (2000). Assessing and attacking workplace incivility. *Organizational Dynamics, 29,* 123–137.

Pearson, C. M., & Porath, C. L. (2004). On incivility, its impact, and directions for future research. In R. W. Griffin & A. M. O'Leary-Kelly (Eds.), *The dark side of organizational behavior* (pp. 23–61). San Francisco: Jossey-Bass.

Pearson, C. M., & Porath, C. L. (2005). On the nature, consequences and remedies of workplace incivility: No time for "nice"? Think again. *Academy of Management Executive, 19,* 7–18.

Pearson, G. (1995). *Integrity in organizations: An alternative business ethic.* London: McGraw-Hill.

Peterson, D. K. (2002). The relationship between unethical behavior and the dimensions of the Ethical Climate Questionnaire. *Journal of Business Ethics, 41,* 313–326.

Phatak, A. V., Bhagat, R. S., & Kashlak, R. J. (2005). *International management: Managing in a diverse and dynamic global environment.* Boston: McGraw-Hill Irwin.

Philips, R. (2003). *Stakeholder theory and organizational ethics.* San Francisco: Berritt-Koehler.

Piliavin, J. A., & Charng, H. W. (1990). Altruism: A review of recent theory and research. *American Sociological Review, 16,* 27–65.

Piper, T. R., Gentile, M. C., & Parks, S. D. (1993). *Can ethics be taught? Perspectives, challenges, and approaches at Harvard Business School.* Boston: Harvard Business School Press.

Post, S. G. (2002). The tradition of agape. In S. G. Post, L. G. Underwood, J. P. Schloss, & W. B. Hurlbut (Eds.), *Altruism and altruistic love: Science, philosophy, & religion in dialogue* (pp. 51–64). Oxford, UK: Oxford University Press.

Postmes, T., Spears, R., & Cihangir, S. (2001). Quality of decision-making and group norms. *Journal of Personality and Social Psychology, 80,* 918–930.

Putnam, L. L., & Mumby, D. K. (1993). Organizations, emotion, and the myth of rationality. In S. Fineman (Ed.), *Emotion in organizations* (pp. 36–57). London: Sage.

Quinn, R. E. (1996). *Deep change.* San Francisco: Jossey-Bass.

Quinn, R. E. (2000). *Change the world: How ordinary people can achieve extraordinary results.* San Francisco: Jossey-Bass.

Radtke, J. M. (1998). *Strategic communications for nonprofit organizations: Seven steps to creating a successful plan.* New York: John Wiley.

Rafaeli, A., & Sutton, R. I. (1989). The expression of emotion in organizational life. In L. L. Cummings & B. M. Staw (Eds.), *Research in organizational behavior* (Vol 2, pp. 1–42). Greenwich, CT: JAI.

Rafter, M. V. (2005, May). Nike opens a window on overseas factories. *Workforce Management, 84,* 17. Retrieved July 25, 2005, from Business Source Premier database.

Randolph, W. A. (2000). Re-thinking empowerment: Why is it so hard to achieve? *Organizational Dynamics, 29,* 94–107.

Rawls, J. (1971). *A theory of justice.* Cambridge, MA: Belknap Press.

Rawls, J. (1993). Distributive justice. In T. Donaldson & P. H. Werhane (Eds.), *Ethical issues in business: A philosophical approach* (4th ed., pp. 274–285). Englewood Cliffs, NJ: Prentice Hall.

Rawls, J. (1993). *Political liberalism.* New York: Columbia University Press.

Rawls, J. (2001). *Justice as fairness: A restatement* (E. Kelly, Ed.). Cambridge, MA: Belknap Press.

Rayburn, C. A. (1997). Vocation as calling. In D. P. Bloch & L. J. Richmond (Eds.), *Connections between spirit and work in career development* (pp. 162–183). Palo Alto, CA: Davies-Black.

Research updates America's view on cell phone etiquette. (2002, September 3). *Business Wire.* Retrieved September 8, 2003, from LexisNexis Academic database.

Rest, J. R. (1979). *Development in judging moral issues.* Minneapolis: University of Minnesota Press.

Rest, J. R. (1986). *Moral development: Advances in research and theory.* New York: Praeger.

Rest, J. R. (1993). Research on moral judgment in college students. In A. Garrod (Ed.), *Approaches to moral development* (pp. 201–211). New York: Teachers College Press.

Rest, J. R. (1994). Background: Theory and research. In J. R. Rest & D. Narvaez (Eds.), *Moral development in the professions: Psychology and applied ethics* (pp. 1–25). Hillsdale, NJ: Lawrence Erlbaum.

Rest, J. R., & Narvaez, D. (1991). The college experience and moral development. In W. M. Kurtines & J. L. Gewirtz (Eds.), *Handbook of moral behavior and development. Volume 2: Research* (pp. 229–245). Hillsdale, NJ: Lawrence Erlbaum.

Rest, J. R., Narvaez, D., Bebeau, M. J., & Thoma, S. J. (1999). *Postconventional moral thinking: A neo-Kohlbergian approach.* Mahwah, NJ: Lawrence Erlbaum.

Rice, D., & Dreilinger, C. (1990, May). Rights and wrongs of ethics training. *Training and Development Journal,* pp. 103–108.

Richmond, L. J. (1997). Spirituality and career assessment: Metaphors and measurement. In D. P. Block & L. J. Richmond (Eds.), *Connections between spirit and work in career development* (pp. 209–235). Palo Alto, CA: Davis-Black.

Riesen, J. (2004, May 3). The struggle for Iraq: Prisoners. *New York Times,* p. A1. Retrieved June 14, 2005, from LexisNexis Academic database.

Ripley, A. (2004, June 21). Redefining torture. *Time,* pp. 49–50.

Ripley, A. (2005, January 24). The DNA dragnet. *Time,* pp. 39–40.

Ritson, M. (2005, April 20). Nike shows way to return from the wilderness. *Marketing* (UK), p. 21. Retrieved July 25, 2005, from Business Source Premier database.

Robinson, M. (2000). Internalizing human rights in corporate business practices. *UN Chronicle, 37,* 38–39.

Roloff, M. E., & Paulson, G. D. (2001). Confronting organizational transgressions. In J. M. Darley, D. M. Messick, & T. R. Tyler (Eds.), *Social influences on ethical behavior in organizations* (pp. 53–68). Mahwah, NJ: Lawrence Erlbaum.

Romano, A., & Guide, K. (2005, July 11). The O'Connor verdicts. *Newsweek,* pp. 28–29.

Rosenfeld, P., Giacalone, R. A., & Riordan, C. A. (1995). *Impression management in organizations: Theory, measurement, practice.* London: Routledge.

Rosenthal, R. (1993). Interpersonal expectations: Some antecedents and some consequences. In P. D. Blanck (Ed.), *Interpersonal expectations: Theory, research, and applications* (pp. 3–24). Cambridge, UK: Cambridge University Press.

Rosenthal, R., & Jacobson, L. (1968). *Pygmalion in the classroom.* New York: Holt, Rinehart & Winston.

Ross, J., & Staw, B. M. (1993). Organizational escalation and exit: Lessons from the Shoreham Nuclear Plant. *Academy of Management Journal, 36,* 701–732.

Ross, W. T., & Robertson, D. C. (2000). Lying: The impact of decision context. *Business Ethics Quarterly, 10,* 409–440.

Rost, J. (1991). *Leadership for the twenty-first century.* New York: Praeger.

Rost, J. (1993). Leadership in the new millennium. *Journal of Leadership Studies, 1,* 92–110.

Rothwell, J. D. (1998). *In mixed company: Small group communication* (3rd ed.). Fort Worth, TX: Harcourt Brace.

Rubin, J. Z., & Brown, B. R. (1975). *The social psychology of bargaining and negotiation.* New York: Academic Press.

Ruschman, N. L. (2002). Servant-leadership and the best companies to work for in America. In L. C. Spears & M. Lawrence (Eds.), *Focus on leadership: Servant-leadership for the twenty-first century* (pp. 123–139). New York: John Wiley.

Salovey, P., Hsee, C. K., & Mayer, J. D. (1993). Emotional intelligence and the self-regulation of affect. In D. M. Wegner & J. W. Pennebaker (Eds.), *Handbook of mental control* (pp. 258–277). Englewood Cliffs, NJ: Prentice Hall.

Saraceno, J. (2004, December 29). White's death sends message to super-sized NFL. *USA Today*, p. 12C.

Scelfo, J., & Nordland, R. (2004, July 19). Beneath the hoods. *Newsweek*, pp. 40–42.

Schein, E. H. (1992). *Organizational culture and leadership* (2nd ed.). San Francisco: Jossey-Bass.

Schick, T. A. (1994). Truth, accuracy (and withholding information). *Public Relations Quarterly*, *7*, 397–410.

Schlenker, B. R. (1980). *Impression management: The self-concept, social identity, and interpersonal relations.* Monterey, CA: Brooks/Cole.

Schminke, M. (Ed.). (1998). *Managerial ethics: Moral management of people and processes.* Mahwah, NJ: Lawrence Erlbaum.

Schultz, H., & Yang, D. J. (1997). *Pour your heart into it: How Starbucks built a company one cup at a time.* New York: Hyperion.

Schwartz, S. H. (1994a). Are there universal aspects in the structure and contents of human values? *Journal of Social Issues, 50*, 19–45.

Schwartz, S. H. (1994b). Beyond individualism/collectivism: New cultural dimensions of values. In U. Kim, H. C. Triandis, C. Kagitcibasi, S, Choi, & G. Yoon (Eds), *Individualism and collectivism: Theory, method and applications* (pp. 85–119). Thousand Oaks, CA: Sage.

Schwartz, S. H., & Sagiv, L. (1995). Identifying culture-specifics in the content and structure of values. *Journal of Cross-Cultural Psychology, 26*, 92–116.

Scileppi, P. A. (2005). *Values for interpersonal communication: How then shall we live?* Belmont, CA: Star.

Seabright, M. A., & Moberg, D. J. (1998). Interpersonal manipulation: Its nature and moral limits. In M. Schminke (Ed.), *Managerial ethics: Moral management of people and processes* (pp. 153–175). Mahwah, NJ: Lawrence Erlbaum.

Seitel, F. P. (1997). *The practice of public relations* (7th ed.). Upper Saddle River, NJ: Prentice Hall.

Sellers, P. (2005, August 22). Retire? No way! *Fortune*, p. 18. Retrieved January 2, 2006, from EBSCOhost database.

Sethi, S. P. (1975). Dimensions of corporate social performance: An analytical framework. *California Management Review, 17*, 58–64.

Shaw, R. B. (1997). *Trust in the balance: Building successful organizations on results, integrity and concern.* San Francisco: Jossey-Bass.

Sheppard, J. A. (1993). Productivity loss in performance groups: A motivation analysis. *Psychological Bulletin, 113*, 67–81.

Sheppard, J. A. (2001). Social loafing and expectancy-value theory. In S. G. Harkins (Ed.), *Multiple perspectives on the effects of evaluation on performance: Toward an integration* (pp. 1–24). Boston: Kluwer.

Shockley-Zalabak, P. (2003). *Fundamentals of organizational communication: Knowledge, sensitivity, skills, values* (5th ed.). Boston: Allyn & Bacon.

Shore, J. (2005, August 27). Play with our name. *New York Times*, p. A13. Retrieved October 4, 2005, from LexisNexis Academic database.

Sims, R. L. (2000). The relationship between employee attitudes and conflicting expectations for lying behavior. *Journal of Psychology, 134*, 619–633.

Sims, R. L., & Keon, T. L. (1997). Ethical work climate as a factor in the development of person-organization fit. *Journal of Business Ethics, 16*, 1095–1105.

Sims, R. R. (1992). Linking groupthink to unethical behavior in organizations. *Journal of Business Ethics, 11*, 651–662.

Sims, R. R. (1994). *Ethics and organizational decision making: A call for renewal.* Westport, CT: Quorum Books.

Sims, R. R. (2002). *Managing organizational behavior.* Westport, CT: Quorum Books.

Sims, R. R. (2003). *Ethics and corporate social responsibility: Why giants fall.* Westport, CT: Praeger.

Singer, P. (2002). *One world: The ethics of globalization.* New Haven, CT: Yale University Press.

Singh, V., Kumra, S., & Vinnicombe, S. (2002). Gender and impression management: Playing the promotion game. *Journal of Business Ethics, 37*, 77–89.

Sison, A. J. G. (2003). *The moral capital of leaders: Why virtue matters.* Northampton, MA: Edward Elgar.

Slavin, B. (2005, April 21). Woman accuses Bolton of harassing her in 1994. *USA Today*, p. 4A.

Social Accountability International. (2005). *Overview of SA8000.* Retrieved August 10, 2005, from http://www.sa-intl.org

Solomon, R. C. (1993). What a tangled web: Deception and self-deception in philosophy. In M. Lewis & C. Saarni (Eds.), *Lying and deception in everyday life* (pp. 30–58). New York: Guilford Press.

Solomon, R. C. (1997). Corporate roles, personal virtues: An Aristotelian approach to business ethics. In D. Statman (Ed.), *Virtue ethics* (pp. 206–225). Washington, DC: Georgetown University Press.

Sorokin, P. A. (1954). *The ways and power of love: Types, factors, and techniques of moral transformation.* Boston: Beacon Press.

Spears, L. C. (2002). Introduction: Tracing the past, present and future of servant-leadership. In L. Spears & M. Lawrence (Eds.), *Focus on leadership: Servant-leadership for the twenty-first century* (pp. 1–18). New York: John Wiley.

Spreitzer, G. M. (1995). Psychological empowerment in the workplace: Dimensions, measurement, and validation. *Academy of Management Journal, 38*, 1442–1485.

Spreitzer, G. M. (1996). Social structural characteristics of psychological empowerment. *Academy of Management Journal, 39*, 483–504.

Spreitzer, G. M., Kzilos, M. A., & Nason, S. W. (1997). A dimensional analysis of the relationship between psychological empowerment and effectiveness, satisfaction, and strain. *Journal of Management, 23*, 679–705.

Starbucks recognized as one of the most valued global brands. (2004, March 30). *Business Wire.* Retrieved May 24, 2004, from LexisNexis Academic database.

Starr, M. (2004, August 16). A long jump. *Newsweek*, pp. 52–53.

Statman, D. (1997). Introduction to virtue ethics. In D. Statman (Ed.), *Virtue ethics* (pp. 1–41). Washington, DC: Georgetown University Press.

Staw, B. M. (1981). The escalation of commitment to a course of action. *Academy of Management Review, 6*, 577–587.

Steinberg, R. J., & Figart, D. M. (1999). Emotional labor since *The Managed Heart. Annals of the American Academy of Political and Social Sciences, 561*, 10–26.

Sternberg, R. J. (2002). Smart people are not stupid, but they sure can be foolish. In R. J. Sternberg (Ed.), *Why smart people can be so stupid* (pp. 232–242). New Haven, CT: Yale University Press.

Stevens, C. K., & Kristof, A. L. (1995). Making the right impression: A field study of applicant impression management during job interviews. *Journal of Applied Psychology, 80*, 587–606.

Storr, A. (1983). *The essential Jung.* Princeton, NJ: Princeton University Press.

Street, M. D. (1997). Groupthink: An examination of theoretical issues, implications, and future research suggestions. *Small Group Research, 28*, 72–93.

Sullivan, J. (2003, August 13). Call it Starbucking, the fine art of hating your local outlet of the Seattle coffeehouse chain. *San Francisco Chronicle*, p. D1. Retrieved May 24, 2004, from LexisNexis Academic database.

Susskind, L., & Field, P. (1996). *Dealing with an angry public: The mutual gains approach to resolving disputes.* New York: Free Press.

Sutton, R. I. (1991). Maintaining norms about expressed emotions: The case of bill collectors. *Administrative Science Quarterly, 36*, 245–268.

Sutton, R. I., & Rafaeli, A. (1988). Untangling the relationship between displayed emotions and organizational sales: The case of convenience stores. *Academy of Management Journal, 31*, 461–487.

Takeuchi, C. L. (2004, July 5). Wal-Mart's gender gap. *Time Canada,* p. 25. Retrieved January 21, 2006, from Business Source Premier database.

Tam, H. (1998). *Communitarianism: A new agenda for politics and citizenship.* New York: New York University Press.

Terrell, K., & Hammel, S. (1999, June 14). Call of the riled. *U.S. News & World Report.* Retrieved August 12, 2003, from Academic Search Premier database.

T'Hart, P. (1990). *Groupthink in government: A study of small groups and policy failure.* Baltimore, MD: Johns Hopkins University Press.

Thomas, D. A., & Ely, R. D. (1996, September-October). Making differences matter: A new paradigm for managing diversity. *Harvard Business Review,* pp. 79–90.

Thomas, E., Taylor, S., Jr., Murr, A., Wingert, P., Clift, E., & Meadows, S. (2005, July 11). Queen of the center. *Newsweek*, pp 24–31.

Thomas, K. W., & Velthouse, B. A. (1990). Cognitive elements of empowerment: An "interpretive" model of intrinsic task motivation. *Academy of Management Review, 15*, 666–681.

Thompson, H. (1999, March 8). The massacre at My Lai. *Newsweek*, p. 64. Retrieved June 23, 2004, from EBSCOhost database

Thoresen, C. E., Harris, H. S., & Luskin, F. (2000). Forgiveness and health: An unanswered question. In M. E. McCullough, K. I. Pargament, & C. E. Thoresen (Eds.), *Forgiveness: Theory, research and practice* (pp. 254–280). New York: Guilford Press.

Tjosvold, D. (1984). Cooperation theory and organizations. *Human Relations, 37*, 743–767.

Tjosvold, D. (1986). The dynamics of interdependence in organizations. *Human Relations, 39*, 517–540

Tobias, A. (1976). *Fire and ice.* New York: William Morrow.

Toffler, B. (2003). *Final accounting: Ambition, greed and the fall of Arthur Andersen.* New York: Broadway Books.

Tompkins, P. K., & Cheney, G. (1985). Communication and unobtrusive control in contemporary organizations. In R. D. McPhee & P. K. Tompkins (Eds.), *Organizational communication: Traditional themes and new directions* (pp. 179–210). Newbury Park, CA: Sage.

Tracy, S. J. (2000). Becoming a character for commerce: Emotion labor, self-subordination, and discursive construction of identity in a total institution. *Management Communication Quarterly, 14*, 90–128.

Tracy, S. J., & Tracy, K. (1998). Emotional labor at 911. *Journal of Applied Communication Research, 26,* 390–411.

Trenholm, S., & Jensen, A. (2004). *Interpersonal communication* (5th ed.). New York: Oxford University Press.

Trevino, L. K. (1986). Ethical decision making in organizations: A person-situation interactionist model. *Academy of Management Review, 11,* 601–607.

Trevino, L. K. (1990). A cultural perspective on changing and developing organizational ethics. In W. A. Pasmore & R. W. Woodman (Eds.), *Research in organizational change and development* (Vol. 4). Greenwich, CT: JAI.

Trevino, L. K., Butterfield, K. D., & McCabe, D. L. (1998). The ethical context in organizations: Influences on employee attitudes and behaviors. *Business Ethics Quarterly, 8,* 447–476.

Trevino, L. K., Hartman, L. P., & Brown, M. (2000). Moral person and moral manager: How executives develop a reputation for ethical leadership. *California Management Review, 42,* 128–142.

Trevino, L. K., & Nelson, K. A. (2004). *Managing business ethics: Straight talk about how to do it right* (3rd ed.). Hoboken, NJ: John Wiley.

Trevino, L. K., & Weaver, G. R. (2003). *Managing ethics in business organizations: Social scientific perspectives.* Stanford, CA: Stanford University Press.

Trevino, L. K., Weaver, G. R., Gibson, D. G., & Toffler, B. L. (1999). Managing ethics and legal compliance: What works and what hurts. *California Management Review, 41,* 131–151.

Trevino, L. K., & Youngblood, S. A. (1990). Bad apples in bad barrels: A causal analysis of ethical decision-making behavior. *Journal of Applied Psychology, 75,* 378–385.

Trice, H. M., & Beyer, J. M. (1984). Studying organizational cultures through rites and ceremonials. *Academy of Management Review, 9,* 653–699.

Troyer, J. (Ed.). (2003). *The classical Utilitarians: Bentham and Mill.* Indianapolis, IN: Hackett.

Turner, N., Barling, J., Epitropaki, O., Butcher, V., & Milner, C. (2002). Transformational leadership and moral reasoning. *Journal of Applied Psychology, 87,* 304–311.

Vaill, P. B. (1998). *Spirited leading and learning: Process wisdom for a new age.* San Francisco: Jossey-Bass.

Valentine, S., & Barnett, T. (2003). Ethics code awareness, perceived ethical values, and organizational commitment. *Journal of Personal Selling & Sales Management, 23,* 359–367.

Van Maanen, J. (1991). The smile factory: Work at Disneyland. In P. J. Frost, L. F. Moore, M. R. Louis, C. C. Lundberg, & J. Martin (Eds.), *Reframing organizational culture* (pp. 58–76). Newbury Park, CA: Sage.

Velasquez, M. G. (1992). *Business ethics: Concepts and cases* (3rd ed.). Englewood Cliffs, NJ: Prentice Hall.

Victor, B., & Cullen, J. B. (1988). The organizational bases of ethical work climates. *Administrative Science Quarterly, 33,* 101–125.

Victor, B., & Cullen, J. B. (1990). A theory and measure of ethical climate in organizations. In W. C. Frederic & L. E. Preston (Eds.), *Business ethics: Research issues and empirical studies* (pp. 77–97). Greenwich, CT: JAI.

Victor, B., Cullen, J. B., & Boynton, A. (1993). Toward a general framework of organizational meaning systems. In C. Conrad (Ed.), *Ethical nexus* (pp. 193–216). Norwood, NJ: Ablex.

Vistica, G. L. (1997, November 24). A quiet war over the past. *Newsweek*, p. 41. Retrieved June 23, 2004, from EBSCOhost database

Waddock, S. A., & Graves, S. B. (1997). The corporate social performance-financial performance link. *Strategic Management Journal, 18*, 303–319.

Wagner-Marsh, F., & Conley, J. (1999). The fourth wave: The spiritually based firm. *Journal of Organizational Change Management, 12*, 292–301.

Waldron, V. R. (1994). Once more, with feeling: Reconsidering the role of emotion at work. In S. A. Deetz (Ed.), *Communication Yearbook 17* (pp. 388–428). Thousand Oaks, CA: Sage.

Wayne, L. (2005a, March 8). Boeing chief is ousted after admitting affair. *New York Times*, p. A1. Retrieved July 27, 2005, from LexisNexis Academic database

Wayne, L. (2005b, March 11). Ousted chief of Boeing gets $2.1 million bonus for 2004. *New York Times*, p. C6.

Wayne, L. (2005c, March 19). Executive involved with chief has resigned, Boeing says. *New York Times*, p. C10.

Weaver, G. R., Trevino, L. K., & Cochran, P. L. (1999). Corporate ethics practices in the mid-1990s: An empirical study of the *Fortune 1000*. *Journal of Business Ethics, 18*, 283–294.

Weaver, G. R., Trevino, L. K., & Cochran, P. L. (1999). Corporate ethics programs as control systems: Influence of executive commitment and environmental factors. *Academy of Management Journal, 42*, 41–57.

Weaver, G. R., Trevino, L. K., & Cochran, P. L. (1999). Integrated and decoupled corporate social performance: Management commitments, external pressures, and corporate ethics practices. *Academy of Management Journal, 42*, 539–552.

Werhane, P. H. (1985). *Persons, rights and corporations*. Englewood Cliffs, NJ: Prentice Hall.

Werhane, P. H. (1999). *Moral imagination and management decision-making*. New York: Oxford University Press.

West, H. R. (2004). *An introduction to Mill's Utilitarian ethics*. Cambridge, UK: Cambridge University Press.

Westneat, D. (2005, March 11). Boeing's message puzzling. *Seattle Times*, p. B1. Retrieved July 27, 2005, from LexisNexis Academic database.

Wheeler, D., Coalbert, B., & Freeman, R. E. (2003). Focusing on value: Reconciling corporate social responsibility, sustainability and a stakeholder approach in a network world. *Journal of General Management, 28*, 1–28.

White, S. S., & Locke, E. A. (2000). Problems with the Pygmalion Effect and some proposed solutions. *Leadership Quarterly, 11*, 389–415.

Whyte, G. (1991). Diffusion of responsibility: Effects on the escalation tendency. *Journal of Applied Psychology, 76*, 408–415.

Wieberg, S. (2005, August 8). Mascot policy will be tough to overcome. *USA Today*, p. 9C.

Wiener, R. L., & Gutek, B. A. (1999). Advances in sexual harassment research, theory, and policy. *Psychology, Public Policy and Law, 5*, 597–518.

Wilmot, W. W., & Hocker, J. L. (2001). *Interpersonal conflict* (6th ed.). New York: McGraw-Hill.

Wilson, F., & Thompson, P. (2001). Sexual harassment as an exercise of power. *Gender, Work and Organization, 8*, 61–83.

Wimbush, J. C., Shepard, J. M., & Markham, S. E. (1997). An empirical examination of the relationship between ethical climate and ethical behavior from multiple levels of analysis. *Journal of Business Ethics, 16*, 1705–1716.

Wiseman, P. (2005, December 9). On the train tracks in Sri Lanka, life does move on. *USA Today*, pp. 15A-16A.

Wood, W., Lundgren, S., Ouellette, J. A., Busceme, S., & Blackstone, T. (1994). Minority influence: A meta-analytic review of social influence processes. *Psychological Bulletin, 115*, 323–345.

Wright, J. P., Cullen, F. T., & Blankenship, M. B. (2002). Chained factory fire exits: Media coverage of a corporate crime that killed 25 workers. In M. D. Ermann & R. J. Lundman (Eds.), *Corporate and governmental deviance* (6th ed., pp. 262–276). New York: Oxford University Press.

Yanay, N., & Sharar, G. (1998). Professional feelings as emotional labor. *Journal of Contemporary Ethnography, 27*, 345–373.

Yukl, G. (2002). *Leadership in organizations* (5th ed.). Upper Saddle River, NJ: Prentice Hall.

Zadek, S. (2004, December). The path to corporate responsibility. *Harvard Business Review*, pp. 125–132.

Zand, D. E. (1972). Trust and managerial problem solving. *Administrative Science Quarterly, 17*, 229–239.

Zernike, K. (2004, June 27). Defining torture: Russian roulette, yes. Mind-altering drugs, maybe. *New York Times*, p. 7. Retrieved June 27, 2004, from LexisNexis Academic database.

Index

About the Author

Craig E. Johnson (Ph.D., University of Denver) is professor of Leadership Studies and director of the Doctor of Management program at George Fox University. He teaches graduate and undergraduate courses in leadership, ethics, management, and communication and is a past recipient of the university's outstanding teacher award. He is the author of *Meeting the Ethical Challenges of Leadership: Casting Light or Shadow* (2nd ed.; Sage, 2005) and the coauthor, with Michael Z. Hackman, of *Leadership: A Communication Perspective* (5th ed.; Waveland Press, forthcoming). His research findings have been published in the *Journal of Leadership Education, Selected Proceedings of the International Leadership Association, Journal of Leadership Studies, Communication Quarterly, Communication Reports, Journal of the International Listening Association,* and *Communication Education.* He has served on the boards of several nonprofit organizations and has participated in educational and service trips to the Czech Republic, Brazil, Kenya, Honduras, and New Zealand.